Power Shifts

CHICAGO STUDIES IN AMERICAN POLITICS

*A series edited by Susan Herbst, Lawrence R. Jacobs, Adam J. Berinsky,
and Frances Lee; Benjamin I. Page, editor emeritus*

Also in the series:

Power Shifts

Congress and Presidential Representation

JOHN A. DEARBORN

The University of Chicago Press
Chicago and London

The University of Chicago Press, Chicago 60637
The University of Chicago Press, Ltd., London
© 2021 by The University of Chicago
Published 2021
Printed in the United States of America

30 29 28 27 26 25 24 23 22 21   1 2 3 4 5

ISBN-13: 978-0-226-79766-3 (cloth)
ISBN-13: 978-0-226-79783-0 (paper)
ISBN-13: 978-0-226-79797-7 (e-book)
DOI: https://doi.org/10.7208/chicago/9780226797977.001.0001

Library of Congress Cataloging-in-Publication Data

Names: Dearborn, John A., author.
Title: Power shifts : Congress and presidential representation / John A. Dearborn.
Other titles: Chicago studies in American politics.
Description: Chicago : The University of Chicago Press, 2021. | Series: Chicago
    studies in American politics | Includes bibliographical references and index.
Identifiers: LCCN 2021007569 | ISBN 9780226797663 (cloth) | ISBN 9780226797830
    (paperback) | ISBN 9780226797977 (e-book)
Subjects: LCSH: Executive power—United States. | Presidents—United States. |
    United States—Politics and government.
Classification: LCC JK516.D427 2021 | DDC 352.23/50973—dc23
LC record available at https://lccn.loc.gov/2021007569

♾ This paper meets the requirements of ANSI/NISO z39.48-1992 (Permanence of
Paper).

For my parents,
Betsy and John B. Dearborn

Contents

Preface: Rethinking a Political Truism

It is nearly instinctual in the political clerisy—and this holds true whether the administration is Republican or Democratic—to portray the president as the elected representative of the entire people, "The People," as it is commonly put, with congressmen portrayed as . . . mere representatives of wards, sections, and districts, thus a cracked mirror of the People.

ROBERT NISBET, 1988[1]

"I pledge to every citizen of our land that I will be president for all Americans, and this is so important to me," proclaimed Donald Trump in the early-morning hours of November 9, 2016, soon after he learned that he had been elected president.[2] The campaign had been unusually contentious, and the outcome came as one of the most shocking political upsets in American electoral history.[3] By invoking the traditional promise of the president-elect, Trump moved immediately to calm the nation, to ease the anxieties of those unnerved by his divisive campaign rhetoric, and to rise to the expectations of the office he had been elected to hold. His words endorsed a common understanding of the uniqueness of that office, that it represents the nation as a whole. The idea that national unity is realized in presidential representation was "right out of a good-government playbook."[4]

As if following a script, two of the other central players in the drama of the 2016 election chimed in.[5] In her concession speech later that day, Hillary Clinton spoke of deference and solidarity: "Donald Trump is going to be our president. We owe him an open mind and the chance to lead."[6] Directly referring to Trump's early-morning pledge, President Barack Obama echoed that call in a Rose Garden address that afternoon: "We are Americans first. We're patriots first. We all want what's best for this country. That's what I heard in Mr. Trump's remarks last night. That's what I heard when I spoke to him directly. And I was heartened by that. That's what the country needs: a sense of unity." Still, Obama spoke of those prospects wistfully, seeming to be none too certain that the president-elect would continue this posture: "I hope that he maintains that spirit throughout this transition, and I certainly hope that's how his Presidency has a chance to begin."[7]

We measure our presidents against this yardstick. The truism that presidents are elected in a nationwide canvas carries the strong presumption that they will take an encompassing view of the affairs of state, that they are uniquely positioned to represent everyone in the country. But notwithstanding Trump's ritualistic invocation of that idea upon his victory, judgments of his performance in adhering to that standard were particularly harsh. "Most presidents believed that their role was to lead the country as a whole, not just a faction," chided *New York Times* White House correspondent Peter Baker in reviewing the first year of the Trump administration.[8] The historian Sean Wilentz accused Trump of a "colossal failure" to "avoid partisan and factional rancor, and . . . unite the country in a great common purpose."[9] A fellow Republican, Senator Jeff Flake (R-AZ), took to the floor of Congress to deliver a blistering speech denouncing Trump on the same basis. He scolded the president for failing to provide "disinterested service to the nation as a whole," and he invoked another Republican president, Theodore Roosevelt, as the embodiment of that ideal of national stewardship.[10] Another reference to TR's uplifting style, this one from the deathbed of former representative John Dingell (D-MI), lamented the degraded state of the presidency under Trump's leadership: "the presidential bully pulpit seems dedicated to sowing division and denigrating, often in the most irrelevant and infantile personal terms, the political opposition."[11]

No doubt, all presidents fall short of our exalted ideal of national representation. Presidents do not shed their political biases or their partisan allegiances on assuming office. It would be reckless for them to ignore their political base. Nonetheless, most presidents have felt compelled to maintain the pretense that they are uniquely representative of all the American people.[12] George W. Bush affirmed that his administration understood that its "job is to represent all of America."[13] "One of the things I learned as president," Barack Obama observed, "is you represent the entire country."[14]

What set Trump apart was not that he failed to represent all the people, but that he quickly lost interest in the idea and even became openly contemptuous of it. Downplaying the importance of reaching out to a wider constituency, Trump speculated, "I think my base is so strong, I'm not sure that I have to do that."[15] Observers across the political spectrum took note, especially during the 2020 election. The incumbent's Democratic opponent, former vice president Joe Biden, offered a sharp contrast to Trump's attitude: "That's the job of a president. To represent all of us, not just our base or our party."[16] But most telling were statements from former officials who had served high in the Trump administration. Decrying Trump's response to nationwide protests responding to police violence against African Americans in 2020, former secretary of defense James Mattis issued a blistering statement: "Donald Trump is the first president in my lifetime who does not try to unite the American people—does not even pretend to try. Instead he tries to divide us. We are witnessing the consequences of three years of this deliberate effort."[17] John Kelly, Trump's former chief of staff, embraced Mattis's critique: "I think we need to look harder at who we elect. . . . Are they willing, if they're elected, to represent all of their constituents, not just the base, but all of their constituents?"[18] Even Trump administration allies concurred with that assessment, if not the concern behind it. "Trump is far more divisive than past presidents," admitted Republican donor and Trump supporter Dan Eberhart. "His strength is stirring up his base, not calming the waters."[19]

Why would President Trump so pointedly abandon what has historically been considered an essential claim to presidential authority? Implicitly, Trump seemed to think that the idea of presidential representation had lost a good deal of its purchase, that it is a less valuable warrant for presidential leadership today than it was in the past. He appeared to believe that he had more to gain by jettisoning that idea in favor a narrower conception of accountability and a more direct connection to his own political supporters. And while Joe Biden, Trump's opponent, stamped his electoral victory over the president with a promise of restoration—"I pledge to be a president . . . who doesn't see red states and blue states [but] only sees the United States"— the 2020 contest exposed just how tenuous that idea had become.[20] The *New York Times* editorial board described it as "a soothing bit of uplift" with a decidedly hollow ring: "in a nation so starkly polarized, what does it even mean?"[21]

At issue here are not just perceptions of Trump's performance in office, but perceptions of the institution of the presidency itself. Two assessments, offered eight decades apart, are instructive. In the first statement, the claim of presidential representation is portrayed as plausible. Because "both houses [of Congress] now tend to consider all legislation from local or regional viewpoints," one newspaper wrote during Franklin Roosevelt's presidency in 1934, "the nation has come to conceive of a President as the one man in Washington who represents the people as a whole."[22] In the second statement, such a notion is dismissed as ridiculous. "No one man—or woman—can possibly represent the varied, competing interests of 327 million citizens," surmised CBS journalist John Dickerson in 2018.[23] Statements like these suggest that the perceived validity of the concept of presidential representation may have changed dramatically over time.

Does that matter? This book argues that it does. If the idea of presidential representation has been losing purchase—if it was perceived as plausible in decades past but is viewed more skeptically today—then prior institutional investments made on the basis of that idea will stand exposed, and actions drawing on those endowments will be called into question.

Consider two controversies about Trump's use of his authority. One involves immigration policy. In 2019, President Trump declared a national emergency at the US-Mexico border in order to get funding for a desired border wall that Congress had denied him. This was widely viewed as an illegitimate use of presidential power. But it was the National Emergencies Act, passed by Congress in 1976, that served as Trump's pretext. The long-standing assumption behind granting emergency powers to the president was that incumbents would use them only to serve the national interest.[24] As Elizabeth Goitein observed in the *Atlantic*, "This edifice of extraordinary powers has historically rested on the assumption that the president will act in the country's best interest when using them."[25]

A second example involves trade policy. Beginning in the 1930s, Congress had delegated sweeping powers over trade to the president, believing that occupants of the White House would have the discipline to act in the national interest by keeping tariff rates low. Trump, however, raised tariffs not only on products made in China, but also on goods made by US allies in North America and Europe. While many presidents have used threats of tariffs in negotiating trade agreements, Trump renounced the free trade orthodoxy that went back decades. When Trump asserted "I am a Tariff Man," he upended the assumption that presidents acting in the national interest on trade meant reducing tariffs through trade agreements.[26] "The Trump administration's trade policy is a disaster," one congressional Republican staffer complained, and "not in the best interest of the United States."[27] Even more provocatively, Trump's own national security adviser, John Bolton, would later bluntly charge that, in trade negotiations with China, there was a "confluence in Trump's mind of his own political interests and US national interests."[28]

In each of these instances, the political significance of the idea of presidential representation was on full display. That idea has been institutionally formative, and in the course of America's political development, it has come back to haunt us. The Trump presidency calls for a renewed look at the powers of the presidency and the ideas that shaped their development. As this book will show, presidential representation is no innocuous truism. Instead, it has been one of the most consequential ideas in American political history.

Introduction: Legislating Presidential Power

No institution of American government has been more profoundly reshaped by ideas than the presidency. And it is not just that the power of the presidency has expanded in accordance with our ideational projections. More striking is that the institution most responsible for the expansion of presidential powers is the one we would expect to be most suspicious of the office. Congress built the modern presidency, and it did so by projecting its own core idea—the idea of national representation—onto the occupant of the White House. It recast the nation's chief *executive* as its chief *representative*.

It is hard at this late date to recapture the novelty of the idea that the president is the nation's representative. The proposition seems to win by default. No other officer in American government can stake such a claim. But the idea that the American government admits of a single national representative is only loosely connected to the constitutional frame, and its successive incarnations have grated in increasingly consequential ways against the rest of the governmental structure. Historically, advocates of presidential representation have been renounced, time and again, as constitutional subversives. The idea is one that has always been suspect and that nevertheless became deeply ingrained in the way we govern.

On its face, the concept is simple: the president is the only officer of the federal government (besides the vice president) selected by a national constituency. But that close association of selection with representation packs a punch. In Congress, lawmakers are elected by districts for the House of Representatives and by states for the Senate. Each branch of the legislature, *as a whole*, represents the nation, but *as individuals*, lawmakers are directly accountable only to parts of it. If selection determines representation, legislators might be thought to pay more attention to the interests of their specific districts or states than to the nation as a whole.[1] A similar observation might be made about the executive branch itself. Most appointed and career officials serve in one or another of the departments and agencies. Together, they encompass all the commitments and responsibilities of the national government, but individually, they might be viewed as beholden to the particular missions and interests that their agencies serve. The president, by contrast, appears directly accountable to the entire citizenry, the unique steward of the national interest.

Of course, talk of representing the whole nation is always something of a conceit. For much of American history, representation discriminated by race and gender. Most people were excluded. Even today, the question of who gets represented and how is a topic of considerable controversy. But this would not be the first time that empirical validity had little to do with the impact of an idea on political life. And the idea that the president is the only institutional actor in America that prioritizes the national perspective is an especially potent one. The potential allure of presidential representation is nicely illustrated in a political cartoon from January 1937 (figure 1.1). Drawing on the "Noah's Ark" story, several features of the depiction stand out for attention. The nation is facing a significant challenge—an impending flood from a major storm. To meet that challenge, Congress is charged with building an ark. However, Congress is surrounded by special interests of all kinds, attempting to distract the nation's legislators from the work that will save us. Only one figure, the president, is dedicated exclusively unto the task at hand. Franklin Roosevelt, here in the figure of Noah, tells Congress, "Pay no attention to them, let's get back on the job."

The implication of the cartoon is as clear as it is significant. The president, being uniquely attentive to the national interest, guides Congress to ignore the special interests competing for its attention and encourages it instead to meet the needs of the country as a whole. No mere axiom, this depiction of presidential stewardship is revolutionary. It challenges the representative legitimacy of the legislative branch.[2] Without the president's guidance, it tells us, Congress will have difficulty focusing on the nation's work and keeping the ship of state afloat.

And if the president bears the primary responsibility for the work of Congress, the new ship will be very different from the old one. Basic governing rearrangements will have to be rethought, and the adaptability of the governing framework will be sorely tested.[3] The idea of presidential representation envisions a shift in the constitutional division of labor, anticipating a relocation of the hub of policymaking from the legislative to the executive branch.

FIGURE 1.1. Jerry Doyle, *Camden Courier-Post* (*Morning Post*), January 7, 1937, 10. © 1937 Gannett-Community Publishing. All rights reserved. Used under license.

Changes commensurate with that new understanding will affect the separation of powers and system of checks and balances.

An enduring puzzle in the history of the relationship between the executive and legislative branches concerns the rise of the institutional presidency. Why did Congress build it, passing authority that seemed securely vested by the Constitution in the legislature to the chief executive? And why, in more recent decades, did it attempt to reverse course and curb that authority? This book pegs these developments to ideas, showing that the changing views of legislators about the legitimacy of presidential representation are essential to how Congress has addressed presidential power over time.

The Institutional Presidency: A Congressional Creation

As a rule, presidents are power maximizers.[4] They are motivated to expand their prerogatives. Whether it is in driving hard bargains with other actors in the political system, centralizing their control over the executive branch, or acting unilaterally, presidential power seeking is persistent and clear.[5] Yet for all the attention consistently devoted to the issue of presidents *demanding* power or trying to attain it for themselves, the more puzzling and consequential change to the presidency in the twentieth century was Congress actively *granting* presidents greater power in the form of new agenda-setting authority and executive branch resources. "One of the striking facts of the modern presidency," noted James Sundquist, "is the extent to which it was built through congressional initiative."[6] Rather than just a presidential "demand side," Sean Gailmard and John Patty observe, the institutionalization of the presidency required a congressional "supply side" that "has received much less focus from scholars."[7]

Congress can legislate presidential power. It did so repeatedly between 1910 and 1949, culminating in several landmark laws that established a new relationship between the executive and legislative branches. The Budget and Accounting Act (BAA) of 1921 made the president responsible for submitting an annual budget to Congress and created the Bureau of the Budget (BOB) (today's Office of Management and Budget [OMB]). The Reciprocal Trade Agreements Act (RTAA) of 1934 allowed the president to enter into bilateral trade agreements without congressional assent. The Reorganization Act of 1939 gave the president qualified authority to reorganize the executive branch subject to legislative veto. It was soon used to establish the Executive Office of the President (EOP). The Employment Act of 1946 made the president responsible for submitting an annual Economic Report to Congress and established the Council of Economic Advisers (CEA). And the National Security Act of 1947 created the National Security Council (NSC), as well as the Central Intelligence Agency (CIA), Joint Chiefs of Staff, and the National Military Establishment, which soon became the Department of Defense.

Cumulatively, these laws created an institutional presidency. The office was broadened, deepened, and more fully articulated. The new edifice exhibited two striking features. First, presidents themselves did not simply seek to become more influential in the lawmaking process. Congress openly enlisted presidential participation in these policy areas by statute. Together, these laws routinized the involvement of *all* presidents in what were erstwhile legislative responsibilities. Legislative leadership by the president was virtually compelled. Second, as part of Congress calling for presidents to play a more significant part in the legislative process, it also granted presidents new re-sources for that role—including more staff, new institutional accoutrements and establishments, and greater expertise to draw on. Congress's augmenta-tion of the organizational capacity of the presidency was monumental.[8]

The implications were correspondingly profound. Although the roles, re-sponsibilities, and capacities of the presidency were by the early twentieth century already growing beyond what was anticipated at the Founding, the institutional presidency inverted the original scheme. Advocates of presiden-tial representation spoke openly of the reversal of roles, now with the presi-dent proposing policies and the Congress offering a check on that officer's legislative ambitions. We all learn that the Founders recognized a need for "energy in the executive," but it is hard to discern in their Constitution a robust idea of the president as a legislative leader.[9] Indeed, the governing arrangements of the Constitution were meant, in part, to constrain the ex-ecutive power. Just as a new "rhetorical presidency" featuring policy-based appeals to the public by presidents was layered on an old Constitution with different expectations of presidential leadership, a correspondingly new in-stitutional presidency was built atop a scheme that had imagined Congress as the "first branch." Dispensing with the need for formal amendments, re-formers endorsed a redeployment of the executive in a new role, promising greater presidential initiative, capacity, and independence.[10]

CONGRESS'S INTERESTS

Why would Congress act as the patron of presidential power? Did its members not recognize that they were acting counter to their institutional self-interest and compromising the legislature's pride of place in republican government?

The predominant explanations for this apparent paradox concentrate on why Congress might determine these actions to be in its own interest after all. First, scholars have pointed to Congress's collective action problem—the difficulty of getting 535 legislators who each have incentives to prioritize their individual careers over institutional prerogatives to solve particular policy problems. Congress, James Sundquist argued, suffers from an "incapacity to act quickly," an "incapacity to plan," and a lack of "centralizing institutions," necessitating a greater role for the presidency to help solve these problems.[11] By these accounts, Congress recognizes its difficulties in acting coherently and delegates authority to the presidency. Second, scholars have cited the role of information as an explanation for the creation of new executive branch resources. It is in Congress's interest, Sean Gailmard and John Patty contend, for presidents to use quality information and expertise in exercising their authority. Therefore, Congress seeks to ensure that such information will be utilized by the president. By placing organizations providing informational capacity directly under control of the president, Congress increases the likelihood of the president choosing to take advantage of these resources in exercising authority. Even if this presidential control comes at Congress's expense, their theory posits, it is worth it in order to have presidents base their decisions on quality information.[12]

These accounts of Congress's own interests provide crucial insights into the institution's role in supplying power to the presidency. Yet they also each face key limitations.

First, a focus on legislators' collective action problems illuminates only one step in Congress's choice to grant authority to presidents. If legislators perceive that they collectively cannot effectively solve a major policy problem, they are then more likely to see a need to improvise and establish new institutional arrangements. That, however, does not in itself explain the choice to delegate authority to the presidency. Any explanation of the *design* of an institutional reform to solve a collective action problem needs to account for the counterfactuals—the alternative arrangements that were not chosen. Which institutional solutions did Congress consider? Which did it choose and why? Presidential empowerment was not the only potential solution to a congressional collective action problem available as legislators debated reforms between 1910 and 1949. Other institutional arrangements with precedent were available, such as the creation of stronger centralized committees, the development of new organizational capacities under congressional control, or the formation of independent agencies or commissions. As this book will show, Congress perceived the localistic incentives and tendencies of individual legislators, arising from their district and state constituencies, as the principal source of the institution's collective action problems. In seeking a correction, Congress bought into the idea of presidential representation. The elegant inverse logic of the idea proved irresistible. If local constituencies led to myopic behavior from legislators, then a national constituency meant that presidents were more likely to act in the interests of the people as a whole. Thus, reformers looked to an empowered presidency as a solution.

Second, Congress's own interest in having the president utilize information and expertise in exercising the office's authority sheds light on another step in its choice to augment the organizational capacity of the presidency. When Congress perceives presidents to already possess authority in a particular policy area, this account suggests, it is then in its institutional self-interest to grant presidents direct control over new informational resources in the executive branch so that presidents are more likely to utilize expertise.

That logic might suffice in the area of national security, where the president's constitutional warrants are particularly strong. But for this explanation alone to be sufficient, we would have to imagine that the president had preexisting authority in all the policy areas in which Congress was legislating. In fact, between 1910 and 1949, in debates over budgeting, trade, reorganization, and employment, Congress knew that it was granting the president *new* authority. I account for this crucial prior step, showing how the idea of presidential representation influenced that choice to formalize presidential responsibility in these policy areas.

Important as it was, the creation of the institutional presidency is also only half the story. Between 1970 and 1984, Congress reconsidered its own role as a patron of presidential power. With varying approaches and outcomes, Congress challenged the role of presidents in the same policy areas in which it had previously expanded their powers. In some cases, it bolstered its own responsibilities and institutional capacities as a way to readdress the perceived imbalance in the relative powers of the legislative and executive branches. The Congressional Budget and Impoundment Control Act (CBICA) of 1974 created a separate congressional budget process and established the Congressional Budget Office (CBO) as a way to counter the president's role in the budget process. The Trade Act of 1974 restored a more explicit role for Congress in trade policy by requiring congressional assent for trade agreements under a new fast-track procedure as a way to counter the president's privileged perspective in negotiating trade agreements. Taking a slightly different tack, the Full Employment and Balanced Growth Act of 1978 (popularly known as Humphrey-Hawkins after its congressional sponsors) added some new requirements for the president's annual Economic Report, but more significantly, it called for a more robust role for the Federal Reserve in economic policymaking and in implementing congressionally established policy mandates. In other cases, Congress rescinded presidential authority entirely. After first renewing a more limited presidential reorganization authority in the Reorganization Act of 1977, Congress ultimately declined to renew such authority after 1984, as legislators reacted to the Supreme Court's determination in *Immigration and Naturalization Service v. Chadha* (1983) that the legislative veto procedure that reorganization authority had relied on was unconstitutional.

This is not to say that Congress was consistent in its rollbacks or that its reforms all operated as intended. Some of these new initiatives ended up ratifying a significant role for the president. Even as the 1974 trade law required explicit congressional assent, its new fast-track procedure significantly privileged the president's perspective in the legislative process by requiring legislators to vote on any agreements without amendment. Similarly, although the War Powers Resolution (WPR) of 1973 attempted to limit presidential war power and recover Congress's national security authority, it ultimately left the president with significant authority.

These variations in outcomes will be considered in due course. The critical point is that Congress took significant action to push back against the institutional presidency. Such actions pose a challenge for the collective action and informational accounts. In the 1970s and 1980s, Congress still possessed these structural disadvantages. What then explains this congressional reconsideration? What had changed was that presidential power was now viewed with deeper suspicion; the old solution had become the problem. As I show, the declining legitimacy of the idea of presidential representation was a crucial influence on Congress's reassessment of presidential power.

CONGRESS'S PARTISANSHIP

Scholars might also turn to partisanship as the primary explanation for Congress's changing approaches to the institutional presidency, depending on conditions of unified or divided government.[13] The expectation would be that during unified government, a shared partisan interest would lead the majority in Congress to grant new authority and resources to a copartisan president. During divided government (likely depending on whether an opposing party controlled both chambers), partisan interests might then dictate that Congress attempt to rescind such authority and resources. At first, this explanation might appear persuasive for laws creating the institutional presidency. The BAA of 1921, RTAA of 1934, Reorganization Act of 1939, and Employment Act of 1946 were all passed during periods of unified party control. Only the National Security Act of 1947 was enacted during divided government. By contrast, the CBICA of 1974, Trade Act of 1974, and WPR of 1973 were all passed during divided government (the Reorganization Act of 1977 and the 1978 Humphrey-Hawkins Act were enacted during unified control).

A closer look at the vote margins, however, tells a different story. First, consider the laws that created the institutional presidency, which might appear to be mostly due to unified government (table 1.1). An earlier version of the BAA had passed in 1920 during divided control (with a Republican Congress and a Democratic president), signaling bipartisan support for reform, and while the 1921 statute was enacted during unified government, it passed with a nearly unanimous vote. The RTAA of 1934, while passed largely with Democratic majorities during unified party control, nonetheless featured support from some key Republicans and dissent from other Democrats. Moreover,

TABLE 1.1. Votes on Laws Creating the Institutional Presidency

Law	Party Control	House Votes (Yea–Nay)	Senate Votes (Yea–Nay)
Budget and Accounting Act of 1921	Unified (Republican)	*House Bill:* 344–9 R: 250–1 D: 93–8 *Conference Report:* 335–3 R: 232–1 D: 102–2	*Senate Bill:* No recorded vote *Conference Report:* No recorded vote
Reciprocal Trade Agreements Act of 1934	Unified (Democratic)	*House Bill:* 274–111 R: 2–99 D: 269–11 *Accept Senate Amendments:* 154–53 Division vote	*Senate Bill:* 57–33 R: 5–28 D: 51–5
Reorganization Act of 1939	Unified (Democratic)	*House Bill:* 246–153 R: 8–148 D: 234–5 *Conference Report:* No recorded vote	*Senate Bill:* 63–23 R: 2–19 D: 58–3 *Conference Report:* No recorded vote
Employment Act of 1946	Unified (Democratic)	*House Bill:* 255–126 R: 58–105 D: 195–21 *Conference Report:* 322–84 R: 114–67 D: 206–17	*Senate Bill:* 71–10 R: 27–6 D: 43–4 *Conference Report:* No recorded vote
National Security Act of 1947	Divided (Democratic President, Republican House and Senate)	*House Bill:* No recorded vote *Conference Report:* No recorded vote	*Senate Bill:* No recorded vote *Conference Report:* No recorded vote

Sources: Congressional Record, govtrack.us, voteview.com.

Note: Votes of lawmakers from minor parties are omitted from party totals.

subsequent reauthorizations of presidential trade authority occurred under both unified and divided government. The Reorganization Act of 1939, while passed by Democrats during unified government, was not a predominantly partisan story. In fact, the main political battle over that legislation occurred among Democrats themselves. A revolt by congressional Democrats derailed the 1938 legislation, and the 1939 statute passed during a session of Congress that featured smaller Democratic majorities in each chamber than had been present in the previous session. The Employment Act of 1946, occurring during unified control, nevertheless passed with an overwhelming bipartisan majority. And the National Security Act of 1947, enacted during divided government (with a Republican Congress and a Democratic president), also was so widely supported that it was enacted with no recorded votes.

TABLE 1.2. Votes on Laws Reconsidering Presidential Authority

Law	Party Control	House Votes (Yea–Nay)	Senate Votes (Yea–Nay)
Congressional Budget and Impoundment Control Act of 1974	Divided (Republican President, Democratic House and Senate)	House Bill: 386–23 R: 180–3 D: 206–20 Conference Report: 401–6 R: 177–2 D: 224–4	Senate Bill: 80–0 R: 29–0 D: 49–0 Conference Report: 75–0 R: 25–0 D: 49–0
Trade Act of 1974	Divided (Republican President, Democratic House and Senate)	House Bill: 272–140 R: 160–19 D: 112–121 Conference Report: 323–36 R: 147–11 D: 176–25	Senate Bill: 77–4 R: 31–1 D: 44–3 Conference Report: 72–4 R: 30–1 D: 40–3
Reorganization Act of 1977	Unified (Democratic)	House Bill: 395–22 R: 129–11 D: 266–11	Senate Bill: 94–0 R: 35–0 D: 58–0 Accept House Amendments: No recorded vote
Full Employment and Balanced Growth Act of 1978	Unified (Democratic)	House Bill: 257–152 R: 24–111 D: 233–41 Accept Senate Amendments: 56–14 Division vote	Senate Bill: 70–19 R: 17–15 D: 53–3
War Powers Resolution of 1973	Divided (Republican President, Democratic House and Senate)	House Bill: 244–170 R: 72–109 D: 172–61 Conference Report: 238–123 R: 75–85 D: 163–38 Veto Override: 284–135 R: 86–103 D: 198–32	Senate Bill: 72–18 R: 22–14 D: 49–4 Conference Report: 75–20 R: 26–13 D: 48–6 Veto Override: 75–18 R: 25–14 D: 49–3

Sources: Congressional Record, govtrack.us, voteview.com.
Note: Votes of lawmakers from minor parties are omitted from party totals.

Second, consider the laws in which Congress reevaluated and challenged the institutional presidency (table 1.2). Though the 1973 resolution on war powers and 1974 laws on budgeting and trade all occurred during divided government, a closer look reveals that they passed with substantial bipartisan majorities. Key congressional Republicans were among their most vigorous proponents. Both the 1977 reorganization law and the 1978 employment law were bipartisan as well, and they were enacted during unified government. Congress also ultimately declined to renew presidential reorganization authority after the Supreme Court declared the legislative veto to be invalid in 1983. Though this initial choice occurred during divided government, the lack of interest in reauthorizing that power was bipartisan, and such authority was never subsequently enacted for presidents even during periods of unified party control. In short, partisanship is not a sufficient explanation for Congress's actions in these episodes.

CONGRESS'S IDEAS

Is there a common thread between Congress's creation of the institutional presidency and its later doubts about its own role in supporting presidential power? Following the patterned rise and alteration of the institutional presidency across several different policy areas points to the formative effect of a specific idea. I argue that the link between these two changing impulses is the idea of presidential representation. To be clear, my claim is not that the perceived legitimacy of the idea of presidential representation by itself *caused* the passage of these laws in either time period. Rather, I argue that the perceived validity of the idea at a given period of time proved decisive in determining the *design* of several of these statutes and the choice of those solutions over other feasible alternatives.[14] Central to legislators' actions were their own understandings of the likelihood of presidents acting in the national interest. This was the essential belief about presidential behavior that Congress relied on in passing laws that enhanced presidential power in the first half of the twentieth century. When Congress began to question that idea's validity in the wake of Watergate and Vietnam, it reversed course and challenged presidential authority.

Congress was by no means simply idealistic or magnanimous in its actions. It candidly recognized its own collective action problem in a number of policy domains and likewise sought to improve the quality of policymaking by incentivizing presidents to utilize expertise. Congress also passed laws to deal with particular challenges, not because it simply set out to change presidential power. Statutes that created the institutional presidency responded to problems such as rising debt (budgeting), the Great Depression and rising tariffs worldwide (trade), the proliferation of executive branch agencies during the New Deal (reorganization), and the influx of returning GIs after World War II (employment). Problems encountered at these critical junctures opened up the possibilities for institutional change, but by themselves, they were not responsible for the subsequent institutional choice. At the core of these seemingly rational choices and efforts to deal with significant national challenges lay an idea: presidents better represent the national interest than legislators. Congress built the modern presidency in the policy areas of budgeting, trade, reorganization, and employment on claims about presidential representation. Lawmakers did more than recognize their institution's collective action problem; they designed these statutes under the influence of an intellectual program of reform that heralded the purported merits of the president's national perspective.

Later, many legislators had partisan reasons to question presidential authority in the 1970s and 1980s. Congress also responded to significant challenges, such as stagflation. But here again, the broadly perceived validity of presidential representation in American political culture was central to Congress's actions. Rising doubts about the idea influenced Congress's reconsideration of the institutional presidency across the same policy areas. The most conspicuous wrinkle in these reform patterns is telling as well. Although national security reform was also associated with the claim of presidential representation, it ran up against the preexisting authority of the president as commander in chief under Article II. That alternative basis for presidential authority constrained the later congressional pushback over war powers.

The Impact of Presidential Representation

The starting point for unpacking the idea of presidential representation is that the president is the only officer of government (besides the vice president) elected by the whole people.[15] But there are multiple ways to interpret this simple truth.[16] One interpretation is *plebiscitary*. In this telling, the president represents the preponderance of opinion and empowers a particular portion of the population. The other interpretation of *stewardship* is more encompassing. Selected by a national constituency that is far flung and heterogenous, the president might be thought of as standing for all citizens, possessing a unique and broad perspective, and focusing on the pursuit of policy outcomes that would reflect the needs of the entire country. In short, the president is the best available institutional embodiment of the national interest.

Though these two interpretations of a representative presidency may be distinguished from each other and may seem to carry very different implications, they are deeply intertwined in both scholarship and the historical record. Moreover, the comparative claim in both conceptions—that the president is the superior representative—arises from a clear institutional origin. As a premise, presidential representation is more plausible in governing systems featuring a separation of powers and an independent executive, rather than parliamentary systems in which the executive is located in the legislature.[17] That separation is what allows proponents of the idea to draw their effective contrast between the "representativeness" of the president and legislators. Juan Linz famously worried that such a separation allows the president or executive to claim independent authority from a separate election, contesting the legitimacy of the legislature as the primary representative of the people.[18] In fact, it permits even legislators themselves to buy into the same premise. Representative William Nathaniel Rogers (D-NH), for example, provided an exemplary statement of the claim when he said to his fellow members of Congress in 1936, "I call to your attention the fact that while a Congressman represents a district—a Senator a State—the President represents the whole United States. He must view the country and the people as a whole."[19]

Assessing presidential representation has become a preoccupation of recent political science. Existing accounts of this idea tend to take either a *behavioral* or a *developmental* approach. The behavioral perspective takes the idea itself as its starting point. For some scholarship along these lines, the idea is a key *expectation* in theories of distributive politics or institutional design. Others seek to interrogate this assumption, using presidential representation as a normative standard by which to judge and measure presidential *performance*. Alternatively, the historical perspective considers the idea's impact on American politics and government over time. The focus here is less on the validity of the idea itself and more on how the idea has mattered to changes to the operation of the American constitutional system.

BEHAVIOR: EXPECTATION AND PERFORMANCE

The idea of presidential representation is a central *expectation* for many scholars studying institutional behavior in America. They describe the president as the only official in government with a focus on the national interest, and they then infer how the president will behave in interactions with other political actors. For these scholars, this supposition is not just about presidents per se. Rather, any actor with a more expansive constituency is expected to behave in a different way from an actor with a smaller constituency.[20] Applying this logic to presidents, scholars generate expectations for presidential behavior compared to other actors in the political system. Presidents are thought to be less likely to respond to interest group pressures than are legislators or executive agency officials, while they are more likely to seek efficient bureaucratic structures and to generally pursue nationally oriented policy outcomes.[21]

Notably, this assumption is fixed and time invariant: the president will be guided by the national interest, while legislators or other bureaucrats will respond to more parochial interests.

Of course, how well presidents represent the nation as a whole is ultimately an empirical question. Seeking to measure presidential *performance*, another group of scholars has interrogated whether the assumption of presidential representation holds in practice. These works set up normative standards of representation and judge how presidents behave compared to them. One standard of performance is *centrism*. The centrist view equates proper presidential representation with the views of the median voter. Positing that presidents should primarily respond to the national median voter rather than to their party's median voter, one group of scholars has largely concluded that presidential representation is, in B. Dan Wood's telling, a "myth." Presidents, they find, behave primarily as partisans, especially in the modern era.[22]

Another standard of performance is *universalism*. This view holds that presidents should avoid serving particularistic interests and instead represent the nation more broadly. Here too presidents are often judged poorly. Scholars have found that presidents prioritize states that are critical to building their Electoral College majority.[23] As Douglas Kriner and Andrew Reeves posit, this need to win swing states in the Electoral College can lead presidents to utilize the executive branch for the pursuit of narrow goals, unevenly distributing benefits related to base closings, trade, disaster declarations, transportation funding, and federal grants.[24] They may even engage in pork barrel spending, the classic criticism of legislators.[25] At the same time, presidents may represent different groups and interests within the population unequally. As James Druckman and Lawrence Jacobs find, presidents favor the views of the affluent and politically well connected, as opposed to responding to aggregate public opinion.[26] In Elizabeth Sanders's view, there has long been "a presidential tilt toward the interests of capital."[27]

Not all evidence points in the negative direction. In evaluations of congressional performance, the distributional consequences of geographic representation and the localistic incentives of lawmakers—especially in the Senate—are well documented.[28] Historically, Congress has aggregated distributive preferences in policy areas such as land distribution, Civil War pensions, tariffs, veterans' bonuses, entitlement expenditures, and taxation.[29] Moreover, some evidence suggests that previous executive experience leads to a different perspective and behavior even for politicians who become legislators. For example, former governors who went on to serve as senators in Congress (during the period from 1983 to 2015) were less partisan than their colleagues who lacked executive experience.[30] Furthermore, compared to legislators, presidents may also be able to exercise a nationalizing influence on proposed legislation in Congress, especially during major wars.[31]

These contributions have provided necessary insights, and research on presidential performance will continue to shed light on the validity of presidential representation. At the same time, in many studies of presidential performance, scholars have a tendency to argue against a straw man. A perfect type of presidential representation is theorized, and the actual operations of the office are judged as failing to meet that standard. The key claim of presidential representation is not, however, an absolute one, but a comparative one, holding that presidents represent the nation as a whole, on average, *relatively* better than do members of Congress. Even as they marshal convincing evidence of presidential particularism, for example, Kriner and Reeves admit that presidents might "routinely take a more holistic, national view than do many members of Congress" on policy choice, while being more particularistic in the implementation of policy.[32] Rather than an absolute normative standard, it is this comparison of the relative performance of the president and Congress that has long been at the core of the idea of presidential representation.

Judging presidential performance also misses the broader consequences of the idea for American political development. The emphasis on performance tends to assume a fixed institutional universe of roles and responsibilities, rather than exploring the possibility that the concept of presidential representation itself may have had an impact on institutional change over time.

DEVELOPMENT: ORIGINS, INNOVATIONS, AND ADAPTABILITY

Current empirical criticism of the validity of presidential representation is symptomatic. The idea has been facing more doubts about its validity for decades. But this hints at a larger point. More than just a belief about presidential behavior or a standard of presidential performance, the concept of presidential representation itself is deeply implicated in the *development* of the American polity.[33] "Political institutions are involved in constant contestation," Josh Chafetz reminds us, "not simply for the substantive outcomes they desire, but for the authority to determine those outcomes."[34] The idea of presidential representation has been a source of legitimation for such institutional changes that have rearranged political authority between Congress and the presidency, altering how our government has functioned. Skepticism of that idea correspondingly exposes those arrangements to critical scrutiny.

Although many scholars agree on the importance of the idea of presidential representation, there is confusion and debate about *when* the idea became politically significant. Andrew Jackson is most prominently credited as the presidential promulgator of this claim, but scholars have nonetheless pointed to different periods of time in describing the rise of the idea of presidential representation to prominence, including the Founding, the Jeffersonian age, the Jacksonian period, and the Progressive Era.[35] One recent account of the American Founding even posits that a concept of executive representation that had developed in England was already embraced by a subset of the Founders who were swayed by the virtues of monarchy.[36] Early presidents also embraced the eighteenth-century notion of the "patriot king," seeking to transcend factions and stand only for the good of the whole nation.[37]

The preoccupation with pinpointing one precise moment of emergence has obscured the more consequential aspects of the idea. A glance at the various times held out as pivotal to the concept's emergence suggests a more significant implication for understanding the relationship between ideas and political development: each inflection point in the development of the idea has been associated with a different reform project.[38] Accordingly, in this book, I posit that the best way to understand presidential representation is through the institutional reforms that correspond to the idea or are thought to be entailed by the idea at different points in time. Once the question is changed from *when* the idea emerged to *what* reforms became associated with the idea, a much clearer picture emerges, both of the history of the idea itself and of its role in institutional change. The idea that the presidency is a representative institution—and the varied implications of that idea—emerged in the course of America's political development, and different institutional innovations become connected to the concept in different eras.

Begin with the Founding. The framers of the Constitution made the popular connection indirect in all institutions of the federal government except the House of Representatives. Legislators, wrote James Madison, were "more immediately the confidential guardians of the rights and liberties of the people."[39] Representation in the Anglo-American political tradition had developed as a means to present local grievances to the nation, formulate legislation, and check executive power.[40] As originally conceived, executive authority had a stronger constitutional basis than a popular one. Selected by the Electoral College, the president—the chief magistrate—was to be an independent officer who would execute the laws, serving also as a check on potential legislative tyranny.[41] Michael Lind goes so far as to suggest that "the idea of the chief executive as chief representative is French, not American."[42]

To be sure, the question of whether executives were representatives at all was, in fact, contested during the Founding era.[43] While in most states "the

governors were not regarded in any sense as 'representatives' of the people,"
in a few states, such as Massachusetts, the governor's "representative potential" was recognized.[44] Some of the framers, such as Gouverneur Morris and
James Wilson, favored direct election of the president by the people, while
most at the Constitutional Convention opposed it.[45] Significantly, Madison
contrasted the American republic with past republics on this point. In some
of the ancient republics, such as Rome, there had been individual officers
"annually *elected by the whole body of the people*, and considered as the *representatives* of the people, almost in their *plenipotentiary* capacity." But the
American government had no single officer elected by all: "The true distinction between these [ancient republics] and the American Government lies
in the total exclusion of the people in their collective capacity from any share in
the *latter*."[46]

The key point for my purposes is not whether all the framers were of the
same mind about the presidency; there was clearly disagreement. It is that
the institutional implications associated with the idea were limited. The understanding of executive representation at the time of the Founding was one
that emphasized *separation*, preserving executive independence and protecting the rights of the people against an encroaching legislature.[47] More ambitious understandings of presidential representation—that the chief executive was a superior national representative, and that the idea might be used
institutionally to *overcome* the separation of powers—came later and proved
transformative.

In the nineteenth century, the larger ambitions associated with the idea
of presidential representation became clearer and more disruptive. A plebiscitary conception of the idea was implicated in both Thomas Jefferson's
creation of a national political party and Andrew Jackson's claim of an electoral mandate to veto the reauthorization of the National Bank and remove
federal deposits from it.[48] Explicitly suggesting that a president could be a
superior representative of the people compared to legislators collectively, the
concept of the presidential mandate was contested for decades between supportive Democrats and suspicious Whigs. The idea took another step toward
becoming more widely accepted once the Republican Party and Abraham
Lincoln—previously a Whig opposed to Jacksonian mandate theory—
invoked the "voice of the people" as having supported the Union cause in the
1864 election.[49]

The institutional innovations attached to the idea in the nineteenth century included presidential vetoes on policy grounds, use of the removal
power, and claims of election mandates. Andrew Jackson pioneered these actions and claimed authority for them from his purported status as America's

chief representative.[50] Vetoing the reauthorization of the Second Bank of the United States partly because it was "incompatible with . . . sound policy," Jackson framed the 1832 election as a "general discussion" on the merits of the bank and hoped to be "sustained by my fellow citizens" in a contest against the will of Congress.[51] After winning reelection, Jackson claimed that he had legitimate authority to remove federal deposits from the bank because "the case was argued to the people" and "the people have sustained the President."[52] Defending his control over the secretary of the treasury through the use of the removal power, Jackson asserted, "The President is the direct representative of the American People, but the Secretaries are not."[53]

The institutional purposes attached to the idea in the nineteenth century were different from those that would be pursued by later reformers. By the early twentieth century, presidency-oriented reformers associated the concept with other entailments that combined to form the basis of the institutional presidency—a formal license for agenda setting in the legislative process and greater executive organizational capacity. This institutional presidency would be able to galvanize the government into concerted action for the national interest. Compared to the nineteenth-century reforms, the entailments of the idea in the twentieth century carried a more direct and candid departure from the original constitutional setup. Even as they had signified clear innovations, the nineteenth-century reforms associated with the idea arguably could more easily claim a firm textual grounding. The president's authority to veto legislation was clearly spelled out in Article I, and the removal power was soon said to be implied by Article II. Likewise, the Twelfth Amendment, adopted to allow the president and vice president to be elected on a party ticket, made it more plausible for presidents to claim a mandate under the workings of the Constitution.[54]

At every stage, however, the idea has had systemic implications, and it has advanced further on a critique of the existing constitutional order. A recent proposal for reform from two political scientists updates and illustrates the point. Decrying the Constitution as a "relic," William Howell and Terry Moe appeal to presidential representation to advance the cause of presidential agenda setting. In their view, the situation is dire, and promoting effective government will require a constitutional amendment. Their proposal would generalize the fast-track authority that presidents have enjoyed over trade policy. Under this process, presidents could submit legislation in Congress that would not be open to amendment by legislators. Moreover, the legislation would be subject to a straight up-or-down majority vote within a limited period of time. Howell and Moe's amendment, which would alter the separation-of-powers design by placing more weight on the proposals of the chief executive, is based explicitly on congressional incompetence and presidential stewardship. Its guiding assumption is that presidents will seek to represent the national interest *relatively* more than members of Congress and that they will, therefore, submit cohesive, nationally oriented legislation for Congress's consideration.[55] Pulling forward a long line of ideational development, Howell and Moe's proposal continues to leverage the concept of presidential representation in pursuit of a constitutional reordering. The idea alleges fatal pathologies in the existing system and claims to provide the cure.

As this book will show, this proposal is only the most recent in a long tradition of reforms based on the idea of presidential representation. The idea has served as the stimulus and intellectual rationale for many a reform agenda. The Howell and Moe proposal is also a reminder that the idea of presidential representation has become most associated with empowering the presidency legislatively.[56] The aim for reformers who have adopted the idea has long been to put the president's thumb on the scale of the legislative process, to use presidential agenda setting for the purpose of guiding legislators to reach outcomes that are in the interest of the entire nation and that they would not otherwise grasp. How much weight might be placed on presidential proposals can vary, but the point is to go beyond the president's Article II authority to periodically recommend measures.

And although presidential representation is most associated with empowering the presidency legislatively, the idea has implications for the president's administrative powers as well. After all, it is the *president's* perspective that is valued. Cabinet officers or other executive officials might be thought of as being too wedded to the particular interests of their own departments and agencies. Therefore, presidents would need some measure of control over the executive branch as a way to ensure that other executive officers cannot submit or advocate for alternative proposals.[57]

The more fully presidential representation is expressed institutionally, the more significant and problematic its intrusions on the government's intended formal arrangements are likely to be. Because providing such institutional means for presidential representation will, by degrees, scramble envisioned constitutional roles, an analysis of this idea's impact on American political development ultimately touches on the adaptability of the Constitution itself.

Plan of the Book

"It seems clear," James Ceaser writes, "that the executive could never have attained its recent status without its first being proclaimed by so many as the nation's only truly representative institution."[58] By contrast, Jeremy Bailey argues this "fairly straightforward consensus" masks the reality "that presidential representation has long been contested and remains unsettled."[59] This book takes up the task of determining whether and how much the idea of presidential representation influenced alterations to the operation and structure of our constitutional system of government. I aim to demonstrate this transformation empirically by considering how political actors apart from the president have viewed presidential power and how Congress's own actions have changed the role of the president. In doing so, I bridge these two viewpoints about the significance of the idea to the office's development. The idea was indeed always contested by political actors at many points in American political history. Yet even as there was contestation over the idea within specific periods of time, there were also broader shifts in the perceived validity of presidential representation in American political culture over time, and it is these shifts that proved consequential for institutional change.

Examining how ideas contribute to institutional change requires a historical institutional approach. I employ a combination of case studies and process tracing to isolate the impact of a particular idea, to consider how that idea affects perceptions of the appropriate bounds of presidential authority in several policy areas, and to compare the durability of such changes over time.[60] My selected cases are used to compare Congress's legislative actions that affected presidential authority both across different policy areas—budgeting, trade, reorganization, employment, and national security—and over two periods of time—the rise of the institutional presidency between 1910 and 1949 and the pushback against it between 1970 and 1984 (table 1.3). This is beneficial for two reasons. First, I can examine the similarities and differences in Congress's approach to presidential power among different policy areas within each period. Second, I can compare changes in Congress's approach to presidential power within the same policy area over time.[61]

TABLE 1.3. Policy Areas and Cases

Policy Areas	Choice, 1910–49: Cases	Durability, 1970–84: Cases
Budgeting	Budget and Accounting Act of 1921	Congressional Budget and Impoundment Control Act of 1974
Trade	Reciprocal Trade Agreements Act of 1934	Trade Act of 1974
Reorganization	Reorganization Act of 1939	Reorganization Act of 1977
		INS v. Chadha (1983)
Employment	Employment Act of 1946	Full Employment and Balanced Growth Act of 1978
National Security	National Security Act of 1947	War Powers Resolution of 1973

The core of this book's argument concerns the role of ideas in political change. Chapter 2 outlines a general framework that shows how ideas can be a common link between institutional choice and durability over time. This framework has two parts. The first part focuses on institutional choice. What would help determine the relative importance of a specific idea to a political outcome, such as the choice of a particular set of institutional arrangements? The second part concerns institutional durability. What would be needed to evaluate the extent to which the durability of a set of institutional arrangements relies on the continued perception of the legitimacy of an idea?

The book's empirical chapters are divided into two parts, covering the rise of the institutional presidency between 1910 and 1949 and Congress's later reconsideration of presidential power between 1970 and 1984. These chapters test these claims across five policy areas in which Congress considered and reconsidered presidential authority. They draw largely on primary source materials from the public record, as well as original archival documents from the congressional papers of lawmakers across the country. Within each individual case, I reconstruct the legislative process involved in the passage of a statute to determine the precise relevance of the idea of presidential representation.

Part 1 examines Congress's creation of the institutional presidency and assesses the extent to which the idea of presidential representation pushed the boundaries of constitutional adaptability. The introduction to part 1 establishes that laws enhancing presidential authority were passed in a context in which the idea of presidential representation was widely understood and discussed in elite political discourse. I then consider the passage of the Budget and Accounting Act of 1921 (chapter 3), Reciprocal Trade Agreements Act of 1934 and Employment Act of 1946 (chapter 4), and Reorganization Act of 1939 (chapter 5), showing that their common assumption was that the president would be less beholden to parochial interests than would members of Congress. Chapter 6 provides a contrasting case, an example of a reform that did not rely on the idea of presidential representation. It shows that the National Security Act of 1947 assumed that the president's national focus should be privileged in issues of security, but relied more heavily for its justification on the president's perceived authority as commander in chief from Article II. This alternative ideational basis for presidential power had significant developmental implications.

Part 2 examines the durability of these reforms in the face of rising doubts about the idea of presidential representation and increased scrutiny from Congress and the Supreme Court, evaluating the extent to which the institutional presidency could be pared back and how much reformers were constrained by Congress's earlier reinventions. The introduction to part 2 establishes that the legitimacy of the idea of presidential representation was widely called into question in public discourse in the wake of Vietnam and Watergate. The remaining chapters show that Congress applied those doubts about presidential representation in reconsidering presidential authority across the same policy areas. I consider the variation in Congress's attempts to reassert authority in budgeting (chapter 7), trade and unemployment (chapter 8), reorganization (chapter 9), and war powers (chapter 10).

Chapter 11 is the conclusion of the book. I reassess the implications of Congress's changing view of presidential authority for our understanding of the relationship between ideas and the politics of adaptability. While Congress's reassertion of its authority affected presidential authority in some policy areas, its more lasting effect was to change the terms of debate over institutional reform. Champions of the unitary executive theory—the controversial and contested idea that the president possesses the entire executive power from Article II—responded to that new emphasis on formalism, seeking to ground presidential authority in original meaning.[62] Finally, I suggest a broader lesson of this book. Ideas gain influence from their ability to repudiate established ideas and institutional arrangements, but the emergence of that opportunity first requires some level of agreement on what constitute the primary problems of our governing institutions.

Ideas and Political Development

> The history of political ideas has been a story of oscillations, of attack and repulse and counter-attack. The dominant thought of one era exerts itself to achieve a political result; in the next, the shortcomings of the achievement invite audacious thinkers to insult an enthroned idol by unfavorable comparisons with old gods which it has displaced.
>
> JOHN DICKINSON, 1930[1]

It's an age-old question: how do ideas impact political change? "There is today a widespread attempt to show the futility of ideas," complained Walter Lippmann in 1914. Most observers of politics today might agree with Lippmann that "you cannot escape ideas."[2] Some might suspect, as the economist John Maynard Keynes asserted, that "ideas . . . are more powerful than is commonly understood."[3] But how ideas affect politics, and how much power they exercise, remains a puzzle. At issue are basic matters of motivation, interest, institutional design, and political reform.

Showing that ideas matter to politics is no simple task. This relationship sits at the center of the longest-standing disputes in the social sciences and humanities. The classic Marx-Weber debate in sociology over the development of capitalism turns on a dispute over the role of ideas.[4] For Marx, history was driven by material conditions, and ideas could not exercise any independent influence on social change: "It is not the consciousness of men that determines their existence, but, on the contrary, their social existence that determines their consciousness."[5] By contrast, for Weber, material conditions alone did not determine how history unfolds, and ideas exercised their own influence on social outcomes.[6] Describing the influence of the "Protestant ethic" on capitalism, Weber wrote, "without the universal diffusion of these qualities and principles of a methodical way of life, qualities which were maintained through these religious communities, capitalism today, even in America, would not be what it is."[7] As Weber put it in his classic metaphor, ideas "have, like switchmen, determined the tracks along which action has been pushed by the dynamic of interests."[8]

An "ideas versus interests" debate rages within political science as well, and sweeping assertions about the distinctions between the two are not hard to find.[9] Are ideas only used instrumentally, with "no independent causal weight" in the determination of actors' preferences and "no motivational force of their own"?[10] Or are ideas central to all political phenomena, "a primary source of political behavior"?[11] If there is any consensus to be found, it is about the difficulty of making the case for ideas. While scholars might "admit that ideas play an important role in affairs of state," writes Peter Hall, "that role is not easily described."[12] Jal Mehta concurs: "specifying how ideas matter is still a considerable task."[13]

The aim of this book is to show how a particular idea—presidential representation—has mattered to American political development. What, then, is an idea? I define an *idea* as a premise about how something in the world works, an assumption that an actor brings to bear on political affairs. Put this way, ideas are "causal beliefs."[14] At their most influential, such beliefs can condition individual and group thought, language, and action.[15] These understandings may also blend the causal with the normative, as is the case with presidential representation. Actors believed the causal logic that presidents represented the national interest and Congress represented local interests. They also thought that empowering the president to speak for the whole nation was inherently desirable for society.

Determining how ideas can serve as one of the drivers of political change is an especially important task for scholars of American political development and thought. "More than other parts of the study of American politics," write Suzanne Mettler and Richard Valelly, "APD scholarship also holds that political ideas matter—that is, that they are independent forces in politics and in the life of the American regime."[16] Or, as George Thomas puts it, "historical political developments are connected to and often rest on political thought."[17]

This chapter takes up the analytic challenge presented by these assertions. I argue that identifying and understanding the *ideational foundations* of institutions, laws, or policies is necessary to make sense of both their creation and their stability over time. By ideational foundations, I mean the implicit and explicit causal beliefs held by key actors about how particular institutional arrangements will function. I outline a framework that establishes the political efficacy of ideas, showing the link between moments of institutional *choice* and the broader *durability* of institutional arrangements over time.

The Political Efficacy of Ideas: A Developmental Framework

American political development scholarship has long been attentive to the role of ideas in politics. Perhaps the most influential works on the matter have focused on the importance of political culture in America.[18] But these works do not take up the task of specifying how ideas can exert a causal influence on specific political developments. Several problems with attempting to demonstrate causality stand out: showing that actors did not just use an idea instrumentally to advance their own interests, ruling out other alternative explanations that do not require ideas, and establishing the extent to which a particular outcome can be explained only with reference to the influence of an idea. As Karen Orren and Stephen Skowronek caution, ideas "may have no effect on" institutions, "and whatever effect they do have will be an empirical question."[19] Any argument that ideas are responsible for a particular political development must meet "high demands on specificity, on precisely determining the empirical referents of ideals and on careful scrutiny of the manner in which they are, or are not, accommodated by government."[20]

How can we move beyond simply asserting that ideas matter and actually demonstrate the persistent importance of ideas to political development? One advance comes from Mark Blyth's examination of the role of economic ideas in institutional change. For Blyth, ideas serve several functions: reducing uncertainty, helping to build coalitions, pushing against existing institutions or policies, and contributing to stability by generating shared expectations about how institutions should function.[21] More recently, Rogers Smith's "spiral of politics" model has suggested several stages through which ideas can influence political development. He calls on scholars to consider how ideas emerge out of changing political contexts, serve as the glue for particular coalitions, and then influence particular policy or institutional choices.[22]

Still, while these studies suggest potential outcomes that should be of interest to a researcher, they are more focused on issues of institutional and policy choice than on the role of ideas in underwriting the durability of a reform. Examining how ideas influence political *development* requires considering a broader temporal range. If "political development[s]" are "durable shift[s] in governing authority," then one must ask how ideas contribute to both the creation of new institutional arrangements and their robustness over time.[23] I build on these works by linking together moments of institutional choice with broader institutional durability. The role of an idea in enacting a reform presumably does not end the moment a particular outcome is achieved. Rather, the idea itself may hold the key to the durability of the revised set of institutional arrangements. In this framework, I suggest a series of attributes that can, in combination, determine the relative importance of particular ideas to political developments.

INSTITUTIONAL CHOICE

Is a particular idea responsible for the choice of a set of institutional arrangements? This is the first principal question that addresses the significance of an idea to a political development. That broad question can be addressed by considering four factors.

Pervasiveness

Is the relevant idea popularized independently of any specific reforms? The answer to this question can help satisfy concerns over endogeneity, addressing the issue of "which comes first, the ideas or the institutions?"[24] If the idea spread *before* the reform was enacted, this would increase the likelihood that the idea exercised independent influence on an institutional choice and was not simply invented to bring about only that specific outcome.[25] To demonstrate this, the political context in which the idea was popularized must be described, and, importantly, particular attention should be given to its diffusion in political discourse among various actors.[26] Of course, an idea of interest does not necessarily have to be entirely new. Ideas can be associated with different purposes and reforms over time.[27]

It may be possible that an obscure idea may influence reform if it finds its way into the mind of the right political figure with power to enact change. But in most cases, establishing that a specific idea has spread throughout political discourse can foster higher confidence that it is significant to reform. An idea that is widely known and understood by political elites, who might be in a position to enact change, is one that is more likely to exercise decisive influence on reform.[28] Of course, it is also possible that a particular idea might be so ingrained in political culture that it would simply be assumed and not need to be stated. This is unlikely to be the case, however, when an idea anticipates a departure from established institutional arrangements. Institutional or policy stability may be able to rest on ideas that are frequently unstated, but challenging the status quo inherently requires argument and justification. Explicit statements of the idea would be expected.

Assumption

Do actors who are in a position to influence a political outcome invoke a particular idea as the rationale for their preferences? The answer to this question can help determine both *which* ideas might be relevant to a particular political choice and *whether* a specific idea served as an assumption made by the actors whose decisions mattered to an outcome.[29] While it might be possible for an unstated idea to influence an actor's decision, evidence of definitive statements about the relevant idea would be more suggestive of its influence on a specific decision.

There are several possibilities as to why an idea might be expressed in debates over reform. First, political actors might cite an idea as a pretense to cover up a motivation of self-interest. This would make for a relatively unconvincing argument of the importance of an idea to a reform. At least, it would not be evidence that the idea itself exercised any kind of influence on its own. More promisingly, political actors' determination of their self-interest might be influenced by their ideas.[30] In this case, even if material interest is important, the relevant idea is still a necessary factor in explaining the outcome. Alternatively, other political actors may have no obvious incentive to cite the idea at all, making their invocation of the idea more likely to not be tied up with their interests. Most significantly, some political actors might invoke an idea as justification for reforms that, in theory, would work against their own self-interest or formal institutional incentives. More generally, finding support for the same idea among actors with a diverse set of interests would also suggest a greater likelihood of their beliefs being sincere.[31]

Political institutions and policies are designed based on certain beliefs about how those arrangements will function.[32] These assumptions—beliefs about causality—can help actors reduce uncertainty in making political decisions, and the most influential assumptions will be widely held.[33] Consider several examples. In forming the Constitution, the framers assumed that an educated populace would be needed to make the government established work in practice.[34] Other common assumptions had more tragic consequences. Throughout much of American history, the assumption that racial diversity was incompatible with democracy was widely held, influencing both colonization movements and later segregation.[35] At the neighborhood level, the assumption that diversity would lead to decreasing property values continually proved a persistent obstacle to overcoming housing discrimination in the twentieth century.[36] More generally, the idea of the United States as chiefly a white settler nation, while sharply contested, has been a tragically enduring image in American politics, both shaping imperial development in the nineteenth and twentieth centuries and continuing to be a major factor in political battles over immigration today.[37] Indeed, ideas were central to American imperialism both on the North American continent and overseas.[38]

There may also be multiple premises that undergird a particular institutional change. For example, when Andrew Jackson broke from the previous presidential practice of issuing vetoes only based on constitutional concerns over legislation and began to veto congressional measures based on policy disputes, he drew on both the nascent idea of the president representing the people *and* Article I, Section 7 of the Constitution for authority.[39]

Selection

Is a reform that corresponds to a specific idea chosen over other alternatives that are not influenced by the same idea? The answer to this question can help determine the extent to which an idea exercised an influence at a key moment of design choice.

Actors are likely to debate and devise multiple alternative institutional solutions to address a particular issue, even if they may perceive a common problem that must be addressed. Thus, the alternatives available to and considered by political actors in a given period should be considered. The influence of an idea might occur in several ways. Ideas could have a negative influence, serving to constrain which alternative choices are viewed as feasible. For example, Aaron Friedberg argues that American traditions of antistatism constrained the emerging post–World War II national security state, resulting in choices that prevented the creation of a garrison state at the dawn of the Cold War.[40] Alternatively, ideas may also have a direct positive influence, determining the choice of one solution over another.[41] For example, Louis Brandeis's idea of regulated competition influenced Congress's choice to create the Federal Trade Commission in 1914.[42]

To be clear, the stimulus for the *creation* of a new set of institutional arrangements may be some triggering event—a crisis or some other pressing problem. But the *design* should be the result of a choice made by key political actors. The creation of executive branch rules to limit communication between White House officials and the Department of Justice and Federal Bureau of Investigation is a case in point. The impulse for reform was the Watergate scandal, but the institutional reform was based on the idea of investigatory independence.[43]

Furthermore, if an idea influenced a particular outcome, the choice of an institutional or policy solution should not be fully explainable without reference to the relevant idea. For example, Daniel Carpenter demonstrates that the autonomy lawmakers granted to some executive agencies and departments depended on their beliefs in those agencies' bureaucratic expertise and capability: "Only bureaucratic legitimacy—the evolving belief among politicians and the organized public in the problem-solving capacities of a select few agencies—explains the evolution of conditional autonomy in the Post Office and Agriculture Departments."[44] Colin Moore shows that early twentieth-century Progressive imperialist administrators—even in the face of considerable obstacles—pursued their goals and ideas of administration in policy in the Philippines, outlawing opium, instituting forestry management, developing an education system, building infrastructure and hospitals, and instituting a civil service. As Moore argues, "it is almost impossible to explain America's approach to imperialism without understanding the role of ideas in shaping the goals of the officials who created the empire."[45] Robert Lieberman illustrates the importance of choices between race-conscious and color-blind ideas for addressing racial inequities to subsequent race policy decisions.[46] The idea of "compassionate conservatism"—blending causal and normative claims—was central to several policy choices of the Republican administration of President George W. Bush, including the No Child Left Behind Act, the President's Emergency Plan for AIDS Relief in Africa, and the creation of the Office of Faith-Based and Community Initiatives.[47]

To be sure, some choices influenced by a particular idea might be only partially achieved. Compromises are often necessary to realize reforms. Nevertheless, even when the reform chosen is the result of a compromise, the idea that underpinned the choice becomes the ideational foundation for that institutional arrangement or policy.

Challenge

What existing institutional arrangements and associated ideas are being challenged by a particular idea and its supporters? The answer to this question can further establish that a particular idea is contributing to political development. Reforms anticipated by an idea constitute a development only if they alter institutions or policies that existed before, and to do this, the idea must indict existing ideas and institutions as problems that need to be overcome.[48] These new arrangements then rely on the relevant idea for legitimacy against the potential counterclaims of alternative ideas.

Competing traditions of constitutional thought in American political development implicitly suggest this point. The successful creation and ratification of the Constitution, for example, required that the arguments of the Federalists refute and prevail over the contrary political ideas of the Anti-Federalists and the previous institutional arrangements of the Articles of Confederation.[49] In a "clash [of] opposing truisms" in the twentieth century, the new idea of a living, flexible Constitution needed to overcome more traditional formalist constitutional reasoning in order to help legitimate the development of the administrative state.[50] Presidential politics has also been illustrative. As Stephen Skowronek shows, those presidents who are positioned to thoroughly repudiate the previous political regime then have the greatest opportunity to reconstruct "the standards of legitimate national government" and establish a durable alternative.[51]

The set of questions surrounding durability are as weighty as those surrounding choice. To what extent does the durability of an institution or policy depend on the continued belief that the ideas underlying it are legitimate? Institutions and their accompanying ideas may not be equally durable. They can exist in tension with each other, with institutions outlasting their underlying ideas or, potentially, vice versa.[52] If the underlying idea itself falls into disrepute, the institutional arrangements may be correspondingly more vulnerable to alteration.

Validity

Does the perceived validity of the idea that supports an institution or policy come into serious question? A widespread shift in belief about the idea's legitimacy would increase the likelihood that institutional or policy choices associated with the idea would face interrogation. As Robert Lieberman argues, political change "arises out of the 'friction' among mismatched institutional and ideational patterns."[53] Therefore, the context in which the idea itself falls into disrepute must be described. To have more confidence that doubts about an underlying idea have a direct influence on new reforms, criticism of the relevant idea in elite political discourse should begin prior to any significant institutional or policy alteration.

While an idea's legitimacy could erode slowly over time, some events could dramatically change perceptions of the idea and expose its flaws in short order. Consider again the case of "compassionate conservatism" during the George W. Bush administration. With this idea serving as "a frame of reference that the American people could use to analyze the administration," the inadequacies of the response to the devastation from Hurricane Katrina and the difficulties of the ongoing Iraq War "cast the administration in a negative light" and helped discredit the idea itself.[54]

Applicability

Do actors who are in a position to influence reform view doubts about the idea as applicable to a particular reform? The answer to this question can determine whether there is an explicit connection between changing ideas and alterations to an institution or policy. Generalized doubt about the idea should be invoked with reference to a particular institution or policy. Perhaps the institution or policy has begun to function in unexpected ways.[55] The connection between doubts about an idea and corresponding institutional changes is also more convincing when a variety of political actors with otherwise competing interests express similar views.

As an example, consider Samuel Huntington's description of how a "gap between political ideal and political reality" has been a recurrent driver of political development in America. Rising doubts about the country's ability to live up to its "democratic creed" of liberty and equality result in widespread cognitive dissonance and expression of collective grievances. These doubts spur recurrent "creedal passion periods" and bursts of political reform: the Revolutionary era, Jacksonian era, Populist-Progressive Era, and 1960s civil rights revolution.[56]

Leverage

With the validity of the relevant idea being questioned, to what extent do other ideas gain leverage over reform? When one of the core assumptions behind a set of institutional arrangements or a policy is seriously challenged, the nature and practical operations of the institution itself are more vulnerable to change on the basis of alternative ideas. These claims might even be those that had previously been overcome in the course of designing an institution or policy, but that are resurgent as the relevant idea falls into disrepute.

This friction among competing ideas can be illustrated with several examples. The decline of the idea of "neutral competence" impacted the authority and role of the Bureau of the Budget, and an opposing expectation of "responsive competence" took hold in the reformulated Office of Management and Budget instead.[57] According to Rogers Smith's "multiple traditions" thesis, there are recurrent competing political traditions in America. Because of this, victories for greater equality are always somewhat provisional, vulnerable to later setbacks. While the liberal tradition might seem predominant in political culture, the ascriptive tradition has periodically been resurgent.[58] More broadly, political movements that lose at key moments in American political history have nonetheless sometimes seen their ideas ultimately have a substantial impact on the development of the polity. Jeffrey Tulis and Nicole Mellow show in their exploration of three constitutional "antimoments"—the Anti-Federalists at the Founding, Andrew Johnson's efforts to thwart Reconstruction, and Barry Goldwater's conservative insurgency in 1964—that such losing ideas can provide a direct blueprint for later political victories.[59]

Applying the Framework

Determining when a specific idea does or does not play a crucial role in the choice and durability of a particular set of institutional arrangements is ultimately an empirical question, and this framework (table 2.1) offers guidelines to make such a determination with higher confidence. In the remainder of the book, I use this framework to provide a rigorous test of the relative importance of the idea of presidential representation to the creation and durability of the institutional presidency.

Part 1 considers the role of the idea of presidential representation in Congress's choices to create different elements of the institutional presidency, answering the questions posed in the first part of the framework. First, was the idea of presidential representation popularized in elite political discourse apart from and prior to any corresponding reforms? Several types of evidence would help show the idea's prevalence in American political culture. In particular, both proponents and opponents of the idea should have recognized its importance. Of course, presidents would naturally claim to represent the

TABLE 2.1. The Political Efficacy of Ideas: A Developmental Framework

Institutional Choice	**Is a new idea responsible for the choice of a particular set of institutional arrangements?**
Pervasiveness	Is the idea popularized apart from specific reforms?
Assumption	Do actors who are in a position to influence the outcome of reform invoke the idea as a rationale?
Selection	Is a reform that corresponds to the idea chosen over alternatives that do not?
Challenge	What existing institutional arrangements and associated ideas are being challenged by this idea?
Institutional Durability	**To what extent does the durability of a set of institutional arrangements rely on the continued perception that its underlying ideas are legitimate?**
Validity	Are there serious challenges that cause a shift in the idea's perceived validity?
Applicability	Do actors view those doubts about the idea as applicable to a particular reform?
Leverage	To what extent do other ideas gain leverage over reform?

nation as a whole. Therefore, I look primarily to the statements of other political actors, such as lawmakers, journalists, academics, and other reformers.
Showing that multiple actors with differing characteristics, such as partisan
affiliation or geographic constituency, state similar claims would attest to
the idea's pervasive influence. The influence of the idea would be especially
clear in cases in which actors who do not have anything obvious to gain from
this idea nonetheless endorse it. These statements should also be present in
a wide variety of sources, including news reports, policy proposals or commission reports, congressional hearings, congressional floor debates, and the
private papers of key actors, such as draft statements and correspondence.
To be sure, some assumptions in political culture may be so widely accepted
as common sense that they do not even need to be frequently stated.[60] But
because the idea of presidential representation was part of a political project
of institutional reconfiguration rather than contributing to institutional con-
tinuity, the actors directly involved would be expected to explicitly offer an
intellectual rationale for their actions.

Two types of statements can be counted as referring to the idea of presidential representation. *Implicit* arguments for presidential representation
contain criticisms of lawmakers or executive branch agencies as parochial
or beholden to special interests, while arguing that the president should have
more responsibility for a policy instead. By promoting a presidential solution
to a problem of congressional representation, such a statement assumes that
the president will be more likely to represent the national interest. *Explicit*
statements spell out the claim of presidential representation directly, laying
out the purported logic that the president is assumed to act only in the interest of the people as a whole because he represents a national constituency.

Second, did actors who were in a position to influence legislation cite the
idea of presidential representation as an assumption for their proposed reforms? Implicit invocations of this idea would constitute important evidence,
but to be convincing, explicit references to presidential representation should
be found in the legislative history behind each law. If that idea influenced institutional design, its influence should be evident as those choices were being
debated, rather than being stated only later. I especially scrutinize the logic articulated by key members of Congress involved in drafting and passing each
law for evidence that figures in a position to have definite influence on the
law embraced the logic of presidential representation themselves. Legislators
undoubtedly act somewhat strategically in any claims they advance for legislation. Yet it is important to note that if these lawmakers were trying to hide
their motives for increasing presidential authority, choosing to praise presidential representation would be a strikingly counterproductive way to do so.

One of the most remarkable findings of this study is that legislators persistently indicted Congress's ability to represent the national interest, doing so across a broad range of issue areas. There was nothing subtle about this. Legislators actively promoted the superiority of presidential government. These debates had implications beyond simple rhetorical flair.

Third, were reforms that corresponded to the idea of presidential representation chosen over other alternatives that did not relate to the idea? To show the idea's influence on institutional design, major elements of the design of these laws should correspond to what these key actors claimed would be necessary to appropriately reflect assumptions about presidential representation. Moreover, these designs should be chosen over other alternatives that would not correspond to the idea of presidential representation. To be sure, any law is still the result of compromise. Not all elements of institutional design may favor the presidency, or go as far as some proponents of presidential representation want. Institutional innovations involving the president would reveal the extent to which each law embraced the assumption of presidential representation, while any limitations imposed would indicate the limits of such change.

Fourth, what existing institutional arrangements and ideas were challenged by the idea of presidential representation and the reforms it anticipated? To show that any new institutional arrangements associated with presidential representation constituted a genuine development, the previous institutional arrangements that were being altered must be specified. Moreover, to show that the idea had some effect, the opposing claims made by those who resisted presidency-oriented reforms should also be described.

Part 2 examines the extent to which rising doubts about the validity of presidential representation affected the durability of the institutional presidency across these same policy areas, answering the questions posed in the second part of the framework. First, did the validity of presidential representation come into question? This would require that evidence of doubts about presidential representation be expressed by a variety of political actors in elite political discourse, apart from any individual law that reconsidered presidential authority. Such statements should be present in a variety of sources, including news reports, policy proposals, congressional hearings, congressional floor debates, and the private papers of legislators.

Second, did actors who were in a position to directly influence reforms apply those doubts about the legitimacy of the idea as a justification for their actions? Statements that cite declining faith in the idea of presidential representation should be made by a variety of legislators, and it is important to highlight those from different parties and regions who nonetheless hold similar views of the idea. Moreover, both advocates of curbing presidential authority and those resisting such changes should recognize the centrality of the idea to debates over reform.

Third, to what extent did other ideas gain leverage over reform? With presidential representation in doubt, opposing ideas would be more likely to have influence over Congress's choices. Statements invoking alternative ideas, asserting Congress's own representational and constitutional claims, should be made by a variety of legislators. Reforms that sought to reassert congressional authority would reveal the extent to which each law embraced those opposing claims, while any limitations imposed would indicate the extent to which presidential authority endured.

The evidence that the idea of presidential representation influenced presidential power over time is, I believe, overwhelming, but I do not think that it speaks for itself. By necessity, the primary evidence for the influence of ideas comes from statements made by political actors about what they were doing and why they were doing it. While there are numerous statements provided throughout this book as evidence for actors' views about presidential representation and the stakes of institutional reform, these are not exhaustive of the historical record for these cases and time periods. Instead, the priority in determining the evidence presented in this book has been to provide different opinions from a variety of sources, and in doing so, to address the key questions posed by my framework. This framework seeks to meet the challenge of assigning causal significance to an idea in changing institutional relationships, and the remainder of the book is organized accordingly.

Institutional Choice: Creating the Institutional Presidency, 1910–49

The presidential type of government which democratic progress is shaping in America is still imperfect. While the presidential office has been transformed into a representative institution, it lacks proper organs for the exercise of that function. . . . No constitutional means are provided whereby [the president] may carry out his pledges.
HENRY JONES FORD, 1898[1]

Is the presidency a representative institution? The answer to this question has changed over time. The presidency was not widely conceived of this way at the time of the American Founding. But by the turn of the twentieth century, the idea that the president represented the people had become prevalent in American political culture. More provocatively, the presidency increasingly was proclaimed to be a superior representative institution compared to Congress, the branch constitutionally established as the closest to the citizenry.

What were the institutional consequences of the rise of this idea? Some, like changes to presidential selection procedures, are beyond the scope of this analysis.[2] Here, in part 1, I consider the role of the idea of presidential representation in Congress's creation of the institutional presidency between 1910 and 1949. The Budget and Accounting Act (BAA) of 1921, the Reciprocal Trade Agreements Act (RTAA) of 1934, the Reorganization Act of 1939, the Employment Act of 1946, and the National Security Act of 1947 were statutes in which Congress consciously enhanced presidential responsibilities and organizational capacities. I argue that the idea of presidential representation was the key influence on laws affecting budgeting, trade, reorganization, and employment policy. National security, by contrast, was more heavily influenced by the perceived constitutional authority of the president as commander in chief.

Of course, political actors other than Congress helped change the role of the presidency in the early twentieth century. Presidents themselves acted as political entrepreneurs, increasingly attempting to direct policymaking and to rally support for legislation.[3] Foreign policy offered new opportunities for presidential leadership on the world stage.[4] The first hundred days of Franklin Roosevelt's administration during the New Deal would further solidify an enduring expectation of a presidency-centered government.[5] Many of the statutes passed by Congress that affected presidential power were spurred on by presidents themselves, other executive branch actors, and a wide range of political reformers.[6]

Nevertheless, the significance of Congress's role in creating the institutional presidency cannot be overstated. Even though presidents and other reformers played important parts, the laws that framed the new presidency were ultimately debated and enacted by legislators. When Congress passed those statutes, it gave the idea of presidential representation institutional form. And significantly, just as much as the idea was an inference about how presidents uniquely could be expected to act in the national interest, the idea was also a critique of Congress and the constitutional order.

Pervasiveness: Faith in Presidential Representation

To demonstrate that the idea of presidential representation was the ideational foundation of a particular law, it is necessary to show (1) that presidential representation was an idea prominent in elite political discourse during this period, (2) that presidential representation was cited as the specific assumption behind the design of a law, (3) that reforms involving the president were chosen over other alternatives seemingly more conducive to Congress's institutional interests, and (4) that the idea of presidential representation pushed against existing institutional arrangements. In this introduction to part 1, I establish that the idea of presidential representation became pervasive in American political culture prior to and during the period in which these laws were enacted.[7]

A NATIONAL FOCUS

At the turn of the twentieth century, only a few decades removed from the Civil War, a decade after the announced "closing" of the frontier in 1890, and shortly after the Spanish-American War of 1898, which signified the nation's emergence as a world power, the United States was perceived as more interconnected than ever before.[8] Advances in industry, transportation, and communication had "made the nation a neighborhood."[9] The American role in World War I in 1917–18 and subsequent ratification of the Nineteenth Amendment in 1920, granting women the right to vote and nearly doubling the size of the national electorate, would also bolster the notion of the United States as a national community.[10] The country was "acquiring a national public sentiment," claimed journalist William Allen White in 1910, and the "average man . . . now finds himself thinking, not merely in cities, not merely in states, but as an American."[11] Still, "national unity," contended Albert Shaw, remained the "transcendent problem" of American politics.[12] And, of course, the Progressives' idea of who constituted the "whole people" excluded many Americans.[13]

A more interconnected nation would require a government that could tackle problems from a national perspective, and in the early twentieth century, Progressive reformers sought to better orient the federal government toward doing just that. The only way to fulfill "the American democratic ideal," asserted Herbert Croly, would be through "an exclusive and aggressive devotion to the national welfare."[14] Prioritizing the general welfare meant focusing less on localities and states and more on the nation, and a recurring refrain of political discourse of the period was that government needed a more holistic outlook. "Once more the issue is raised between state and nation," noted Frank Buffington Vrooman, "whether the part is greater than the whole."[15] "National problems," Walter Weyl emphasized, "cannot be solved by any governmental unit less than the nation."[16] "This is the penalty of democracy," reflected Jane Addams, "that we are bound to move forward or retrograde together."[17]

The Progressive vision of a nationally focused politics, tackling issues facing the whole country, encountered an obstacle: locally oriented politics. And the chief source of that type of politics was believed to be the institution of Congress. The legislative branch was the subject of constant Progressive scorn, with legislators perceived as incapable of looking beyond their localities to think about what the nation as a whole needed. While British members of Parliament were thought to focus on the national interest, American members of Congress were perceived as representing only districts or states.[18] Congress, wrote Woodrow Wilson, was characterized by "hide-and-seek vagaries of authority."[19] Croly derided the institution as the stronghold of mere "special and local interests."[20] Yale president Arthur Twining Hadley lambasted a legislature in which "equity between the different parts becomes in their minds a more prominent consideration than the general interests or safety of the whole, which they are willing to trust Providence to take care of."[21]

With Progressives demanding a focus on national issues over local ones and congressional representation itself viewed as a hindrance, an opportunity arose for another idea. Reformers not only decried the ostensible ills of members of Congress focusing on local interests; they sought to embrace its inverse as a solution. At all levels of government, reformers increasingly believed that executives held the key to guiding government to a more holistic focus. For states, Croly advocated a form of government in which "the executive [would] become essentially a representative agency."[22] Gubernatorial leadership in state legislation was increasingly viewed as being in the interests of the people as a whole.[23] "Executive leadership," wrote Mary Parker Follett, "may reduce the power of legislatures, but it will increase the power of the electorate."[24] Running for governor of New York in 1906, Republican Charles Evans Hughes stated a rationale for his candidacy on that basis: "I desire to see the government at Albany administered solely in the interests of the people of the state and in the interests of all the people of the state."[25]

For the federal government, governing in the interests of all the people meant greater presidential leadership. Drawing forward nineteenth-century Jacksonian claims about the president being the direct representative of the people as a whole, reformers also posited that the president was the only institutional actor in the federal government with a national focus. On that basis, reformers advocated for more presidential influence in legislative policymaking, and they promised to rework constitutional relationships to this end.

Presidents, of course, had an institutional and political interest in promoting this idea. Claiming to represent the national interest would confer more legitimacy—and potentially more power—on the office. Most famously, former Republican president Theodore Roosevelt wrote that the president "was a steward of the people bound actively and affirmatively to do all he could for the people."[26] But other presidents of both parties increasingly spoke of the importance of the office as a representative institution. The presidency, wrote former Democratic president Grover Cleveland, was "preeminently the people's office," and it was "only in the selection of the President that the body of the American people can by any possibility act together and directly in the equipment of their national Government."[27] "The President is himself a representative of the people and selected by all of them, as distinguished from congressmen and senators, who are representatives of states and districts," explained former Republican president William Howard Taft. Like Jackson before them, these presidents recognized how their own representative warrants could be contrasted with those of legislators. "It is thus natural," Taft continued, pressing the implication, "that the President should not infrequently have the sympathy and support of all the people as against the representative, legislative bodies."[28] For Democratic president Harry Truman, this would become an explicit campaign theme in 1948. In contrast to "a special interest Congress," Truman argued, "the Office of the President represents the people. He is elected by all the people."[29]

More importantly, the idea advanced in other quarters. The sheer variety of political actors and observers across the political spectrum who expressed support for the purported national perspective of the presidential office—politicians in various offices in both parties, journalists, academics, even novelists—underscored the widespread impact, recognition, and understanding of the idea in American political culture. Observers agreed that the presidency was now widely conceived of as a representative institution. "Now," the British Liberal politician James Bryce observed, "the President is deemed to represent the people no less than do the members of the legislature."[30] The president, asserted Columbia president Nicholas Murray Butler, "directly represents the sovereign people."[31] Americans, contended Simeon Baldwin, would "speak by the chief magistrate of the republic."[32]

The inference drawn from the notion of the presidency as a representative institution was also widely endorsed. Both Butler and Baldwin, for example, pressed the point that the president better represented the people as a whole than did legislators. "As matters stand to-day," Butler insisted, "states and syndicates have senators; districts and local interests have representatives; but the whole people of the United States have only the President to speak for them and to do their will."[33] "The President of the United States is the only public officer," stressed Baldwin, "who may be expected to keep his mind wholly free from local prepossessions."[34] In fact, in standing "for the nation," concurred Jeremiah Jenks, the president would be "the only possible representative" who could "capture the public imagination."[35] Even a staunch defender of congressional prerogatives, Representative Samuel McCall (R-MA), was forced to admit the ubiquity of the idea in the public sphere: "The claim of President Jackson that the President was the direct representative of the whole people is to-day very often heard."[36]

A more significant indication of how the idea had become widely accepted came from two speeches at elite universities, in which both speakers decided that presidential representation was a concept worth impressing on their audiences. Underscoring the idea's increasingly bipartisan appeal, the respective speakers would be future opponents in the 1916 presidential election. "Only the president represents the country as a whole," lectured then Princeton president and future Democratic president Woodrow Wilson at Columbia in 1907: "he speaks for no special interest."[37] His later Republican opponent agreed. The then governor of New York and soon-to-be Supreme Court justice Charles Evans Hughes told a Harvard audience in June 1910 that it was "out of the conflicts between competing interests or districts [that] the Executive emerges as the representative of the people as a whole." In contrast to legislators, the executive "commands a position of influence which is not embarrassed by district limitations."[38]

Support for the idea and associated critiques of Congress were also present in newspapers around the country. Too often, claimed one *New York Times* report, "Congress had been amenable to special interests incompatible with the public good."[39] For the *Dearborn Independent*, congressional parochialism threatened the legitimacy of Congress as a representative body: "The public is coming more and more to look on members of Congress as *'getters'* and not *'doers,'* as *agents to rather than representatives in the government*."[40] While "Congress is especially susceptible to pressure from organized minorities and from sectional interests," began a column in the *Kansas City Star*, "the president represents the whole nation."[41] Presidents could also be faulted for leadership that was insufficiently bold for the unique representative role that they held. In a critique of William Howard Taft, the *Newark Evening News* reminded its readers that "he is the one representative of the whole people, their trustee."[42] "Only the President represents the Nation," summed up the *Outlook*.[43]

Within a few decades, presidential representation even found its way into textbooks and novels. In political science, the claim would be presented as common sense. "The President is the friend of the people," proclaimed one study of American government in 1948, as "it is he who labors to make the United States a better place in which to live. The most outstanding Presidents have recognized this extralegal position which they hold and have attempted to fill it as completely as possible."[44] Echoing this perspective, another textbook described the president as "the Synthesizer of the General Will."[45] In some of the most popular political novels of the twentieth century, even fictional politicians invoked the idea. "The President is the servant of every citizen in the country," said the presidential dictator Buzz Windrip in *It Can't Happen Here*, and "it's absolutely true I do want power, great, big, imperial power—but not for myself—no—for *you!*"[46] The comparison between the representative standing of the president and that of legislators was explicit in *Advise and Consent*. In one scene, the president confronted a Utah senator and sharply questioned his claim to speak for the national interest: "My charter runs from Hawaii to Cape Cod and the Gulf to Alaska. Yours is bounded by the state of Utah. Are you saying your right to judge is superior to mine, or that your judgment is superior to mine?"[47]

INSTITUTIONALIZING PRESIDENTIAL REPRESENTATION

The Progressives' ambitions went far beyond simply expressing the claim that presidents uniquely represented the entire nation. Progressives sought to institutionalize it and transform how American government worked. One individual who exemplified this reform effort was Henry Stimson. Over the early decades of the twentieth century, Stimson, a Republican, would twice serve as secretary of war, first under President Taft and then under Democratic president Franklin Delano Roosevelt, and would also hold the position of secretary of state under Republican president Herbert Hoover. As a well-respected government official, Stimson also would play a significant role in spurring on the development of the institutional presidency even while out of office.

After Taft's defeat in 1912, Stimson had recently lost his job as secretary of war. Under the circumstances, one might have imagined that Stimson, as a Republican, would be bitter about the loss to Democrat Woodrow Wilson. At the very least, Stimson would not have been expected to turn around and seek to further empower the office that Wilson now held. Yet this was exactly what Stimson set out to do. From his experience in government, Stimson decided that his time would be well spent advocating changes to the relationship between the presidency and Congress. The president, Stimson believed, needed a strong power of legislative initiative.[48]

The key assumption supporting Stimson's vision was the idea of presidential representation. In conducting research to prepare for making a speech on government reform, Stimson scribbled this premise in his notes: "the Executive by nature of Election represents nation at large." Just as significantly, Stimson also noted in a fragment the purported problem of congressional representation. Members of Congress, he jotted down, had a "Responsibility only to District whereas injury may be done to whole country."[49]

Soon these would be the prominent themes in a speech Stimson delivered in Philadelphia in May 1913. The title and subtitle of the speech—"Initiative and Responsibility of the Executive: A Remedy for Inefficient Legislation"— made Stimson's views clear. While the subtitle referred to the problem of congressional representation, the main title held out the proposed solution of executive leadership in legislation. These themes were stated more directly in the speech itself. Stimson indicted the legislative branch for its purported localistic tendencies. "In a body which is supposed to represent the *nation*," Stimson said of Congress, "we find that the interests of the nation are being constantly subordinated to local interests." The cure, he argued, was to be found in the presidency. Stimson explicitly laid out the inference behind granting the president a stronger legislative initiative power. "Nowhere more than in the United States is the Executive the representative of the nation at large," he proclaimed. "Not only do his duties impose upon him constantly the necessity of a nation-wide viewpoint," Stimson enthused, "but he is, in this country, also directly responsible to the electorate of the whole people."[50]

While Stimson praised Woodrow Wilson for speaking directly to Con-

gress for the first time in over a century, he argued that making new "machinery" was needed so that such "cooperation will become normal and natural
and not dramatic and extraordinary." In other words, presidential leadership
needed to be institutionalized. Such executive initiative might take several
institutional forms. It could attempt to achieve some form of cabinet government, allowing the president to have executive branch officials advocate for
the administration's policies on the floor in legislative debate. It could take the
form of a direct presidential privilege to introduce bills in Congress. Or such
efforts could be targeted at reforming two policy areas that Stimson found
to be especially in need of the president's national perspective—budgeting
and the tariff. Regardless of the precise form, the overall thrust was clear: the
president should have formal legislative agenda-setting authority.[51]

Stimson's speech stands out as significant for several reasons. To begin
with, it is possible to identify how Stimson's own perspective on presidential
representation was cultivated. He had read the works of the political scientist Henry Jones Ford, who chronicled the development of the presidency
as a representative institution. Specifically citing "Ford's brilliant studies" in
his handwritten notes, Stimson also listed Ford's books in a bibliography of
works consulted in writing his speech.[52] Moreover, Stimson's advocacy was
also notable in that he expressed support for the idea of presidential representation prior to the enactment of congressional laws creating the institutional presidency. In fact, championing the idea during both Republican and
Democratic administrations over the subsequent decades, Stimson would
prove to be a key voice in support of congressional efforts in budgeting and
trade that granted the presidency new authority.

When the political scientist whose works were an inspiration for Stimson's views, Henry Jones Ford, wrote that "the presidential office has been
transformed into a representative institution" but "lacks the proper organs
for the exercise of that function," he too was seeking to privilege the president's purported national perspective in policymaking.[53] Though reformers
did not agree on all proposed remedies to tap that unique institutional standing, most focused on giving the president more formal authority to initiate
legislation. Correspondingly, they sought to give the president greater organizational capacity—more staff, expertise, and information in the form of
new institutions in the executive branch.

With prescribed agenda-setting authority, the president would propose
bills that would purportedly best consider the needs of the whole country.
This connection to Congress would also establish a more formal role for
the president in the legislative process. Reformers continued to assert over
the coming decades that this would force the Congress to better think of the

national interest. Without a presidential initiative, Stimson bemoaned, "we have eliminated the officer who is representative of the whole people and who is responsible to them and who proposes legislation from their viewpoint."[54] Walter Lippmann went so far as to assert that "a congressman who is deeply concerned with the national interest will always desire strong leadership by the President."[55] Harold Laski agreed: "The only person responsibly charged with thinking and planning in terms of the whole Union is the president."[56]

In order to maximize the potential of that agenda-setting authority, the president would also need new executive branch resources and some level of control over administration. The separate departments and agencies were viewed as uncoordinated. They could communicate views to Congress that did not necessarily reflect the perspective and preferences of the president. Therefore, reformers thought enhancing the president's organizational capacity was necessary to manage the executive branch, provide access to more expertise and information so that he could be informed about national problems, and ensure that Congress would consider only presidential proposals. Describing a proposed executive budget process, for example, William Willoughby explained that presidential initiative could not work "unless the chief executive is definitely recognized as the head of the administration."[57] More generally, Pendleton Herring connected the president's authority to the organization of the administration: "The increased power of the President means, of course, an increase in the importance of the bureaucracy. Consistency in the formulation of presidential policy involves an intelligent and efficient arrangement of the whole administrative service."[58] It was also assumed that executives would feel akin to experts in focusing on the whole nation. In Hadley's view, economists and other experts would have "a corresponding advantage in advising the executive," who "regards himself as a representative of the whole people rather than of small sections of the people."[59]

CONSTITUTIONAL IMPLICATIONS

Reformers viewed the idea of presidential representation as contrasting with republican political thought about representation and legislating from the time of the American Founding. "Our fathers used to speak of their representative assemblies as the refuge of the liberties of the people," noted Stimson in his 1913 speech, but "there is danger now that we shall come to think of them as the refuge of the powerful special interests of business."[60] Acknowledging the traditional suspicion of executive power in America, the theologian Lyman Abbott nevertheless challenged that notion directly. The president "cannot be a peril," he pronounced, because of the office's accountability to the people:

"he is himself but the instrument and the servant of self-government."[61] For one author in the *North American Review*, this amounted to an ironic twist in American political thought about executive power and representation: "The President, paradoxically enough, has become the people's agent for keeping the people's representatives up to their job."[62]

With this Progressive reformulation contrasting with the framers' understanding of executive power, it was no surprise that the reforms associated with presidential representation had obvious constitutional implications. Creating more organizational capacity for the president could plausibly claim support in the executive power vested in the president by Article II, but it would still be necessary for Congress to actually bring it about. Providing such informational expertise to presidents would also potentially give their proposals greater weight, affecting the balance of power between the presidency and Congress. More boldly, though the president possessed authority from Article II to recommend measures to Congress, the push to have presidents set the congressional agenda—to institutionalize presidential initiative—directly challenged legislative prerogatives.

Proponents of such authority explicitly acknowledged that the president's legislative powers from the Constitution were insufficient to ensure that the Congress considered the president's national perspective. In Ford's view, Andrew Jackson had established the veto power as a representative tool in the nineteenth century. The president could veto legislation determined not to be in the national interest. But, to Ford, "the correlative function, the legislative initiative, still dependent as it is upon congressional acquiescence, has shown no access of strength."[63]

Some thus envisioned essentially inverting the legislative process: the president would propose legislation, and Congress would decide whether to accept it. "Without such an initiation," wrote John Burgess, "the veto power does not give the President an equal part in the legislative power."[64] Rather than Congress passing laws and the president reacting by signing or vetoing, the president, argued Gamaliel Bradford, "should himself" submit legislation "for acceptance or rejection" by Congress. In other words, "the veto should be applied the other way."[65] When Bradford attended the address of Charles Evans Hughes at Harvard in 1910, which extolled the virtues of an executive representing the people as a whole, he unsurprisingly reacted to the speech with enthusiasm. "It is impossible to refrain from expressing the intense pleasure which I received from your address today," Bradford immediately wrote to Hughes.[66]

As they sought to grant the president some sort of formal legislative initiative, reformers consciously took direct aim at the separation of powers itself.

Stimson ridiculed a formalistic adherence to that doctrine as being outdated: "The theory upon which it is based has been completely abandoned not only in the government of which Montesquieu wrote, but in all other homes of effective parliamentary institutions. It lingers on here in the United States, the fount of most of our troubles, yet cherished as if it were a veritable ark of the covenant."[67] Similarly, an article in the *Dearborn Independent* mocked "the technical observance of the 'division of powers' set forth in the Constitution" when, for all practical purposes, the nation was increasingly prepared to hold the president "responsible" for legislative outcomes.[68]

To varying degrees, then, the reforms associated with presidential representation self-consciously stretched from the original constitutional frame, seeking to essentially alter how the machinery of the Constitution could be put to use. Thus, they were dependent on a corresponding notion that the Constitution was a "living" document, capable of new institutional adaptation.[69] This was the takeaway of one paper on executive and legislative power presented at the first annual meeting of the American Political Science Association in December 1904: "the American President has all of the work which the British Prime Minister and the Cabinet perform, but he is at present subject to all the hindrances of a system calculated on the needs of the eighteenth century. To do away with these anomalous and obstructive legal conditions is the problem of the immediate future."[70] Indeed, the connection between a new vision of the presidency and a notion of constitutional flexibility was even more explicit in Howard Lee McBain's influential book *The Living Constitution*: "The prime function of the President is not executive at all. It is legislative."[71]

Rather than minimizing the connection between presidential representation and constitutional critique, Ford celebrated it: "The greatness of the presidency is the work of the people, breaking through the constitutional form."[72] The implication of Ford's enthusiasm was profound. Breaking through the constitutional form to accommodate presidential representation involved some belief that the idea was valid, suggesting that any corresponding institutional reforms would have some degree of dependence on that concept's continued legitimacy.

Part 1

Did the prominence of the idea of presidential representation in political discourse influence Congress in creating the institutional presidency? How did this influence vary across the policy areas of budgeting, trade, reorganization, employment, and national security? To what extent did the idea's institutional entailments challenge the existing constitutional order? These are the questions addressed in the chapters of part 1. Chapters 3–6 examine to what degree the idea of presidential representation was the specific assumption behind the laws creating the institutional presidency, analyze the alternative institutional choices that Congress could have made that would not have involved the presidency, and consider the established institutional arrangements and associated ideas that reforms associated with the idea needed to overcome.

Presidential Budgeting

*When you have decided upon your budget procedure you have decided upon the form
of government you will have as a matter of fact.*

EDWARD A. FITZPATRICK, 1918[1]

Congress's passage of the Budget and Accounting Act (BAA) of 1921 arguably
marked the beginning of the "modern presidency."[2] Making the president
responsible for submitting a budget to Congress each year and creating a Bureau of the Budget (BOB) in the executive branch, the law was the first in a series of statutes in which Congress would act as a patron of presidential power.

The enactment of the BAA poses two puzzles. First, the BAA shows the
institutional presidency emerging earliest on what might otherwise be considered its most unlikely constitutional ground. The intimate connection that
had developed between finance and representation in the Anglo-American
political tradition stretched back to Magna Carta, with parliamentary assent
becoming a condition for appropriating money and raising taxes over subsequent centuries.[3] In the United States, this connection was formalized in
Article I of the Constitution. Revenue bills would originate in the House of
Representatives, giving the power of the purse to the chamber closest to the
people.[4] The question thus arises as to what circumstances and arguments
could have led the House to compromise this vital advantage.

Second, the specific timing of the law's passage presents a notable paradox.
The initial proposal for presidential budget reform was made by Republican
president William Howard Taft's Commission on Economy and Efficiency
in 1912. Coming in the midst of Progressive enthusiasm for executive power,
their plan to bolster the president's role in budgeting was perhaps unsurprising. But Congress did not pass a law providing for a presidential budget
until 1921—after World War I, after the repudiation of Democratic president
Woodrow Wilson, and after public reaction against Progressivism had set in.
At a time when "the American people seek . . . the resumption of constitutional and representative government," in the words of budget reformer Sen-

ator Medill McCormick (R-IL), one might have expected the president's role to recede.[5] To be sure, World War I had brought about a severe debt problem, but solutions that might have avoided presidential involvement in budgeting were conceivable and considered. Yet instead, Congress formalized presidential initiative in the budget process and augmented the president's organizational capacities with the creation of the BOB. In effect, Congress accepted that institutionalizing presidential leadership was necessary for even a return to "normalcy."[6]

What explains this initial step in Congress's creation of the institutional presidency? While existing explanations for the BAA's passage illuminate key aspects behind the law's passage, each faces limitations in accounting for the type of reform enacted. Some have pointed to Congress seeking to solve its collective action problem in budgeting.[7] Indeed, Congress explicitly acknowledged this as an issue. But the collective action problem alone was not, in itself, sufficient for Congress to decide specifically on a presidential solution. Other alternatives that would not have involved the president, such as centralizing the committee process or giving more authority to the treasury secretary, were feasible and had precedent. Congress may also have wanted presidents to utilize information and expertise in making decisions and exercising their powers in budgeting.[8] But while this account is sufficient to explain why Congress wanted to place the BOB under presidential control, it is insufficient to explain why Congress would grant presidents a new and formalized responsibility in budgeting in the first place.[9] A partisan explanation, focusing on the existence of a unified Republican government, does not explain the BAA's passage in 1921. Budget reform had first passed during divided government in 1920, and the margin of passage in 1921 was overwhelmingly bipartisan.[10] The proximate cause of the law's passage was rising debt from World War I. But this factor alone cannot explain the particular design that Congress chose for budget reform.[11] Finally, an explanation focused solely on the idea of efficiency is inadequate.[12] Simply seeking a more efficient budget process would not in itself require a presidential solution. Beneath the amorphous consensus on the goal of efficiency, reformers possessed a clear underlying assumption about how presidents would behave in budgeting. In effect, presidential representation was the premise behind the notion of executive efficiency.

The design of the BAA is explained by the currency of a different idea. Congress's principal design assumption in crafting the BAA was the idea of presidential representation. While the concept of presidential representation had been connected to political developments in the nineteenth century—including presidential vetoes based on policy grounds, use of the

removal power, and claims of electoral mandates—the institutional purposes attached to the idea in the twentieth century were new and distinc-
tive. Presidency-oriented reformers, such as Henry Jones Ford, increasingly
associated the concept with two other entailments that combined to form
the basis of the institutional presidency—a formal license for agenda setting and greater executive organizational capacity. It was no coincidence that
Ford followed up his 1898 call to provide "proper organs" for the exercise
of the presidency's function as "a representative institution" with substantial
advocacy for a presidential budget.[13] "By so much as [the president's] power
of initiative is abridged," Ford wrote in 1910, "the sovereignty of the people is
impaired."[14] Both of these entailments were debated in considering the BAA
and acknowledged in its passage. By making the president responsible for
initiating the annual budget process and creating the BOB, the statute reveals the extent to which the idea of presidential representation had become
legitimized by 1921 and the terms on which constitutional relationships were
reconfigured.

At issue in this chapter is a pivotal moment in American political development, an instance in which Congress did not simply tolerate a presidential
pretension, but candidly acknowledged its own institutional incapacity and
promoted the institutionalization of presidential remedies. I argue that the
idea of presidential representation was not just a vehicle used instrumentally
to pass the BAA, but that the act was instead utilized to advance a new conception of American government. Even as they debated different kinds of reforms, contemporary observers understood that the choice of a "budget procedure" would effectively determine "the form of government" Americans
would have "as a *matter of fact*."[15] As the introduction to part 1 has shown, the
idea of presidential representation animated reformers prior to their settling
on budget reform as their primary vehicle, and it was taken up by key actors
at all stages of the reform process—proposing reforms, considering legislation, and implementing the new law. Given the historical and constitutional
connection between legislative representation and finance, the significance of
conceiving of the president as a representative of the whole people to reforms
in budgeting is hard to overstate.

This chapter proceeds as follows. First, I show that the core assumption
behind the proposals for a presidential budget, culminating in the BAA of
1921, was that the president's purportedly unique national perspective should
be privileged in policymaking as a way to guide members of Congress in
overcoming their own localistic interests and passing a budget focused on the
nation as a whole. Second, I examine the different alternatives considered for
budget reform, focusing on how the presidential budget and the BOB were

devised to specifically take advantage of the promised benefits of presidential representation. Third, I demonstrate how the BAA pushed against established institutional arrangements, showing the extent to which the reforms anticipated by the idea of presidential representation overcame opposing claims of congressional representation and constitutionality, especially Congress's power of the purse. Finally, I briefly consider the impact of the BAA on American government and indicate how some parts of the act proved to be more provisional than others.

Assumption: The President's National Perspective

Progressives used the language of "efficiency" in pursuing budget reform.[16] Efficiency—"the idiom of [that] generation," as F. Scott Fitzgerald wrote—was a nebulous concept encapsulating many reform impulses.[17] Some viewed the concept as promising economical spending, while many Progressives viewed it in terms of broader social goals.[18] But efficiency alone was not a rationale for a specifically presidential cure for the nation's alleged budgetary sickness. Debates about budgeting, from the local to the national level, necessarily involved questions and claims about representation.[19]

Proposals to involve the president in budgeting, leading to the final version of the BAA of 1921, asserted that the president was the most likely political actor to propose efficient budgets. This claim itself relied on an assumed logic of presidential representation. To show this, I demonstrate how a wide variety of actors who supported a presidential budget shared at all stages of the reform process an understanding that the president, representing a national constituency, would propose budgets best taking into account the needs of the nation as a whole and avoid unnecessary spending.

For budget reformers, the promise of presidential representation stood in stark contrast to the problem of Congress's perceived inefficiency in budgeting. Individual legislators were viewed as localistic in orientation, seeking money for their respective districts and states without consideration of a national perspective. As Charles Wallace Collins wrote in his budget reform proposal, "local influences—the influences which each Member feels from his own district or his own State—permeate our financial methods."[20] "Nearly every congressman," concurred William Bennett Munro, "has some project for spending public money in his own district, and if it is not recommended in the estimates of some executive department, he endeavors to get it wedged into one of the omnibus enactments."[21] Prominent Republicans also admitted to spending problems despite their party controlling Congress. Representative James Tawney (R-MN), the chairman of the House Appropriations Committee, stated in 1909, "In no period except in time of war have the expenditures of our National Government increased so rapidly . . . as these expenditures have increased during the past eight years." Senator Nelson Aldrich (R-RI), the chairman of the Senate Finance Committee, agreed: "The rapidity with which our national expenditures have increased within the last three years is a source of anxiety if not of alarm."[22] Nor was Congress the only source of angst. Executive branch agencies routinely overspent their budgets, requesting further appropriations from legislators to make up the deficiency.[23]

Accompanied by proposals that the president should submit a budget, these critiques of Congress as parochial and of individual executive departments as myopic relied on an implicit assumption of presidential representation. While many reformers "frequently urged" economy as a rationale, Edward Fitzpatrick critically observed, the "contemporary discussion takes practically for granted that there is an inevitable connection between what is called responsible government and the so-called executive budget." Though a skeptic of a presidential budget, Fitzpatrick recognized the argument being made. "Since legislators are representatives of small districts and the executive is representative of the state or the nation," he panned, the "responsibility for budget proposals must obviously be placed in the executive. *This is the way the argument is presented by the advocates of the executive budget plan.*"[24]

Beyond criticizing congressional inefficiency, proponents of budget reform had more idealistic expectations for presidential accountability and stewardship. They explicitly touted the president as best able to embody the nation, serve as its overall spokesman, focus on national priorities, and alert the whole country to the importance of seemingly mundane aspects of budgeting. The leading protagonist of the budget reform movement, Frederick Cleveland, argued that democracy would be better served by being able to hold an executive accountable for governance. An executive budget— accounting for past policy decisions, assessing present financial conditions, and engaging in long-term planning—would be a means to this end, allowing the public to properly evaluate its leaders. As Cleveland stated, "The only person or persons who can formulate and submit for consideration a plan or program for the government as a whole is the President and his advisors."[25] Similarly, Henry Jones Ford argued that a presidential budget would be necessary "to subordinate particular interests to the general interest."[26] Ford had offered "a prescription according to the spirit of the times," raved one book review: "It is necessary that our Executive should act as Steward of the Public Welfare."[27]

No mere sideshow to arguments about efficiency, this broader conception of presidential representation was present at the genesis of the reform programs that led to the BAA of 1921, exercising a crucial influence on the law's design. Two of the proposals that influenced the BAA were the 1912 report of the President's Commission on Economy and Efficiency (PCEE), spearheaded by Frederick Cleveland, and the 1919 proposal of the Institute for Government Research (IGR), authored by William Willoughby. Though differing in some particulars, they shared the goal of establishing a presidential budget based on an assumption of presidential representation. The PCEE was set up by President Taft, who later wrote that, as "the one whose method of choice and whose range of duties have direct relation to the people as a whole and the government as a whole," any president would likely "feel the necessity for economy in total expenditures."[28] An executive budget, concurred the PCEE in its report, would "enable the *President, as Chief Executive and representative of the people at large*, to get before the country a definite proposal."[29] In the IGR's proposal, Willoughby argued that an executive budget would allow the president to help Congress rise above its localistic tendencies and consider "the general interests of the government as a whole."[30]

These claims about a presidential budget were made not just in academia and in reform proposals. They became prominent in Congress, where legislators could affect the direction of reform. A candid analytical memo on budgeting, belonging to the bill's sponsor, Senator McCormick, underscored that the executive budget was premised on presidential accountability to the nation: "Advocates of a budgetary system for the United States are agreed on the point that the President . . . should be made responsible to the people for the preparation of the budget estimates and for the financial programs embodied therein."[31] In floor debate, Representative Joseph Byrns (D-TN) emphasized that, under the proposed budget legislation, "the President . . . an elective officer of the United States, is made responsible to Congress and to the country."[32] Most notably, the House sponsor of the bill and chairman of the powerful Appropriations Committee, Representative James Good (R-IA), emphasized that the budget legislation "assumed that the President, being the only official of the United States that is elected by all the people . . . must lay out a work program for the Government."[33]

Implicitly and explicitly, reformers stated the importance of presidential representation to a new budget process, and they sought to grant the presidency an initiatory responsibility and organizational capacity commensurate with its allegedly superior representative standing. In the politics of reform, the language of efficiency would fail to submerge these structural stakes.

Selection: Involving the President

Before passage of the BAA, presidential budgeting was not the only institutional arrangement proposed to address rising debt. Other arrangements that would not have involved the president were considered and had precedent. The solution involving the president was a choice, one that indicates the influence of the idea of presidential representation on reform.

Pre-BAA budget processes mostly excluded the president. The original act establishing the Treasury Department had been unique in specifying the secretary's responsibilities to Congress. In the early years of American government, Secretaries of the Treasury Alexander Hamilton and Albert Gallatin had wielded influence over the estimates.[34] Despite Andrew Jackson's subordination of the Treasury in the Bank War, there was no stipulation that the president would have a role in budgeting.[35] Executive branch departments and agencies generated their own estimates. Presidential influence over those estimates in the nineteenth century was irregular and not formalized, dependent on individual presidents taking an interest.[36] After the Civil War, the House made its new Appropriations Committee responsible for reviewing estimates, though the process was soon decentralized again.[37] By the early twentieth century, budgeting involved individual departments and agencies submitting nonrevisable estimates to the treasury secretary to be sent to the House. Neither the president nor the treasury secretary was responsible for individual estimates or coordinating among departments. Congress reigned supreme. Various committees, especially Ways and Means and Appropriations, considered and revised the estimates for particular departments. But no part of government holistically oversaw financial matters: "at no time does any single committee or board or other legislative or executive agency view the finances as a whole. The financial legislation of Congress is therefore lacking in the national point of view."[38]

Well into the twentieth century, alternatives not involving the president were considered. Some in Congress had offered legislative budget alternatives instead, including the proposal of Representative J. Swagar Sherley (D-KY) for a committee that would report estimates of available revenue, or the plan of Representative John Fitzgerald (D-NY) to centralize the appropriations process by granting the Appropriations Committee full jurisdiction over expenditures.[39] Speaker Champ Clark (D-MO) privately admitted to Representative Sherley, a legislative budget advocate, that he wanted to find "some kind of a budget arrangement," but, even with a Democratic president in office, he was "not in favor of turning the whole thing over to the Executive Department."[40] Former Speaker Joseph Cannon (R-IL) also advocated for centralizing the committees rather than involving the president: "I believe that the House of Representatives should have one committee with jurisdiction over appropriations, and that the House should stand firmly for its budget, because it is the one branch of Congress to which the Constitution committed this responsibility and the one which the people hold responsible for the budget, which includes taxation as well as expenditure."[41] In addition to considering addressing the issue solely through changes to the committee process, Congress nearly gave authority to prepare budgets to the treasury secretary, an office with which Congress historically had a close relationship. "There are some of us," wrote Senator McCormick, "who believe, and believe very earnestly, that the Secretary of the Treasury must be made a veritable Minister of Finance, surveying the field of revenue and expenditure."[42] Furthermore, some states and cities had commissions to propose budgets, rather than the elected executive, an alternative that was also discussed in congressional hearings.[43] Finally, Congress could also have considered creating its own institutional resource for budgeting expertise like the later Congressional Budget Office.

The push for a presidency-oriented solution began in earnest with President Taft's efforts, utilizing an appropriation granted by Congress in 1910 to study the possibility of budget reform. Taft argued that it was his "responsibility" to seek reform because he would be "held accountable to the public."[44] Writing to his brother about his push to study budgeting, Taft claimed to "have gone further into reform than most Presidents, especially . . . in economy."[45] After legislators had appropriated funds, Taft revealed the scope of his ambition in choosing Frederick Cleveland to lead the inquiry. Cleveland did not disappoint, suggesting the need to centralize executive branch authority. Pleased, Taft expanded the inquiry to a full commission.[46] The two principal innovations proposed by the commission—an executive budget and a Bureau of Administrative Control—pushed for increased presidential influence. However, congressional concern over the presidential tilt of the PCEE's proposals sank budget reform efforts during the Taft administration.

With Democrat Woodrow Wilson assuming office in 1913, the prospects for an executive budget briefly appeared brighter. The new president had been initially viewed as likely to continue the commission's work, even discussing it with Cleveland.[47] But despite his keen interest in budget reform and public administration, Wilson deferred to his congressional supporters in supporting the strictly legislative solution of a single committee controlling all appropriations.[48] Indeed, Representative Sherley had sought to impress on Wilson as a presidential candidate the desirability of the legislative budget solution.[49] Because his vision of executive-led government required strong party discipline to accomplish a legislative program, "Wilson traded administrative leadership for congressional leadership."[50]

Though disappointed, Taft correctly predicted that the commission's recommendations would influence future reforms.[51] The "wide publicity" of Taft's efforts helped the budget reform movement make progress.[52] While a variety of budget systems were adopted at the state level, many states increasingly gave budget responsibility to governors—the "popularly elected chief."[53] In their 1912 platforms, both major parties acknowledged budgeting as an issue, with Democrats demanding a return to "simplicity and economy" in government and Republicans praising Taft's "earnest effort" toward "greater economy and increased efficiency."[54] But whereas neither party made an explicit commitment to particular budget reforms in 1912, both embraced specific proposals in their 1916 platforms. For the time being, however, a partisan division emerged. Democrats favored a legislative budget system, with the House "initiating and preparing all appropriation bills through a single committee," while Republicans now praised Taft's "oft-repeated proposals" for a presidential budget as "necessary to effect a real reform in the administration of national finance."[55] Republican nominee Charles Evans Hughes, who by 1916 had long spoken of the virtues of executive representation, called for "a responsible budget, proposed by the executive."[56]

A crisis would finally precipitate legislative action. Rising debt from World War I—the total debt skyrocketed from $1 billion in 1916 to over $25 billion by 1919—exposed Congress's inability to halt the growth in expenditures and gave the movement to enact a presidential budget momentum. Citizens also had an increasingly direct stake in federal finances under the new system of income, corporate, and inheritance taxes.[57] Whereas "the ordinary taxpayer" had been relatively unaffected by the "system of indirect taxation," Representative Good explained, "the number of corporations and persons who are affected by direct taxes is rapidly increasing and with that increase there will come an increased demand for the practice of economy and efficiency."[58] Recognizing Congress's failure to control the deficits, the House Select Committee on the Budget, chaired by Good, urged the adoption of a presidential budget in 1919. Notably, this recommendation was made at a time of divided government. President Wilson, who previously had supported budgeting through a single appropriations committee, later announced his concurrence.[59] Proposals favoring presidential participation in budgeting now preempted alternatives that excluded the president, such as the earlier proposals to have a single committee review departmental estimates or to centralize the appropriations process.

Both the 1920 and the 1921 versions of the budget legislation contained reforms meant to privilege the president's national perspective: a presidential budget and a Bureau of the Budget. However, President Wilson vetoed the first act in 1920 over other concerns, viewing Congress's ability to remove the comptroller general through concurrent resolution as violating the president's removal power under Article II. Despite Wilson's veto—which was not a rejection of presidential budgeting—it was clear budget reform would soon pass in some form. Both party platforms moved closer to a presidential cure in 1920. After previously favoring a legislative budget, the Democratic platform now sought to place responsibility on the treasury secretary to prepare the budget "as the representative of the President."[60] Republicans again called for "an executive budget."[61]

Entering office alongside a Republican Congress for unified government in 1921, President Warren Harding sought to deliver a promised deficit reduction. Ironically, though he had pledged to seek "normalcy," Harding realized he needed new tools for presidential leadership. He confessed that he sought a fundamental departure: "The Fact that a thing has existed for a decade or a century—that things have been done in a certain way for a generation— must not be accepted as proving that it ought to continue that way."[62]

The House and Senate overwhelmingly passed budget reform in 1921, though they initially continued to have differences. First, the House placed an independent BOB solely under presidential control, while the Senate placed it again in the Treasury Department. Second, the House bill continued to allow for removal of the comptroller general without the president's approval, while the Senate bill provided for a joint resolution requiring presidential approval.[63] In the conference compromise, the BOB was placed in the Treasury Department, but the director and assistant director would be appointed by the president without Senate consent and placed under the president's direct authority. Furthermore, though Congress retained an independent audit, it agreed to provide for removal of the comptroller (who would hold office for fifteen years during good behavior) through a joint resolution requiring the president's signature.[64]

Increased debt, along with the new system of direct taxation, were proximate causes of the BAA's passage. But explaining the law's design requires accounting for the persistent influence of the idea of presidential representation. Promoting a presidential solution in reaction to the perceived problem of congressional parochialism, the 1921 law's provisions for presidential agenda setting with a presidential budget and new executive organizational capacity through the BOB were explicitly thought to utilize the president's purported national perspective. The law also prohibited any other members of the administration from submitting appropriations requests without a congressional demand to do so.[65] However, Congress rejected proposals to require a supermajority vote for any congressional increase of the president's budget.

A PRESIDENTIAL BUDGET

Congress's ultimate choice of a presidential budget in the BAA, over those other alternatives considered during a decade of debate over the issue, marked an acceptance of presidential representation. From the PCEE report in 1912 to debates over the BAA between 1919 and 1921, proponents of the presidential budget had consistently invoked the rationale that only the president could overcome the localistic incentives of legislators and prod Congress to consider budgeting from a national viewpoint. The PCEE envisioned the annual presidential budget as including a summary message; summaries of general finances, expenditures, and estimates; and suggestions for changes in law to facilitate "greater economy and efficiency."[66] Without that kind of budget initiative, the commission argued, the president lacked a tool for keeping in touch with popular feeling and for guiding Congress in focusing on a national perspective:

> Without a definite method of getting his concrete proposals before the country the Executive, as the one officer of the Government who represents the people as a whole, lacks the means for keeping in touch with public opinion with respect to administrative proposals—both the Congress and the Executive are handicapped in thinking about the country's needs.[67]

Under the commission's proposal, Congress would then be responsible for taking action on "definite proposals" submitted by the president.[68]

The IGR proposal also embraced the same logic for the presidential budget as a guide to Congress. And though William Willoughby focused more on the president's responsibility to provide information to Congress than his keeping in touch with the public, he also praised the improved accountability that the presidential budget would offer. It would allow citizens to exercise "a real popular control" on "their representatives, legislative and executive."[69] However, because the PCEE had faced resistance for the broad scope of the presidential agenda-setting power it envisioned, Willoughby sought to head off similar criticism. Therefore, he rejected a presidential monopoly on budgetary agenda setting—which would have prohibited congressional amendments to the president's proposal—in favor of a revisable presidential budget that Congress could alter through the proposed new budget committees in each chamber.[70]

The hearings of the House Select Committee on the Budget in 1919 featured a parade of witnesses explaining to legislators the link between the executive budget and the president's unique national perspective, and lawmakers themselves recognized the connection. Former representative J. Swagar Sherley—who had argued for a legislative budget involving a committee on estimates and also raised the possibility of giving more responsibility to the treasury secretary while still in Congress—testified that the president should set the agenda in budgeting.[71] Shortly after Sherley's reelection loss in 1918, William Allen, the director of the Institute for Public Service in New York City, had written to urge Sherley to promote the executive budget: "I hope that you will consider it advisable to have Congress formally urge the President to organize for budget estimating."[72] "The legislative body," Sherley subsequently told lawmakers, "should not undertake the forming of a budget until after action by the executive branch."[73] As Sherley admitted, "every Member of Congress is required through the pressure of his constituency at times to undertake action in the way of voting of moneys that perhaps his pure, disinterested judgment might not entirely recommend."[74] Representative John Nance Garner (D-TX) reflected on the same difficulty, arguing that Congress should see only the president's budget rather than individual department and bureau proposals. "Congressmen are human beings," Nance observed, "and liable to be influenced."[75]

Other witnesses explained that the executive budget relied on the premise of presidential representation as well. Frederick Cleveland elaborated on the logic behind the proposal to the committee:

> The assumption that lies back of the suggestion that the Executive should be held responsible is this: . . . The Executive is the one man that is elected by the people at large and represents the whole country. . . . The viewpoint of his vision must be countrywide. . . . He must be in a position of coming to have some definite program or plan that is comprehensive.[76]

Former secretary of war Henry Stimson concurred that the presidential budget was desirable because "the Executive brings to bear . . . the viewpoint of the Nation as a whole as against the [legislature's] view of an aggregate of disputants."[77] Though Stimson still had doubts that Congress would go as far as he wanted in budget reform, he wrote privately to Leonard Wood, "I was glad to find signs of appreciation on their part of the fact that times have changed, and old methods will not do any longer."[78]

The hearings clarified the growing consensus among reformers and law-makers that the president should be granted a formal role in the budget process and augured a significant reform, even as it hinted at what limits would be imposed. The president, emphasized Representative Good, would initiate the budget process, while Congress would retain the ability to amend the budget and would have an independent audit.[79] Praising the Select Committee for recommending a presidential budget, Stimson wrote to Good, "I was very much pleased to see from the press report that your committee has placed all of the responsibility for the formulation of the budget upon the executive, and that you propose to establish the necessary machinery to enable him to discharge that responsibility."[80]

In debates over both the 1920 and the 1921 versions of the budget legislation, lawmakers themselves emphasized that the president was being made responsible for proposing a budget and recognized this reform's reliance on the president's national perspective. The "chief advantage" of the legislation, asserted Byrns, was that it increased presidential accountability by "fix[ing] in the most direct and positive way upon the President the responsibility for all the estimates submitted" and allowed "the people [to] know who is responsible."[81] Highlighting that "new responsibility," Representative Martin Madden (R-IL) argued that "the President, being the only elective official that represents all the American people, is the only man upon whom the responsibility should be placed."[82] The president "ought to frankly and fully let the country know what his policy is," stated Representative Edward Taylor (D-CO): "He will have the necessary machinery, and he should do the work and give the country the benefit of his power and opportunity to save the people's money and get the credit for it if he does and be blamed for it if he does not."[83] "The responsibility is laid on the President to outline a policy," emphasized Senator McCormick, the Senate sponsor of the bill.[84]

Overall, the BAA of 1921 contained the most essential component that advocates of budget reform had long sought. Congress's passage of an enhanced presidential role in an Article I power indicated the influence of the budget reform movement. While Congress rejected a supermajority requirement to increase the budget beyond the president's request, the law institutionalized presidential budgetary initiative.[85] It ensured that the president's purportedly national perspective would make it before Congress for its consideration.

THE BUREAU OF THE BUDGET

To ensure that any executive budget would actually reflect the views of the president, reformers also sought to augment the president's organizational capacity in the executive branch. The final version of the BAA would provide this in the form of the BOB.

In the PCEE's original proposal, the president's control over the executive branch would have been augmented by a new—and unsubtly named—Bureau of Administrative Control. As "the central information plant for the Government," the bureau would help the president and cabinet know "the current problems and conditions that require immediate consideration." Among the functions performed by the bureau would be auditing and budget preparation. Crucially, to ensure the president's own views rather than agency perspectives went before Congress, the budget would "be formulated in a central office which is responsible directly to the President and not under any one department."[86]

Though the PCEE's plan had included a proposed bureau, its more notable feature had been a potentially strong agenda-setting power that had intimidated members of Congress. In the IGR's budget plan, Willoughby shifted to emphasizing the president's managerial role, rather than bearing down on Congress. He focused attention on making the president more clearly the head of the executive branch, which might appear less constitutionally threatening given the president's executive power under Article II. Nevertheless, Willoughby viewed this as a departure, noting that the treasury secretary had been the original officer directed by Congress to prepare budget estimates in 1789. Initially, Willoughby observed, "Congress had no intention of establishing the President in the position of head of the administration."[87] Thus, for Willoughby, "the fundamental basis for effecting this reform" was "the new conception now entertained regarding the President as the responsible head of the administration."[88] Unlike the British, who recognized the Treasury as the superior authority in financial matters, Willoughby wanted it to be "definitely established by law that the President is the sole authority by whom requests for the grant of funds for the executive and administrative branches of the government shall be made of Congress."[89] To ensure budget proposals reflected only the president's views, a new budget bureau would be placed "under the immediate authority and direction of the Chief Executive."[90]

Advocates of a new budget bureau testified to Congress that their aim was to ensure that the president's budget reflected his perspective, rather than that of individual executive departments. Willoughby explained the logic of giving the president, assisted by a budget director, the responsibility of preparing the budget, as opposed to giving it to the treasury secretary, a member of the cabinet. "The one thing that we want," Willoughby told lawmakers, "is that the President shall not only be responsible in the minds of Congress for formulating a definite program but that everybody in the United States should recognize that he has that responsibility and subject him to criticism when he exercises it." Placing "the responsibility squarely upon the President," Willoughby continued, meant that, "in order to meet that responsibility, he will have to dominate his Cabinet."[91] The treasury secretary would be unable to subordinate other departments and agencies: "It would be very difficult for the head of one department to effectively supervise or control his colleagues sitting around the table with him." Instead, a separate budget officer, who would not be a member of the cabinet and "would simply perform the duties for the President," was needed.[92]

Other witnesses concurred with providing the president a budget director and bureau on these grounds. While he had previously considered the idea that the treasury secretary, who was "more peculiarly the officer and agent of the Congress" than any other cabinet member, should have responsibility to revise the budget estimates, former representative Sherley admitted he had changed his mind: "the more I think about that the more I have come to doubt the wisdom of such a provision." Instead, only the president, assisted by a "close executive officer," should "determine what involves not only a question of expenditure, but through expenditure, the question of administrative policy on the highest sense."[93] A budget bureau, Henry Stimson affirmed, would be beneficial because it would "multiply the power of the President over his subordinates."[94] Another former member of the PCEE, Frank Goodnow, advocated for a new "Executive Secretary of the President." Only an empowered subordinate directly under presidential control, Goodnow believed, could effectively "stand up under the demands of the spending departments."[95] Assistant Secretary of the Navy (and future Democratic president) Franklin Delano Roosevelt also called for an officer "directly under the President himself" to prepare a budget. Foreshadowing his own administrative reform efforts in the 1930s, he hoped a budget system would augment presidential control over the administration: "The President ought to have someone who could come into my department at any time and see how I am running it, for his own satisfaction."[96] Such presidential control, these reformers trusted, would prevent the individual departments and agencies from compromising the president's unique institutional perspective in budgeting.

The 1920 version of the legislation granted the president such organizational capacity by authorizing the establishment of a Bureau of the Budget. However, this provision was the subject of a dispute between the House and Senate bills. In the conference compromise, the BOB was placed in the Treasury Department, and the treasury secretary was made the BOB director, responsible for preparing the president's budget. Senator McCormick explained that the Senate had agreed with the House on "fixing upon the President the ultimate responsibility" for "the annual budget" but preferred the treasury secretary to draft it. A separate budget officer, some senators believed, might threaten the status of the rest of the cabinet. "If the President were to maintain the opinion of the director of the budget against that of the head of the department upon any serious issue," argued the Senate's report on the House bill, "the resignation of the member of the Cabinet would naturally follow."[97] Since many reformers had advocated for a separate officer directly under the president to prepare the budget, this was a shortcoming. Representative Byrns, for example, had stated the importance of having a separate budget director who would be "in harmony with the President and his policies, because . . . every appropriation to a certain extent carries with it a question of policy."[98]

The opportunity for a more presidency-oriented BOB emerged from President Wilson's veto of the 1920 bill over unrelated concerns involving the process to remove the comptroller general. In the final version of the BAA of 1921, the BOB was still not solely a presidential agency as the House wanted, as it was placed in the Treasury Department. Yet the House achieved a significant victory, as the BOB director was established as a separate officer directly under the control of the president. Praising the conference report, Representative Good declared the outcome to be a triumph over the Senate, telling lawmakers that "all of the changes have gravitated toward the original provisions of the House bill." Good emphasized that the goal was to give the president the most direct control over the BOB that the Senate would accept. The location of the BOB as an institution "mattered very little" to the House, he argued, given that it would not be subject to the treasury secretary's control. While he admitted that it "would have been better not to have put in the words 'in the Treasury Department,'" Good asserted that this was mostly "an idle phrase." Instead, "the real meat in the section is the power granted," which was "only" to "the President." Notably, the legislation avoided any requirement for Senate confirmation for the director and assistant director because those positions would be "peculiarly the President's staff," and this would ensure the budget "reflected [the president's] sentiment." Moreover, the director could be changed at any point, especially with new administrations, because "the President would want his own budget officer who entertained his ideas of economy."[99]

Other lawmakers recognized this connection between having a separate budget director under the president's direct authority and ensuring that the administration's budget proposal reflected the president's own views. John

Nance Garner, in particular, was enthusiastic. The budget director, he suggested, could become "the second largest man in the executive department." He relished a potential scenario in which the budget director and the treasury secretary disagreed on the estimates:

> He will be able to look at the Secretary of the Treasury and say, "You will cut out this expenditure. This is what I am going to abolish." "Who is this that is speaking to me?" "It is the representative of the President of the United States himself."[100]

Thus, the BAA of 1921 marked a major leap forward in the creation of the institutional presidency. Establishing the BOB to ensure that the president's views would be predominant in the annual budget, the BAA endorsed greater presidential control over administration in statute.

THE GENERAL ACCOUNTING OFFICE

While Congress substantially empowered the president with an executive budget and the BOB, it still sought to check that power. The institutional mechanism would be the audit, performed by a new General Accounting Office (GAO) (today called the Government Accountability Office). Even the strongest presidency-oriented bills that Congress had considered envisioned granting Congress control of the audit.[101]

Proponents of the presidential budget explained the importance of the audit to legislators in the House hearings on budget reform. The comptroller should be independent of the president, Representative Good argued, "so that his criticisms can be at all times free from Executive interference."[102] In essence, Willoughby suggested, "the office would be really an agency of the legislature."[103] Even the strongest advocate of presidentialism in budgeting, Frederick Cleveland, noted that "the audit and control of expenditures in any event ought to be so organized for, and developed, that Congress would have an independent source of information."[104]

Under the 1920 version of the legislation, the comptroller general—the head of the GAO—could be removed by concurrent resolution. This meant that the president's approval would not be required in order for Congress to remove the comptroller.[105] President Wilson thus vetoed the bill, charging that it infringed on the president's removal power.[106] The 1921 legislation changed the concurrent resolution to a joint resolution, ensuring that the president would have the opportunity to veto an attempt by Congress to remove the comptroller.

With the establishment of the GAO and the audit, the president did not simply gain power at Congress's expense. Instead, "the independent audit was Congress's quid pro quo for the President's budget bureau."[107] These were the terms on which Congress was willing to accept the new system of presidential budgeting.

Challenge: Congress's Power of the Purse

Presidential budgeting was vulnerable to charges that it would interfere with the power of the purse that belonged to Congress and especially to the House of Representatives. At the Founding, the connection between finance and representation that had developed in the Anglo-American political tradition was formalized in Article I, as revenue bills would originate in the House of Representatives, giving the power of the purse to the chamber perceived as closest to the people.[108] As James Madison famously argued in *The Federalist*, "This power over the purse, may in fact be regarded as the most compleat and effectual weapon with which any constitution can arm the immediate representatives of the people."[109] Treasury secretaries had wielded some influence early on, but any presidential influence over executive branch estimates before the 1921 act was irregular and not institutionalized.[110] Thus, the innovation of a presidential budget—even if it was fully amendable by Congress—was a substantial departure from previous ideas about and institutional arrangements for budgeting.

Key reformers did not hide the fact that presidential budgeting raised constitutional issues. Instead, they pressed the implications and identified the separation of powers as an obstacle to be overcome. Henry Jones Ford described budgetary issues as "symptomatic of [a] general constitutional disease" in which "our national representative assembly fails to discharge this constitutional function successfully." The House, the primary locus of budget initiation, was simply not up to the task.[111] Significantly, the PCEE's 1912 report also described how its vision of presidential budgeting would depart from American constitutional precedents. The report noted that "executive authority" in other nations possessed "powers of initiation and leadership," while "legislative authority" possessed "merely powers of final determination and control." Because the United States had this relationship backward, the "use of a budget would require that there be a complete reversal of procedure by the Government."[112] Of course, the president's Article II authority to recommend measures could give some constitutional cover for this new procedure.[113] But the PCEE had deemed that Article II provision insufficient.[114]

For a time, objections to these visions of a constitutional departure sank reform efforts. Despite the PCEE's name focusing on "economy" and "efficiency," its scope of inquiry had revealed a broader and bolder ambition, provoking backlash even before the commission completed its work. Both executive branch agencies and Congress resisted the commission. Conscious of its traditional relationship to Congress, the Treasury Department only grudgingly cooperated with Frederick Cleveland when President Taft personally intervened.[115] Stimson, Taft's secretary of war, would later testify to Congress in 1919 about the resistance of departments to the PCEE's work: "I do not want to tell tales out of school, but I remember very vividly the feeling of semiresentment that the average head of the department had when these fellows came burrowing around, as he thought, asking questions and trying to help him in the management of his department."[116] In 1912, Congress pushed back against the commission by rejecting a $250,000 funding request, giving instead $75,000 and stipulating that the appropriation pay no more than three salaries.[117]

After hampering that study, Congress rejected its grandiose plans. The presidential budgeting proposal, involving mainly an Article I power, portended a significant change to constitutional relationships. The proposed Bureau of Administrative Control, which would be used to implement a new budget system, likewise would alter the relationship of the departments to Congress. But the budgeting recommendations provoked more congressional resistance.[118] Democratic committee chairmen "humanely disposed of" its report.[119] Furthermore, when Taft tried to impose the new budget process in 1912 on a recalcitrant Congress by directing departments to submit their estimates in the manner prescribed by the commission's recommendations, Congress countered by requiring submission of the estimates according to procedures under existing law. The move was intended to ensure that the PCEE's proposal "had been killed."[120] Taft responded by submitting estimates to Congress himself to complement the standard budget procedure, but Congress took no action on his message. As the *New York Times* noted, the Appropriations Committee chairman, Representative Fitzgerald, "voiced the point that the President's proposal was an invasion of legislative prerogatives."[121] Finally, though Taft sought to extend the commission even after losing in the 1912 election, Congress refused to extend the appropriation past June 1913.[122]

Political calculations did help fuel this defense of congressional prerogatives. Between the authorization of the PCEE and its report, Democrats had ended Republican unified party control by winning the House in the 1910 midterm elections. Moreover, House rules had been decentralized after the revolt against Speaker Cannon in 1910, giving back more authority to individual legislators and making it even less likely that they would surrender prerogatives to the president.[123] But revealingly, the commission faced resistance because it had clarified the ambition behind institutionalizing presidential initiative. The potential scope of the president's proposed initiative power was also ambiguous. By citing Britain's budget process as a model, the report seemed to leave open the possibility that the president would present a plan allowing for no congressional amendments, a reform that went further than Congress was willing to consider. House members recognized that their constitutionally granted powers were at stake.[124]

At the same time, members of the House also recognized that "many of their influential constituents" approved of Taft's efforts. Therefore, they offered an alternative that was understood to preserve congressional prerogatives. House Democrats would "propose to have a budget," reported the *Times*, "but not one controlled by the President."[125] Advocating his plan for a legislative budget, Representative Sherley called Congress "the only logical representative of a free people."[126] "I want again to congratulate you," wrote one citizen to Sherley, "on the proposal which bids fair to secure proper responsibility in Government money matters without attempting to change the Committee System of doing business." That committee system, noted the writer significantly, "seems to be natural to us Americans."[127]

When the IGR decided to prioritize budget reform in 1916, it responded to Congress's defensiveness over its own constitutional prerogatives. In fact, the IGR trustees chose former PCEE member William Willoughby as director over Frederick Cleveland because they believed that Willoughby would be the more effective political operator with Congress to achieve budget reform.[128] Willoughby took the PCEE's report as a starting point for reform, but by making it clear that the presidential budget could be amended by Congress, the IGR's proposals were presented in a reconfigured, less confrontational form.[129] This was a concession to Congress's prerogatives. Though he preferred the strong executive powers of the British system, Willoughby recognized that Congress was unlikely "to make such a radical change." Thus, he expressed a strategic preference: "the system proposed goes as far as it is believed that Congress is prepared to go at this time."[130]

Still, even a less confrontational version of the presidential budget could be portrayed by critics as a threat to Congress's prerogatives. Former House Speaker Cannon warned, "I think we had better stick pretty close to the Constitution with its division of powers well defined and the taxing power close to the people."[131] The challenge that any kind of presidential budget signified to Congress's own power was underscored in the House's hearings on budget reform in 1919. When Samuel Lindsay, the vice chairman of the National Budget Committee, attempted to downplay changes to Congress's role in budgeting, Representative Byrns confronted him. "I do not know of anything," observed Byrns, "that would tend more to put Congress under the domination of the Executive." Justifying it as a necessity, Lindsay admitted the scope of the proposed change. "It is true," he admitted, "you are centralizing the power of initiation in the Executive that does not vest there now, and you are limiting the power of initiation that now vests in individual Members of Congress." "We either do not need a budget system at all," contended Lindsay, "or you have to face that issue."[132] Even Byrns, who would be a supporter of the BAA, admitted his worries that House members would lose too much power, wondering if it would be "entirely democratic to take away from the membership of the House . . . who are directly responsible to the people and who are elected by the people, any voice whatever with reference to appropriations."[133]

Ultimately, despite earlier resistance that cited constitutional claims, rising debt from World War I made legislators more receptive to the need for change, and reformers who had been agitating for a presidential budget based on an assumption of presidential representation had a solution at the ready. The resistance arising from the established sets of institutional arrangements and related ideas did lead to some compromises in the legislation that headed off moves toward even more presidential empowerment. But on the whole, the impact of the idea of presidential representation is evident from the arrangements and ideas that had to be overcome to achieve a new departure in budgeting. Congress had self-consciously granted the president a significant part of its most cherished power.

Conclusion: Presidentialism in the Service of Normalcy

The BAA of 1921 contained substantial innovations inspired by the idea of presidential representation, marking a recognition in statute that the president was the nation's chief representative. Not only did Congress choose to formally involve the president in proposing a budget for the first time; it provided a budget director and Bureau of the Budget under presidential authority (even if it was initially located in the Treasury Department until 1939).[134] Congress did reject the notion of allowing the president's budget to be increased only by a congressional supermajority, revealing the limit to which it was willing to empower the president. Still, given its Article I prerogatives, the House's eagerness to ensure the president's views would prevail in budget proposals is remarkable. Rather than granting a presidential agenda-setting power that would limit congressional amendments, the House focused on the president's control of the BOB, touching on an Article II power. Legislators passed a law based on an assumption that the president's national constituency would make him more likely to seek greater economy in expenditures.

The significance of the new budget system for the presidency was soon apparent. With the BAA's passage in 1921, a paradox arose—the prospect of using the presidency to return to normalcy. The Progressive Era had been characterized by bold attempts at presidential leadership.[135] Yet despite the reaction against Progressivism, Congress and President Harding discovered that fiscal retrenchment required its own increment of presidentialism. Satirically describing this new presidential responsibility, F. Scott Fitzgerald wrote that "a good President ought to be able to tell just how much we could afford."[136]

Though the law was supposed to apply to the 1923 fiscal year, the Harding administration boldly decided, without formal authority, to implement it early and devise a budget for 1922.[137] The conservative Harding admitted to aggressively using the presidency to "restore sane and normal ways again." He focused on "binding together" those "departments and independent establishments which formerly . . . operated independently of one another."[138] The new budget director, Charles Dawes, nudged Harding to adopt a stronger view of presidential authority. Dawes underscored the significance of using the new budget process: it "marks the passing (and is intended so to do) of the old system."[139] The law ensured departments would be "made to better accord with the plan which the President had established."[140] Though Dawes was criticized by some for placing the BOB's focus too much on reducing costs and not on broader policy ends, he unquestionably viewed the new budget process as enhancing presidential accountability: "Nothing should be allowed to withdraw the attention of the public from the duty and powers of the President."[141]

Enthusiasm for using this new budgetary authority continued unabated after Dawes left his post. Harding put his own business-oriented spin on presidential representation: "what we are doing is not for ourselves . . . not for the President . . . but for the people—the stockholders of this great business."[142] Seeking to ensure that only the *presidential* perspective would be put before Congress in budget proposals, Harding warned executive branch employees that testifying with estimates "in excess of the Executive recommendation" would be "sufficient reason" for being fired.[143] His successor, Calvin Coolidge, issued the same warning: "[Harding] admonished you against the advocating of an estimate before the Congress and its committees in excess of the executive recommendation. . . . This law must be observed."[144] Harding, Dawes, and Coolidge implemented the law in a manner that augmented presidential authority.

The BAA of 1921 marked a significant achievement in constitutional adaptation, the new budget system a shift toward a more presidency-centered government in America. It was the first step in Congress's creation of the institutional presidency, part of a broader series of reforms that would alter the separation of powers. Beyond putting together the budget, the new BOB soon took on broader roles, serving to assist the president in assembling a legislative program and unilateral actions.[145] The president was widely seen as a budget leader for the nation.[146] Indeed, "it is recognized," wrote one observer at midcentury, "that the whole shape and pace of the economy may be decided by the scale and character of the President's proposals."[147] Reflecting on the act's significance decades later, one scholar called it "probably the greatest landmark in our administrative history except for the Constitution itself."[148]

As transformative as the BAA of 1921 was, it had a latent vulnerability. In the era in which the BAA passed, the notion that the president uniquely represented the national interest was widely accepted in elite political discourse. But what if that premise lost its perceived validity? In the late 1960s and early 1970s, the legitimacy of the idea of presidential representation came under attack. The implications for a budget system that had presumed the president possessed an exclusive national perspective—and had pushed against strong congressional claims to the power of the purse—were potentially profound. Chapter 7 will consider the fate of the system set up by the BAA once its guiding assumption came under fire.

4

Presidential Economic Policymaking

But whatever the method of meeting the situation, the remedy in all cases is in principle the same; the initiative is transferred from territorial delegates who represent local and special interests to the executive who in theory represents the whole nation. This is a political revolution which is temporarily necessary in any grave crisis and is permanently necessary if the modern state is to discharge the great task of regulating the national economy.

WALTER LIPPMANN, 1934[1]

Citizens expect presidents to take a lead role in economic policymaking. Occupants of the White House are held responsible by the public for the performance of the economy, regardless of how much influence they actually wield.[2] But while economic stewardship by the president is a public expectation, it was not a constitutional expectation. Congress institutionalized that responsibility in the presidency.

Legislators expanded and formalized the president's economic responsibilities with the passage of the Reciprocal Trade Agreements Act (RTAA) of 1934 and the Employment Act of 1946. These laws granted the presidency authority in trade and employment, a combination that cemented the president's leading role in economic policymaking. While presidents in the early twentieth century had themselves already taken a more active role in economic management, these two laws signaled a substantial shift. Congress willingly chose to endorse presidential leadership in statute. The RTAA granted new and substantial power to the presidency by authorizing the incumbent to negotiate bilateral trade agreements with other nations and reduce tariff rates by up to 50 percent. In effect, the president both set *and* executed the agenda in tariff making. The Employment Act made the president responsible for submitting an annual Economic Report to Congress, including legislative recommendations, and created the Council of Economic Advisers (CEA) in the Executive Office of the President (EOP). These were major developments in Congress's creation of the institutional presidency.

Why did Congress choose to grant this authority and organizational capacity to the presidency? A persuasive account of the passage of the RTAA might focus on regional interests. Legislators representing agrarian periphery regions favored lower tariff rates, while those representing industrial core areas generally resisted them.[3] But while the influence of regional interests may broadly explain the coalitions for and against the tariff legislation, it cannot explain the design decision to grant the president substantial trade authority. Coalitions of periphery legislators favorable to lower tariffs had previously acted unilaterally to reduce rates, rather than delegating such authority to the president. The rationale for the law's design requires another explanation.

A strong case for an informational account can be made to explain the passage of the Employment Act. Seeking to ensure that the president utilized information and expertise in proposing economic legislation and reporting on the state of the economy, Congress granted the president control over the new CEA and even placed it directly in the EOP.[4] But Congress did not place the CEA under presidential control because it perceived the president as having substantial preexisting authority over economic policy. Rather, the Employment Act itself constituted an effort by Congress to grant and formalize presidential responsibility in that domain. Thus, any account of the Employment Act must first explain the assumptions behind Congress's choice to recognize and formalize the president's economic role.

Additionally, partisanship alone cannot explain the design of these laws. In trade policy, the RTAA received few Republicans votes, continuing a long-standing pattern of Democrats seeking lower tariff rates and Republicans favoring protectionism. Still, five Republican senators did vote in favor of the legislation.[5] More importantly, the enactment's design was a new development, and both proponents and opponents of presidential trade authority notably agreed that the more holistic viewpoint of a president would likely promote an institutionalization of lower tariff rates. In employment policy, each iteration of the legislation that culminated in the 1946 law passed with substantial bipartisan margins, suggesting that partisan disagreements were not a principal influence on the law's design.[6]

Without accounting for the role of ideas, explanations for the RTAA of 1934 and Employment Act of 1946 are limited. I argue that in both statutes Congress again consciously recognized the idea of presidential representation and worked that assumption into the design of reforms that established new presidential responsibilities and capacities. To be clear, my claim is not that the idea of presidential representation itself directly caused the passage of these two laws. Congress was prompted to consider tariff reform in 1934 in response to the Great Depression and the collapse of world trade. Its passage of the Employment Act in 1946 was motivated by the fear of a recession, as the United States faced the prospect of post–World War II reconversion and an influx of returning GIs. But the design of each law and the choice of institutional solutions involving the president over other alternatives directly corresponded to the assumption that the president would act based on a unique national perspective in policymaking.

This chapter proceeds as follows. I broadly compare the creation of the institutional presidency and the provision for presidential authority in economic policy in both trade and domestic economic policy. For each policy area, I first show that the idea of presidential representation was specifically cited as the core assumption behind the legislation. Second, I examine how reforms involving the president were chosen over other potential alternatives that would have potentially corresponded to greater congressional authority. Third, I demonstrate that the reforms that corresponded to the idea of presidential representation pushed against established institutional arrangements. Finally, I conclude by briefly considering the different paths of development these reforms took in subsequent decades.

Presidential Trade Authority: The RTAA of 1934

Congress transformed the tariff-making process with the passage of the RTAA of 1934, transferring significant control over one of Congress's fundamental powers to the presidency.[7] Legislators changed the institutional location of tariff making by removing direct control over tariff rates from Congress and granting substantial authority to the president.[8] In doing so, Congress altered the trajectory of American political development.

The tariff had been a defining political issue between the parties and regions of the country in Congress. In the words of James Sundquist, "more than any other single topic," the tariff "had engrossed [Congress's] energies for more than a hundred years."[9] Democrats in Congress, particularly those from the South and the West, had largely favored lower tariff rates, while, after the Civil War, Republican legislators, particularly from the East, used high tariff rates to protect domestic industries and hold their electoral coalition together.[10] Moreover, even as the United States had begun to develop an empire overseas, it retained protectionist tariff policies.[11] As E. E. Schattschneider famously documented, the tariff law that passed a few years before the RTAA, the Smoot-Hawley Tariff Act of 1930, was an infamous case of congressional particularism, raising tariffs to extraordinary heights.[12]

A drastic decline in trade by 1934 served as the impulse for a reconsideration of the tariff process.[13] The *New Republic* bemoaned the state of world trade and the economy: "The world is desperately sick, and the United States is sickest of all."[14] In the 1932 campaign, Democratic presidential candidate Franklin Delano Roosevelt had criticized congressional logrolling in tariff making and pledged a reduction in rates.[15] In early 1934, Secretary of State

Cordell Hull, who in his congressional career had long sought freer trade and worked on tariff and tax legislation, drafted a bill that would change the tariff-making process.[16] President Roosevelt soon requested new authority from Congress.[17] Unlike the 1930 tariff law, the new bill would not require an investigation and recommendation by the Tariff Commission to justify any presidential action. It allowed for the negotiation of reciprocal bilateral agreements, in which the president could reduce duties by up to 50 percent but could not place dutiable articles on the free list or remove articles from the free list. The administration had wanted even more power for the president, but it sought to act strategically to ensure congressional passage.[18]

Notably, scholars have debated whether the president's national perspective was a major consideration behind the design of the RTAA. Some dispute that presidential representation was a meaningful assumption behind the passage of the law, focusing on the role of partisanship.[19] Others have suggested that presidential trade authority was based on the notion that presidents would be more likely to seek freer trade.[20] In my account, the decision to substantially alter the tariff-making process by involving the president and coupling consideration of both imports and exports was not simply a response to declining world trade. To be sure, immediately lowering tariffs as a way to stimulate world trade and economic growth was the main goal. But by embracing a solution with the assumption of presidential representation in mind, supporters of presidential trade authority consciously sought to *institutionalize* lower tariffs and promote freer trade. The influence of the idea is revealed in the explicit statements made in congressional debates, the choice of a reform involving the president, and the established institutional arrangements that were disrupted with the creation of presidential trade authority.

ASSUMPTION: THE PRESIDENT'S NATIONAL PERSPECTIVE

For proponents and opponents alike, the core assumption behind the RTAA was that the president, being elected by a national constituency, would be predisposed to reduce tariffs rates and promote freer trade. This presumption gained traction from the contrast made between the president and members of Congress. Lawmakers were widely understood to be beholden to local interests and, therefore, were perceived as being unreliable in support of lower tariff rates. As Senator Harry Byrd (D-VA) quickly announced after the tariff measure was proposed, "I am . . . convinced, after seeing juggling in Congress . . . that for the present, at least, it is far preferable to have these trade agreements made by the President, who can take into consideration what may be the best for the interests of the Country as a whole."[21]

In congressional hearings on the proposed legislation, lawmakers and witnesses laid out the logic of presidential representation repeatedly. In the context of unified Democratic government, it was perhaps unsurprising that Democratic lawmakers praised the president as the best representative of the nation. Representative Ralph Lozier (D-MO) told senators that the bill would allow "the President, acting for the welfare of the whole country as distinguished from the selfish localism of any particular community," to make trade agreements with tariff rates "unhampered by considerations which control a Member of Congress."[22] Another prominent bill supporter, Representative Jere Cooper (D-TN), asserted that the president "is the best representative of the American people, because he represents the whole people."[23]

A more unexpected statement of support for presidential representation came from a key witness testifying before the House Ways and Means Committee. The chairman of the Tariff Commission, Robert Lincoln O'Brien, had been appointed to his position by former Republican president Herbert Hoover. It was thus a surprise to the committee when he voiced his steadfast support for the bill.[24] Replying to a question about the president from Cooper, O'Brien drew a clear contrast between the institutional perspective of the president and that of legislators:

> It is true he is the only elective officer who represents the entire body politic. You gentlemen represent districts, and the Senators represent States, and the President is the one who represents all of the people of the country, and to that extent that gives him a judicial status to handle these questions.[25]

Moreover, O'Brien connected his understanding of presidential representation with the expected policy change that would result from presidential trade authority. He explained that his testimony focused on the likelihood of "lowering tariffs" under the proposed bill because "there seems to be no worry about the President's use of that power in raising tariffs."[26]

This rationale for the design of the legislation was also articulated in congressional floor debate. In the House, Representative Robert Doughton (D-NC), the sponsor of the bill and chairman of the Ways and Means Committee, emphasized that the president could be trusted in matters of tariff making because of his national constituency: "We Representatives are elected by people of certain districts; the Senators represent States; but the President is elected by all of the people and has the welfare of all the people at heart."[27] The president's accountability to the nation, Representative Thomas Cullen (D-NY) assured his colleagues, ensured that there could be no fear that the president would abuse the proposed trade authority. Because "the President represents the United States as a whole," he professed to have "no patience with that kind of criticism, whether it is too much power to grant the President." Failure to pass the bill, Cullen warned, would mark a defeat by the very forces of congressional parochialism that the legislation was meant to supersede. Defeat would "appear to many" to be the result "of those sectional interests which through the means of logrolling and back-scratching have brought congressional tariff-making into disrepute."[28]

The Senate discussion of the bill likewise focused on the expected behavior of the president in exercising trade authority. Senator Pat Harrison (D-MS), the chairman of the Senate Finance Committee, managed the bill on the Senate floor. Seeking to criticize the act, Senator Charles McNary (R-OR) asked Harrison whether the president would use trade authority to favor one part of the country over another: "Will it be used to the preference of the South and the detriment of the West? Will it be used to help the East, and will the Middle West be left untouched?" In response, Harrison asserted that the idea of presidential representation was, in essence, common sense. "Of course, that requires no discussion on my part," Harrison replied dismissively, "because the Senator does not believe that the President of the United States . . . would permit, in negotiating any trade agreements, that they should be employed to the disadvantage of one section as against another, or of one class against another." Instead, Harrison chided, "the President would deal fairly with every section and with all interests of the country."[29]

These statements of faith in presidential representation from congressional Democrats might seem to principally reflect only their partisan interests in granting power to a Democratic president. Moreover, Democrats like Doughton, Harrison, Lozier, and Cooper were from periphery regions naturally disposed to want lower tariff rates. More revealing, then, was that key Republicans agreed on the significance of the connection between the president's national constituency and the expectation of lower tariff rates. Representing a periphery state, Senator Arthur Capper (R-KS) also hoped to lower the tariff. He lambasted congressional parochialism as an obstacle: "Logrolling is inevitable. . . . We jam together, through various unholy alliances and combinations, a potpourri or hodgepodge of section and local tariff rates. . . . I see no reason to believe that another attempt would result in a more happy ending." Given his disgust with congressional representation in tariff making, Capper was willing to bet that presidential representation would prove superior. "I have no assurance, though I have some hopes," Capper admitted, "that a President responsible to the Nation as a whole can and will enter into trade agreements from the national viewpoint." "But," he affirmed, "I do have grave doubts, judging from past experience, that the Congress can write a national tariff act."[30]

Perhaps even more remarkable was the view of the leading opponent of the proposed bill in the House. Representative Allen Treadway (R-MA) was a typical eastern supporter of high protective tariffs, and he feared the possibility of lower tariff rates. It was thus significant that Treadway agreed that presidential representation was likely to lead to lower rates because it prioritized a more national view. "Members should bear in mind," Treadway warned, "if they vote advance approval of [future presidential] trade agreements by this bill, that they may be voting the death of some industrial or agricultural activity in their district; unimportant, perhaps, in the national picture, but in many cases the lifeblood of a local community."[31]

Democrats also made it a point to portray even Republican presidents as more favorable to free trade than their congressional counterparts. In the House, Representative Lozier invoked Treadway to argue that even Republican presidents would be likely to act as national stewards in tariff making. Lozier asserted that if Treadway were to become president, the office would change his perspective on tariffs: "when [Treadway] was clothed with Presidential responsibility . . . he, though a militant Republican, would carefully consider the arguments for and against the application of this formula to any particular industry."[32] Taking the same tact, Senator Harrison invoked Republican president William McKinley's final speech at the 1901 Pan-American Exposition in Buffalo, which had called for greater openness in trade, in Senate debate over the RTAA. Harrison read a portion of McKinley's "strangely prophetic" address:

> The period of exclusiveness is past. The expansion of our trade and commerce is the pressing problem. . . . Reciprocity treaties are in harmony with the spirit of the times; measures of retaliation are not. If perchance some of our tariffs are no longer needed for revenue, or to encourage and protect our industries at home, why should they not be employed to extend and promote our market abroad?[33]

For Harrison, that statement showed that presidents of both parties—even McKinley, who had been an architect of high tariffs—had recognized the need for freer trade in the national interest while in office.

SELECTION: INVOLVING THE PRESIDENT

The choice to empower the president over other potential methods of tariff making also indicates the influence of the idea of presidential representation on the passage of the RTAA. While the Great Depression was the proximate cause of the RTAA's passage, the law's specific design hinged on an expectation that presidents, owing to their unique national standing, would be more likely to lower tariff rates.

Bilateral Reciprocal Agreements

The central innovation of the RTAA was to allow the president to negotiate bilateral trade agreements. With this authority, the president could potentially lower tariff rates on particular goods by up to 50 percent.[34] By statute, the president would not just set the agenda in tariff making. He would determine the entire policy.

For congressional Democrats, seeking to empower the president was a new move. When in power in the past, congressional Democrats had lowered tariff rates on imports without any corresponding consideration of US exports. In 1894 and 1913, during two previous periods of unified Democratic government, Congress had acted to lower tariff rates unilaterally. Certainly, the Democratic Congress of 1934 faced a vastly different economic situation. High domestic unemployment and rising trade barriers across the world during the Great Depression constricted Congress's ability to decide tariffs by itself.[35] But the response of Congress in 1934 to create presidential trade authority signaled an attempt to institutionalize lower tariff rates and freer trade, making a resurgence of congressional protectionism less likely in the future.

Advocates of the bill connected their support of presidential trade authority with the premise of presidential representation. Predictably, this was the rationale given by members of the Roosevelt administration to support a presidency-oriented reform over continued congressional tariff making. The intellectual force behind the RTAA, Secretary Hull, cited his extensive experience as a legislator working on tariff reform to argue that Congress was unequipped to handle tariff making in a time of economic emergency.[36] When asked by Representative John McCormack (D-MA) if the bill would vest power in "the only man whose constituency is the whole country," Hull responded affirmatively.[37] Secretary of Agriculture Henry Wallace testified that it was "totally impossible for Congress to handle this matter from the standpoint of the national welfare."[38] "The President, if elected by all the people, is the man whom the public chooses to trust," concurred Assistant Secretary of State Francis Sayre. If the president could not be trusted, "then we might as well abdicate and close up shop."[39]

Democratic lawmakers explained their choice to depart from the previous method of tariff making on the same basis. Granting this trade authority, asserted Representative Doughton, would allow the president to "extend his efforts toward bettering our trade with foreign countries, and thereby further promote the general welfare of all the people." In the context of the Depression, Congress could not "delay creating the necessary machinery."[40] Senator Marvel Mills Logan (D-KY) also invoked the president's unique institutional standing. "Who is most interested in bringing peace and happiness and prosperity to the people of the United States of America?" Logan asked. "The answer is obvious: The President of the United States of America. Everything is at stake so far as he is concerned."[41]

If members of the Roosevelt administration and congressional Democrats were already assumed to support presidential trade authority on partisan grounds, a more surprising intervention came from a prominent Republican. Former Republican secretary of war and secretary of state Henry Stimson startled observers and upset a number of Republican senators by making a prominent radio address to support granting such authority to a Democratic president.[42] But his support was consistent with his long-standing agitation to empower the president as "the representative of the nation at large."[43] Believing that Congress was "entirely ineffective" at setting tariff rates and too responsive to local interests, Stimson linked the design of the bill to the earlier Budget and Accounting Act (BAA) of 1921, another presidency-oriented reform he had supported years earlier. Moreover, he declared himself "not impressed with the objection that it would give undue or dictatorial powers to our Executive."[44] "I dislike to differ with the leaders of my own party," Stimson admitted privately, "but it seems to me that never did the country need independent and constructive leadership more than it needs it now."[45]

Supporters of the trade legislation counted Stimson's support as a significant boost to their efforts. "It was," wrote one confidant to Stimson, "not only a patriotic but a most courageous thing that you, the most influential member of President Hoover's cabinet, should be willing to express yourself at a time when such an expression will mean so much."[46] "It came at just the right moment," wrote a grateful Assistant Secretary of State Sayre, "and I am sure will do much to help in pushing through the program. . . . It was a strong and splendid move on your part and I want you to know how much it is appreciated."[47] As manager of the trade bill, Senator Harrison soon made a point of citing Stimson's "eloquent radio address" during subsequent Senate floor debate.[48]

Congress also declined several alternatives that would have curtailed the extent of the presidential trade authority granted by the RTAA. Though there were discussions of relying more on the Tariff Commission, this alternative was rejected. Its chairman, Robert O'Brien, told lawmakers that the commission should not be "a source of primary power" because the decision over rates was "a question of such ramifications that it belongs very much higher up than with the Tariff Commission."[49] Congress could have required the president to negotiate treaties that would be subject to Senate consent, rather than relying on executive agreements that could bypass such a requirement, as many critics pointed out. Some legislators also tried to require congressional assent to presidential agreements or, at least, to give Congress a legislative veto through which legislators could disapprove of those agreements. But amendments to that effect were defeated in both the House and the Senate.[50] Proponents of the RTAA argued that restricting presidential trade authority would compromise the mission of lowering tariffs.

Duration of Presidential Authority

One potentially strong limitation was added to the bill before it passed. Proponents of the bill had emphasized that it was a response to an economic emergency, and this came with a cost. As amended, the final version of the bill limited the president's authority to negotiate bilateral agreements to three years from the date of the legislation's enactment. As Representative Doughton explained, the amendment was adopted "to show that the bill is only an emergency measure."[51] Assistant Secretary of State Sayre admitted the Roosevelt administration's strategic preference in agreeing to this limitation: "I think this bill goes as far as we can appropriately ask."[52] Still, any trade agreements reached by the president would remain in force unless specifically "terminated in accordance with the terms of the agreements themselves."[53] Indeed, the House and Senate rejected amendments that would place limits on the duration of agreements themselves.[54]

For presidential trade authority to be maintained over time, Congress would have to pass legislation renewing it. But despite this limitation, opponents of the RTAA recognized that Congress might not reclaim its tariff prerogatives and that presidential trade authority would likely be institutionalized through consistent reauthorizations. "It seems to me," warned Representative Isaac Bacharach (R-NJ), that "once [the president] got the power, it would be hard to take it away from him."[55] "While the bill is to be in force for only 3 years," testified Fred Brenckman for the National Grange in the Senate hearings, "the prospects are if it is passed, the people will never regain the power they now have to frame their own tariff laws."[56] Regardless of the emergency duration, opined Representative Roy Woodruff (R-MI), the bill would become "permanent legislation." He warned that "any power turned over to the present occupant of the White House is also turned over to all those who shall come after him."[57] These concerns would prove prescient, as trade authority would be renewed for subsequent presidents.

Public Notification and Consultation

A second limitation imposed in the final bill was a minimal nod to concerns that localistic perspectives would be bypassed in presidential tariff making in favor of only a national perspective. The Senate adopted an amendment requiring the president to give a notice of intent to negotiate in order to allow time for public comment. It also stipulated that the president would consult with the Tariff Commission, State Department, Agriculture Department, and Commerce Department before concluding a bilateral agreement.[58]

Initially, the bill's champion in the House opposed such a consulting period. Representative Doughton dismissed the possibility that the president would ignore affected constituents: "What reason do you have to apprehend the President of the United States, elected by all the people, a representative of all the people, would turn a cold shoulder and a deaf ear to an industry of any kind essential to American life and American business?"[59] But opponents of the legislation were unwilling to take that leap of faith. Senator Frederic Walcott (R-CT) objected "that the people aggrieved [by tariff changes] have no way of presenting their side of the case."[60] Reacting to such concerns, Senator Harrison sought an accommodation. He explained that "to allay the fear that the needs and desires of private business interests might be ignored or that ill-considered action might be taken," the amendment would make it "compulsory on the Chief Executive to give public notice of intended negotiations so that interested persons may have an opportunity to present their views."[61] In the House, Doughton decided to accept the additional "safeguard, so that any interested party could be heard, and the President may obtain advice from all proper sources."[62] Though the public notification and consultation requirement was a compromise, it detracted little from the overall authority being granted to the president in the RTAA. The president would not be bound in any way to act on any advice or the perspective of those commenting on proposed trade agreements.

CHALLENGE: CONSTITUTIONAL STRETCHES

The RTAA's embrace of presidential representation pushed hard against an established set of institutional arrangements and associated ideas about the tariff, Congress, and the Constitution. The charges aimed at the proposed legislation by opponents indicated potential vulnerabilities. Critics of the RTAA's provision for presidential trade authority argued that Congress was a more direct representative of the people than the president. Moreover, they posited that the bill entailed constitutional departures, including bypassing the requirement of Senate consent for treaties and delegating Congress's constitutional authority to tax to the president.

Perhaps most remarkably, even proponents of the RTAA admitted these implications, indicating the extent of the transformation they sought. In a revealing floor speech, Representative Lozier acknowledged the departure from constitutional expectations that the RTAA would entail but spoke of the increased expectations of presidents and dismissed legislators' constitutional concerns. The separation of powers "in theory," he noted, was to be "watertight." Nonetheless, he lectured, "some of our greatest thinkers . . . have pointed out that in practice such a divided authority is unworkable." Lozier also admitted that the president's role under the RTAA would grow beyond constitutional expectations: "Theoretically, under the Constitution, a President is expected to recommend the legislation to be considered by Congress and then keep his hands off. The people of America expect more of their President." Dismissively waving away the objections of other representatives, he chided, "Of course, it is easy on the floor of Congress . . . for some Members to be oracles on constitutional law." Instead, he challenged those who questioned the bill's constitutionality to pass it anyway: "A man who really believes a proposed law is unconstitutional . . . does not worry about its passage. He knows in course of time, its invalidity will be declared, and in the meantime, he lets things ride and allows the procession to go by." The greater risk, Lozier contended, was not acting to utilize the presidency in a time of crisis. If the bill failed, "we may be deprived of its benefits, and we may never know just how much we have lost."[63]

Congressional Representation and Tariffs

Defenders of congressional tariff making sought to preserve legislative primacy, and they declared Congress the better representative of the American people. The legislative process in tariffs, Representative Daniel Reed (R-NY) explained, allowed concerned citizens the "full opportunity to be heard through their representatives" in Congress.[64]

In fact, out of frustration with the constant emphasis on the superiority of the president's perspective, some legislators explicitly defended their localistic orientations as a positive good. Representative Treadway proudly defined himself as the "representative of a certain area" and argued that proponents of the presidential perspective "ought to look at the picture from the viewpoint of a congressional member a little bit."[65] Senator Huey Long (D-LA) also defended the benefits of localistic representation. Positing that logrolling was beneficial for the nation, Long stated, "I have stood for a tariff when it affected commodities produced in my own State and in which my State was interested, except that I have been a little bit broader, realizing that I had to be reciprocal and vote for a tariff on the other man's products in order that we might have one on ours." By granting authority to the president, he warned, Congress was essentially abdicating its tariff responsibilities: "We ought to have passed the resolution saying, 'Be it resolved by Congress that we have passed a law letting the President do whatever he pleases. Now we are going to quit and go home.'"[66]

Defenses of congressional representation also came from outside of Congress. "It is the feeling of the mining industries," reported A. W. Dickinson on behalf of the American Mining Congress, "that they wish tariff matters to be handled as in the past, so that they may appeal to the Representatives in Congress."[67] While admitting that "logrolling may have its evils," F. E. Mollins, the secretary of the American National Live Stock Association, warned against "altering the well-known and 100-year maintained policy" of congressional tariff making.[68] A Democrat from Hartford bemoaned the fact that "the Congress, which directly represents the people of the country, would be willing . . . to relieve itself of this sacred trust."[69]

Like some legislators who opposed the RTAA, other skeptics of the legislation also admitted their parochial self-interest in resisting the legislation. A resolution of the Home Market Club, sent to Representative Doughton, stated opposition to "a measure which delegates a power that, by the stroke of a pen, might readily be the means of wiping American industries out of existence."[70] Testifying to the House on behalf of the US Potters Association, John Dowsing admitted that he viewed the tariff "from an angle, representing my own industry." This prompted a sharp rebuttal from Representative Doughton: "Would you say the welfare of the entire country should be neglected in the interest of your own industry?"[71]

Despite pleas to preserve the influence of Congress, amendments meant to address a direct concern of the bill's embrace of presidential representation—that it would result in the destruction of local industries in the name of the national good—were rejected in the House and Senate.[72] Both proponents and opponents of the bill recognized that its passage amounted to a repudiation of congressional power and local representation in tariff making.

Executive Agreements versus Treaties

The debate over the RTAA also clarified that institutionalizing presidential representation in tariff making envisioned a significant departure from constitutional expectations. The use of executive agreements deliberately avoided the requirement of Senate consent for treaties.

Proponents of the bill admitted this evasion. They justified bypassing the Senate by arguing that assembling a two-thirds majority for the passage of any trade agreement would be nearly impossible. "Our treaty-making process," observed Senator Bennett Champ Clark (D-MO), "is too cumbersome to permit of its use in trade negotiation."[73] Representative McCormack also pointed out that "treaties, subject to the approval of the Senate, have been rather unsuccessful."[74] Reflecting on his experience as a former Tennessee congressman, Secretary of State Hull emphasized that many trade treaties had been "filibustered to death in another body, as we are accustomed here in the House to say."[75] Hull would later be even more blunt in his memoirs: "It was generally agreed that only this type of executive agreement could succeed. Treaties, which had to be submitted for Senate approval, were hopeless if they contained substantial tariff reductions."[76]

In circumventing the prescribed constitutional route for congressional involvement in foreign trade, advocates of the RTAA also admitted that they sought to follow the practice in other developed nations by allowing the executive to negotiate tariff agreements. Criticizing this rationale, Representative William Evans (R-CA) complained that "we have yet in this country a written Constitution and they have not."[77] Representative Treadway also protested that the bill meant that "Congress abdicates its right of control over international matters, trade agreements, if you want to call them that, but in reality treaties."[78] In the House hearings, Treadway remonstrated to Hull that the requirement of Senate consent for treaties was "another clause of the Constitution which seems to be going into the discard in anticipation of this legislation." Hull conceded to the departure he was proposing. Congress, he asserted, must decide whether the economic situation "would justify either branch of Congress or both in giving authority to the executive department in advance to perform certain functions which would ordinarily be reviewed by one branch of the legislative department."[79]

While Hull admitted attempting to bypass the Senate, other RTAA supporters sometimes highlighted their efforts inadvertently. Advocates of using executive agreements instead of treaties sometimes slipped into referring to those trade agreements as treaties. In the House hearings, Assistant Secretary Sayre made this mistake. When Representative Thomas Cochran

(R-PA) pointed out that Sayre had used "the expression treaty agreement and trade agreement," Sayre replied, "It is possible I have used the word 'treaty' when I meant 'agreement.' I may have been careless." Representative Treadway then emphasized that he was "quite certain" Sayre had "used the words 'treaty agreement,'" to which Sayre replied, "I beg that it be allowed to be altered to 'trade agreement.'" This prompted a dispute over whether the witness could revise his use of the term "treaties" in the documented record of the hearings.[80] A similar episode took place during Senate floor debate. Describing how the president could lower tariff rates, Senator Harrison mixed up the distinction, saying, "the President could then negotiate treaties, and so forth, that might reduce that rate further." Senator William Borah (R-ID) pounced on the mistake: "did the Senator say 'negotiate treaties'?" Senator Arthur Vandenberg (R-MI) quickly joined in: "Yes; that was his language." Chastened, Harrison corrected himself: "I did not mean 'negotiate treaties.' I meant he could enter into these reciprocal trade agreements."[81] The mixup of the terms "agreements" and "treaties" by proponents underscored the bill's move away from previous constitutional practice.

The Power to Tax

The extent to which the RTAA potentially stretched from previous constitutional arrangements was also questioned on the issue of taxation. Because tariffs had traditionally been used as a principal way to raise revenue, the proposed legislation was vulnerable to charges that it took away the House's constitutional primacy under Article I to initiate revenue-raising measures. As one businessman complained in a letter to Representative Doughton, the bill "involves a radical departure . . . in that it takes away from the Congress the control of revenues and duties."[82]

Two of the most prominent Republican critics of the RTAA emphasized the tax issue. "Under the Constitution, article 1, section 7," argued Representative Treadway, "all bills for raising revenue shall originate in the House of Representatives." "This bill is originating in the House, is it not?" Secretary Hull dismissively replied.[83] But Treadway continued to press the point in floor debate. Because the measure "delegates to the President discretionary legislative power in tariff making," Treadway characterized it as "an unconstitutional delegation of the supreme taxing power of Congress."[84] Senator Borah argued that the legislation degraded Congress's position under the Constitution. The question of "where the taxing power should rest," stressed Borah, had been "a burning theme throughout the story of Anglo-Saxon civilization." Even if a particular tariff or trade deal was in "the interest of the

Nation as a whole," it was still "a tax." Pointing to what he interpreted as original constitutional meaning, Borah asked, "Is not the making of a tariff a legislative power? Has it not been so since the hour when the Constitution was framed?"[85]

Republicans were not the only legislators to raise concerns about Congress's taxing power. Representative Finly Gray (D-IN), who was supportive of lowering tariff rates and agreed "with the object and purpose and the policy of this legislation," nonetheless gave a long speech dissecting the constitutionality of the bill. He echoed both of the key critiques made by the bill's opponents. "The Constitution provides," Gray stated, "that all revenue measures shall originate in the House of Representatives . . . and further that all treaties must be agreed to by the Senate by two-thirds vote." But the tariff legislation ignored those provisions, and Gray charged the proponents of the bill with constitutional evasiveness. "In the maneuvers here today, to evade the express, explicit, and plain provisions of the Federal Constitution," he complained, "we are told that the agreements contemplated are not treaties to be confirmed and that measures producing revenue are not revenue measures to be originated in the lower House of Congress." Regarding the tax concern specifically, Gray also emphasized that, contrary to any claims about presidential representation, members of the House "remain nearest to the people."[86]

Some of the legislation's prominent supporters sought to minimize the significance of any effect on Congress's tax powers. Senator Alben Barkley (D-KY) argued that there was "a vast difference between delegating to the President . . . the power to levy taxes, and delegating to him the authority, as the agent of Congress, to enter into negotiations and agreements in regulating the commerce of the United States with foreign countries." Placing emphasis on Congress's ability to delegate authority in a manner of its choosing, Barkley explained how other institutional solutions for tariff making, such as independent commissions, could have been possible: "Congress has the power and the right . . . to set up the machinery or the agency by which its mandate may be carried into effect. The agency which we set up here is the President of the United States."[87] Supporters of the bill also pointed to the flexibility provision of the earlier 1930 Smoot-Hawley tariff, which allowed the president to raise rates up to 50 percent upon the recommendation of the Tariff Commission.[88]

However, the RTAA's opponents focused on explaining why the new proposal stretched beyond this earlier provision. Representative Treadway argued that the 1930 law had prescribed more precise rules for when the president could act, meaning the president "merely carries [Congress's will] into execution." He asserted that the new bill had "no particular guidance and rules" in allowing the president to make a determination of rates when negotiating with another country.[89] Treadway also cited the RTAA's primary champion, Secretary of State and former representative Cordell Hull (D-TN), as having complained previously that the flexibility provision gave "such additional authority to the President as would practically vest in him the supreme taxing power of the Nation."[90] Representative Clarence Hancock (R-NY) acknowledged that the flexibility provision of the 1930 tariff had responded to criticism of "logrolling methods" and meant that "the President, who represents all our districts, may with the assistance of the nonpolitical Tariff Commission correct the inequalities of the law." However, he criticized the new bill for asking "Congress to give [the president] absolute authority, beyond his constitutional functions."[91]

In the face of criticism on constitutional grounds, some RTAA supporters chose to be forthright in admitting that they were likely intruding on Congress's powers of taxation. The move was justified, they contended, because of the economic emergency and the potential benefits of the president's national perspective. Representative McCormack confessed that "this legislation in an emergency would be constitutional, while in normal times I have my doubts."[92] Senator Clark acknowledged that tariffs were "as much a tax as any excise or income tax ever imposed." But for Clark, the localistic behavior of members of Congress necessitated a departure: "by our own stupendous folly," legislators had "deliberately created the present deplorable situation," meaning that "a mere reduction of our tariff taxes . . . will not reopen the markets of the world to our products" unless the president could negotiate bilateral agreements.[93] A more dramatic statement came from a periphery Republican, Senator Capper. While admitting that "the traditional way of changing our tariff schedules is through Congress rewriting the tariff act," Capper blasted opponents for relying on constitutional objections in their attempt to derail the bill: "the Constitution is the last refuge of the obstructionist."[94]

Some outside of Congress also argued that the problems of congressional localism should outweigh any constitutional qualms about the legislation. The *Hartford Courant* noted that "such delegation of authority [to the president] would seem contrary to the constitutional provision that Congress alone shall have the power to levy duties." But, it emphasized, previous tariffs had been so bad "that a growing number of people are prepared to welcome any move that will take authority over the tariff away from the greedy sectional forces that dominate Congress."[95]

The passage of the RTAA amounted to a repudiation of these concerns about stretching from the expected workings of the Constitution. That the president was gaining greater authority over tariffs, which many in Congress had perceived to be strictly their legislative power, was not in doubt. The legislation was a significant step toward institutionalizing presidential authority in tariff making. The president's national perspective was to be privileged in making trade agreements on the assumption that such agreements would best serve the national interest and promote free trade. The law, along with subsequent reauthorizations of the trade authority, gave the presidential substantial power in a crucial area of economic policymaking.

Presidential Economic Stewardship: The Employment Act of 1946

Congress's passage of the Employment Act of 1946 marked another institutionalization of the president's economic responsibilities to the nation. The law bolstered the president's agenda-setting authority by making the president responsible for submitting an Economic Report to Congress each year, and it augmented the president's organizational capacity by establishing the Council of Economic Advisers.[96] Like the RTAA of 1934, the design of the statute revealed Congress's conscious decision to require presidential involvement in economic policymaking, relying again on an assumption of presidential representation.

An intellectual push to make government embrace the goal of full employment had long been underway by the mid-1940s, but the prospect of returning American GIs at the end of World War II spurred Congress to consider how to formalize federal economic responsibility.[97] Embracing Keynesian economics, advocates of full employment were influenced by a variety of proposals, including the Beveridge report in the United Kingdom, FDR's proposed economic Bill of Rights, and calls from FDR and Secretary of Commerce Henry Wallace for the United States to create sixty million jobs to handle the return of America's World War II soldiers.[98] Opponents of that effort warned against the purported dangers of government planning.[99]

Much of the dispute surrounding the legislation would be over the bill's policy declaration.[100] From the initial introduction of the Full Employment Bill of 1945 to its passage as the Employment Act of 1946, the policy aim changed from achieving "full employment" to attaining "maximum employment, production, and purchasing power."[101] But deliberations over what the federal government's declared policy in employment should be raised other issues as well. The debates involved fundamental questions of institutional design and the appropriate division of responsibilities between the executive and legislative branches.

The political context of the mid-1940s was not as favorable to presidential power as it had been amid the Great Depression in 1934. Congress was motivated to counter its perceived decline vis-à-vis the executive branch during the Depression and World War II.[102] In 1943, conservatives had shown hostility to the concept of executive planning by eliminating the National Resources Planning Board.[103] More significantly, in 1946, Congress wholly reconsidered its internal organization and relationship to the executive branch with the passage of the Administrative Procedure Act (APA) and the Legislative Reorganization Act (LRA).[104] The LRA marked Congress's attempt to exert greater control over the executive branch, even raising the prospect of a legislative budget system. However, in reforming its committee system to match the executive branch structure, it ended up focusing more on its supervisory and oversight role. The APA set up a rule-making process for administrative agencies, provided judicial oversight over agency actions, and extended due process protections to those affected by agency decisions.[105] Together with the LRA and APA in what Karen Orren and Stephen Skowronek have dubbed "the system of '46," the Employment Act marked Congress's attempt to better plan for a national economic program.[106]

While the RTAA had used the presidency to replace congressional involvement in tariff making, the Employment Act sought use utilize the president's holistic perspective to help guide Congress to better legislative outcomes in the national interest. Given the congressionally oriented thrust of the day, the debates over the institutional arrangements of the Employment Act and the final outcome are revealing. Once again, Congress acted to institutionalize presidential responsibility for national economic policymaking.

ASSUMPTION: THE PRESIDENT'S NATIONAL PERSPECTIVE

In its assumptions and design, the Employment Act was modeled after the earlier Budget and Accounting Act of 1921. Just as the BAA had assumed that the president would propose budgets to Congress that took into account the needs of the nation as a whole, the Employment Act was premised on the assumption that the president possessed a unique national perspective that should be privileged in economic policymaking.

A variety of key congressional figures spoke to the significance of the president's national focus, especially as a rationale for the Economic Report. Senator James Murray (D-MT), for example, was a sponsor of the original version of the Full Employment Bill and remained one of the principal advocates of even the altered legislation. Shortly before the final passage of the law, Murray connected Congress granting formal responsibility to the president with the idea of presidential representation, telling senators in congressional debate that this was the significance of the act's enactment. "The effect of this act," Murray proclaimed, "is to underscore the responsibility of the President as the elected representative of the entire country, and as head of the executive branch of the Government."[107] The original sponsor of the House version of the bill, Representative Wright Patman (D-TX), stated that the president would propose "goals toward which he feels we should strive" and that these proposals would deal with "the economy as a whole."[108] Expressing confidence that the law "will be of benefit to the country as a whole," Representative John Cochran (D-MO) noted that once again Congress was choosing to formalize presidential responsibility in statute: "Again, we are passing legislation that is placing a new responsibility upon the President."[109]

The localistic orientation of lawmakers was also contrasted with the viewpoint of the president. One exchange in the legislative hearings between Representative Carter Manasco (D-AL), the chairman of the House Expenditures Committee, and A. S. Goss, the master of the National Grange, captured this comparison: "Mr. Goss, don't you think the President is in much better position to know the needs of the people than is the Congress?" Goss's reply described the different perceived incentives of legislators versus those of the president. While individual legislators would better "know the needs of the people" in their "local communities," the president would be "in better position to know the general situation so far as the Government is concerned."[110] Perhaps more notable was the view of Senator Robert Taft (R-OH), a critic of the earlier version of the full employment legislation. Taft also admitted that a presidential employment proposal could be beneficial to overcome Congress's own lack of a holistic perspective: "I don't say that is not a wise thing to do. I have noticed a noticeable lack of planning in congressional action."[111]

The assumption of presidential representation was not repeated as frequently in these debates as it was in those over the RTAA. But in a context in which Congress was thinking of asserting its own institutional prerogatives, these statements emphasizing the president's focus on the economy as a whole were striking.

SELECTION: INVOLVING THE PRESIDENT

In the Employment Act of 1946, Congress made a deliberate choice to formalize presidential responsibility in economic policymaking over other alternatives. In the earliest iteration of the legislation in 1944, Congress itself was made responsible for developing economic proposals.[112] But there was soon widespread agreement that the president should report on the economy and propose policies. This choice directly corresponded to the assumption that the president would focus on the needs of the whole nation, and it sought to tap the president's perspective as a way to guide Congress in policymaking. Once Congress had decided to formalize that presidential responsibility, it then chose to grant the president control over the newly created Council of Economic Advisers. However, Congress's deference also had limits. The act provided that CEA members would need to be confirmed by the Senate, and it also established a Joint Committee on the Economic Report in Congress.

Economic Report of the President

"We believe that Congress owes it to the country and to the world not to let us go planless into another economic crisis," wrote two New Hampshire summer residents to Senator Charles Tobey (R-NH), a cosponsor of the Full Employment Bill of 1945.[113] Congress's efforts on this front took the form of enlisting the president's help. The initial vision was that the president would submit a National Production and Employment Budget to Congress. This economic budget would forecast economic performance for the coming year, estimate the size of the labor force, estimate aggregate investment and expenditure in the country, and provide legislative recommendations to meet the needs of the nation.[114] For many of the bill's supporters, such as the Union for Democratic Action, the presidential economic budget was "the key to the bill."[115] The call to make the president responsible for such a report was also supported by most legislators. As Representative George Outland (D-CA) wrote to other lawmakers, "the idea of having a National Budget of this type has been generally accepted."[116] By the time the bill passed Congress as the Employment Act of 1946, the provision had been rechristened as the Economic Report of the President. But the significance of the new mechanism was the same: the institutionalization of presidential initiative was premised on the notion that presidential recommendations would be formulated in the interests of the entire country.

Congress designed the initial provision for a presidential economic budget to correspond with the State of the Union message. Nonetheless, this innovation signified a departure, as Congress was stipulating in statute that presidents could no longer avoid taking a lead role on economic issues. Introducing the Full Employment Bill to the Senate in January 1945, Senator Murray explained that the National Production and Employment Budget meant that the president would have the "responsibility" to "report to Congress . . . on the extent to which the economy is providing jobs for all."[117] Without such a provision, argued Senator Murray, "it would be impossible for the Government to grapple intelligently with the employment problem and develop a consistent and carefully planned economic program."[118] In the Senate hearings on the bill, Senator Robert Wagner (D-NY) also placed the responsibility of setting economic goals for full employment on the president. It "directs the President each year" to consult widely and come up with the budget: "This sets the goal."[119] The economic budget, Wagner suggested, "would serve as a guide in the enactment of sound and progressive legislation."[120] Supporters of this provision chastised opponents of the legislation who worried that too much power would be granted to the president. "I am willing to let the President exercise the discretion which the terms of the bill provide in connection with economic planning for full employment," emphasized Senator Wayne Morse (R-OR), "because I am satisfied that the alternatives offered by opponents of the bill will not be helpful in preventing depressions."[121]

In congressional hearings on the employment legislation, witnesses expressed their understanding that the proposed economic budget would provide a holistic perspective on the economy. Testifying before the Senate, the Congress of Industrial Organizations (CIO) president Philip Murray stated that "the President should regard the preparation of a national budget as an obligation to meet the needs of the American people."[122] A. S. Goss, testifying for the National Grange, enthused that president's economic budget was "the heart of the bill" and that it would be "through this legal means that we take steps to muster all our resources to meet the Nation's needs."[123] The president's economic budget and accompanying legislative proposals were also viewed as a way to spur debate that would focus on the economy as a whole. As Major General Philip Fleming, an administrator for the Federal Works Agency, argued, "the country could not fail to gain in understanding from annual debates embracing the whole state of the economy rather than debates upon fragmentary sections of it."[124] By placing "the responsibility in one place," suggested Millard Rice, the national service director of Disabled American Veterans, the bill "focuses attention on these problems."[125]

The design assumption of the president's economic budget was also explicitly compared to the rationale behind the earlier BAA of 1921. The director of the Bureau of the Budget (BOB), Harold Smith, contended that the new economic budget was "a logical further step."[126] It would "provide a mechanism through which and by which we can have public debate of all of the factors that are involved" with the national economy.[127] Smith also equated the way Congress then considered economic measures with the fragmented state of the federal budget process prior to the BAA's passage: "Pieces of legislation too often have to be considered without sufficient regard for the consistency of the Government program as a whole." By contrast, the new provision would allow Congress to consider the president's "entire economic and fiscal program."[128]

Of course, the president already possessed authority to recommend measures to Congress under Article II of the Constitution. This led to clashes in the House Committee on Expenditures over whether the specific provision for a presidential economic budget was necessary and to disputes over its significance. The most notable critic along these lines was an influential one, Carter Manasco, the committee's chairman. But while Manasco consistently minimized the procedure's significance, others reacted to his critique by arguing that stipulating presidential responsibility was a new and consequential development. In the hearings, Manasco asked BOB director Smith whether "the President possesses at this time all the authority that is granted him in this bill." Smith answered by pointing to the difference between the president having discretion under Article II to submit economic requests to Congress and being given a statutory responsibility for that function: "He would be presenting such estimates without a definite procedure recognized and adopted by the Congress. I think that is a very important difference."[129] Moreover, the "appraisal and recommendations" of the budget were "of such importance" that "they should be transmitted not merely at the discretion of the President, but should become part of his statutory responsibility."[130] Smith again likened the proposed procedure to "the Budget and Accounting Act—a very definite procedure."[131] In other words, Smith viewed the proposal as a way to formally institutionalize presidential responsibility for the economy. Similarly, in response to Manasco's position, Representative John Cochran argued, "that is different," suggesting that the bill gave the president "the power for planning—advance planning." Presidents would assuredly possess that authority, Cochran stipulated, only with "legislation of this character."[132] Leading support for the bill on the floor, Manasco again argued that the president "can submit a budget any day he wants to, he can transmit a message to the Congress any day he wants under our Constitution."[133] But Representative Walter Judd (R-MN) highlighted the importance of expecting all presidents to take that action to help guide Congress, rather than leaving it only to their discretion: "this bill makes it also a duty for him to do it."[134]

The provision for a National Production and Employment Budget would be changed to an Economic Report, but the alteration did not change the fact that the legislation called for the president to act as an agenda setter.[135] As Representative Cochran explained to the House, the report would still "contain all of the basic elements which were called for in the original bill" but would not be "described by the misleading name of national Budget."[136] Senator

Barkley, who chaired the conference committee to reconcile the House and Senate bills, also stipulated that using "the term 'economic report'" would avoid confusion "with the President's annual budget message." The president would remain responsible for making "any recommendations he may see fit to make to Congress to carry out" the act's declared policy.[137] Senator Murray concurred, stressing that "the content of the national production and employment budget has not been changed in any material fashion."[138]

The strength of the president's new authority in domestic economic policy was different from the sweeping trade authority the president had gained in the RTAA. Senator Joseph O'Mahoney (D-WY), for example, minimized the importance of the president's "job budget," positing that it would "be for the Congress, the representatives of the people chosen in the constitutional way, to determine what they shall do about it."[139] Senator Murray also observed that Congress had the right to "substitute its own program for full employment."[140] Nonetheless, like the BAA of 1921, the act's significance was that Congress granted the president more agenda-setting authority with the aim of guiding Congress in the legislative process. As Democratic president Harry Truman stated upon signing the law, "Congress has placed on the President the duty of formulating programs designed to accomplish the purpose of the Act."[141] Moreover, the president's Economic Report "provides an opportunity for all our citizens to judge the merits of the analysis and proposed action."[142]

Council of Economic Advisers

Even after the decision to make the president responsible for proposing an economic program, Congress still considered bolstering its own role more than that of the president. It was not certain that the CEA would be placed under presidential control.

Indeed, the CEA had not even been in the original bill. But from the start, one initial stipulation had suggested that lawmakers were thinking of how to ensure that the economic budget would reflect national priorities and not be utilized as a vehicle to advance the interests of any particular government department. The initial legislation called for the budget to be prepared in the EOP, standing above the separate parts of the executive branch. As Senator James Murray explained, "the National Budget transcends in scope the activities and responsibilities of any one department. . . . Its development properly belongs in the Executive Office of the President."[143] Testifying for the CIO, Philip Murray underscored that the economic budget would ultimately be the president's responsibility to assure such consideration of the overall economy: "No more specific responsibility should be given by law to one Cabinet officer than to another" in order to ensure consideration of "all the objectives for all the people."[144] Fleming, the Federal Works Agency administrator, also argued that "the President would be enabled to arm himself in advance with complete information about all relevant economic factors having a bearing upon the welfare of the American people."[145]

Initially, the BOB was expected to assist the president with this function. However, not all were satisfied with the bill's lack of advising specifics or the assumption that the BOB would adopt another major planning function. Though supportive of the bill, Ralph Flanders, the president of the Federal Reserve Bank of Boston, testified that a "Commission on Full Employment" should be created with members "chosen as representatives of the general public interest" and who were "the ablest men to be found." It would be "headed by a representative of the President."[146] Representative Cochran also showed interest in having an economic board but was sure to stipulate that it should be "answerable to the President and not an independent agency."[147]

The House bill soon provided for this sort of institutional capacity, proposing a three-member Council of Economic Advisers. Representative Manasco noted that a majority of the House Expenditures Committee felt the president "should have some machinery to make continuing studies of our economic problems." Furthermore, he explained that it was desirable that "a separate agency not connected with any of the old so-called bureaucratic agencies should make these studies."[148] For Representative Cochran, this new "machinery" would help the president "get the proper information," which would, in turn, help the president in his role as national representative. The president would "be enabled to keep the Congress advised and make such suggestions as he deems necessary not only for the benefit of private industry, but for the benefit of all the people of the country."[149]

Yet not all were convinced the CEA should be under the influence of the president, and some legislators attempted to prevent that outcome. For a time, the legislation was amended to make the CEA's own analyses available to Congress, rather than just to the president.[150] This would have undermined presidential authority over the CEA by allowing Congress to question the assumptions behind the president's Economic Report. Auguring a potentially even more substantial change away from presidential authority, Representative Everett Dirksen (R-IL) sought to make the CEA completely independent of the president, allowing it to propose its own economic recommendations. "Why," Dirksen asked, "should we not have an independent agency outside of the office of the President to make an inventory, to make a survey, to ascertain the conditions that have a bearing upon unemployment, and then to make a recommendation that shall involve every factor and every incentive?"[151] Representative Judd agreed, wanting the CEA "to be an independent agency, not in the Executive Office of the President."[152]

The final legislation tilted back toward presidential control of the CEA. Lawmakers who wanted a more independent institution did succeed in amending the legislation to require Senate consent of the three members of the CEA. But they otherwise failed to make the CEA independent.[153] Moreover, legislators decided not to require that the CEA's internal analyses be available to Congress.[154] Legislators who supported these moves did not shy away from underscoring their significance. Explaining that the conference bill "drops the provision that the reports, studies, and recommendations of the President's economic advisers should be made available to the joint committee," Representative Cochran argued it was "a distinct improvement because it emphasizes the fact that the council is not an autonomous agency, but that its sole purpose is to provide the President with essential assistance and information on economic matters."[155] If the CEA's recommendations were available to Congress, Senator Murray observed, it would have given the CEA "an independent status apart from the Presidency." Instead, Murray stressed, Congress had chosen to place responsibility on the president to make yearly economic recommendations, as opposed to "placing the responsibility in the hands of planning boards" apart from the president. The implication, Murray emphasized, was that the CEA was "entirely subordinate to the President," had "no independent nor autonomous authority," and would be subject to the president's removal power.[156]

The Senate's discussion of the CEA offered another perspective on how lawmakers viewed the role of the president under the legislation. Senator Guy Cordon (R-OH) questioned why the bill had not stipulated that the CEA be composed of representatives of "the three great divisions of effort in this country, namely, agriculture, management or industry, and labor." Responding, Senator Barkley said that proposal had been discussed in conference committee, but the conferees had "decided that if the law were to make it mandatory for the President to appoint a representative of each of the three groups, the appointees would automatically consider themselves as spokesmen and representatives of their respective groups." Instead, Barkley asserted that the CEA needed to support the president in taking a national view: "the President would choose men who would be able to speak in a broad way for all the people." Echoing Barkley's view, Senator Taft, who supported the conference report after "struggling with the bill," expressed his hope that the CEA's members "would not be merely representatives of any particular group." Barkley again emphasized that the president's appointees must "be men of such outstanding ability and experience that they would be representing the whole country."[157]

Even Congress's stipulation that members of the CEA be "exceptionally qualified to analyze and interpret economic developments" was viewed as helping the president take a national viewpoint.[158] As the first CEA chairman, Edwin Nourse, would explain, the CEA's function was to help the president take a view of the whole economy without regard to special interests: "the Council would furnish a means of comparative and integrating study of segmental policies with a view to assisting the President in charting a course which would promote the well-being of the whole economy."[159] And even as legislators wanted the president to listen to economic experts, they had ensured that the economic recommendations proposed to Congress would reflect the president's views, making an explicit choice to subordinate the CEA to the president by placing it in the EOP and declining other alternatives that would have granted the CEA more independence.[160]

Joint Committee

As much as it strengthened presidential authority, the Employment Act did feature an attempt by Congress itself to better consider the needs of the country as a whole. That innovation was the creation of the Joint Committee on the Economic Report. Consisting of seven members each from the House and Senate, the Joint Committee would review the president's recommendations and make its own recommendations to Congress as a whole. This underscored a limitation on presidential power in the Employment Act: presidential proposals could be completely altered by the Joint Committee if it desired. Still, as much as this feature of the legislation reflected the worries about executive aggrandizement emerging in the mid-1940s, the Joint Committee also underscored that the president was now expected by statute to submit an economic program. Even as he stressed that "Members of Congress are the representatives of the American people," Murray noted that the Joint Committee's main purpose was to bridge the separation of powers: "the provision for a joint congressional committee to analyze the President's overall program has been hailed as a distinct contribution to the improvement of congressional operations."[161]

Indeed, the Joint Committee's creation drew on a common critique that had generally worked to the benefit of the presidency. The constant emphasis that the Joint Committee would provide Congress its own ability to take a nationally oriented view of the economy was an implicit concession to criticisms that legislators were localistic.[162] In describing the Joint Committee on the National Budget provided for in the original Full Employment Bill, Senator Murray pointed to the need for Congress to take a holistic perspective: "At present, there is no arm of the Congress that has the responsibility of considering all the elements in the Federal Budget, or the relationships between the Federal Budget and the national economy." The Joint Committee "is created to study the National Budget in its entirety."[163] Nourse, the first CEA chairman, likewise concurred that the Joint Committee's aim was to overcome congressional localism. Its purpose, Nourse wrote, was "to study national policy as an integrated whole and to raise the level of its economic statesmanship above local and pressure-group politics."[164]

Moreover, in creating a forum for lawmakers to consider presidential proposals, the Joint Committee's function recognized a unique role for the president. As Murray put it, the president's proposal would set the terms of national debate: "Both the general public and Members of the Congress themselves need regular information on the status of the various measures that make up the President's full employment program."[165] Representative Cochran concurred, explaining that the committee would "analyze the President's economic report and attempt to coordinate the activities of the various committees of Congress affecting the full-employment program."[166]

CHALLENGE: CONSTITUTIONAL STRETCHES

In seeking to accommodate the purported merits of presidential representation, the Employment Act furthered the institutionalization of presidential government. Proponents of the measure defeated criticism that the presidential Economic Report interfered with Congress's principal responsibility to initiate legislation.

Critics understood that the employment legislation would formalize the president's responsibility for economic stewardship, moving beyond any presidential initiative to recommend measures envisioned under Article II. In hearings on the legislation, George Terborgh, the research director of the Machinery and Allied Products Institute, criticized the bill for its "easy assumption that all economic proposals having to do with full-employment policy are to originate in the executive department of the Government." Because it was "clearly taken for granted that the real initiative . . . shall lie with the White House," the bill was "a fresh example of the abdication by Congress of its own proper function originating legislation and legislative policy, in deference to the 'papa-knows-best' tradition established during the last decade and a half."[167] John Snyder, the director of war mobilization and reconversion, also directly criticized the claim of presidential representation.

"Congress is much better informed, by its large membership," he argued: "You wouldn't at all want to have just one man telling this country what it should do or shouldn't do. You want a broad representation."[168]

Some legislators shared this skepticism. Representative Charles Gifford (R-MA) complained that the provision required the president to intrude on legislative power: "You tell him to study all the conditions, then bring in a report as to what he thinks we ought to do. In my opinion, it is time that the Congress itself should say what we ought to do." Reflecting on congressional experience during the New Deal, Gifford observed, "I should hesitate to give more Presidents a chance to plan for me."[169] More exaggeratedly, Representative Frederick Smith (R-OH) complained that the bill would "centralize all planning in Washington in the hands of a single individual . . . just as all planning of the Soviet regime is presently centralized in Moscow in the hands of Stalin."[170]

Defying this criticism, the enacted legislation formalized presidential agenda setting in economic policy, adopting a similar structure to the BAA of 1921. Despite greater congressional skepticism of presidential authority by the mid-1940s, the act again signified a congressionally authorized expectation of presidential stewardship. In David Mayhew's estimation, "The Employment Act of 1946, edited to congressional size though it was . . . gave this Keynesian regime authorization and shape. It was a presidency-centered regime."[171]

Conclusion: Economic Presidentialism, Foreign and Domestic

The RTAA of 1934 and Employment Act of 1946 were each influenced by an assumption that the president's national perspective should be privileged in economic policymaking. Showcasing the adaptability of American government, the statutes institutionalized that idea through different institutional forms and to different degrees. In allowing the president to negotiate bilateral agreements to reduce tariff rates that would not be subject to congressional approval, Congress chose to have the president supplant legislators in trade. The RTAA gave the president substantial power to match this representative role, moving beyond constitutional expectations for tariff making. In giving the president the responsibility to submit an annual Economic Report and creating the Council of Economic Advisers, Congress looked to the president to guide legislators in developing economic legislation with a national perspective in mind. The Employment Act too sought to bridge the separation of powers.

Each law altered the operations of American government. In trade policy, the RTAA and subsequent reauthorizations of presidential trade authority resulted in an institutionalization of lower tariffs and a broad shift toward free trade. As Douglas Irwin summarizes, "In making an unprecedented grant of power to the executive, the RTAA changed the process of trade policymaking and put import duties on a downward path."[172] Though the time limits imposed on presidential trade authority meant that presidents had to periodically request its renewal, Congress regularly reauthorized that authority from 1934 through the mid-1960s. Notably, a Republican president, Dwight Eisenhower, soon embraced such trade power, solidifying more bipartisan support for free trade. Furthermore, subsequent renewals would continue to invoke the purported benefits of presidential representation. In 1939, for example, the Roosevelt administration again communicated to its congressional allies that Congress should keep "its attention [on] the forces constantly at work here in Washington to obtain inordinate benefits for special interests at the expense of the country as a whole."[173] Congress, Secretary Hull affirmed, would still have a problem with "log-rolling."[174] Later, presidents began to enter multilateral agreements under the 1947 General Agreement on Tariffs and Trade (GATT), which aimed for more substantial reductions in trade barriers around the world. In 1962, the president was granted the most expansive leeway yet to reduce tariffs and also gained new executive organizational capacity in trade. Congress established the special representative for trade negotiations, a Senate-confirmed position, to focus on negotiating trade agreements, rather than relying on the secretary of state.[175] President John Kennedy then located that officer in the EOP, confirming it would "be directly responsible to the President."[176]

In employment and economic policy, the operation of the institutions created by the Employment Act indicated a relative consensus on a standard set of economic goals for the federal government to pursue. The act underscored that economic management was now a responsibility of the president, signaling that "henceforth an administration that failed to achieve acceptable macroeconomic performance was a failed administration." Under the institutional setup of the act, federal fiscal policy also proved more responsive to addressing unemployment.[177] And though the CEA's influence waxed and waned over the decades, it would exercise a meaningful influence on presidential economic policymaking.[178]

However, a central difference continued to emerge between these realms of presidential economic policy. Though increasingly connected to foreign affairs, tariffs were still largely viewed in domestic terms in 1934. But after the RTAA's enactment, tariff rates and trade agreements would become a core tool of presidential foreign policy. As one scholar noted, "In 1932, President Hoover could say that tariff policy was wholly domestic policy; no President would ever say that again."[179] This had potential implications for the durability of presidential power in trade. As a constitutional matter, while tariff-making authority clearly belonged to Congress under Article I, foreign policy gave the president a more plausible claim to authority under Article II. And as a practical matter, the increased importance of trade to the US and world economy portended the endurance of significant power for the president in that area. By contrast, while the expectation of presidential economic leadership was a lasting one, employment policy nonetheless remained a domestic economic issue, potentially making it easier for Congress or the Federal Reserve to wield more significant influence in the decades to come.

How dependent were the different institutional forms that supported presidential economic policymaking on the legitimacy of presidential representation? What were the implications of tariff policy becoming a key element of foreign policy? Chapter 8 will examine the politics of Congress's reconsideration of the institutional presidency in trade and employment.

Presidential Reorganization Authority

The President has the advantage that if delegated the necessary authority by the Congress he may, if he so elects, ignore sectional interests and pressure groups.
LEWIS MERIAM, 1939[1]

Presidents and their defenders make many claims to bolster their authority. Among the most prominent are the unitary executive theory and the idea of presidential representation. Both claims figured prominently in the debates in the late 1930s over whether the president should be granted authority to reorganize the executive branch, leaving Congress with a choice about whether to accept either idea as a basis for institutional reform.

These ideas are not mutually exclusive. They can be intertwined, and both have served as rationales for the president's removal power. At the same time, however, unitary and representational claims can also be distinguished as justifications for different types of institutional changes.[2] The unitary executive theory, popularized in recent decades in conservative legal and political circles, asserts that the president possesses all of the executive power through the vesting clause of Article II of the Constitution.[3] Those who embrace it agree that the president can control the entire executive branch through the removal power, and they argue that presidential claims in this regard have been consistent and unchanging over time.[4] Unitary theory, though contested, is an originalist claim about the Constitution. Institutionally, it envisions top-down presidential control of all departments and agencies. By contrast, the idea of representation, as has been noted in previous chapters, is largely a developmental claim. The notion that the president is the steward of the entire citizenry has been associated with various institutional reforms, competing for supremacy with the claim that Congress is the better representative of the people. The idea anticipates institutional arrangements that would allow for the president's purported national viewpoint to have a larger role in policymaking.[5]

Who should reorganize the executive branch? The answer to this question changed in the 1930s. Though in the nineteenth century reorganization was mostly perceived as a congressional responsibility, acquiring reorganization authority and deciding the organization of the executive branch became a goal of presidents in the twentieth century.[6] Having focused more on responding to the Great Depression than on reorganization, Democratic president Franklin Delano Roosevelt decided to address his confessed weakness in administration in 1936, enlisting Louis Brownlow, Charles Merriam, and Luther Gulick to study the issue.[7] The potential scope of that authority was vast, implicating both unitary and representational claims. It included a range of possibilities from simply shuffling bureaus to different departments in the executive branch, to the more significant potential of undermining the independence of the regulatory commissions, or even to the extraordinary prospect of creating or abolishing entire departments.

In reaction to the proliferation of agencies during the Great Depression, Congress granted the president a qualified reorganization authority under the Reorganization Act of 1939, another significant step in the development of the institutional presidency.[8] Other accounts have explained this choice with reference to Congress's collective action problem or to provisions for presidential control over informational capacities associated with powers the president already possesses.[9] But to understand the law's design and implications, those assessments must contend with issues that were central to the debates in Congress: presidential versus congressional representation, the structure of the government, and the constitutional division of labor. The reorganization authority created in 1939 amounted to a new presidential power, and the design of the law had a specific intellectual rationale.

Perhaps the strongest alternative account for the passage of the act might appear to be partisanship. The law passed during unified Democratic government on a mostly partisan vote.[10] One might hypothesize that congressional Democrats simply wanted to give Roosevelt, a fellow partisan in the White House, more power. But the battle over reorganization authority was not predominantly a partisan story. In fact, the main political conflict occurred among Democrats themselves.[11] A revolt by congressional Democrats sank the 1938 version of the plan, and the 1939 legislation passed during a session of Congress that actually featured reduced Democratic majorities in the House and Senate. Moreover, even prominent southern Democrats in Congress could be found on both sides of the issue. Rather than partisanship, the politics over reorganization were largely driven by fundamental concerns over institutional design.

The defeat of the reorganization proposal of FDR and the President's Committee on Administrative Management (PCAM) in 1938 and the passage of a compromise law in 1939 is a well-known tale, and its significance has been debated.[12] In this chapter, I advance the novel claim that the failure of the PCAM's proposal and the first reorganization bill in 1938 signified a congressional rejection of institutional innovations that invoked a formalistic claim about the president's executive power, an idea that later became known as the unitary executive theory. Specifically, Congress rejected presidential control over the independent regulatory commissions and the audit. Conversely, in passing a different reorganization bill in 1939, Congress accepted and accommodated institutional adjustments based on the idea of presidential representation. Congress created a special process for reorganization plans in which presidents would submit proposals that would be enacted unless both chambers of Congress voted to disapprove those plans through a legislative veto by concurrent resolution. This procedure, departing from constitutional expectations, was both implicitly and explicitly justified based on an assumption of presidential representation: Congress was too bound to parochial interests to effectively reorganize the executive branch, so only a nationally oriented president could do the job.

My argument is not that the idea of presidential representation itself caused the passage of executive reorganization. Rather, I contend that the idea influenced the *design* of the 1939 law. I show that the unitary executive theory and idea of presidential representation were each associated with different aspects of reorganization, and I chronicle how Congress, having cause to be dubious of both claims, ultimately responded differently to them. While it might seem that reorganization of the executive branch naturally would be a presidential responsibility, that assumption is symptomatic of how far we have come in presidency-centered thinking about government. In fact, against the unitary claim, Congress possessed a strong case for control and oversight of the executive branch from its enumerated and implied powers under Article I, Section 8, and from its prerogative to vest the appointment of inferior officers in the president, the courts, or the heads of departments under Article II, Section 2. Against the idea of presidential representation, Congress expressed wariness of a presidential agenda-setting power that went beyond the Article II provision for the president to recommend measures. Given ample reason for congressional skepticism, it is important to understand the theoretical rationale behind the change that the 1939 law authorized.

This chapter proceeds as follows. First, I demonstrate that both the unitary executive theory and the idea of presidential representation were associated with different aspects of the reorganization proposals. The president's purported national perspective was the rationale behind presidential reorganization authority itself. Second, I recount the alternative institutional choices considered during the debates over reorganization. I show that Congress rejected institutional arrangements associated more with the unitary claim, while it ultimately accepted solutions corresponding to presidential representation. Third, to show that the solution associated with presidential representation amounted to a new development, I discuss how the proposal for presidential reorganization authority had to overcome established institutional arrangements and claims about Congress's constitutional powers to determine the structure of the executive branch. Finally, I conclude by briefly considering the immediate impact of presidential reorganization authority on the broader development of the institutional presidency.

Assumptions: The Unitary Executive and Presidential Representation

Both the unitary executive theory and the idea of presidential representation were assumptions at the core of the primary proposals in the debate over reorganization. Two prominent studies of executive reorganization, undertaken by the PCAM and the Brookings Institution respectively, considered these ideas, though they reflected different institutional perspectives. The PCAM—composed of Brownlow, Merriam, and Gulick—considered the question of reorganization broadly and reflected the president's point of view. By contrast, Brookings, with its mission set by the congressional committee of Senator Harry Byrd (D-VA), focused more narrowly on individual agencies and the congressional priority of economy.[13] The reports diverged on one fundamental assumption, while converging on another. Brookings disagreed with one of the central claims of the PCAM—that the president was vested with *all* executive power under Article II—and instead asserted that Congress had substantial constitutional authority over the organization of the executive branch. However, each plan revealingly accepted the claim of presidential representation, differing only on the degree of reforms that idea should entail. For Congress, the question would be the extent to which legislators endorsed either idea and its associated institutional reforms.

THE PRESIDENT'S EXECUTIVE POWER

The PCAM report, unveiled in January 1937, made five general recommendations: (1) expanding the White House staff, (2) strengthening "managerial agencies," including "those dealing with the budget, efficiency research, personnel, and planning," as "arms of the Chief Executive," (3) extending the merit system to all non-policy-determining positions and reorganizing the civil service system, (4) placing all executive branch agencies within the regular department structure, and (5) changing the audit system.[14] The report mixed an originalist claim about the vesting clause, emphasizing presidential control of the executive branch, with the developmental claim of presidential representation, focusing on the president's connection to the public and unique national perspective.

Of course, the PCAM did not use the phrase "unitary executive" itself, and it did not embrace all implications of the president possessing the entire executive power in the way that the conservative legal movement later would. For example, the report sought to replace the Civil Service Commission with a single civil service administrator who would "be responsible to and hold office at the pleasure of the President," providing "unity, energy, and responsibility." But the PCAM also envisioned that administrator as a hybrid position, appointed both on the basis of competitive examination and subject to Senate consent. And the PCAM advocated an extension of merit protections, which goes against the unitary theory's claim that all executive branch officers should be removable by the president.[15] But if unity in the executive is a continuum, the PCAM proposals constituted a bold and explicit shift in that direction. The fourth recommendation of the report, especially, relied on a unitary reading of Article II. The Supreme Court in *Humphrey's Executor* (1935) had recently delivered a setback to FDR by determining that the president's removal power did not apply to the independent commissions.[16]

The PCAM claimed that the Constitution intended the executive power to belong only to the president. Articulating the core claim of the unitary executive theory, the PCAM pointed to "the constitutional principle of the separation of powers, which places in the President, and in the President alone, the whole executive power of the Government of the United States."[17] Introducing the report, FDR likewise stated a unitary claim about the purported meaning of Article II. "The plain fact," he contended, "is that the present organization and equipment of the executive branch of the Government defeats the constitutional intent that there be a single responsible Chief Executive."[18]

Addressing issues involving the independent commissions and the audit, the PCAM embraced a formalistic insistence on what functions were part of the executive power and which functions were distinguishable from it. In exercising "duties of administration," the independent commissions "ought to be clearly and effectively responsible to the President." Meanwhile, the performance of "judicial work" by the commissions "ought to be wholly independent of Executive control."[19] The PCAM also held that the existing state of the audit system featured an "unsound and unconstitutional division of executive authority."[20] The General Accounting Office (GAO) and the comptroller general possessed powers that belonged to the president: "The settlement of accounts and the supervision of administrative accounting systems are executive functions; under the Constitution they belong to the Executive Branch of the Government." Instead, only the postaudit, the review of expenditures after they had already occurred, "should operate under legislative direction."[21]

Responding to the PCAM proposal, the Brookings Institution rejected its unitary assertions and insistence on formalism. "The Federal Constitution," its report to Congress emphasized, "does not permit complete executive centralization nor the establishment of a perfect hierarchical organization."[22] A lack of unitary control was an innate feature of the Constitution's separation of powers. "In a system of separated powers," the report argued, "a tendency naturally exists for the legislative body to make certain agencies independent or semi-independent of the Chief Executive."[23]

Thus, the formalistic claims about the president's possession of the executive power and the proper division of powers among the branches of government were disputed even before Congress itself considered these different reorganization plans. But while the unitary claim was contested, the two principal proposals would agree on a different assumption that served as a rationale for presidential reorganization authority.

THE PRESIDENT'S NATIONAL PERSPECTIVE

The Reorganization Act of 1939 assumed that the president's national perspective was necessary to overcome the resistance of lawmakers who were focused on particular departments or bureaus and to achieve a rational reorganization of the executive branch. Throughout debates over reform, key actors stated this understanding of the president's unique institutional standing.

Congress had, in fact, briefly legitimized an association between presidential representation and reorganization at the height of the Great Depression, passing the Economy Acts of 1932 (under Republican president Herbert Hoover) and 1933 (under FDR). Under the 1932 law, the president could issue reorganization orders subject to a one-chamber legislative veto by concurrent resolution. This legislative veto, allowing Congress to scuttle presidential plans through a disapproval vote that would not require any assent by the president, was a novel invention.[24] But Hoover found his efforts toward reorganization thwarted by the Democratic House. Under the 1933 law, Congress could reject presidential plans only through a joint resolution, meaning that it had to pass a bill disapproving of a reorganization plan that could be vetoed by the president. FDR possessed this authority until 1935.[25] While efficiency was the proclaimed goal, the assumption behind both laws was that only the president could rise above the pressures facing legislators and executive branch officials to achieve reorganization. In floor debate in 1933, Representative John Miller (D-AR) told his colleagues that, unlike Congress, "the President represents all and will not be moved by any partisan consideration nor sectional desire."[26] Senator Arthur Vandenberg (R-MI) argued that Congress "must place authority and responsibility [in the president], and then demand results."[27] Though the reform was temporary, Congress had made a notable departure.

Thus, by the late 1930s, there was precedent to argue that presidential representation could serve as a basis for reorganization authority. "We cannot call ourselves either wise or patriotic," FDR had argued, "if we seek to escape the responsibility of remolding government to make it more serviceable to all the people and more responsive to modern needs."[28] Unsurprisingly, the PCAM embraced this idea. Each member of the committee viewed reorganization authority through the lens of the president's purported national perspective. Writing about his experience a decade later, Brownlow explained that "the President has become the supreme servant" of the people, expected to realize "their purpose, their plans, and their aspirations."[29] In his political science writings, Merriam chronicled the development of the idea of the president's representative role under Andrew Jackson.[30] In the twentieth century, Merriam posited, stronger executives had emerged at all levels of government because of "the demand of the people for vigorous and effective leadership against strong special groups."[31]

The PCAM's report stated the overall rationale for reorganization based on the logic of presidential representation. The president would overcome localistic and special interests in Congress and in the executive branch departments and agencies themselves. As the PCAM stated, "The President is indeed the one and only national officer representative of the entire Nation."[32] In his accompanying message, FDR argued that reorganization authority would help the president "carry out the will of the Nation."[33] Overall, the PCAM's goal amounted to an institutionalization of presidential representation: "Our national will must be expressed not merely in a brief, exultant moment of electoral decision, but in persistent, determined, competent day-by-day administration of what the Nation has decided to do."[34]

Given that its charge came from the president, the PCAM's embrace of this line of argument was to be expected. More revealing, then, was the position taken by the Brookings Institution. Despite having been commissioned by Congress and the reorganization skeptic Senator Byrd to study reform, the Brookings Institution embraced the same core assumption that, unlike legislators, the president could be counted on to act in the national interest.

The Brookings report pointed to congressional representation as the problem, comparing Congress to a family whose members care only about their "divergent interests" rather than "matters affecting the family as a whole."[35] The report also recognized the president's major stake in reorganization because he was "held by the people responsible for administrative results."[36] It further supported augmenting the role of the Bureau of the Budget (BOB), the institution created by the Budget and Accounting Act (BAA) of 1921 to help the president avoid getting bogged down in the supposedly parochial perspectives of individual executive departments.[37] Elaborating in a subsequent Brookings Institution book that called for Congress to delegate reorganization authority to the president, Lewis Meriam articulated the logic of presidential representation as keenly as the most fervent presidentialist. "[The president] is not the representative of a state or a congressional district," stated Meriam. "His constituency is the entire country and his position is such as to give him a sense of responsibility to the whole people. He may therefore take a national as distinct from a sectional point of view."[38]

These claims were not limited to studies of reorganization. Some in the media also presented the contrast between the perspective of legislators and that of the president on reorganization as a common-sense proposition. Since "the vested interests of Congressmen in patronage, and of separate bureaus in their own prerogatives, have always prevailed against the public interest in efficiency," noted one article in the *New Republic,* "students of the subject have come to the conclusion that nothing would ever be done unless the President were given authority to do it."[39] The *New York Times* compared the problems of Congress in reorganization to its earlier stumbles in tariff policy: "In these matters, as in the matter of detailed tariff changes, log-rolling invariably appears."[40] The journalist Arthur Krock echoed the same argument: "If the Federal Government is ever to be practically and soundly set up and administered, the President and not Congress will have to do the reshuffling. That is in the nature of the case."[41]

Most importantly, these claims about the president's national perspective being the key to effective government were central to the legislative debates over reorganization authority. The most important legislator to invoke the idea was Senator James Byrnes (D-SC), who sponsored the legislation and emphasized that "the purpose of the Reorganization Bill is to make Government a more efficient instrument for accomplishing the will of the people."[42] Chairing the Select Committee on Government Organization, Byrnes advocated having "the President of the United States, who was chosen by the people," undertake reorganization, rather than relying on legislators. In response to a rhetorical question from the reorganization skeptic Senator Byrd over whether Congress was also "chosen by the American people," Byrnes stressed the geographic limitations of lawmakers: "No, each Congressman is chosen by the people of his district."[43] Other lawmakers also articulated the importance of presidential stewardship. Representative Jed Johnson (D-OK) acknowledged that congressional parochialism prevented reorganization, as the "departments and agencies are too powerful" owing to their "many friends in and out of Congress."[44] And Senator Lister Hill (D-AL) pointed to a speech by Solicitor General Robert Jackson to explain the logic of presidential representation: "The President has every citizen of the United States as a constituent, but every Senator or Representative is primarily a representative of a section, however much he may desire to take a national view."[45]

Notably, congressional Democrats who supported granting the president authority to reorganize the executive branch were not simply acting out of partisan loyalty. Some of the key supporters of executive reorganization, such as Representative Lindsay Warren (D-NC) and Speaker William Bankhead (D-AL), opposed the president's concurrent effort at judicial reorganization, FDR's ambitious plan that would have enlarged the Supreme Court. Recounting a "strictly confidential" conversation between himself and Bankhead in a memo, Representative Warren wrote that since they both feared that judicial reorganization might pass the House on the strength of votes from "nearly every northern [D]emocrat," they decided to try to delay a vote on that legislation as a way to buy time to let opposition to the measure grow. "Both of us said we hated to break with the President, as we were two of his Asst. Floor Managers in the 1932 Convention," Warren wrote, but they were each committed to opposing the plan: "I told him that I would rather be defeated than to vote for the President's bill. The Speaker reached over and took me by the hand and said: 'Lindsay, they are exactly my sentiments.'"[46]

But while Warren and Bankhead opposed the judicial reorganization plan, they both were prominent advocates of presidential reorganization authority for the executive branch. Indeed, Warren would become the sponsor of the House bill, and he explained that the chief feature of reorganization authority was that it would make the president accountable to the nation. Describing the "splendid bill" in a letter to his cousin, Warren wrote, "If it becomes a law it will put the President on the spot to either do a good job in effecting economies and promoting efficiency or admit failure."[47]

Selection: Constitutional Divergence, Representational Convergence

The respective influence of the unitary executive theory and the idea of presidential representation would be demonstrated by Congress's choice of institutional reforms. The proposals made by the PCAM to place the independent regulatory commissions in the executive branch and to change the audit system were based on unitary claims, while presidential reorganization authority was premised on the president's national perspective. The Brookings plan, presented to Congress in August 1937, rejected the PCAM's unitary reforms. But, foreshadowing Congress's choice in the 1939 legislation, its proposal for a presidential reorganization authority subject to legislative veto embraced the logic of presidential stewardship.

Though the initial prospects for reorganization appeared promising, the first reorganization bill based on the president's proposal was defeated in April 1938. That appeared to deal both the unitary executive theory and the idea of presidential representation a significant blow. The independent regulatory commissions had already been exempted from reorganization in the bill, but the change to the audit system still faced significant criticism. The congressional floor debate also revealed concerns over allowing the president a share of what many congressmen perceived to be legislative power over structuring the executive branch. With the concurrent controversy over FDR's judicial reorganization plan, and the specter of executive authority spreading in Europe as an international backdrop, executive reorganization faced stiff resistance.[48] "I hear," wrote one bemused citizen to Senator Byrnes, "that there is a helluva lot of hullabaloo around the President's plan for changing the gov't departments."[49] A blunter warning was delivered in a telegram to Representative Warren: "Better drop this bill like a hot coal."[50]

A second attempt, shorn of the unitary provisions, focused on the idea of presidential representation itself. The new bill—exempting the independent regulatory commissions and some other bureaus from reorganization, while also avoiding changes to the audit—signified a retreat from unitary assertions. The proposed bill also did not create new departments, and it left the Civil Service Commission in place.[51] What was left in the bill relied on the logic of presidential representation: the president could submit reorganization plans to Congress, subject to legislative veto by majority vote through concurrent resolution. Those plans could abolish agencies or transfer functions but could not eliminate government functions or create new departments.[52]

UNITARY REFORMS: THE INDEPENDENT COMMISSIONS AND AUDIT

The PCAM's proposal to place all agencies, including the independent regulatory commissions, within the regular departmental structure of the executive branch relied explicitly on a unitary reading of Article II.[53] Placing the independent regulatory commissions—"a headless 'fourth branch' of the government"—in departments was said to fulfill original constitutional intent.[54] "It will reestablish," contended the report, "a single Executive Branch, with the President as its responsible head, as provided by the Constitution."[55]

Taking away the independence of the commissions would have fundamentally altered one of the major achievements of the Progressive Era.[56] For example, the Interstate Commerce Commission, Federal Communications Commission, Federal Power Commission, Federal Trade Commission, Securities and Exchange Commission, and Federal Reserve Board of Governors all would have suddenly been brought under the potential influence and direction of the president. This was bound to raise significant opposition. "We are particularly opposed," wrote A. L. Reed of the Southwestern Compress and Warehouse Association, "to the suggestion that the Interstate Commerce Commission be made subservient to one of the executive departments of the government."[57] "We cannot," concurred C. A. Cannon, the president of the Cannon Mills Company, "afford to have other than an impartial body composed of competent Commissioners and answerable only to Congress."[58] Still, for other influential observers, this feature of the PCAM report was attractive. Woodrow Wilson's former secretary of the Navy, Josephus Daniels, wrote to Representative Warren with a more positive assessment of that part of the proposal: "I am not much of a believer in commissions and boards. I believe in a single man."[59]

At the same time, the PCAM also took aim at the functions of the General Accounting Office, which was viewed as an agent of Congress. It sought to increase executive control over most aspects of the existing audit system. The PCAM distinguished between a preaudit authority and a postaudit authority. The report opposed allowing the comptroller general in the GAO to perform a preaudit, through which he could potentially reject requests for expenditures of funds by executive officials.[60] The PCAM held that this constituted an infringement on the president's constitutional authority:

> The removal from the Executive of the final authority to determine the uses of appropriations, conditions of employment, the letting of contracts, and the control over administrative decisions, as well as the prescribing of accounting procedures and the vesting of such authority in an officer independent of direct responsibility to the President for his acts, is clearly in violation of the constitutional principle of the division of authority between the Legislative and Executive Branches of the Government. It is contrary to article II, section 3, of the Constitution, which provides that the President "shall take Care that the Laws be faithfully executed."[61]

The PCAM also dismissed the notion that allowing the comptroller—"who is not responsible to the Chief Executive"—to make decisions on expenditures was worthwhile, asserting that the loss of effective executive control outweighed any financial benefit: "Rulings by an independent auditing officer in the realm of executive action and methods, even when they seem wise and salutary, have a profoundly harmful effect. They dissipate executive responsibility."[62]

Instead, any authority of the comptroller, other than the postaudit, would be placed in the Treasury Department. As the PCAM saw it, "the authority to prescribe and supervise accounting systems, forms, and procedures in the Federal establishments should be transferred to and vested in the Secretary of the Treasury." Furthermore, the report held that "claims and demands by the Government of the United States or against it and accounts in which the Government of the United States is concerned, either as debtor or as creditor, should be settled and adjusted in the Treasury Department."[63] Only the postaudit, "an examination and verification of the accounts after transactions are completed," was properly a legislative function, and the PCAM wanted an independent auditor general to conduct a postaudit for Congress.[64]

In contrast to the PCAM, the Brookings Institution report rejected the institutional entailments associated with these unitary claims. It resisted executive control of the independent regulatory commissions. Because the commissions had legislative functions—"They do what Congress would if it had the time"—and judicial functions—"resembl[ing] the courts" in adjudicating disputes—they could not, observed Brookings, be "viewed from the viewpoint of the Executive alone."[65] Thus, the commissions were to be left alone. Brookings likewise opposed changes to the audit system, viewing it as a tool of Congress and not the executive.[66] "The major issue between our group and the President's committee is on the question of where the control should be located to prevent an illegal or unauthorized expenditure," testified Lewis Meriam for the Brookings Institution: "Auditing control should, in our judgment, be independent of the executive branch of the Government." As Meriam warned legislators, "if Congress should delegate the power of settling accounts to the Executive, it would allow the executive branch of the Government to audit its own accounts."[67]

In the first attempt at passing a reorganization bill, the reforms that drew on unitary claims faced the most opposition from members of Congress. Testifying in hearings on the legislation, Louis Brownlow revealingly could not assure legislators that the independence of the commissions from the president could be guaranteed if they were placed in departments. Asked whether the president would have the power to abolish the Federal Trade Commission with an unrestricted reorganization authority, Brownlow admitted, "Well, he might." Moreover, while Brownlow argued that the independent commissions would still "have a semi-autonomous status in the department," he nonetheless noted that "they would report to the President through the department head."[68]

Legislators also rebuffed the idea that the preaudit should be performed in the Treasury Department. Representative John Cochran (D-MO) emphasized that the GAO "was set up as an agency of the Congress, not as an agency of the executive branch." To Cochran, the preaudit simply carried out Congress's legislative intent: "The Comptroller General does not take control; he simply says, 'Yes', or 'No.' If the law is not worded so it will permit the expenditure the Comptroller General will say so." While A. E. Buck testified for PCAM that "we would have a very thorough audit by the Bureau of Fiscal Control, in the Treasury Department, before the payment had been made," Representative John Taber (R-NY) complained that if the treasury secretary were made responsible for "a preaudit of all accounts and all payments," the postaudit would be "of no value whatsoever." "I think Congress has a right to appropriate money and say exactly how that money is to be spent," Senator Byrd declared. "And that money should not be spent unless the restrictions and regulations placed on it by Congress are obeyed."[69]

Reflecting this resistance, the Senate bill exempted the independent regulatory commissions from presidential reorganization authority. But though it had eliminated one unitary provision, the bill still contained other unitary elements, including creating an auditor general, eliminating the comptroller general, and having the Bureau of the Budget perform the preaudit. Proponents of the bill defeated an amendment from the reorganization critic Senator Byrd to protect the comptroller general. The bill passed the Senate with the changes to the audit intact.[70]

Nonetheless, the bill's defeat in the House in April 1938 signaled Congress's rejection of the institutional reforms associated with unitary theory. Instead, Congress's decision on a second attempt at reorganization in 1939 would be based more directly on the purported merits of presidential representation. The new bill pulled back from unitary assertions, again exempting the independent regulatory commissions and some other bureaus from reorganization and also now avoiding changes to the audit. The proposed bill also dropped the idea of replacing the Civil Service Commission with a single civil service administrator responsible to the president.[71]

ACCOMMODATING PRESIDENTIAL REPRESENTATION:
REORGANIZATION AND THE LEGISLATIVE VETO

The final design of the Reorganization Act of 1939, creating a presidential reorganization authority subject to legislative veto by a two-house concurrent resolution, was chosen from among multiple alternatives. Of course, Congress could simply have kept its primary responsibility to reorganize the executive branch itself, as some resisting presidential reorganization authority wanted. Alternatively, some lawmakers sought to either strengthen or weaken Congress's potential check on presidential reorganization authority, either requiring the president to gain positive assent for reorganization plans or allowing the president to veto Congress's disapproval of plans.

In its report, the PCAM criticized the existing executive branch organization, which mirrored the organization of congressional committees, as serving parochial interests. "The departments themselves and groups of citizens interested in particular activities," the PCAM observed, "often seek to settle such disputes by direct appeals to the Congress, there again only to find the same or almost the same differences represented in the jurisdictional jealousies of congressional committees."[72] Instead, the PCAM advocated presidential responsibility for "the continuous administration reorganization of the Government."[73] This would require a sweeping agenda-setting power to overcome resistance in Congress and determine "the effective division of duties among the departments."[74] Under the PCAM's bold vision, such a reorganization authority would be subject to no expiration and would provide for both the establishment and the abolition of agencies, including entire departments.[75] Reorganization, Charles Merriam argued to lawmakers, would be the next "step" to bring the presidency "up to date."[76]

The Brookings Institution agreed with the PCAM's diagnosis of congressional representation as an obstacle to achieving a rational reorganization of the executive branch. It also viewed the presidency as having the potential to better represent the national interest. But Brookings was wary of the scope of reorganization authority that the PCAM proposed. In exchange for giving "sufficient powers" to the president, argued Lewis Meriam, Congress should have "compensating . . . devices for holding him responsible."[77] Meriam's chosen solution essentially granted the president an enhanced agenda-setting power to improve the chances of enactment of a reorganization plan: the president would issue executive orders for reorganization subject to a legislative veto by concurrent resolution (in either one or both chambers). The president could "with safety" be given such power, posited Meriam, because "the system of checks and balances would be preserved."[78] Preserved perhaps, but adapted to have a presidential tilt.

Members of Congress understood that presidential reorganization authority was an institutional device meant to overcome the perceived problems of congressional and bureaucratic parochialism. Senator Pat Harrison (D-MS) cited resistance from legislators and cabinet officers as evidence that Congress could not overcome particularistic interests, arguing, "you have got to give this power to the Executive if anything is to be accomplished."[79] Senator Joseph Robinson (D-AR), the initial chairman of the hearings on reorganization, agreed that giving the president "the authority to make the reorganization" was "probably the only way a reorganization ever can be made."[80] After Robinson's death, his successor as chairman of the hearings, Senator Byrnes, admitted congressional incompetence at achieving executive reorganization: "Congress has been trying to merge bureaus for 150 years, but it has not succeeded up to this time." If it were "left to the Congress," no changes would be made.[81] The PCAM's director of research, Joseph Harris, later outlined the same logic in a private memo to Byrnes. Expressing the importance of Congress "delegat[ing] this authority to the Chief Executive," Harris invoked the limitations of lawmakers: "The main reason is that Congress is subject to such strong bureaucratic pressure that it is unable to do the job. Regardless of whether we like it or not, the history shows conclusively that this is the fact."[82]

Though some lawmakers, such as Senator Byrd, resisted new presidential authority, the more notable division among legislators proved to be over the extent of the proposed power, not whether delegating such authority was necessary. In hearings on the reorganization proposals in 1937, lawmakers were inclined to favor the Brookings approach to devise presidential reorganization authority, opposing the more expansive vision of the PCAM. They sought to add checks—exemptions, a legislative veto, and a limitation on how long such authority would last before requiring congressional reauthorization. Though initially opposed by the PCAM, the legislative veto served as an accommodation to the idea of presidential representation, allowing the president strong reorganization authority but preserving a potential congressional check on it. Senator Robinson preferred this to the PCAM's alternative, in which Congress would primarily rely only on the budget process to check the president.[83] Persuaded that the legislative veto was necessary to win congressional approval, Gulick later defended the device against criticism from Senator Byrd, who worried that presidents could nullify Congress's ability to exercise the veto by continually issuing reorganization orders and overwhelming Congress with changes.[84]

Questions arose in 1938 over which form, if any, the legislative veto should take. Senator Marvel Mills Logan (D-KY) argued that if a president's plan avoided a legislative veto, that would functionally be the equivalent of attaining congressional consent: "does not Congress determine whether his Executive order shall go into effect?" Opposing this legislative veto, Senator Josiah Bailey (D-NC) responded to Logan that he would vote for reorganization only if the legislative veto were changed to require positive congressional *assent* to a presidential proposal, as opposed to avoiding congressional *dissent*: "If the Senator from Kentucky will offer an amendment saying that the acts of the President shall not be valid until approved by the Congress, I shall be very happy and will very quickly vote for the bill."[85] Seeking to diminish the president's agenda-setting advantage, Senator Burton Wheeler (D-MT) offered an amendment requiring a majority of the House and Senate to approve reorganization plans within ten days of submission, but it was narrowly defeated.[86]

Managing the bill, Senator Byrnes instead sought to ensure that reorganization orders would take effect unless both chambers voted them down via joint resolution. Because a joint resolution required presidential assent, blocking a president's reorganization plans would essentially require support from two-thirds of lawmakers in both chambers, the threshold for overcoming a presidential veto.[87] As Byrnes proclaimed, "I am confident that if the executive departments are not reorganized until Congress does it, they will never be reorganized." Moreover, he emphasized the president's constituency as reassurance for granting such authority: "the same people who elected the Senators and Congressmen elected the President and the people have just as much confidence in the ability of the President to reorganize the departments."[88]

But there was still concern over the appropriate balance between presidential reorganization authority and Congress's ability to respond. In an effort to mollify the opposition, a compromise was devised in the House between the Byrnes and Wheeler positions on the extent of the advantage given to presidential reorganization proposals. Despite arguments over the constitutionality of the provision, the House passed the amendment of Representative Frank Kniffin (D-OH) to allow both chambers of Congress to override a reorganization plan via a concurrent resolution, rather than a joint resolution.[89] This meant that the president would not be able to veto Congress's disapproval resolution. FDR approved the compromise, even after declaring only days earlier that such a use of a concurrent resolution—"only an expression of Congressional sentiment"—would be unconstitutional.[90] Speaker Bankhead defended the legislative veto as an adequate check on presidential power, emphasizing that Congress would "for 60 days" be able to decide "whether the recommendations of the President shall stand or not."[91] And Representative Warren argued that, compared to the Senate bill, "the House Bill is surrounded by every safeguard and protection."[92] Yet despite the apparent compromise in having the bill privilege the president's reorganization plans, the measure still lost narrowly on a motion to recommit in April 1938.[93]

The next attempt to pass presidential reorganization authority in 1939 proceeded along the same lines. Once again, the bill featured a legislative veto based on a concurrent resolution. House bill sponsor Representative Warren admitted that Congress was actively deferring to the president, who would undertake the "reorganization of the government under a review by Congress."[94] Considering some legislators thought that, under Article I, Congress was responsible for reorganizing the executive branch, promising a "review" of presidential actions with the chance to vote against them was far from a ringing endorsement of legislative supremacy.

Another procedural alteration, aimed at mollifying congressional concerns, essentially conceded that reorganizing was a legislative power. As Louis Brownlow would later recount, the bill made "the President an agent of the legislature." Rather than using executive orders, reorganization plans would be "published as statutes" if they avoided congressional disapproval. Presumably tongue-in-cheek, Brownlow explained that the duty of proposing reorganization plans had been placed "upon a legislative agent who merely happened to be the President of the United States."[95] The move underscored the significance of the institutional adaptation that the legislation entailed.

Supporters of the 1939 bill defeated multiple attempts to weaken the presidential agenda-setting advantage that would be granted for reorganization plans. Amendments that would have required a congressional majority to vote in favor of reorganization, rather than avoiding a negative judgment, were defeated. The House rejected the amendment of Representative Richard Kleberg (D-TX) to that effect. He had criticized the bill's "devious methods" and asserted it was wrong for Congress "to accept a position where by negative action only can they express the wish of the people or the voice of those whom they represent." Representative Warren countered that "anyone who wants to see reorganization in the Government cannot support this amendment," implicitly suggesting that only the president could achieve that goal.[96] In the Senate, Senator Wheeler nearly succeeded with the same amendment, attempting to require an affirmative vote from Congress. Joseph Harris, the PCAM's director of research, privately warned Senator Byrnes, "Some of the senators are in favor of reorganization if a measure can be passed which grants no authority whatever to the President, and under which there is little or no chance of actual reorganization."[97] After initially passing 45–44, the amendment was reconsidered the following day and defeated 44–46. Another amendment in the House from Representative Hatton Sumners (D-TX), allowing just one chamber to veto a presidential plan, also narrowly failed.[98] The House majority leader, Sam Rayburn (D-TX), argued that those "who really want reorganization" should require a two-chamber veto, making a presidential plan harder to reject.[99]

Though pared back from the ambition of the PCAM, the final law provided for an executive reorganization authority, subject to legislative veto, for two years before requiring congressional reauthorization.[100] Congress had rejected the formalistic unitary assertions that sought to provide a more hierarchical executive branch structure. But it had essentially inverted the legislative process in order to tap the purported benefits of the president's national purview. The president would propose plans that would take effect unless Congress vetoed them. The setup was a testament to how reforms associated with presidential representation envisioned the reworking of constitutional relationships between the legislative and executive branches.

Challenge: Constitutional Stretches

Precisely because presidential reorganization authority was such an institutional adaptation, it was vulnerable to formalistic claims that, under the Constitution, Congress was primarily responsible for deciding on the organization of the executive branch. Under powers outlined in both Article I and Article II, Congress could create agencies, fund them at will, set the terms of appointments for officers, and vest certain powers in those officers. As the "constitutionally designated source of national policy," note Karen Orren and Stephen Skowronek, Congress "can assert its will in administration [through] program design."[101]

Proponents of presidential reorganization authority admitted, often openly, sometimes grudgingly, that their vision stretched beyond the constitutional structure. Far from only providing the opportunity to shuffle some bureaus, FDR saw reorganization as one facet of achieving constitutional change.[102] Somewhat incongruously with their formalistic assertions about the executive power, FDR and members of the PCAM embraced the notion of a "living" Constitution, seeking to change the way government worked without formal amendment. Amid battles over both judicial and executive reorganization, FDR sought to impress his view of the Founding document on Congress: "it is patriotic as well as logical for us to prove that we can meet new national needs with new laws consistent with an historic constitutional framework clearly intended to receive liberal and not narrow interpretation."[103] For Charles Merriam, democracy and constitutional flexibility were intertwined: "the doctrine of the flexibility of the Constitution developed as part of the general democratic movement."[104] Before working as part of the PCAM, Gulick had envisioned a change to the constitutional separation of powers. Under a "new theory of the division of powers," Gulick argued, "the executive will be called upon to draft the master plan."[105]

The president and the PCAM brought these understandings of the Constitution to the task of reorganization. Privately, FDR admitted to Gulick that he was seeking reforms through reorganization rather than formal constitutional amendment: "there is more than one way of killing a cat, just as in the job I assigned you."[106] But there was no hiding what the president was up to. As journalist Arthur Krock reported when FDR unveiled his reorganization proposal, "The President, in December 1936, decided that the amendment process requires too much time for the country's needs and security."[107] A disgruntled South Carolinian picked up on the scope of the transformation the reorganization legislation portended, asking Senator Byrnes, "why not let the people speak thru a proposed constitutional amendment"?[108]

Opponents of presidential reorganization authority emphasized that Congress would be delegating away its own legislative power. As even the PCAM admitted, since the Constitution "sets up no administrative organization for the government," reorganization involved legislative power: "the administrative organization of the Government to carry out 'the executive Power' thus rests upon statute law."[109] This point was not lost on the proposal's critics. Opposing the 1938 bill in floor debate, Senator Bailey claimed reorganizing as "legislative power . . . our power," and he attacked the bill for taking that power "from ourselves, to whom it belongs," and giving it "to one single, sole man, who, until we do transfer it, never had or enjoyed one particle of it."[110] Bailey emphasized that reorganization was a "constitutional power of ours," hoping it would remain "in the hands of the duly elected constitutional representatives of the American people."[111]

As the 1938 bill faced increased resistance, FDR was forced to rebut accusations from opponents that he sought dictatorial power. Issuing an extraordinary letter, FDR denied that he had the "qualifications" or "inclination to be a dictator."[112] The letter backfired. Representative Hamilton Fish (R-NY), for example, turned FDR's words against him. "The President says he does not want to become a dictator," Fish mocked. "If this bill is voted down, it will not even give President Roosevelt a chance to become a dictator." However, Fish warned ominously, if the bill passed, "we shall have a government of the people, by the President, and for the President."[113] "It is not a question of whether Roosevelt wants to be a dictator," stated one telegram sent to Representative Warren, "but whether you are going to do your duty and guard the liberties of the people so he cannot be a dictator."[114] A postcard to Warren was unambiguous in its criticism: "Some Congressmen may be rubber stamps by choice. Many Congressmen have been rubber stamps in fact. All Congressmen will be rubber stamps by law if the Reorganization Bill passes."[115] And as he spearheaded a stunning defeat of the House bill in 1938, Rules Committee chairman John Joseph O'Connor (D-NY) asserted that the measure was nothing short of "an attempt to compel Congress to surrender its rights."[116]

The 1939 reorganization bill faced the same objections that it delegated Congress's constitutional responsibilities to the president. Representative George Dondero (R-MI) complained that "the representative branch of the Government has surrendered its function to the Executive of the Nation."[117] Accusing the bill's proponents of giving "a purely legislative function" to the president, Representative J. William Ditter (R-PA) also sought to remind his colleagues that FDR could not be trusted. Citing the "brazenness" of the president's "Court-packing proposal," "discredited reorganization bill," and "pitiless purge," he asked, "Have not our suspicions been aroused?" The new bill, he concluded, remained a creature of the PCAM, leaving "little doubt" as to its true purpose: "In a nutshell the findings were that economy and efficiency could only come by increasing Executive power, even though such increases were contrary to the limitations and separations prescribed by the Constitution."[118]

Proponents of presidential reorganization authority also went beyond the Article II provision for the president to recommend measures to Congress. They stacked the deck in favor of those presidential recommendations, only giving Congress a chance to prevent presidential reorganization plans from taking effect through a legislative veto rather than requiring congressional assent. Remarkably, this solution was embraced despite questions over its constitutionality even among its advocates. Lewis Meriam candidly acknowledged that he was unsure of the legislative veto's constitutionality, as "the constitutionality of such a delegation has been debated but it has not been decided by the courts."[119] While Representative Charles Gifford (R-MA) opined that the legislative veto procedure might better withstand judicial scrutiny than just giving the president broad reorganization authority with no congressional input at all, C. M. Hester, testifying alongside members of the PCAM, admitted, "we have given that question very careful consideration and we have been unable to find any authority establishing the proposition that Congress, by silence, can legislate."[120]

Thus, presidential reorganization authority and the legislative veto were recognized as testing the adaptability of the constitutional frame. The process created by the Reorganization Act of 1939 amounted to a complete legislative inversion: the president would propose reorganization plans that would become law unless Congress took action to disapprove of them.

Conclusion: Presidentialism without "Radical Amendment"

The significance of the passage of the Reorganization Act of 1939 would quickly become evident in its implementation. While Representative Warren claimed that "no one has any idea" how the authority would first be utilized, Congress would soon discover FDR's ambitions for its use.[121] FDR used the new authority to establish an Executive Office of the President (EOP) and to transfer other functions into a new Federal Security Agency, the forerunner to the Department of Health, Education, and Welfare.[122] The EOP would provide the president with "adequate machinery" to manage the executive branch as a whole. The constituent parts of the EOP would be physically located next to the White House in the old State, War and Navy Building. Importantly, the EOP would assist with presidential agenda setting, allowing the president to inform Congress "with respect to the State of the Union" and recommend "appropriate and expedient measures."[123]

Both Brownlow and Gulick connected the idea of presidential representation to the establishment of the EOP in a 1941 public administration symposium on the subject. Brownlow asserted that an enhanced presidential role was necessary because "the legislature [had] lost its ability to take a coherent view . . . of the nation." Moreover, Brownlow noted that Congress had, in essence, itself bolstered the status of the presidency and agreed to the new EOP: "this new institution was created, not by the President alone, but with the concurrence, and presumably the blessing of the Congress."[124] Gulick declared that the creation of the EOP was "one part of America's answer to the taunt of the dictators that democracies cannot meet the demands of the modern world and still remain democratic."[125]

The president also transferred the BOB from the Treasury Department into the new EOP. By moving what was understood to be a presidential agency out of a department that had historically maintained a close relationship with Congress, FDR used his new reorganization authority to correct a perceived flaw in the earlier BAA of 1921. Both the PCAM and the Brookings Institution had envisioned a broader role for the BOB, viewing it as positioned to avoid the parochialism of departments or agencies. As the PCAM report explained, the BOB director was "one of the few Government officers in a position to advise the President from an over-all, as opposed to a bureau or departmental, point of view."[126] For Lewis Meriam, placing the BOB "directly under the president" would allow it to be "entirely independent of any Cabinet officer."[127] With FDR's action, the BOB would be tasked with additional responsibilities beyond assisting the president in planning a budget, including developing plans for future reorganizations and clearing both proposed legislation and executive orders. The BOB director Harold Smith explained that the bureau would "help the President develop a suggested program of action for the consideration of Congress."[128] Brownlow noted that the move to the EOP allowed the BOB to better serve "as an engine to aid [presidents] in coordinating general legislative programs."[129]

Thus, the Reorganization Act of 1939 was a decisive moment in the development of presidential government in America, with the EOP becoming the centerpiece of the institutional presidency. As implemented, the statute helped expand and routinize the involvement of the president in the legislative process and augmented the president's organizational capacity, acknowledging the president's "newfound leverage as orchestrator of the nation's policy commitments."[130] It was also a comparatively substantial shift of power to the presidency by Congress. The agenda-setting authority for the president that the reorganization statute provided did not simply supplant congressional authority in the way that the RTAA had accomplished in tariff making. But it was different from the presidential initiative provided by the earlier BAA of 1921 and the later Employment Act of 1946. In reorganization, presidential stewardship did not just guide Congress to better consider the national interest; it forced Congress to disapprove of the plan to avoid it automatically becoming law.

In this way, the Reorganization Act also was a unique achievement in constitutional adaptability. Establishing the EOP, asserted Clinton Rossiter, had saved the Constitution "from radical amendment."[131] Moreover, the reorganization process adopted in 1939 was reauthorized, with some alterations, by subsequent Congresses between 1945 and the early 1980s.[132] That innovative process continued to utilize the legislative veto as a central mechanism for the inversion of the relationship between the legislative and executive branches. The consequences of Congress's choice to accommodate presidential representation through the invention of the legislative veto would come to the fore in the 1970s and 1980s. Ironically, by that time, it was the originalist claim of the unitary executive that was newly on the rise. Meanwhile, the idea of presidential representation had faltered, and constitutional originalism in the judiciary threatened a challenge to the reinvention to the separation of powers that reorganization had entailed. Chapter 9 will explore the politics of the congressional and judicial reconsideration of presidential reorganization authority.

Presidential National Security Authority

The key idea in my mind . . . is that after all this whole set-up is to improve our national
security, and by the Constitution, the President has that responsibility.

FLEET ADMIRAL E. J. KING, 1947[1]

In 1949, the Commission on the Organization of the Executive Branch of
the Government, known as the Hoover Commission, referred to the idea of
presidential representation as it advocated the reorganization of the recently
created National Military Establishment and National Security Council. "The
president," the Hoover Commission reported to Congress, "as the single
member of the executive branch answerable to the electorate, is ultimately
responsible to the American people for the formulation, execution, and coordination of foreign policies."[2] It would seem natural for the new national security reforms Congress established as part of the institutional presidency in
1947 to rest on an assumption of presidential representation. As chapters 3–5
have shown, when Congress passed laws addressing presidential authority
in budgeting, trade, reorganization, and employment policy, presidential
representation was the organizing premise behind the formalization of new
presidential authority and the creation of new organizational capacities in the
executive branch.

But there was a crucial distinction. In those other policy domains, Congress had perceived itself as granting *new* or, at the very least, enhanced authority to the president. In the area of national security, however, Congress
thought that the Constitution already provided the necessary foundation for
the innovations it had in mind. Indeed, to some degree, providing new resources to support the president and coordinate national security policy inherently would *condition* the president's power in that realm.[3] Of course, Congress itself possessed clear constitutional authority to organize the executive
branch and provide for the raising of the armed services. But as Fleet Admiral
E. J. King noted in testimony to lawmakers, the president was understood to

have substantial constitutional authority over national security and foreign policy by virtue of being commander in chief. This difference had substantial implications for Congress's consideration of national security reform.

The National Security Act of 1947, along with the 1949 amendments to that law, sought to bolster the government's capacity to take a holistic outlook on national security, a desire that dated back to the Progressive Era.[4] The disaster of Pearl Harbor in 1941 had heightened perceptions about the need for reform. But arrangements made to coordinate across military services and departments during World War II, such as the State-War-Navy Coordinating Committee, Office of War Mobilization, and Office of Strategic Services, had not been institutionalized.[5] By the end of World War II, key actors across the government sought to achieve greater coordination in the national security apparatus.

Though by the mid-1940s Congress was becoming more concerned about its own authority compared to that of the presidency, its choice of institutional reforms in the realm of national security continued its earlier pattern of bolstering the organizational capacity of the chief executive. As Amy Zegart argues, these institutional arrangements were not simply "foisted on a reluctant Harry Truman by a public-spirited Congress."[6] The 1947 law established a National Military Establishment (NME) headed by a secretary of national defense, while still preserving substantial authority for the separate service secretaries. It also created the Central Intelligence Agency (CIA) and Joint Chiefs of Staff. Finally, the law's establishment of the National Security Council (NSC) in the executive branch was another congressional contribution to the multidecade creation of the institutional presidency. The later 1949 amendments to the law reconstituted the NME as the Department of Defense (DOD), augmented the authority of the office of secretary of defense, and removed the service secretaries from the NSC.

The passage of this law is a familiar tale.[7] Other accounts understandably focus on how the law was impacted by the politics of the battle between the Army and Navy over armed services unification. To be sure, major bureaucratic interests among the military services and their supporters were at play. Advocates of unification included the Democratic president Harry Truman and Army Chief of Staff (and soon secretary of state) George Marshall. Opponents of unification included Secretary of the Navy James Forrestal, the businessman Ferdinand Eberstadt, and some congressional patrons of the Navy, such as Representative Carl Vinson (D-GA) and, before his electoral defeat in 1946, Senator David Walsh (D-MA).[8] But the National Security Act also stands out for other reasons when the broader development of the institutional presidency is considered.

Notably, partisanship was not a significant factor in the law's passage. The Republican former secretary of war and former secretary of state Henry Stimson, who had long advocated reforms supporting presidential government, argued to Congress that national security reform "deals with an issue in which all partisan feelings are entirely irrelevant."[9] The votes on both the 1947 law and the 1949 amendments bore this out. Both the respective House and Senate versions of the bill in 1947, and the ultimate conference report, passed without recorded votes.[10] Additionally, the amendments to the law in 1949 passed without a recorded vote in the Senate and overwhelmingly in the House.[11]

My aim in this chapter is to identify the claims that the institutional reforms enacted in the law rested on. The National Security Act of 1947 was another statute in which Congress enhanced presidential responsibilities and organizational capacities, but unlike in other policy areas, the president was already perceived to have substantial authority over national security from Article II as commander in chief. Because of the president's preexisting authority, an informational account explains the law's design. Congress wanted to ensure that presidents would utilize expertise in national security decision-making, a move that could inherently condition the president's authority. Thus, legislators placed the new NSC under direct presidential control.[12] The bill may have been, in the words of Senator Raymond Baldwin (R-CT), "a compromise of ideas," but it was a compromise reached on a playing field that already advantaged presidential authority.[13] Presidential representation was not irrelevant to debates over the law, but it would not be the act's primary premise.[14]

This chapter proceeds as follows. First, I examine two of the potential assumptions behind national security reform. While this effort responded to the perceived need for a more holistic perspective in national security, I show that the central claim cited as a basis for reform was the president's constitutional authority. Second, I consider the institutional choices Congress made to involve the president. I chronicle the creation of the Department of Defense and the position of secretary of defense, examining to what extent the claims of presidential representation and the president's authority as commander in chief proved influential on that reform. Turning directly to the institutional presidency, I explain the creation of the NSC, focusing on what assumptions supported its creation. Third, I consider the extent to which the act pushed against existing institutional arrangements and constitutional claims. Finally, I conclude by considering the implications of the contrast between the National Security Act's ideational foundations and those of other laws creating the institutional presidency.

Assumptions: Holism and Constitutionalism

The effort to reform the national security system reflected a consensus that a holistic perspective was needed for the formation and implementation of foreign and national security policy. As Douglas Stuart stresses, the disaster of Pearl Harbor had been instrumental in making national security the "unchallengeable standard" by which foreign policy would be determined and judged.[15] National security was just that—*national*. Reformers "talked more expansively about the national interest" and "used the phrase 'national security' more frequently than ever before."[16] Congress wanted to make this kind of coordination an expectation of all presidents, but at the same time, its efforts to provide institutional forms that would ensure an overall perspective on national security issues had to accommodate the president's constitutional authority.

AN ANCILLARY CLAIM: PRESIDENTIAL REPRESENTATION

Actors in various institutional positions—journalists, officials in executive departments, the president, members of Congress—repeatedly invoked the need for a broader perspective on issues of national security. "If only we could consider our foreign relations as a whole," Walter Lippmann lamented, "it would save us no end of embarrassment and confusion."[17] The *New York Times* argued that reforms were necessary "to see the whole defense problem as a single picture" and to provide for "over-all planning."[18] Trying to overcome Army-Navy disagreements over unification, President Truman told both the secretary of war and the secretary of the Navy that they needed to focus less on the needs of their departments and services and more on the "whole picture."[19] In congressional hearings, Secretary of the Navy Forrestal argued that a law would be needed to provide "for the coordination of the three armed services," and "more important than that," it would provide "for the integration of foreign policy with national policy."[20]

Lawmakers themselves also echoed these concerns. Addressing his New Hampshire constituents, Senator Styles Bridges (R-NH), a member of the Senate Armed Services Committee, asserted that foreign policy was "not something abstract" but "affects every citizen."[21] Senator Henry Cabot Lodge Jr. (R-MA) criticized the separate group behavior of the military services for detracting from this focus on the whole, saying, "It is all right for college boys to cheer themselves hoarse about Annapolis and West Point or Harvard and Yale, but when manhood is reached that sort of rivalry and separatism seems utterly out of place."[22] And Representative Frank Keefe (R-WI) complained that while "the mustering of the entire country" was needed, "no agency of Government is charged with over-all responsibility. . . . Each has a partial answer to the plaguing questions which must be answered."[23]

This obsession of reformers with constructing a national security apparatus that would have a more holistic perspective was associated with presidential representation. Given that the critique of both legislators and the military services was that they were too parochial in their outlook, it was unsurprising that some reformers would look to the president as a corrective. The most direct influence of that claim came from one of the chief architects of the reform, the political scientist Pendleton Herring.[24] In his academic work, Herring frequently criticized members of Congress for being responsive to organized pressure groups that each advocated for putting its own "interest before the interest of the 'people,'" resulting in a "neglect of the national welfare of the country."[25] Instead of finding "a unified conception of the public interest," posited Herring, "blocs in Congress bargain and logroll." These parochial interests were likewise reflected in the bureaucracy, as "single bureaus are loyally supported by their congressional sympathizers."[26] In contrast to the "heterogeneous group of individuals responsible to local machines and special interests" in Congress, the president—the "chief representative"—was responsible to "an over-all constituency whose mass verdicts often differ from the dictates of pure localism."[27]

Herring connected this understanding of the presidency to the problem of national security. The "presidential office is the keystone" to the nation's "preparation for defense," he wrote, but more "systematic organizational support" was needed.[28] While "in normal times" localistic bargaining in Congress might be acceptable, "at times of real crisis such bargains may be too dear."[29] Looking to the post–World War II world, Herring warned against allowing Congress to reassert itself too far at the expense of presidential leadership. Asserting that "localism is tenacious and hinders our need to deal with issues that far transcend state or national boundaries," Herring sought to achieve greater presidential control over administration, especially in national defense, to push back against localistic congressional behavior or agencies that seek to "stand for a particular purpose or viewpoint."[30] Administrative rationality was necessary for promoting the national welfare: "Consistency in the formulation of presidential policy involves an intelligent and efficient arrangement of the whole administrative service."[31]

The constitutional role of the president as commander in chief was also connected to the president's representative role through the principle of civilian control of the armed forces. Senator Baldwin, for example, noted that effective civilian control of the armed forces relied on an assumption that "the President of the United States is bound to be, as he should be, responsive to the will of the people."[32] Similarly, Senator Wayne Morse (R-OR) argued that control over that officer and over the military was ensured by presidential representation. "The ultimate political control resting in the people of the country," Morse argued, would "manifest itself if anyone under this bill should attempt to engage in arbitrary or abusive power." "I am not at all fearful," he asserted, "so long as the President of the United States remains the civilian controller of our Military Establishment."[33] In another instance, the claim of presidential representation was invoked to push back on the charge that the legislation would increase the risk of eventual military domination of policymaking. When Marine Corps Brigadier General Merritt Edson warned of this risk, Senator Leverett Saltonstall (R-MA) responded sharply: "Do you not overlook . . . the President of the United States and his responsibility to the citizens as a whole . . . when you make those assumptions here in the United States?"[34]

To some extent then, the National Security Act reflected assumptions about presidential representation that were dominant in elite discourse of the period.[35] But while the idea of presidential representation was referred to in debates over national security reform, it was not the core assumption behind the law.

THE PRIMARY CLAIM: COMMANDER IN CHIEF

The National Security Act of 1947 and the 1949 amendments depended far less on presidential representation than did the other laws that created the institutional presidency. Instead, the core claim behind the reforms was that the president, as commander in chief, had responsibility for foreign affairs and national security.[36] "You cannot, under the Constitution, set up a second President of the United States" in national defense, Democratic president Franklin Delano Roosevelt had emphasized in 1940, as "the Constitution states one man is responsible."[37] Pendleton Herring enthused that American democracy was prepared for "dangerous periods" because the "true champion of its ideals is also the commander in chief of its military might."[38]

Lawmakers in both parties left no doubt that they viewed the president's role as commander in chief as a sufficient basis for the national security reorganization they had in mind. Senator Baldwin noted that the Founders had "provided that the civilian head of State, the President, should be the Commander in Chief of the armed forces, as he still would be under this bill." Whatever reforms legislators might desire, "Congress cannot change the Constitution" in that respect.[39] "We all know," declared Representative James Wadsworth (R-NY), "that under the Constitution of the United States the President, in addition to his duty to execute the laws, performs two other very, very important functions. One, he conducts the foreign relations of the United States; and, two, he is Commander in Chief of the armed forces."[40] "Under no conditions," emphasized Representative John McCormack (D-MA), "does [the statute] infringe upon or invade the powers of the President as President or as Commander in Chief. This is clearly the intent of Congress."[41]

As will be shown, these perceptions of the president's constitutional role in foreign policy and national security directly influenced the design of the National Security Act. Whereas other laws creating the institutional presidency had relied on a developmental claim of presidential representation, the National Security Act rested on perceptions of the constitutional meaning of the commander in chief clause.

Selection: Reconciling Coordination with Command

Two of the primary issues in national security reform were the battle over unification and the push to enhance the executive branch's organizational capacity to consider national security issues. The unification fight concerned whether the military services would be placed in one department and under the authority of a single secretary. The creation of a new institution in the executive branch to coordinate national security policy received wide support. For both reforms, Congress would need to reconcile its desire to provide for greater coordination of national security policy with the primacy of the president's authority as commander in chief.

UNIFICATION AND THE SECRETARY OF DEFENSE

The most contested issue in debates over national security reform was unification of the armed services. With President Truman supporting the move, the disagreement over that possibility was primarily between the Army and Navy and their respective patrons in Congress. While this fight arose out of different conceptions of self-interest between the services, two claims were accommodated by the various reform proposals. First, any reform of the existing separate service department structure needed to focus on the overall defense picture for the president, rather than prioritizing compartmentalized viewpoints. This reflected the ancillary influence of the idea of presidential

representation. Second, and more consequentially, it was clear that any reform addressing unification would draw on and accommodate the president's
prerogatives as the commander in chief.

The Army-Navy Game: Contesting Unification

The Army and Navy disagreement over national security reform was rooted
in a fight to protect the interests of each service, but it also arose from the
different organizational cultures, purposes, and conceptions of appropriate
command structure ingrained in each service.[42] Organizationally, the Army
favored a hierarchical structure of command, while the Navy featured a more
horizontal structure.[43] The positions of the Army and Navy on the institutional form that post–World War II national security reform should take
reflected these differences: the Army wanted unification; the Navy sought
coordination.

The Army's idea of unification was to have a single defense department
under the leadership of a single secretary. The plan's chief proponent was
Army Chief of Staff George Marshall.[44] President Roosevelt had pushed off
Marshall's efforts at unification during World War II, though congressional
hearings in 1944 had brought the dispute between the Army and Navy out
into the open.[45] Under FDR, a former assistant secretary of the Navy, the
Navy was the nation's preeminent service. But with FDR's death, the Navy
feared a loss of position under President Truman, who had served in the
Army and favored unification. In particular, the Navy was concerned about
the implications of unification for the Marines Corps, which faced hostility
from the Army, and for naval aviation with the likely creation of an Air Force
as separate coequal service branch.[46] Furthermore, the Navy faced the potential of being outvoted by the Army and new Air Force in any unified defense
department.[47]

In a direct challenge to presidential authority, the Navy opposed Truman's
preference. Recognizing the need for something substantive with which to
oppose the Army's unification plan, Secretary Forrestal commissioned businessman Ferdinand Eberstadt to produce a report outlining a Navy alternative for national security reform.[48] Disputing the Army's position, Eberstadt
argued that a single unified defense department would not improve national
security. While unification "looks good on paper" and "sound[s] good in
words," he contended, prioritizing "the one-man decision" would "minimize the tremendous benefits that arise from the parallel, competitive, and
sometimes conflicting efforts which our system permits."[49] Instead of a single

defense department, Eberstadt proposed a council on national security that would coordinate among the three military services to help the president in determining foreign policy.

Despite the Navy's opposition, President Truman "made it plain" that he wanted "an alter ego or deputy to deal with him about all the problems of the armed services and to relieve him of reconciling service differences and of discussing service details with two or three separate Secretaries." In the eventual compromise, the Army succeeded in getting its preferred position of a single civilian secretary of national defense, but the Navy was promised protections for its functions, including the Marines and naval aviation. Moreover, at least initially, the service departments would still be administered separately.[50]

Holism and the Secretary of Defense

The logic of focusing on the overall needs of the nation, rather than on the needs of any particular service, permeated the debates over unification. Even the initial name of the new defense organization indicated this rationale. Under the National Security Act of 1947, the new organization was to be called the National Military Establishment, rather than a department. The "choice of the word 'establishment,'" reported the *New York Times*, was the result of an Army-Navy compromise, avoiding an official "creation of a new over-all 'department,' to which the Navy had objected."[51] By not referring to it as a department, the act also indicated that the NME was meant to focus on a broader view of defense than a single department might provide.

Throughout the debates over reform, the secretary of national defense, the head of the NME, was envisioned as an officer who would assist the president in considering defense from a holistic perspective. Calling for unification in December 1945, President Truman argued that the existing defense structure was too compartmentalized: "up to the present time, the makeup and balance of our Armed Forces have not been planned as a whole." Because future wars would be "sure to take place simultaneously on land and sea and in the air," argued Truman, "our combat forces must work together in one team as they have never been required to work together in the past." Truman also reminded lawmakers of his own congressional background. "From experience as a member of the Congress," stated Truman, "I know the great difficulty of appraising properly the over-all security needs of the nation from piecemeal presentations by separate departments appearing before separate congressional committees at different times." Congress would benefit from that overall perspective as well: "It is only by combining the armed forces into a single department that the Congress can have the advantage of considering a single coordinated and comprehensive security program."[52]

The connection between the establishment of a defense secretary and a holistic outlook was a refrain throughout Congress's consideration of reform. Executive branch and military officials echoed Truman's reasoning. Bureau of the Budget (BOB) director James Webb compared the proposed secretary's potential perspective to his own. Rather than taking the view of a particular department, the secretary would "provide a focal point from which the national-defense program can be seen as a whole."[53] Because "the field of national defense is a single field," argued Secretary of War Robert Patterson, responsibility for it "should be concentrated, not divided as at present."[54] "My own feeling is that the problem of national defense should always be presented in the rounded form from one brain," Army Chief of Staff Dwight Eisenhower asserted.[55] Lawmakers themselves also invoked this understanding of national security reform in congressional floor debate. Senator Morse stated that the secretary would consider "the over-all problem of national security impartially and on a broad basis," serving as "a principal assistant to the President."[56] And Representative Walter Andrews (R-NY) envisioned the secretary as serving as "the full-time delegate of an overburdened President."[57]

The Commander in Chief and the Secretary of Defense

Though the purpose of a new secretary position was to support the president in taking an overall view of national security issues, constitutional claims dominated discussions about the extent of the authority that the proposed secretary would possess. Opponents of the unification plan argued that the secretary position might *interfere* with the president's constitutional authority. Proponents of establishing that position argued that the secretary would *support* the president in exercising his constitutional authority. Nearly everyone, however, agreed on the fundamental point: the president already possessed the authority. At issue was how to best support the president.

Current and former executive branch and military officials stipulated that the secretary would assist the president, but that the position would have no formal constitutional authority on its own. Eisenhower told Congress that it was "all right to say, 'We have the President as Commander in Chief,'" but he reminded them that the president could not realistically make all decisions regarding national security.[58] The defense secretary would "be a powerful officer," stated former secretary of war and former secretary of state Stimson, "but it should be observed that he is given no powers which do not already belong to the President as Commander in Chief." Instead, the necessity was attributable to other demands on presidential time: "we all know that the President even now is much overworked, and that he cannot permit himself to become entirely preoccupied by his duties as Commander in Chief."[59] Making perhaps the strongest claim that the secretary would assist the president in carrying out his constitutional responsibilities, President Truman argued that "the President, as Commander-in-Chief, should not personally have to coordinate the Army and Navy and Air Force. With all the other problems before him, the President cannot be expected to balance either the organization, the training or the practice of the several branches of national defense. He should be able to rely for that coordination upon civilian hands at the Cabinet level."[60]

Legislators from both parties would embrace the call for a defense secretary to assist the president in carrying out constitutional duties. If Congress failed to provide the president with such a secretary, asserted chairman of the Senate Armed Services Committee Chan Gurney (R-SD), it "would be tantamount to restraining the Commander in Chief from the most efficient possible performance of the responsibility which the Constitution places upon him."[61] Senator Lister Hill (D-AL) likewise emphasized that the secretary would serve as the agent of the president as commander in chief: "unification of general direction, supervision, and administration resides in the single secretary as the direct delegate, agent, servant, or lieutenant of the constitutional Commander in Chief."[62]

Subordinating the Service Secretaries

Some compromises were made in the 1947 law that limited the authority of the new secretary. Congressional and Navy ambivalence about the proposed new position of secretary of national defense was reflected in that office's lack of clear statutory superiority over the service secretaries of the Army, Navy, and Air Force. That choice would soon prove unworkable.

Members of Congress, particularly those viewed as patrons of the various services, were initially unwilling to clearly delineate control over the services by the new secretary. Senator Bridges worried about the creation of a "super-Secretary and the tremendous powers that he has over the three." In particular, Bridges wanted to ensure that the service secretaries retained access to the president: "You have to trust somebody and I will trust, as far as possible, the President of the United States, because he is Commander in Chief in time of emergency." Senator Millard Tydings (D-MD) viewed the service secretaries maintaining access to the president as a sufficient safeguard for the interests of each service: "So you have really got two umpires. You have got a pre-liminary umpire [the secretary of national defense], whose decision stands provided that the big umpire [the president] does not overrule him. But you have always got, as you have now, the same access to the big umpire."[63] Navy Secretary Forrestal took that right of appeal one step further, noting that if such appeals were made, Congress would likely know about it.[64]

Maintaining the right of the service secretaries to appeal to the president was promoted as a safeguard, but from the president's perspective, it was a shortcoming. The goal of unification was to help the president gain an overall view on national security policy. It remained, of course, the constitutional prerogative of the president as commander in chief to ask for the opinion of the service secretaries on any issue, but the 1947 law had allowed for the in-verse. It granted these subordinates a statutory right to complain to the chief executive about any and every decision made by their superior.

It did not take long for Congress to change its mind. In 1949, Truman criticized the 1947 law for not giving enough authority to the defense secre-tary: "the Act fails to provide for a fully responsible official with authority adequate to meet his responsibility, whom the President and the Congress can hold accountable." Therefore, he asked Congress "to convert the Na-tional Military Establishment into an Executive Department of the Govern-ment, to be known as the Department of Defense; and, second, to provide the Secretary of Defense with appropriate responsibility and authority, and with civilian and military assistance adequate to fulfill his enlarged respon-sibility."[65] The Hoover Commission suggested several moves to subordinate the service secretaries to the secretary of defense. The secretary of defense would be included on the NSC, but the service secretaries would be excluded. Service secretaries would be prohibited from appealing decisions of the sec-retary on budgetary matters directly to the president, the BOB director, or Congress. Overall, the secretary would have more authority over the defense establishment.[66]

In response, the 1949 amendments to the National Security Act stipulated more authority for the secretary of defense over the rechristened Department of Defense. The secretary would "be the principal assistant to the President in all matters relating to the Department of Defense." Representative Vinson reemphasized Congress's intent that "under this law the Secretary of Defense is to have clear-cut authority to run the Department of Defense." Notably, even as Congress empowered the secretary with more authority over the De-partment of Defense, it made sure that it did not grant the secretary a broader purview. While the Senate had sought to define the secretary as the "Presi-dent's principal assistant 'in all matters relating to the national security'" in the statute, the House "changed the 'national security' to the 'Department of Defense.'" As Representative Vinson stated, "obviously the Secretary of Defense is not the President's principal adviser in all manners related to the national security."[67] That responsibility would belong to the NSC, which was directly a part of the institutional presidency.

THE NATIONAL SECURITY COUNCIL

The provision for the NSC was originally offered as an alternative to armed forces unification, a strategic proposal made by the Navy to hold off its least desired outcome. The proposal envisioned coordinating national security decision-making, rather than providing a unified structure. Despite its origins in the battle over unification, however, it soon came to be a relatively uncontroversial, core feature of the National Security Act.[68] The NSC was another instance of Congress building the apparatus of the institutional presidency by granting the president new organizational capacities for the management of national security issues.

The creation of the NSC was analogous to the BOB in the Budget and Accounting Act of 1921 and the Council of Economic Advisers in the Employment Act of 1946. For those two laws, the development of this capacity was associated with Congress also delegating authority to the presidency based on an assumption of presidential representation. The NSC was also devised to assist the president in taking a holistic view of national security issues, a way to improve coordination among the relevant entities in the executive branch. But its design did not rely on the idea of presidential representation. Because any kind of coordination of national security policy could be interpreted by presidents as an infringement on their preexisting constitutional authority, the NSC was placed under presidential control. This was underscored by Congress in a series of decisions. The law would not provide for congressional access to NSC reports; it would not place the new secretary of defense as the chair of the NSC; and it would not attempt to force the president to chair meetings or be bound in any way by NSC decisions. All these choices reconciled this new institutional creation with Congress's perception of the preexisting authority of the president as the commander in chief.

Holism and the NSC

By the mid-1940s, reformers had long envisioned creating an institutional mechanism to help the president coordinate among departments and agencies in the executive branch and to make decisions in national security from a holistic viewpoint. Before US entry into World War II, for example, political scientist Lindsay Rogers had called for "machinery to coordinate diplomatic, military, naval, economic and financial policy" that would "be divorced from routine departmental detail" and "advisory to the President."[69] The specific instigation for such a council came from Secretary of the Navy Forrestal, who had charged Eberstadt (assisted by Pendleton Herring) with producing a report on national security reform.[70]

Eberstadt argued that problems in national security policy were the result of purported "defects of coordination" and "gaps between foreign and military policy." A lack of overall perspective hampered US national security: "We have concluded that these faults were due principally to lack of appropriate and seasoned mechanisms and of adequate plans, policies, and procedures for coordination; lack of clear understanding and appreciation by one group or individual of the relation of others to the over-all job."[71] Given his assignment from the Navy secretary, Eberstadt unsurprisingly concluded that unification of the services was not the way to achieve a needed holistic perspective. In fact, he even suggested that there would be constitutional issues with that approach: "It is obviously impossible to unify all these elements under one command, short of the President." Instead, he sought to create a formal coordination mechanism for the three cabinet-level service secretaries, resulting in a "harmonious whole."[72]

That coordination would be provided by the NSC, which Eberstadt argued "would be the keystone of our organizational structure for national security." The council would integrate foreign and military policy, being "charged with the duty of (1) formulating and coordinating over-all policies in the political and military fields, (2) of assessing and appraising our foreign objectives, commitments and risks, and (3) of keeping these in balance with our military power, in being and potential." The NSC "would be a policy-forming and advisory, not an executive, body." The council would also have a "permanent secretariat" for informational and staff capacity, and it would supervise a newly formed Central Intelligence Agency.[73] Notably, this vision for the NSC departed from the statutory design of the BOB and CEA, the other establishments in the institutional presidency. Under Eberstadt's plan, the president would be a member of the council as chair, alongside permanent members that would include the secretary of state and the three service secretaries.

Strikingly, antagonists from different sides of the unification debate all articulated the purpose of the NSC in similar terms. In congressional testimony, Navy Secretary Forrestal described the NSC as "a paramount feature of the bill," providing "for thorough integration of our foreign policy with our military policy."[74] Secretary of War Patterson likewise said that the principal functions of the NSC "shall be to advise the President on integration of foreign and military policies and to enable the military services and other agencies to cooperate more effectively in matters relative to national defense."[75] General Carl Spaatz of the Army Air Forces emphasized that "national security is a larger concept than military defense," and that the NSC would help determine "unified action."[76] And the former secretary of war Stimson praised the "wise and proper step" of establishing the NSC "for the assistance of the President in those matters of national security which transcend the strictly Military Establishment."[77]

The overall picture to be provided by the NSC also applied to intelligence gathering, with the Central Intelligence Agency established by statute under the auspices of the NSC. Lieutenant General Hoyt Vandenberg, the director of central intelligence for the then existing Central Intelligence Group, distinguished the need for "national" intelligence from that for "departmental" intelligence. Providing this perspective, he argued, required an independent standing and institutional location for the CIA: "National intelligence is that composite intelligence, interdepartmental in character, which is required by the President. . . . National intelligence is in that broad political-economic-military area, of concern to more than one agency." Only such a holistic perspective, which would "transcend the exclusive competence of any one department," would allow "the President and appropriate officials [to] draw a well-rounded picture on which to base their policies."[78] By locating the CIA under the auspices of the NSC, rather than placing it in the State Department, Congress endorsed this emphasis on transcending any parochial departmental viewpoints.[79]

The Commander in Chief and the NSC

The NSC's structure was viewed as encouraging coordination and collective decision-making among key actors in the executive branch. But the council would also be assisting the president fulfill what was believed to be a core constitutional function of the president. Thus, the NSC's placement under presidential control resulted from this congressional perception of the president's authority as commander in chief.

This rationale was invoked when the NSC was discussed in congressional hearings. For Fleet Admiral King, the NSC's role in providing recommendations, but not determining policy, showed that the core assumption of the proposal "was that the President is supported in his constitutional power."[80] The chairman of the Armed Services Committee, Senator Gurney, emphasized that the NSC "reports directly to the President," not to the new secretary of national defense.[81] When asked by Senator Baldwin whether the NSC should have any executive powers, Ferdinand Eberstadt testified that the NSC should not "have any executive powers whatsoever." Rather its function was as "an advisory body and a coordinating body."[82] The point was repeatedly made: the NSC was to help the president discharge a perceived constitutional responsibility for national security, not to take over the function or provide a greater role for Congress in executive decision-making.

Congressional floor debate confirmed this interpretation of the NSC's relationship to the president. Explaining why the new secretary of national defense would not be made the chair of the NSC, Senator Gurney cited the president's constitutional role: "We do not wish to take away from the President, in any shape, manner, or form, his constitutional duty as Commander in Chief of the armed forces." The secretary should not have "overall authority" over the NSC, since the council was being "established to advise the President on security problems."[83] Senator Baldwin also explained that he had changed his mind from wanting the secretary of national defense to serve as chairman or vice chairman of the NSC because it would "place him in a position of too much power and authority."[84] Wanting the president to utilize the NSC for information and coordination, Congress ensured presidential authority over the new institution in the statute.

The NSC Staff and APNSA

Despite its genesis owing primarily to the fight between the Army and Navy, the NSC was immediately proclaimed to be a vital reform. Foreshadowing his extensive use of the NSC as president, Eisenhower praised its creation as meeting what had "always been an urgent need."[85] The establishment of the NSC, argued journalist Arthur Krock, was "the most important creation of the law."[86]

Still, despite Congress accommodating presidential authority in creating the NSC, the possibilities for how it could enhance presidential national security powers took some time to become apparent. Recognizing that Congress's idea of coordination could infringe on presidential decision-making, President Truman was initially wary of the council. He did not regularly utilize the NSC until the Korean War, as "he thought his presence might imply a delegation of authority which he did not intend."[87] In fact, this had been the reason why the statute did not attempt to *require* presidential participation on the council. Noting concerns about avoiding infringement on the president's authority, Fleet Admiral King had explained, "This is my way of implementing that. . . . [The president] can sit in when he sees fit."[88]

Truman had reason for concern about the new NSC. As the new secretary of national defense, Forrestal sought to assert his influence, wanting to chair the NSC in the absence of the president and to locate the council in the Pentagon. Truman rebuffed those efforts.[89] Forrestal's temptation to use the NSC as a mechanism for cabinet government ran contrary to presidential purposes and the authority of the commander in chief. Truman later contrasted his view of the NSC with that of Secretary Forrestal:

> Secretary of Defense Forrestal for some time had been advocating our using the British Cabinet system as a model in the operation of the government. There is much to this idea—in some ways a Cabinet government is more efficient—but under the British system there is a group responsibility of the Cabinet. Under our system the responsibility rests on one man—the President. To change it, we would have to change the Constitution.[90]

An additional problem for Truman was that the compromise the statute had endorsed, in which both the defense secretary and all three service secretaries had seats on the council, proved unworkable, confusing lines of authority.[91] As Senator Chapman Revercomb (R-WV) had presciently warned, if the service secretaries were on the NSC together with the secretary of national defense, the secretary would not actually "have authority to coordinate them."[92] The 1949 amendments to the National Security Act soon corrected this issue, bolstering presidential authority over the NSC. Accepting the recommendations of the Hoover Commission, Truman called on Congress to remove the service secretaries from the council: "The Secretary of Defense should be the sole representative of the Department of Defense on the National Security Council."[93] Even more significantly, Truman enhanced the status of the NSC by placing it in the Executive Office of the President in August 1949. The former home of the Army, Navy, and State Departments, the Old Executive Office Building now became the physical location of the NSC, with proximity to the White House signaling its influence. Truman began to call and attend more NSC meetings in 1949 as well.[94]

Two other developments revealed how the NSC could bolster the president's foreign policy prerogatives: the utilization of the NSC staff and the creation of the assistant to the president for national security affairs. While much attention had been given to the statutory composition of the NSC, the true resource for presidents proved to be the NSC staff. This staff would provide the president with relevant information and recommendations that would not be from the perspective of any one department.[95] As Truman described it, the NSC "built a small but highly competent permanent staff which was selected for its objectivity and lack of political ties" and would last across administrations.[96] Soon, the NSC staff became more important to the president than the council itself.[97]

The other key development was the creation by Republican president Dwight Eisenhower of the position of special assistant for national security affairs (today the assistant to the president for national security affairs [APNSA]) in 1953, which was not subject to Senate confirmation.[98] As the first national security adviser, Robert Cutler continued to place an emphasis on the NSC's "advisory only" role. The priority was providing the president information and recommendations from an overall viewpoint: "The Council's purpose is to integrate the manifold aspects of national security policy (such as foreign, military, economic, fiscal, internal security, psychological) to the end that security policies finally recommended to the President shall be both representative and fused, rather than compartmentalized and several." The NSC was a congressional creation, noted Cutler, but it was up to the president how to utilize it: "The Congress provided the vehicle, but it is in the President's discretion to do with it what he wishes." The role of the APNSA would be to take divergent views and clarify them for presidential decision.[99] By giving the NSC staff a greater role in drafting policy memos and creating the APNSA to chair NSC meetings, the NSC became "an effective instrument of presidential policy, responsible to the Oval Office."[100]

With the passage of the National Security Act and its implementation, the president was once again given clear responsibility for a policy area and new capacity to take a purportedly overall viewpoint in policymaking. "The primacy of the president in the determination of foreign policy," surmised James Sundquist, "was formally, if tacitly, acknowledged in the 1947 legislation creating the National Security Council." The law made the NSC responsive to the president, not to Congress. The president would formulate policy and take action, leaving the legislature to play a more reactive role.[101] Congress had deferred to the president's perceived constitutional authority in creating a new part of the institutional presidency.

Challenge: Accommodating Constitutional Claims

In debates over national security reform, some political actors also raised constitutional concerns that presidential power would be enhanced at the expense of Congress. With that concern in mind, Congress notably acted to reaffirm its own constitutional authority to establish the functions of each of the armed services. But by and large, the predominant constitutional issue raised in designing the institutional forms of the National Security Act was ensuring that there would be no interference with the president's preexisting authority. The law was a test of how far Congress could go in institution-alizing presidential authority over national security without infringing on constitutional prerogatives. This resulted in Congress designing a law that provided it minimal influence over national security deliberations in the ex-ecutive branch.

To be sure, different interpretations of where foreign policy authority most prominently resided under the Constitution were plausible.[102] "The Constitution is not at all precise in its allocation of foreign affairs powers between the two branches," noted the Hoover Commission in 1949.[103] But the perception that the president had unique responsibility over foreign affairs, even while remaining disputed, had a long history. In 1800, then representa-tive (and future Supreme Court chief justice) John Marshall (F-VA) famously told Congress that the president was the "sole organ of the nation in its ex-ternal relations, and its sole representative with foreign nations."[104] In *U.S. v. Curtiss Wright Export Corp.* (1936), Justice George Sutherland's opinion af-firmed the "very delicate, plenary and exclusive power of the President as the sole organ of the federal government in the field of international relations—a power which does not require as a basis for its exercise an act of Congress."[105] Of course, some in Congress would contest the sweeping extent of those claims. But by the mid-1940s, presidential dominance of foreign policy was already widely accepted.

RECONCILING THE INSTITUTIONAL WITH THE PERSONAL

Detractors of the position of secretary of defense argued that the secretary might actually infringe on the president's constitutional authority, claiming that the secretary would make choices that could only belong to the presi-dent. Some even said establishing the secretary position would be a step toward military dictatorship.[106] This constitutional skepticism was a center-piece of the Navy's initial criticism of unification. Ferdinand Eberstadt had raised the prospect that unification under a single secretary could "infringe upon the authority of the President," which was "fundamentally unaccept-able."[107] Melvin Maas, the president of the Marine Reserve Officers Associa-tion, argued that the "radical departure in our democratic system" of having a defense secretary would interfere with the people's will. "The President is subject to the electorate of the country," said Maas. "The people choose him to be their military leader along with being President."[108]

While these claims were used instrumentally by the Navy and the Marines to defend their interests, their concerns forced a response from advocates of unification. Those who supported creating a secretary had to tread carefully around the president's constitutional authority. One revealing admission on this front came from another Navy official, speaking at a time when the Navy was trying to push back on any kind of unification plan. "The President cannot be relieved of his constitutional responsibility," said Fleet Admiral Chester Nimitz. Rather than posing a threat to presidential control, "a single Secretary . . . will never make a decision on a disputed point, or on any important point, no matter how unified the thought flows up to him, without consulting and being guided by the individual who is ultimately responsible . . . the President."[109]

Lawmakers also repeatedly pledged that the creation of the position of secretary would reconcile the goal of offering the president a more holistic perspective on military policy with avoiding any interference in the president's constitutional authority. In hearings on national security reform, Senator Baldwin admitted the need "to avoid any possibility that this Secretary, this single Secretary shall in any way become the Commander in Chief of the Armed Forces, which, under the Constitution is delegated entirely to the President."[110] In floor debate, Baldwin argued that the legislation accomplished this task. "The Secretary," he argued, "in no way will diminish the responsibility and authority of the President, but he will merely provide the President with an impartial assistant to view national security problems from the over-all standpoint, rather than from that of any one element of the armed services."[111] Taking aim at those critics who warned of the secretary as a military dictator, Representative Chet Holifield (D-CA) also downplayed the notion that the secretary had too much independent authority. The legislation provided "no super-Secretary, no commander in chief possessed of operational control of all our armed forces, but merely an administrative head serving under the President."[112]

The president's authority as commander in chief also posed an issue for the creation of the NSC and potential congressional input into its operations. Eberstadt's original plan had envisioned the president participating in meetings of the NSC and viewed it as a policymaking body. But presidential participation in all NSC meetings could risk appearing to bind the president to collective NSC decisions, a potential infringement on the president's constitutional authority.[113] Moreover, Eberstadt's provision that the NSC would produce "annual reports to the President and to Congress" posed potential issues of control over its work.[114] Congressional access to such reports raised the prospect that the NSC would not simply be advising the president, but that Congress could use its advice to ascertain and highlight any departure between the president's actions and NSC recommendations.

The potential impact of the NSC on the president's constitutional authority needed to be addressed. Secretary of State George Marshall, the former Army chief of staff and proponent of unification, opposed the NSC plan because of concerns about infringing on the president's constitutional authority. Reflecting such concerns, President Truman and the BOB thus worked to change the proposal to clarify that the NSC was an advisory, not a policymaking, body.[115] And though the Senate version of the bill initially put the secretary of national defense, rather than the president, in charge of the NSC, the House changed this provision to affirm presidential control.[116]

There was also a limited challenge on the floor in Congress to the easy assumption that the NSC was meant to support the president alone in exercising authority over foreign affairs and as commander in chief. Representative Thomas Owens (R-IL) expressed concern that Congress would not be involved in presidential foreign policy decisions made in consultation with the NSC. Indeed, he noted that some lawmakers had considered placing members of Congress directly on the council itself—an outcome that would have been a significant challenge to the president's own constitutional authority. In a more limited move, Owens sought to increase congressional access to the NSC's work. He proposed an amendment to make any NSC recommendations and reports available to the House Speaker and president of the Senate. Notably, Owens defended this proposal on the grounds of congressional representation, emphasizing that those "close to the people" should be able "to judge for themselves." Owens also challenged originalist assertions about the president's authority as commander in chief, observing that the "bill would create a council such as we have not had in the history of our Government." And he complained that "there has not been one word said about the Congress, the representatives of the people themselves, having one word to say about the plans that are being made 1 year or 2 or 3 or 4 years ahead." The amendment would be "a safeguard which the people need." But his efforts were in vain, as the amendment was rejected.[117] The Senate also rejected an attempt to require congressional access to the NSC's budgetary deliberations.[118]

Instead, Congress severed the NSC from congressional control in order to increase the likelihood that the president would utilize it as a resource for policymaking. The price of coordination was unity.

CONGRESS'S POWER OF THE PURSE

A primary interest of Congress in reforming the national security system was budgeting efficiency, similar to its motivation in passing the BAA of 1921. "The objectives of economy and efficiency," said Under Secretary of War

Kenneth Royall, "are implicit in the act."[119] Debates over the extent of the authority of the secretary of defense over budgeting pitted presidential authority against Congress's Article I claims to primacy in setting budgets and raising the armed forces.

Proponents of unification suggested that the secretary, having a broader perspective than the services, would be able to help the president in keeping military spending estimates under control. Secretary of War Patterson argued that unification was the only way to "reduce to a minimum the duplications that are frequent today" and to "give economy" by proposing "a comprehensive plan for national defense."[120] General Eisenhower posited that "the person that is going to show you, from a disinterested, over-all viewpoint, where the savings can be made, will be the Secretary."[121] Similarly, Senator Baldwin enthused that "the Secretary of National Security is charged with preparing an over-all budget for the national security, and this for the first time in the history of our country."[122]

Despite this enthusiasm for unification's potential to realize efficiency, Congress at first gave the president, through the new secretary, only incomplete control over budget proposals for the military services. This signaled Congress's intent to exercise its own constitutional authority over budgeting. From the perspective of presidential authority, the initial National Security Act had shortcomings compared to the BAA of 1921. Senator Bridges sought to require the secretary of national defense to justify deviations in proposed budgets for the separate services to Congress.[123] Provisions were made so that the service secretaries could complain to the president about their budget proposals. Even more notably, the defense spending requests of both the secretary of national defense and the separate service secretaries would be included in proposals to Congress. Rather than seeing the budget "with only what the President says is necessary for these departments," Senator Gurney explained in describing the process, "Congress will be fully informed of the request of the service secretary, the administrator of the individual department, then the recommendation of the National Security Secretary, and finally of the President himself."[124] Gurney presented this distinction as a way to preserve Congress's prominence in the formation of national security policy: "Congress must retain its power to regulate national security, under the Constitution, wherein it is provided that Congress shall provide for the common defense. The power of the purse is all-important." Thus, Congress had provided for its ability to understand the preferences of each service separately: "the budget must be sent to Congress not just as the National Secretary wants, but in minute detail as to the manner in which the secretaries of the branches of the service make their requests to the National Security Secretary."[125]

Other lawmakers noted that this move undermined the presidential budget initiative established in 1921. The Appropriations Committee chairman, Representative John Taber (R-NY), worried that the provision "supersedes the Budget and Accounting Act of 1921. . . . The practice has always been that the President would submit these budget estimates when the Congress met, and the Congress would consider them on their merits." Rather than providing only a presidential budget, Taber complained, the bill "amends that law and provides that there shall be submitted to the Congress, first, what the President in his budget shall submit; second, what the Secretary of Defense may submit; and third, what the heads of the three departments themselves should submit." Taber thought it would be "a great deal better" for the presidential budget to be preserved, offering "some protection for the people of the United States."[126]

Significantly, Congress quickly reconsidered this provision in the 1947 law and reaffirmed the setup of the BAA of 1921 for defense spending in 1949. Bolstering presidential influence over the budget process in defense spending, Congress acted to ensure that budget requests reflected the views of the president. The 1949 amendments required that the secretary of defense must approve any request for additional appropriations by a service secretary to the BOB, the president, or Congress.[127] Senator Claude Pepper (D-FL) noted the gravity of this choice: "I say that it is a great power which we place in one man, if he may determine, before the question ever gets to the Bureau of the Budget, what each service shall have, or what it may ask for, or even how it may appeal to public opinion with regard to what is in the public interest and to the greatest advantage."[128]

RAISING AND MAINTAINING THE ARMED FORCES

By granting the president and secretary of defense substantial authority over military spending estimates, Congress empowered the president. However, Congress did preserve its own constitutional authority by placing one substantial limitation on the authority of the secretary of defense. By extension, Congress sought to draw a distinction between its own constitutional claims and those of the president as commander in chief. The 1949 statute reaffirmed limitations on the secretary from "taking any combatant functions assigned to the Army, the Navy, or the Air Force and abolishing it, transferring it, consolidating it, or reassigning it." This meant that the Marine Corps and naval aviation, priorities of the Navy's chief patron in Congress, Representative Vinson, would be protected from reorganization or abolition.[129] Senator Baldwin affirmed that he "would not stand for a bill which would give to the Secretary of Defense the power to determine what the components and the functions and the missions of the armed services of the United States should be," because this constitutional authority "to raise and support armies, to provide and maintain a navy" belonged to Congress. Emphasizing the role of the Army, Navy, and Air Force, Baldwin maintained that "the defense of our country must rest, like an old-fashioned milk stool on three sturdy legs."[130]

By specifying the functions of the respective services, Congress made a statement about its own constitutional authority for raising and organizing military forces. Ensuring that the individual services and their functions would be preserved would durably affect the structure of the military for decades to come. But beyond this, Congress did little to carve out its own role in national security policymaking in the 1947 law. The president's authority as commander in chief had crowded out Congress's own claims in the politics of reforming the institutional apparatus for American national security.

Conclusion: Presidentialism on an Alternative Foundation

Part 1 of this book has sought to examine the extent to which Congress's creation of the institutional presidency was influenced by the idea of presidential representation. In examining the National Security Act, I have taken care to distinguish between institutional reforms that were heavily influenced by the idea of presidential representation and those that were not. Laws creating the institutional presidency in the policy areas of budgeting, trade, reorganization, and employment all relied on the assumption of presidential representation. But the National Security Act of 1947 and amendments of 1949 rested primarily on a claim of the president's perceived authority as commander in chief. Those two statutes reconciled new institutional forms and responsibilities with the president's preexisting constitutional authority.

In the Cold War, presidents would exercise US power on a global scale.[131] Increasingly, they had an organizational capacity for independent action, including the utilization of the institutional apparatus of the DOD and NSC. The influence of the NSC, in particular, reached new heights with the powerful APNSAs Henry Kissinger and Zbigniew Brzezinski in the 1970s.[132] Indeed, the prominence of the APNSA position in that decade was suggestive of the implications of presidential national security authority not inherently relying on the idea of presidential representation. By that time, Congress would come to doubt the assumption of presidential representation that had under-lay many of its earlier choices for presidential authority.

Would the decline of the legitimacy of presidential representation affect presidential authority in national security in the same way as in other policy areas? Would the alternative foundation that these reforms rested on have any implications for the durability of presidential authority over national se-curity? Chapter 10 will examine the politics of this attempted congressional pushback against presidential authority over national security.

Institutional Durability: Reconsidering the Institutional Presidency, 1970–84

The meaning of the Presidency in the American political equation has changed.
JEFFREY HART, 1974[1]

Congress created the institutional presidency in an era in which the idea of presidential representation pervaded national political discourse. In the policy areas of budgeting, trade, reorganization, and employment, its choices to institutionalize policy responsibilities for all presidents and, correspondingly, to augment the president's organizational capacity were influenced by the premise that the president could best act in the national interest. In national security reform, Congress also institutionalized presidential responsibility, but in doing so, legislators needed to accommodate the president's constitutional authority as commander in chief.

This idea, and the reforms that drew on it, altered the trajectory of American political development. Along with complementary efforts toward greater policy leadership by presidents themselves, the result was a shift toward presidential government with a new division of labor layered over the written constitutional frame.[2] The new authority that presidents wielded was consequential. Presidential reorganization authority, for example, was used to establish the Executive Office of the President in 1939, the Department of Health, Education, and Welfare (forerunner to the Department of Health and Human Services and the Department of Education) in 1953, and the Environmental Protection Agency in 1970.[3] Presidential trade authority was utilized to reduce tariffs and steadily usher in an era of freer trade, with presidents living up to the expectations of the authority they had been granted.[4] Cumulatively, these laws formed the statutory basis for the expectation of a presidential program—an "institutionalizing of the initiative," in the words of Richard Neustadt—with all presidents expected to routinely propose legislation to Congress.[5] Presidential representation had moved from its status as a critique of the constitutional order to becoming the ideational foundation of a new institutional order. The institutional reinvention that the idea had anticipated, that Congress had enacted, and that presidents now put to work testified to the adaptability of American government.

At the beginning of the 1960s, the idea of presidential representation not only maintained its status as political wisdom; it appeared to portend an even greater shift toward presidentialism. "We will need in the Sixties," then senator John Kennedy (D-MA) proclaimed early in the 1960 presidential campaign, "a President who is willing and able to summon his national constituency to its finest hour."[6] Yet soon, rather than presidential representation bringing the nation to "its finest hour," the legitimacy of the idea began to come into question. By the early 1970s, the notion that the president could be counted on to always act in the national interest was under attack from all quarters.

The formative significance of a political idea is clearest once faith in it is dispelled. Stripping the institutional presidency of its ideational foundations exposed all that had been built on them. The institutional consequences were immediate. But ensuing developments suggested as well the difficulties of simply reversing course. What had been a sense of open-ended adaptability gave way to the anxieties of entrapment and an emphasis on constraint.

What were the institutional consequences of questioning the idea of presidential representation? To what extent was Congress constrained by its own reinvention of American government as it reassessed the desirability of presidential power? In part 2, I consider how rising doubts about the validity of the idea affected Congress's reconsideration of the institutional presidency. Between 1970 and 1984, Congress attempted to adjust the institutional arrangements in each of the areas in which it had formerly invested presidential authority. Statutory reconsideration is evident in the War Powers Resolution of 1973, the Congressional Budget and Impoundment Control Act of 1974, the Trade Act of 1974, the Reorganization Act of 1977, the Full Employment and Balanced Growth Act of 1978, and a 1984 act to ratify all previous reorganization plans. The Supreme Court's decision in *Immigration and Naturalization Service v. Chadha* (1983), voiding the use of legislative vetoes—a device placed in many statutes allowing Congress to reject actions taken by the president or executive branch agencies without presidential input—as unconstitutional, also affected Congress's reevaluation of presidential reorganization authority.

I show that Congress pushed back against presidential authority consistently on the basis of doubts about presidential representation, but that the effects of this reconsideration differed across policy areas. In some areas, as in budgeting and domestic economic policy, Congress bolstered institutional arrangements to counter the authority of the president. In others, as in re-organization, Congress would reduce and, ultimately, rescind presidential authority. Still, in other areas, as in trade and war, Congress would leave the president with significant authority intact. Congress's own claims of repre-sentational superiority and constitutional primacy were increasingly influ-ential as presidential representation came into question, but the ability and willingness of legislators to press forward with the full implications of those claims was constrained both by the president's constitutional authority and by the practical realities of governance. Congress's "resurgence" against the presidency was a halting, uneven affair.[7]

To examine the impact of rising doubts about presidential representa-tion's validity on the arrangements of the institutional presidency, I consider (1) the criticism of the idea of presidential representation in elite political dis-course during this period, (2) the extent to which the assumptions embod-ied in earlier reforms were questioned, and (3) how much increased leverage opposing claims about congressional authority and constitutional legitimacy gained over subsequent institutional reforms. In this introduction to part 2, I chronicle the changes in the perceived validity of presidential representa-tion prior to and during the period in which these laws were enacted.

Validity: Lost Faith in Presidential Representation

To the extent that there was a "basic political consensus" in American politics in the mid-twentieth century, events in the late 1960s and early 1970s would dispel it.[8] The rights revolution of the 1960s took aim at the long-standing inequalities in representation that had always excluded many Americans from being a part of the "whole people," while the counterreaction to these advances fueled political conflict and foreclosed a restoration of consensus.[9]

In some ways, the role of the presidency in responding to the civil rights movement in the 1960s might have marked a defining achievement toward fulfilling the president's claim to represent *all* the people. Yet ironically, this was the period in which the validity of presidential representation came into question. The strained relationships between presidents and the social move-ments of the 1960s and 1970s undoubtedly contributed to the erosion of that idea.[10] But the more abrupt shift in views of presidential representation would be primarily driven by two events. "Vietnam and Watergate," as one 1976 assessment of presidential power by the *New York Times* would repeat-edly state, changed perceptions of presidential stewardship.[11] First, the pro-longed and unpopular Vietnam War, prosecuted by Democratic president Lyndon Johnson and perpetuated by Republican president Richard Nixon, eroded the credibility of the presidency. Second, the revelations of the Watergate scandal proved devastating to the notion that the president could be counted on to rise above narrow political concerns and to act in the national interest. The values of "truthfulness" and "integrity," Pierre Rosanvallon has argued, are essential to maintaining the belief that a political leader acts in the general interest.[12] Vietnam and Watergate left the presidency exposed on both counts, combining to undermine faith in the office as the primary force for good government in the American system.[13]

To be sure, claims of presidential representation did not disappear. The idea would continue to be invoked in elite political discourse among presidents, lawmakers, journalists, and other political observers. But it was no longer taken as an article of faith. Instead, it was persistently questioned and increasingly dismissed as naïve. Whereas an earlier generation had looked to the presidency as a solution to the difficulties of parochialism in American constitutional government, a new generation of reformers held that the presidency was now the problem. Correspondingly, reformers argued that Congress needed to restore its own constitutional authority.

In the early twentieth century, political scientists had been among the leading scholars praising the virtues of presidential stewardship, and by mid-century, that notion had acquired the status of scholarly common sense. "In a relative but real sense," Richard Neustadt confidently wrote, "what is good for the country is good for the President, and *vice versa.*"[14] It was thus all the more striking that the rising doubts about the idea of presidential representation were chronicled by contemporary scholars. Samuel Huntington, for example, viewed this as a momentous shift. "Since Theodore Roosevelt," he argued, "the presidency has been viewed as the most popular branch of government." But "in the 1960s . . . the tide of opinion dramatically reversed itself: those who previously glorified presidential leadership now warn of the dangers of presidential power." That reversal, Huntington contended, would have consequences: "Probably no development of the 1960s and 1970s has greater import for the future of American politics."[15] In his own assessment of the state of American government, Theodore Lowi agreed, reporting that "faith in the presidency as a representative majority rule came almost completely unstuck during the late 1960s and thereafter."[16] "Too much has been made by too many presidents and by too many scholars," the political scientist and former White House staffer Thomas Cronin concluded, "of that ancient but partial truth that only the president is the representative of all the people."[17] Mocking this reversal, one writer in the *National Review* observed, "The last 50 years of trendy political science have been a terrible mistake, it seems."[18]

More importantly, these doubts were becoming more prominent in discussions of the relationship between the presidency and Congress by legislators themselves. One example was an address entitled "The Congress and America's Future," delivered by Representative Charles Mathias (R-MD) at Brigham Young University in 1965. Mathis noted the continued influence of presidential representation: "To some, Congress now appears to represent only the local and provincial interests of America, while the President seems to speak for the nation as a whole." "We often hear that Congress is not even really representative," he continued. But, in Mathias's view, the validity of these ideas was changing: "This criticism is fast outliving its relevance." In his telling, the increasing complexity both of the problems facing government and of the national government itself demanded not just a single-minded focus on the national interest from a president, but a closer relationship between the people and congressional representatives: "As national problems become more intricate and government becomes more impersonal, Congress will find itself more harassed and more essential as the representative of the people."[19] A Republican lawmaker might be expected to criticize presidential representation at the height of the Democratic "Great Society" programs. Still, the same rationale would be expressed by Senator Edmund Muskie (D-ME) a few years later. Addressing "questions about the nature of the Presidency and its distance from the American people," Muskie wrote to one citizen, "Unfortunately, the growth of our nation's population and the increased complexity of the economic and social problems we face has made it impossible for any one individual to remain closely in touch with every aspect of national life."[20]

Another legislator's change in views encapsulated the sudden and swift decline in faith in presidential representation. In 1961, Senator J. William Fulbright (D-AR) had described "the achievement of consensus" as "preeminently a task of Presidential leadership." Only the president, contended Fulbright, "can rise above parochialism and private pressures." Moreover, Fulbright echoed earlier Progressives in his critique of the Constitution: "The President is hobbled in his task of leading the American people to consensus and concerted action by the restrictions of power imposed on him by a constitutional system designed for an eighteenth century agrarian society far removed from the centers of world power." To Fulbright, it was "imperative that we break out of the intellectual confines of cherished and traditional beliefs and open our minds to the possibility that procedural adjustments in our system may be essential to meet the requirements of the twentieth century."[21] But, influenced particularly by Vietnam, Fulbright became a sharp critic of the presidency under both the Democratic administration of Lyndon Johnson and the Republican administration of Richard Nixon.[22] In 1966,

Fulbright warned of the risk of "confusing Presidential convenience with the national interest."[23] By 1973, Fulbright scolded Nixon for echoing the same claim. "If the President really has no confidence in the judgment of the Congress," Fulbright chided, "he ought to propose a constitutional amendment and say just what he is saying here, that the Congress no longer represents the country [and] it represents special interest[s], therefore, we abolish the right of Congress to determine policy."[24]

The media also recognized the change that was afoot. Despite Richard Nixon winning forty-nine states in the 1972 presidential election, substantially bolstering his claim to represent the whole nation, a January 1973 cover of *Time* declared a "Crisis in Congress." As the headline of the story asserted, presidential authority was the "crack in the Constitution," one that Congress needed to address. The magazine's editor in chief, Hedley Donovan, drew a contrast between congressional and presidential representation, arguing that the stakes of any contest between the presidency and Congress would be over "whether a democratic society puts some value on collective wisdom as opposed to centralized individual [presidential] wisdom, and whether the Congress can make a more constructive contribution to public policy."[25]

The Congressional Research Service (CRS) formally recognized the salience of that question. In 1974, the CRS sponsored an intercollegiate debate topic that addressed the rising doubts about presidential authority. The subject was "Resolved: That the Powers of the Presidency Should Be Curtailed." As part of that program, the CRS provided students with scholarship questioning the fundamental assumptions behind the presidency. The accompanying reading materials included numerous critiques of the presidency, such as Louis Fisher's criticism of the idea of presidential representation: "It is a crude generalization, of course, to depict Congress as the servant of selfish interests while idealizing the President as the one who acts for the nation as a whole."[26]

These claims were also echoed in letters from citizens to legislators, particularly during the Nixon administration. "To my understanding," wrote one citizen to Senator Edmund Muskie in 1973, "the Congress is the most representative branch of the government and the executive branch is the least representative."[27] Some questioned whether the president actually could be counted on to effectively represent the national interest. "People in greater numbers," asserted a New Hampshire resident to Senator Norris Cotton (R-NH), "are beginning to believe that Richard Nixon is exploiting the Presidency and in other regards acting contrary to the best interests of the nation."[28] "Are we suppose[d] to accept gratefully whatever [the president] decides is best for the nation?" asked another citizen rhetorically in a letter to Senator Thomas McIntyre (D-NH).[29] Though a Republican president was in office, a self-described "55-year-old Republican Wasp" nevertheless complained: "This country is too big and complex for one-man rule."[30] In addition to questioning whether presidential representation was a valid idea, some who wrote to Congress made the connection between changes to the powers of the office and how the presidency was perceived over time. "All that has been needed," lamented one citizen, "was for an amoral man to win the White House and abuse the power accumulated by his predecessors and handed him and them by the Congress."[31] "Every administration, regardless of which party it is, takes more power," complained a Kansas resident to Senator Bob Dole (R-KS).[32] Summing up the shift in perceptions of the presidency, one letter observed that the institution "no longer can demand the unconditional positive regard of the American people."[33]

With the validity of presidential representation coming into question, the idea of congressional representation was being rehabilitated. "Congress *is* the most representative of our national political institutions," Richard Fenno affirmed.[34] But even more significantly, calls for congressional primacy were accompanied by assertions of the value of constitutional formalism. The Constitution's separation of powers, the constitutional feature that Progressive supporters of presidential representation had identified as an institutional obstacle to overcome, was now viewed as holding the solution to the nation's problems. In his famous "Time for Choosing" speech in 1964, Ronald Reagan had criticized the view that the president "must be freed" from "the restrictions" imposed by an "antiquated" Constitution "so that he can do for us what he knows is best."[35] Soon, one of the primary champions of the presidency, Arthur Schlesinger Jr., would raise similar concerns in the defining book on the presidency of the 1970s, *The Imperial Presidency*. "The constitutional Presidency—as events so apparently disparate as the Indochina War and the Watergate affair showed—has become the imperial Presidency," Schlesinger warned. A "shift in the *constitutional* balance" away from Congress and toward the presidency was now the problem.[36] Acknowledging the widespread attention on the relative balance of power between the legislative and executive branches, the *New York Times* looked to the Constitution for clarity on the direction reform should take, drawing its readers' attention to the specific provisions in Articles I and II about congressional and presidential authority.[37]

REINFORCING THE SHIFT

The decline of the idea of presidential representation was cemented by other evolving political conditions. One change was that more political issues became contested at the national level, making the distinction between the purported national perspective of the president and the local perspective of lawmakers appear less significant to many political observers.[38] Indeed, one journalist went so far as to claim that the lawmakers had changed in their orientation from local to national issues:

> The men and women elected to Congress in the sixties and the seventies are, for the most part, a different breed from their predecessors. They are less parochial. . . . They are elected as much on national and international issues as they are on local matters, and they must answer to their constituents as much for their stands on issues discussed on the network news as for their success or failure in filling the local pork barrel.[39]

Accompanying the nationalization of politics and policymaking was a newly restored electoral competitiveness between the parties for control of the federal government. For most of the mid-twentieth century, control of Congress had been uncontested, "with the Democrats becoming something of a 'party of state' at the congressional level."[40] Starting in the early 1980s, however, gaining control of Congress became a more attainable goal for both parties. This quickly began to change the incentives of legislators, particularly in how they interacted with the president. With political parties needing to focus on promoting their own brand, while at the same time undermining the reputation of the opposing party, bipartisanship became more difficult to achieve.[41] This had corresponding implications for the ability of presidents to appear to stand for the national interest and guide Congress to such an outcome. As presidents attempted to influence policymaking in Congress, their leadership made policy issues subject to more, not less, partisanship. As Frances Lee has written, presidents became "dividers, not uniters."[42] In fact, one early indicator of the declining faith in presidential stewardship among legislators had come in 1966, when the opposition party delivered a formal response to the president's State of the Union address for the first time.[43]

Both issue nationalization and increased electoral competitiveness combined to intensify political polarization. Driven especially by the post–civil rights revolution party realignment in the South, conservatives and liberals increasingly became sorted into the Republican and Democratic parties, making bipartisan compromises among legislators more difficult.[44] This had the effect of further challenging the credibility of presidents to stand for the national interest. For many political actors who actively sought to sharpen distinctions between the parties, the desirability of even seeking a national consensus was becoming suspect.[45] More ideologically cohesive parties also focused legislators' attention on national issues, again undermining the claim that the president was the sole actor with a national perspective.[46] A correspondingly more fractured media environment made it difficult for presidents to speak for the whole nation.[47]

Presidents, in turn, were more incentivized after the 1970s to govern as partisans, drawing on plebiscitary claims to represent particular groups of Americans.[48] Ironically, the decline in faith that presidents were truly representing the people in the late 1960s and early 1970s contributed to this development. In both parties, reformers changed the selection procedures for presidential candidates to rely on primaries, increasing the role of ordinary voters in choosing the party standard-bearer.[49] Bringing presidential candidates closer to the people *within* the party strengthened the plebiscitary claims of presidents, but it ultimately undermined the ability of presidents to *transcend* their parties in representing all the people. As presidents became more identified with their parties and the parties became more identified with their presidents in the public mind, claims of stewardship appeared less plausible.[50]

Presidents did not just give up their claim of stewardship, and the idea remained a regular feature of American politics. But the idea had become hollowed out, and the transformative ambitions associated with it were blunted. As early as the 1980s, presidential administrations implicitly acknowledged this change. Recognizing the declining legitimacy of the idea, the Reagan administration made a sharper "distinction between [the president's] political role as the chief representative of the people and his constitutional duty to protect the office of the presidency."[51] Thus, conservatives began to increasingly emphasize the unitary executive theory, believing it would provide a more solid constitutional basis for presidential prerogatives.[52] Unitary theory also had the advantage of focusing presidential power on what was increasingly the principal terrain of contestation for policymaking—administration. Even as they did not necessarily embrace the unitary theory as constitutional doctrine, Democrats likewise became enamored of the virtues of "presidential administration."[53] As a political premise, unitary theory would absorb a more plebiscitary, partisan conception of presidential representation and fuse it to an originalist claim about the president's possession of all the executive power.[54] What was once an audacious conception of the presidency as the representative of the national interest and "the leader of all the people"—an idea that transformed the institution and American government in the twentieth century—had been diminished to being, in the words of the *New York Times*, "so, well, old-fashioned."[55]

Part 2

On its own, changes to the perceived legitimacy of presidential representation might appear trivial. But in the hands of Congress, this shift had consequences for the experiment in constitutional adaptability that the institutionalization of presidential representation had yielded. How did those doubts affect Congress's reconsideration of the institutional presidency? To what extent could Congress change or roll back presidential authority across different policy areas? These are the questions addressed in the chapters of part 2.

Chapters 7–10 examine the consequences of the decline of the idea of presidential representation, consider the extent to which the opposing claims of congressional representation and constitutionality had leverage over reform, and compare the durability of presidential authority within and across the policy areas of budgeting, trade, employment, reorganization, and national security. These chapters demonstrate that, with doubts about presidential representation prevalent, earlier reforms were left more susceptible to charges of illegitimacy. The variation in pushback partly reflected degrees of vulnerability to a constitutional critique. Presidential authority perceived as intruding on Congress's Article I legislative powers—including in budgeting, trade, reorganization, and employment—would face significant pushback. The results of that pushback, however, varied. On balance, Congress was more likely to bolster its own capacity or the authority of other institutions in an effort to rival or even diminish the significance of the president's authority. Outright reversions of presidential authority were rare, and in trade, presidential authority even received a boost. At the same time, presidential authority over the executive branch, foreign affairs, and national security was viewed through the lens of Article II by many members of Congress and proved resilient.

Congressional Pushback against Presidential Budgeting

When the rights of the Congress are in any way impinged upon, it is the rights of the people that are being affected. We represent the people and I hope we will take the responsibility upon ourselves to get our house in order so we can retain and fully exercise our power of the purse.

REPRESENTATIVE JAMIE WHITTEN (D-MS), 1973[1]

The 1970s began with a new push toward presidentialism in budgeting. Presidential authority over the executive branch, particularly over the appropriations requests made by agencies and departments, had already been enhanced as a result of the passage of the Budget and Accounting Act (BAA) of 1921, the relocation of the Bureau of the Budget (BOB) into the Executive Office of the President (EOP) in 1939, and Congress's decision to pull back from an attempt to create a legislative budget in 1946.[2] Republican president Richard Nixon went further, seeking to increase his influence over federal spending in two ways.

One move was organizational. Using presidential reorganization authority in 1970, Nixon reorganized the BOB—the principal component of the institutional presidency created by the BAA of 1921—into a new Office of Management and Budget (OMB). The OMB was to become "a center for policy formulation."[3] Beyond the "budget function," the OMB would have an enhanced role in "fiscal analysis." Nixon invoked a familiar justification for his action to Congress, stating, "The national interest requires it."[4] The OMB's expanded role promised to make the bureaucracy more responsive to the presidential viewpoint.[5]

The second move was to alter and expand the use of impoundments. While many presidents had withheld funds for some small appropriations, Nixon's actions were of a different magnitude. He targeted congressional appropriations amounting to a significant portion of the federal budget, gutting programs for infrastructure, the environment, and social welfare in the name of the national interest. This was not trimming around the margins; it was a claim of authority to dismantle programs established by Congress and defy the will of legislators.[6] With a resounding reelection victory in 1972, winning forty-nine of the fifty states, Nixon dared Congress to second-guess who spoke for the nation.

But Congress was no longer buying it.[7] The move toward greater presidential control over the budget process proved short-lived, halted by the passage of the Congressional Budget and Impoundment Control Act (CBICA) of 1974.[8] In part, the law was an immediate response to Nixon's OMB reorganization and extensive use of presidential impoundments. Thus, the law restricted the use of impoundments by establishing a process for the president to secure congressional approval for any rescission of funds or to specify circumstances for any fund deferrals. Two of the principal components of the statute, however, sought a more significant change in the long-standing institutional arrangements of budgeting between Congress and the presidency. The aim was to change the relative balance of power between the legislative and executive branches and to tilt things back in Congress's favor.

One reform touched on the president's agenda-setting authority in budgeting. The establishment of a congressional budget process and creation of new budget committees in each congressional chamber indicated Congress's intent to develop an agenda of its own. Newly fortified with the institutional wherewithal to create a "congressional" budget for the nation, legislators would no longer have to work within parameters set by the president. To be sure, there were limits to this pushback. The president's own authority to submit a budget to Congress was not rescinded. The new budget process did not displace the old one; it was an add-on, a new reform layered somewhat awkwardly over the old one. Nonetheless, its key features were designed to strengthen the legislators' hands and increase congressional power. A new Congressional Budget Office (CBO) was to evaluate the president's proposal for Congress. New House and Senate budget committees would pass their own budget resolutions for consideration in their respective chambers. Once each chamber passed its concurrent resolution on the budget, a conference committee would negotiate a final budget to be approved by Congress in a reconciliation process (avoiding the possibility of a Senate filibuster). The final bill would then be presented to the president for approval or veto.

A second set of reforms looked to match the president's organizational capacity. The CBO was to give Congress its own budgetary expertise, reducing its dependence on the information provided by the OMB. Moreover, in another law passed that year, Congress sought to increase its own influence on the OMB by requiring Senate consent for the director and deputy director, ending the ability of the president to select his own budget advisers without congressional input. All told, the pushback against the president's budgetary powers may have had the ironic effect of moving the OMB further toward Nixon's alternative conception of the agency as a strong arm of administrative management and presidential control over the rest of the executive branch. The emphasis on management would soon become manifest in the rise of regulatory review.[9]

Congress had established the president's initiative in the budget process in 1921, so what prompted its efforts to pull back on that arrangement in 1974? Existing accounts that seek to explain the development of the institutional presidency would not predict Congress's reaction against presidential budgeting. First, explanations focusing on Congress's collective action problem in budgeting—the difficulties of getting 535 legislators to focus on keeping spending under control—would not envisage Congress's efforts to diminish the significance of the presidential budget.[10] Between 1921 and 1974, Congress had not suddenly cured itself of the challenges of having so many legislators involved in the budgeting process. Yet legislators nonetheless decided to alter the institutional process that had been meant to solve that collective action problem. Second, accounts emphasizing the role of information—arguing that Congress would give the president control over new informational capacities to ensure their use—also would not predict the outcome of the 1974 law.[11] Specifically, Congress decided to create the CBO in order to give the legislative branch its own separate source of expertise, independent of the president and executive branch. Finally, the outcome of the 1974 law also cannot be explained on the basis of partisanship. Although the legislation was indeed passed in a period of divided government, the votes in both the House and the Senate were thoroughly bipartisan.[12] Moreover, notwithstanding the Republican in the White House, many of the primary proponents of the budget reforms were Republican legislators. Nixon, who had previously opposed and threatened to veto congressional budget reform, agreed to the act only weeks before resigning as a result of Watergate.[13]

An ideational account provides the link between the earlier creation of the presidential budget in 1921 and the later congressional pushback in 1974. The declining legitimacy of presidential representation was essential to this change. Of course, doubts about this idea's validity were hastened by the Watergate scandal. But legislators did not seek to constrain only Nixon; he was out of office soon enough. Rather, legislators acted to diminish the budget authority of all presidents thereafter. The effort sought to reaffirm Congress's claim to represent the nation and to reassert the constitutional prerogatives of the legislative branch in budgeting.

This chapter proceeds as follows. First, I detail how rising doubts about the validity of presidential representation had a direct impact on legislators' changing perceptions of presidential budgeting. Second, I examine the extent to which claims about congressional representation and constitutional prerogatives influenced the reform. Finally, I offer an overview of the long-term effects of the 1974 reforms and the limitations Congress faced even in utilizing its new budget process.

Applicability: Doubting the President's National Perspective

The questions raised about the validity of presidential representation in the general political discourse of the early 1970s had significant implications for presidential budgeting. Whatever their stance on the desirability of potential congressional budget reform, legislators recognized that the president's role in the budget process was intertwined with the assumption of presidential representation. While opponents of Congress's efforts would continue to invoke that assumption, proponents of congressionally oriented reform viewed doubts about whether the president could be counted on to act in the national interest as applicable to budgeting.

Defenders of presidential budget authority spoke of the president's responsibility as a national steward in language that the earlier Progressives would have recognized. President Nixon justified his role in budgeting, including his extensive use of impoundments, by asserting that he was the only institutional actor possessing a national perspective. "Congress represents special interests," Nixon argued, but "I am going to stand for that general interest."[14] This also was the official stance of the Nixon administration. "Congress represents many interests and, at times, speaks for each of them," Deputy Attorney General Joseph Sneed testified to lawmakers. Sneed chided legislators that their purported representation of local interests meant that Congress could not control the overall budget: "the correlative weakness of this strength is its frequent inability to pursue integrated fiscal policies which will keep taxes in proper step with expenditures."[15] Administration officials invoked these types of claims in correspondence with legislators as well. Calling for fiscal restraint in federal employee pay in a letter to the Senate majority leader, Mike Mansfield (D-MT), OMB director Roy Ash portrayed the president as attempting to guide Congress to a focus on the national interest: "I trust the Senate will support the President's recommendation in the best interests of all Americans."[16] Lawmakers who supported Nixon's impoundments turned to the same justification. Senator Milton Young (R-ND) asserted that legislators were still too localistic in their orientation: "the proper thing for any Member of Congress to do is to spend more, more for more programs. He could be elected forever doing that."[17]

Invocations of presidential representation worried some critics who had grown skeptical of the idea's validity. Senator J. William Fulbright (D-AR) fretted that citizens might not recognize Congress's stake in budgeting and would view legislators as petty for pushing back against presidential authority. "I have a feeling," he warned, "that many people think we as members of the House and Senate are just being quarrelsome about our personal prerogatives, that we are not really concerned about the Constitution or the government. . . . That is the feeling I get and I don't know what to do about it." Fulbright was pessimistic that Congress could fight against impoundments and for budget reform if the debate centered on whether the president better represented the national interest: "[The president] will say it is improvident, that it is special interests. . . . He can say he is representing a national interest and no special interest."[18] A lawmaker in the House agreed. "In the current confrontation between Congress and the White House, the Executive is pictured as clear, precise, exact, and prudent when it comes to budgetary matters," lamented Representative Samuel Stratton (D-NY), whereas "Congress, on the other hand, is pictured as profligate, bumbling, inexact, sloppy, and devoid of any capacity for tight managerial control."[19]

Fulbright and Stratton need not have worried. Both Republican and Democratic lawmakers made it clear that they would not be cowed by that claim. The dissent among the Republicans was especially notable given that a member of their party occupied the White House. While the Senate minority leader, Hugh Scott (R-PA), blandly asserted that "despite impoundment[s], the Republic will continue to survive," other legislators in his party did not follow his lead.[20] One particularly notable discontent was Senator Bill Brock (R-TN), a leading advocate of congressional budget reform. Congress, not the presidency, argued Senator Brock, was "the branch of government which is most directly reflective and responsive to the American people" and was therefore "their instrument of reform."[21] More pointedly, Representative Victor Veysey (R-CA) argued that Congress could not simply assume that the president would produce a better overall budget: "the time has passed when we can pass that responsibility to the White House and expect the President to balance the budget."[22]

More predictably, Democrats criticized the president. Nonetheless, it was significant that they did so by directly questioning the validity of presidential representation. Senator Thomas McIntyre (D-NH) implied that the president was not a responsible steward of the nation's finances, writing to a New Hampshire constituent that "the President's proposed budgets for the past four years have recommended a deficit of over $100 billion dollars—certainly the largest, by far, for any comparable period in our history."[23] Others took on the claim with a degree of humor. Senator Sam Ervin (D-NC) questioned the idea by suggesting that the collective election of lawmakers gave Congress the same claim to representing the nation as the president. "Aren't Members of the Senate and the Members of the House elected by exactly the same people that elected the President?" he asked rhetorically. "That is my impression," Senator Fulbright replied dryly.[24] Ervin then suggested that the president should read "Dale Carnegie's book on 'How to Win Friends and Influence People'" but later observed that Nixon could not yet have "read the volume on winning friends, for he still makes such uncomplimentary remarks such as saying that Congress represents special interests."[25]

Despite the levity, congressional Democrats were determined to push back on the president's claim. One of the most direct confrontations over this claim was between Senator Edmund Muskie (D-ME) and OMB director Ash during congressional hearings on budget reform. Muskie took Ash to task for repeating Nixon's claim about presidential representation. Repudiating the notion, Muskie asserted that presidents could be beholden to special interests:

> Now, would the President demand executive power on the grounds that this Congress is influenced by special interest groups? I resent that. And I must say that a statement on your part is a temptation to me to pursue that line with respect to examples of special influence in the executive branch. . . . On my part I believe we are [as] motivated by the general interest, as anyone in the executive branch, and I think it ill becomes the executive branch beginning with its principal spokesman, the President, to accuse Congress of being primarily motivated by such special interest considerations.[26]

House Speaker Carl Albert (D-OK) also took on the administration's claim, depicting such criticism of Congress as invalid. "The President seems to have no sense of duty to the people who he is supposed to represent," Albert observed, even though he "talks about Congress being controlled by special interests and likes to present himself as the defender of the public interests." Albert contended that "those special interests" that Nixon attacked as influencing legislators "turn out to be school children who need books to read and nutritional food to eat; older Americans who can't afford to go to the hospital; and urban residents who can't find or afford a decent place to live."[27] In Albert's telling, it was the president who was out of touch with the needs of his own national constituency.

A variety of other figures shared legislators' skepticism of the validity of presidential representation in budgeting. The Georgia state superintendent of schools, Jack Nix, took the opportunity of testifying before Congress to rebut President Nixon's claim. "I know the President has said that 'the Congress represents special interests,' and that he 'represents the nation's general interest,'" he stated, but "I suggest that the President's impoundment of these particular [education] funds is testimony that the opposite is true."[28] Perhaps most strikingly, the Federal Reserve chairman Arthur Burns, appointed by Nixon to that position, testified to Congress about "the importance of not centralizing power too much in any one place," confessing, "I sometimes feel, perhaps, too much power has been given to the President."[29]

Leverage: Rethinking Constitutional Relationships

In November 1965, NBC News aired a television special report titled "Congress Needs Help." Signaling initial cracks in the foundation of the idea of presidential representation, the written study commissioned for the special report made the case for the importance of localistic congressional representation in budgeting. "If the Presidency were the only representative institution in the political system," it stated, "disadvantaged groups in the society would have far less ability to make their grievances known." Representatives and senators, being "highly sensitive to . . . the views and grievances" of their constituents, offered "a sensitive and continuous reading of public interests." When "majority coalitions are formed in Congress," the report continued, "much more than a bare majority of the population is represented in the coalition." Calling for the establishment of a "joint committee on fiscal policy to provide a comprehensive view of federal revenue and expense" and the creation of "an analytical budget information service," the report previewed the prescriptions that became the basis for the institutional reforms of the 1974 law.[30]

It also previewed part of the intellectual rationale behind these changes. The Vietnam conflict and Watergate, along with Nixon's aggressive actions in budgeting, had changed perceptions of how much presidents could be counted on to act in the national interest. With that idea in question, lawmakers and others reasserted counterclaims—that Congress was the superior representative of the people and that it constitutionally possessed the power of the purse—that proponents of presidential representation had overcome with substantial success decades before.[31] In considering budget reforms, Congress moved beyond just criticizing the rise in presidential impoundments and questioned the wisdom of the entire system established by the BAA of 1921.

CONGRESSIONAL REPRESENTATION:
THE PEOPLE'S BRANCH

In discussing the need for greater congressional authority in budgeting, legislators from both parties did not just question the president's claim to represent the national interest. They also reasserted the collective claim of Congress to represent the nation. As the party in control of Congress, Democrats were of course eager to assert the representative claim of the legislative branch. Senator Walter "Dee" Huddleston (D-KY) put the point succinctly: "Congress represents the will of our people much more directly than the executive branch."[32] Representative Ogden Reid (D-NY) warned that "the people's branch of the government—notably the House—can increasingly become irrelevant if we don't have certain powers of the purse refurbished and restored."[33] "Nothing," asserted Representative Stratton, "is more important today to the continued survival and vitality of the Congress as the people's branch of the Federal Government than that we should find the means to achieve absolute control over the Nation's budgetary practices."[34]

Despite being in the minority in Congress, key Republicans made similar claims. One of the leading Republican supporters of budget reform made the claim of Congress's ability to represent the nation as fervently as any Democratic legislator. "We have the opportunity now," argued Senator Brock, "to restore congressional prerogatives of the people's branch. It is the people's branch." Brock called for new institutional arrangements to ensure that it would be "the legislative branch that does establish the national priorities of this Nation."[35]

Public claims of the superiority of congressional representation were echoed in legislators' correspondence as well. In response to a citizen from Minnesota who supported Nixon's impoundments, Senator Muskie disputed Nixon's claim to a superior representation of the nation compared to Congress. "I am quite well aware that President Nixon won reelection, and has the approval of the people of this country," wrote Muskie. "However," he continued, "Congress, which . . . appropriated the funds, also was elected by the same voters, and presumably also has their approval." Congress was the proper branch "to set national priorities by establishing spending levels for various programs."[36] Senate majority leader Mansfield received letters from his Democratic Caucus colleagues that also emphasized Congress's own claim to represent the nation in budgeting. Senator Russell Long (D-LA) wrote that Congress was the branch "charged with determining national priorities."[37] And Senator Thomas Eagleton (D-MO) stated that it was "incumbent upon us to make every effort to change budget priorities to align them with the current needs of the people and the nation."[38]

The importance of Congress's claim to represent the nation in budget reform was echoed in the wider public sphere as well. "If you can develop procedures that will enable Members of Congress to vote on an overall fiscal policy that adequately reflects congressional priorities," Federal Reserve chairman Burns testified to lawmakers, "you will revitalize representative government in this country."[39] For the *New York Times*, reform would be an opportunity for Congress itself to stand for the nation as a whole. An editorial suggested that the new congressional budget process "should help put public interest above special interests in shaping the Federal budget, the focal point of national economic, social and military decision-making."[40]

CONSTITUTIONAL AUTHORITY:
THE POWER OF THE PURSE

While legislators asserted their own claims to represent the nation better than the president, that claim could still be contested. Less ambiguous was a more formalistic claim, an assertion that budget reform was necessary to allow Congress to restore its Article I constitutional power of the purse. Critics charged that Nixon's use of impoundments violated this power. While a president might legitimately impound funds for an "item appropriation," wrote one journalist, "it is quite another thing for a President to use the impoundment of appropriated funds offensively or aggressively—as Mr. Nixon is now doing—to change the whole direction of government and to nullify legally legislated policies without resort to accepted constitutional practice."[41]

Critics of presidential power in budgeting also went beyond targeting impoundments. In both parties, legislators suggested that the system established by the BAA of 1921 had gone too far in the presidential direction and that a restoration of Congress's constitutional authority was required. Senator Edward Gurney (R-FL) placed blame for presidential budgetary pretensions on congressional delegation: "The blame for the crisis of power in which we find ourselves must be placed upon ourselves, the Congress. We have given discretionary budget authority to the executive through such legislative precedents as . . . the Budget and Accounting Act of 1921."[42] Similarly, Senator Robert Byrd (D-WV) pointed to the BAA as the genesis of the slippage of congressional spending powers: "In the more than 50 years since the Budget and Accounting Act was passed the Congress has permitted its 'power of the purse' under the Constitution gradually to slip away or diminish."[43] While

"the Executive branch has acquired almost the whole of the initiative in matters involving coordination of federal financial policy," noted Senate majority
leader Mansfield in a meeting of Senate Democrats, "that is not as it should
be under the Constitution."[44]

Such claims marked a decisive turn away from the more critical views
of constitutional formalism held by many presidency-oriented reformers in
prior decades. Formalistic reasoning was now invoked by both Republican
and Democratic lawmakers to support Congress's budget reform. Representative Richard Fulton (D-TN) compared the president's claim of standing
for the people unfavorably with the authority of the Constitution: "Others in
our Government claim to be operating under mandates from the people. Let
us not fail to remember that the ideals of our Constitution are a mandate of
unassailable veracity."[45] "At stake is the constitutional role of the Congress as
the guardian of the Treasury," asserted Representative Joel Pritchard (R-WA):
"Article I, section 9, of the Constitution clearly assigns the spending power
to the Congress."[46] The legislation promised "a reversal of the accelerating
erosion of the congressional purse power," enthused Senator Charles Percy
(R-IL), promising nothing short of "a reassertion of our correct role in the
American plan of government."[47]

Legislators even invoked the framers' original constitutional meaning.
"Our Constitution's framers understood best how to avoid tyranny," declared
Senator Lawton Chiles (D-FL).[48] "Our Founding Fathers expected," asserted
Representative John Zwach (R-MN), "that we as men of stature would also
assume the full weight of responsibility and do our share to keep the budget
and the country fiscally sound."[49] Such claims were also invoked out of the
public spotlight. Writing to a California resident, Senator Muskie emphasized that Congress's "obligation under the Constitution is to set national
priorities in spending," which was "not an obligation that the executive can
demand for itself, nor is it one that Congress can abdicate."[50] Legislation to
create a congressional budget process, wrote Senator Ervin to Senator Mansfield, would "restore the balance and establish the necessary machinery to enable the Congress to handle its constitutional role in controlling spending."[51]
"Certainly," Senator Harrison Williams (D-NJ) likewise wrote to Mansfield,
"Congress' position should be preeminent in this process as was intended
under the Constitution."[52]

This turn toward formalism in budgeting also occurred in the wider public sphere. The New York Times stressed that "in this country, Congressional
supremacy on fiscal matters is clearly set forth in the Constitution and in
the Federalist papers." Rather than arguing for congressional budgeting "in
ideological or programmatic terms as a liberal might," the Times emphasized

that the debate should focus on "the enduring place of Congress in a stable constitutional order."[53] In a protest on Capitol Hill by three thousand elderly citizens wearing "Senior Power" buttons, Nelson Cruikshank, the president of the National Council of Senior Citizens, called for Congress to "stand up like men and take back the powers given to you by the Constitution."[54]

And perhaps most strikingly, former executive branch officials also spoke of the need for Congress to reassert its constitutional authority. Robert Mayo, the president of the Federal Reserve Bank of Chicago and a former BOB director, told Congress that it had "an opportunity to restore the congressional share of overall fiscal responsibility to its rightful place in the balance of governmental powers."[55] Another former BOB director, Charles Schultze, warned that it was "absolutely vital for the Congress to get its hands around its own budget" to avoid "the power of the purse [becoming] less and less important."[56] "Congress will never reach its constitutional place in our system of government," wrote former secretary of the treasury Joseph Barr to Speaker Albert, "unless it adopts a unified rather than a fragmented approach" to budgeting.[57]

A CONGRESSIONAL BUDGET PROCESS

For lawmakers, the reassertion of Congress's representational claims and insistence on its constitutional authority was not just rhetoric. The move to restrict the president's use of impoundments by requiring congressional approval for proposed rescissions within forty-five days and limiting any deferrals of funds showed Congress's intent. Indeed, efforts by defenders of presidential budgeting to approve of the use of presidential impoundments failed. When Senator William Roth (R-DE) sought to amend the congressional budget bill to allow the president to impound funds unless Congress specifically voted to approve release of the money, his fellow partisans, Senator Percy and Senator Jacob Javits (R-NY), joined with Senator Ervin to defeat the amendment.[58]

Beyond the issue of impoundments, the terms of the debate about budgeting made it clear that the 1974 legislation would be a test of the extent to which the claims that opposed presidential representation—that Congress best represented the people and that it possessed the constitutional power of the purse—could be made practical in institutional expression. The first way this was achieved was to create a separate congressional budget process. The statute sought to allow Congress to enhance its own agenda-setting authority and increase its ability to focus on the budget in holistic, as opposed to piecemeal, fashion. The new House and Senate budget committees would propose budgets for their respective chambers to consider as concurrent resolutions, and a final budget, negotiated by a conference committee, would be voted on by the Congress through the reconciliation process.[59]

The president's budget initiative, dating back to the BAA of 1921, was viewed as having granted the president a significant advantage in setting the agenda. Congressional lawmakers from both parties were acutely aware of the institution's previous reliance on budgets presented by the president. Because "the very impact of [the president's] budget is so powerful," asserted Senator Hubert Humphrey (D-MN), "it is 95 percent passed by the time it gets here."[60] "Congress has relied too heavily upon the national budget prepared by the Executive Branch," concurred Representative Jack Brooks (D-TX), and "in practice, that budget has all too often become equivalent to a determination of national priorities."[61] Republicans agreed with their Democratic colleagues. "All of us must share the blame," said Representative Paul Findley (R-IL): "We have tended to take the easy way out. It is easier to appropriate money piecemeal from the President's budget requests than to adopt a budget ourselves."[62] "We have been in the habit of operating generally within the parameters set by the Executive," admitted Representative Robert Bauman (R-MD).[63]

Lawmakers did not react to their past reliance on the presidential budget by rescinding the president's authority. Instead, the proposed congressional budget process was envisioned by legislators in both parties as a way to counter the president's budget and make it less determinative of national priorities. Indicting the earlier BAA of 1921, Representative Charles Thone (R-NE) argued that such a reform was "more than 50 years overdue. . . . When Congress 52 years ago gave the executive branch power to control all agency requests and to prepare an overall budget, a capability to cope with overall budgets should also have been given to the legislative branch."[64] "Congress in the past has left basic budget decisions to the Executive," Speaker Albert told the Democratic Study Group, but "this bill represents a reclaiming of budgetary authority from the Executive."[65] "Our spending," enthused Representative Wayne Owens (D-UT), "can be based on a congressional budget each year, rather than a Presidential document."[66] The new budget process, emphasized Representative Bauman, would "place the Congress in the driver's seat."[67] Indeed, legislators connected this reclamation of budgetary initiative to their broader congressional project of pushing back against presidential government. "If Congress is to regain control of Government," argued Senator Henry Bellmon (R-OK), "it is absolutely essential that we first seize control of the budgetary and appropriations process."[68]

The establishment of budget committees in each chamber was viewed as a way to make Congress itself more effective at focusing on national priorities. It signified a direct attempt to respond to the chief argument for presidential representation, which held that legislators could serve only local interests. Representative Joel Broyhill (R-VA) explained that Congress needed to match the president's claim of focusing on the whole nation:

> The executive branch is forced to view the budget in terms of overall objectives. It must weigh priorities, and make choices which are consistent with policy goals, the economy and other public considerations. . . . In contrast, the Congress has allowed its own budgetary procedure to be fragmented and uncoordinated. . . . The achievements of the Joint Study Committee on Budget Control represent a major guidepost in helping us find our way out of the fiscal maze in which we have wandered like some blind giant for so many years.[69]

"In place of the present loosely coordinated process," stressed Representative Howard Robison (R-NY), the new congressional budget process would provide "the capability to treat the budget as a whole entity and to recommend a correspondence between expenditures and revenues."[70] The act, concurred Representative Harold Donohue (D-MA), "responds to the need for the Congress to restore to itself its separate power to determine and declare priorities in national spending."[71] Representative Brooks even rebuked the claim that the president was entitled to any kind of privileged agenda-setting authority on the basis of possessing a national perspective: "The ordering of national priorities is not an Executive function, but a Legislative function."[72]

Other current and former officials in the federal government testified to Congress about the importance of providing an institutional means to take an overall view of budgeting. Under the existing process, opined Arthur Burns, the Fed chairman, lawmakers "have no opportunity to express the wishes of their constituents on choices such as what total expenditures should be. . . . Choices of this type are of greater importance to the electorate as a whole than the single proposals on which congressional votes actually occur."[73] Asked by Representative Al Ullman (D-OR) whether he agreed with "our effort to establish a mechanism in Congress whereby Congress would establish an overall program of revenues and expenditures, and thereby have a mechanism for fitting the parts into the whole," Burns replied, "I endorse that wholeheartedly. I think it is absolutely essential."[74] Former BOB director Schultze also implored Congress to develop its own process by which it could take a holistic view on the budget: "A process has to be devised which makes the individual spending actions of the Congress consistent with a reasonable total and, conversely, makes sure that the total which Congress authorizes and votes is consistent with the individual actions." As Schultze observed, this would allow Congress to better match the president's budget: "In the executive branch, whether you like the results or not, at least that is done."[75]

As the budget committees were being set up after the passage of the 1974 law, the refrain of taking a national perspective continued to be a major theme for legislators. As Edmund Muskie prepared to lead the new Senate Budget Committee, he explained the importance of this to his new committee colleagues in a memo: "the Committee must develop within itself the capacity to make and support its policy decisions on budget priorities. The Committee will undoubtedly be called upon to defend whatever position it takes in setting national priorities."[76] On the House side, the effort of Representative Bella Abzug (D-NY) to gain a seat on the new House Budget Committee expressed a wider conception of congressional representation. Writing to Speaker Albert, Abzug first emphasized a pluralistic view of representing urban interests: "As a Representative from the most populated urban area in the nation, I believe I can bring to the Budget Committee an awareness of urban needs and problems that will be essential in helping the Committee to plan a fair and well-balanced budget." At the same time, recognizing the spirit behind the new law, she hastened to add, "In addition, I have occasion to be in touch with all sections of the country and the population and feel that I can add a national perspective to the Committee's planning."[77]

The new congressional budget process responded to the claims that legislators made in response to the declining legitimacy of presidential representation and gave those ideas new institutional form. Still, the reform also indicated limits to Congress's pushback against presidential authority. While the CBICA "reorganizes our procedures to wield effectively the [budget] power which is ours," Senator Percy noted, "we do not interfere with the President's ability to formulate his own budget recommendations."[78] Another potential limit was the reconciliation process. Ironically, permitting the budget to bypass a Senate filibuster would become a tool to allow major legislation pushed by the president to pass Congress on a majority vote. Finally, the new budget committees did not displace the role and authority of other relevant committees, such as Appropriations. The result was "recurrent jurisdictional conflict."[79]

THE CONGRESSIONAL BUDGET OFFICE

Improving Congress's power relative to the presidency was also the principal goal of the other reform in the 1974 law. Just as Congress sought to match and rival the president's initiative in budgeting by creating its own congressional budget process, it also sought to correct another imbalance in organizational capacity. Lawmakers were tired of relying on the OMB for budget estimates and wanted a budgetary office of their own. Thus, the second key reform of the 1974 law was the establishment of the Congressional Budget Office.

Members of Congress from both parties expressed resentment of the OMB, viewing it purely as a tool of presidential power. Responding to the idea of having Congress rely on the OMB's figures for its new budget process, Senator Brock warned, "I am afraid it would rather than enhance the power of Congress, diminish it. . . . It would place us, as we are today, at the disposal and the mercy of a huge and talented staff for which we have no counterpart to give us alternative suggestions."[80] Instead, argued Senator Humphrey, Congress needed to "be in a position to act independently, to make our own choices, gather our own data, do our own analysis, and propose our own policy alternatives."[81] Senator Javits advocated creating what would be, "in effect, a Budget Bureau responsible to the Congress."[82] "We need our own congressional office of management and budget if the Congress is to be on equal footing with the White House," implored Senator George McGovern (D-SD) more bluntly.[83]

The broad role Congress envisioned for the CBO, helping legislators to have a more national perspective, was elaborated on by Senator Lee Metcalf (D-MT). The CBO would have several functions. Most obviously, the office's "primary responsibility" would be to assist with the dual budget proposals. It would "service the budget committees in their analysis of the President's budget" and help with "their development of the legislative budget resolutions." The CBO would also have a "scorekeeping function," evaluating proposed bills for their potential effects on government revenue and spending. Furthermore, the CBO would offer a projection "with respect to the economic impact of alternative levels of revenues and spending for the coming fiscal year to provide Members with a range of information by which they may determine what would be the appropriate deficit or surplus in light of the economy." Here too, the aim was to provide "every Member with an economic analysis independent of the Executive—of spending and revenue alternatives—including revenue losses attributable to tax expenditures.[84] Of course, the authority of the CBO in conducting these analyses would depend on its perceived objectivity and expertise. As Robert Mayo, the Chicago Federal Reserve Bank president testified, the institution would need to be "a highly professional group, beholden to no one except its own dedication to objectivity of budget policy."[85]

THE OFFICE OF MANAGEMENT AND BUDGET

Along with passing the CBICA of 1974, Congress passed a law in the same year amending the BAA of 1921 to make the OMB director and deputy director positions subject to Senate confirmation.[86] With this act, Congress indicated its recognition of the growing role of the OMB as an arm of presidential power, and it sought to grant itself some additional degree of influence over that part of the institutional presidency. However, considering the intensity of criticism legislators directed at the OMB as being subservient to the president, the challenge was limited.

The battle to set a new requirement that the OMB leadership receive Senate confirmation did briefly take aim at the OMB as an institution. In the midst of Congress's debate over the possibility of involving the Senate in the appointment process, President Nixon appointed Roy Ash as OMB director. With that action, Nixon filled the position before Congress had the chance to change the process. In response, the House and Senate passed a bill that would abolish the OMB entirely. The idea was then to immediately reconstitute the institution, making the leadership subject to Senate confirmation. However, Nixon vetoed the measure as a threat to the president's removal power. The Senate overrode Nixon's veto, reflecting the chamber's hostility toward the OMB, but the House failed to do so. As a result, revised legislation, applying only to future directors and deputy directors, was then passed.[87]

Lawmakers' efforts to adjust the requirement for the OMB's leadership stemmed from their concerns over the institution's growing power. Senator Metcalf, sponsoring the confirmation measure, said that the OMB had "become a superdepartment with life or death powers over the expenditure of funds, the development of programs, the management of Government, and the careers of Federal employees." "This is not any academic exercise in political science as to appointment powers with respect to the President's office," he asserted, but instead was an issue of "the exaggerated power of the executive branch."[88] "It is plain," bemoaned Senator McGovern, "that the Office of Management and Budget has evolved as a priorities-and-political arm of the White House, with a single loyalty to the President."[89] Writing to a Maine constituent, Senator Muskie stressed, "The Directorship of OMB is the second-most important office under this Administration."[90]

Despite this recognition, the best Congress felt it could do in this realm was to make the officers subject to Senate confirmation. "The purpose of this legislation," affirmed Representative Brooks, "is to reinstate the constitutional right, obligation, and responsibility of the Congress to evaluate the qualifications of the two top officers in what has become possibly the most powerful office in the executive branch, second only to the President him-self."[91] The OMB "deserves Senate confirmation of its top officers even more" than many other parts of the executive branch, argued Representative Chet Holifield (D-CA), "considering its vital role and far-reaching influence in governmental affairs."[92] At the same time, lawmakers recognized their limi-tations in addressing OMB's power. Reacting to the assertion of Representa-tive John Melcher (D-MT) that there had been "a gradual accumulation of awesome power" at the OMB, Representative Frank Horton (R-NY) noted that, in an essential sense, the OMB's managerial authority now inherently belonged to the president: "I think the concern you have, John, is that the awesomeness is the awesomeness of the Presidency." Since "the OMB role is a role that the President has," Horton observed wryly, "the only solution I see is to ask for confirmation of the President."[93] Beyond stipulating Sen-ate confirmation of the OMB leadership, there was little Congress could do to specify how the president used such a key component of the institutional presidency. Abolishing the OMB appeared a step too far.

Congress's real complaint stemmed from misunderstanding or even downplaying the congressional intent of the earlier BAA of 1921. Metcalf called the earlier BOB only a "small agency of accountants which was trans-ferred to the Executive Office from the Treasury Department some 34 years ago to help the President prepare a budget."[94] "The OMB is not some mysti-cal or magic instrument reserved exclusively for Presidential use," argued Holifield: "We should not lose sight of this basic fact: that central budgeting was developed for the convenience of the Congress."[95] The understandings of Metcalf and Holifield about the minimal presidential orientation of the BOB were belied by the reality that Congress had intended the BOB to adopt the president's perspective and to enhance the president's managerial capac-ity over the executive branch. As Representative Horton correctly pointed out, Congress had envisioned a broad role for the BOB in 1921: "At that time it was indicated that it would be an arm of the President, and it was being strengthened; it was to be given not only budget authority, but also manage-ment authority."[96] Moreover, while Holifield was right that Congress per-ceived itself as benefiting from central budgeting, that reform assumed that the president's national purview was the key to guiding Congress to a better budgetary outcome. The criticisms about presidential authority over OMB underscored how the Congress of 1974 was making decisions at a time during which it did not inherently trust presidents, while the Congress of 1921 had actively looked to the president as the agent of reform.

Ultimately, Congress's halting attempt to push back on the OMB under-scored the difficulty of rescinding the managerial power of the institutional presidency, authority that could easily fit under the president's Article II purview. While the significance of the president's budget proposal would decline after the passage of the 1974 law, the managerial role for the OMB flourished. The OMB's Office of Information and Regulatory Affairs (OIRA) enhanced presidential power over the executive branch and agency policy-making through regulatory review. This was consistent with what would become a more general shift to a formalistic understanding of the separation of powers. While the process was formalized in 1981 with an executive order by Republican president Ronald Reagan, presidents had already begun pushing to use regulatory review as a managerial tool in the 1970s. By instituting a cost-benefit analysis on any agency regulations, presidents were subsequently able to exercise more centralized control over policymaking in the executive branch. In effect, with a decline in the primacy of the presidential budget, the OMB's main function was converted into what was arguably an even more powerful role—determining the implementation of policy. Regulatory review became institutionalized as a core feature of modern presidential power.[97]

Conclusion: The Limits of Congressional Restoration

The CBICA of 1974 showed both the vulnerability of reforms based on the idea of presidential representation and the limits of Congress's attempts to restore its own authority. With the creation of a separate congressional budget process, layered over previous arrangements, the influence of the presidential budget over Congress was diminished.[98] And by giving Congress its own "information base" and providing cost estimates on proposed legislation, the CBO further eroded presidential control over budgeting.[99] Presidents and their administrations quickly recognized that change. "We are increasingly a minor player" in the budget process, noted Stuart Eizenstat, the head of the Domestic Policy Staff for Democratic president Jimmy Carter.[100] However, besides the new Senate confirmation requirement for its leadership, the OMB was left in place, and its importance to presidential authority over the executive branch and policymaking would only grow as the focus of presidential power and policymaking increasingly turned to the bureaucracy.

The experience of two later Republican presidents soon underscored the subsequent limits on the president's budgetary stewardship. At the beginning of President Reagan's first term, it briefly appeared that presidential primacy in the budget process might be restored. Congress bought into the budget proposal of OMB director David Stockman. But when that budget was shown to have relied on unrealistic GDP growth and inflation control projections, Congress—including Republican legislators—subsequently pronounced all

Reagan's budget proposals "dead on arrival." The experience cemented the practice of the presidential budget becoming more of a wish list and tool of political mobilization rather than a managerial blueprint: "The FY1983 plan initiated the practice of using unrealistic budgets as a tool of presidential power."[101] The presidential budget changed from "an authoritative guide to national policy" into more of a "bargaining chip."[102] Reagan's successor, Republican president George H. W. Bush, attempted to stand above the fray in budgeting in 1990, breaking his pledge not to raise taxes in order to come to a budget agreement with Democrats in Congress. But Bush lost reelection partly as a result, underscoring "the difficulties of depoliticizing the deficit in the cause of the national interest."[103]

Yet while Congress might have succeeded in diminishing presidential influence over the budget, it also discovered the limits it faced in restoring its own authority. Indeed, Congress's struggles to actually utilize its new budget process were foreshadowed by some proponents of the CBICA of 1974. Before Senator Muskie became the new Senate Budget Committee chairman, one adviser had bluntly warned him of the risk that the new committees would not work: "the budget committees may not work. While hopefully they will, the fact remains that they may not."[104] Representative Bauman had also presciently warned his colleagues that the institutional reforms of the CBICA would require a Congress committed to making them work as intended: "the Budget and Impoundment Control Act will give us the tools we need to approach the budgetmaking process in a responsible and organized fashion. But we must use these tools effectively. If we approach them as troublesome annoyances and work around them, then budget control will be a sham."[105]

Both warnings presaged what would become a decades-long record of poor congressional performance. Competing more successfully with the president in budgeting did not translate into congressional effectiveness. Congress almost never passed budget resolutions on time and in many years did not do so at all, relying on continuing resolutions instead. Periodic funding gaps and government shutdowns from the 1970s onward provided high-profile evidence of Congress's inability to utilize its own budget process.[106] Thus, the congressional budget process has long been viewed as fundamentally "broken," making it "difficult for Congress to serve as a responsible steward of the nation's resources."[107]

SECOND THOUGHTS: THE LINE ITEM VETO ACT OF 1996

The dysfunction of the new congressional budget process led to a reconsideration of the purported merits of presidential representation. As budget deficits grew in the 1980s and 1990s, it had become clear that Congress's priorities in budgeting were not easily aligned with deficit reduction. And as the Republican Party and a conservative ideological approach to fiscal policy came to set the terms of political debate, presidential representation became the animating idea behind a different institutional reform, drawing strength from renewed criticisms of individual legislators as being too localistic.

A line item veto was proposed to allow presidents to rescind specific items in appropriations bills, a reform that amounted to a statutory impoundment authority. Its proponents bemoaned the post-1974 budget process for having gone too far in limiting presidential authority. Though the CBICA of 1974 may have been a "necessary reaction to an imbalance in the way that the executive branch and the Congress operated in terms of spending money," posited Senator Dan Coats (R-IN), it had created "an imbalance in the other direction."[108] Legislators again spoke of their inability to take a holistic approach to budgeting. "Members of Congress will always load up appropriations bills with pork," asserted Senator Bob Dole (R-KS), so "the man in the Oval Office should be able to slice it off when there's too much fat."[109] Bemoaning fiscal mismanagement by Congress, Senator John McCain (R-AZ) wrote to Dole, "if we don't give the President [a] line item veto, we might as well take the taxpayers' money to the edge of town and burn it."[110]

A short-lived change was enacted in 1996.[111] In the aftermath of the 1994 Republican takeover of the House and Senate, Congress took up the line item veto proposal. The reform had been a part of the "Contract with America," spearheaded by Newt Gingrich (R-GA), which had also pledged Republicans to a balanced budget amendment. Though Democratic president Bill Clinton was in office, Republican legislators nonetheless embraced the logic of presidential representation in response to what they viewed as the failure of the congressional budget process. "We need to allow the President—even a Democratic one—the ability to veto waste and pork or line items that have not been properly considered or sufficiently justified," stated Senator Trent Lott (R-MS).[112] "The line-item veto bill," argued Senator Bob Smith (R-NH), "will give the President—who has a national constituency with a national interest—the tool he needs to cut projects that serve a narrow constituency with a special interest."[113] While many Democrats opposed the reform, some key legislators offered support. "The line-item veto will give the President a tool, if he chooses to use it, to raise the profile of wasteful, special-interest spending—to expose it to the light of public scrutiny," suggested Senator Joe Biden (D-DE).[114] Upon signing the act into law, President Clinton affirmed this logic, stating that the tool would "permit Presidents to better represent the public interest."[115]

This was a striking reversal of fortune for presidential representation. The idea's resurgence in budgeting arose from the combined limitations of the congressional budget process and the increased political focus on deficits. But even for many supporters of the reform, the post-1970s doubts about counting on the president to represent the national interest remained. Senator John Chafee (R-RI) admitted that the "potential for abuse by the President is great."[116] Senator Biden also elaborated on his ambivalence, explaining why he opposed an alternative plan to pass the line item veto as a constitutional amendment. Such a move, Biden warned, would commit the government to an "unknown and practically unalterable course and fundamentally shift the balance of power in a way that could not, absent another amendment, be changed back." For Biden, the possibility of presidential abuse was a significant concern: "We now have Presidents who are viewed as not being vindictive or not strong enough or weak . . . but we will have another Lyndon Johnson down the road. We will have another Franklin Roosevelt or Richard Nixon in the heydays."[117] These concerns were also invoked by opponents of the line item veto. In his testimony to Congress, Robert Reischauer, the CBO director, expressed skepticism of the validity of presidential representation: "history suggests that Presidents who support reductions in one area in the budget often favor increases in other areas. They would then be expected to use the item veto to free up resources provided in appropriation bills and redirect them to spending on their own priorities."[118]

Arguments against presidential representation and in favor of congressional representation were insufficient to prevent the reform. Instead, the reform proved more vulnerable to critiques on formalist grounds. Indeed, even as the law passed by a comfortable margin, legislators were well aware that a statutory line item veto might face constitutional problems.[119] Senator Byrd, a veteran of the 1974 budget fight, reminded his colleagues that "the control over the purse is the ultimate power to be exercised by the legislative branch to check the executive."[120] Representative Paul Kanjorski (D-PA) complained that "there seems to be a basic distrust for the basic document, the Constitution of the United States."[121]

The Supreme Court soon held that this new innovation associated with presidential representation had strayed too far from the constitutional structure. The Line Item Veto Act of 1996 was struck down in *Clinton v. City of New York* (1998) as a violation of the presentment clause. As Justice John Paul Stevens wrote for the majority, the line item veto essentially allowed the president to amend laws that had already passed. "There is no provision in the Constitution," he noted, "that authorizes the President to enact, to amend, or to repeal statutes." Moreover, "the Article I procedures governing statutory enactment were the product of the great debates and compromises that produced the Constitution itself."[122] An "ecstatic" Senator Byrd declared it "a great day for the Constitution of the United States," while Representative David Skaggs (D-CO) opined that "the Supreme Court has saved Congress from itself."[123]

AN ENDURING CRITIQUE

Once again, institutions associated with presidential representation in budgeting had proven vulnerable to formalist critiques. Congress's preeminence in budgeting from the Constitution was underscored again by the court's decision, leaving those who sought a line item veto to wrestle with how to make it pass constitutional muster.[124] Presidential influence in determining federal spending priorities would remain diminished. "The president's budget is just a nice book," Representative Bill Flores (R-TX) said of Republican president Donald Trump's proposed budget in 2018: "It's good to know where their priorities are, but the ones that make a difference are the ones here."[125]

Yet while the president's budget initiative became a less influential agenda-setting lever, this also afforded presidents a different opportunity for a more partisan era. With less influence came less responsibility. Presidents can signal priorities and use the budget as a negotiating tactic, all while pinning any budgetary problems on Congress. In effect, Congress is now indicted politically for asserting its constitutional prerogatives without delivering, while presidents can lecture legislators about their parochial irresponsibility in comparison to their own national perspective.

In the end, the twisted course of these developments appeared to leave Congress boxed in on all sides. The budget debates of the early 1970s show that institutional arrangements that rely on the idea of presidential representation are vulnerable to dismissal on any and all evidence that the president cannot be counted on to act in the national interest. Moreover, budget reforms associated with that idea also proved vulnerable to formalistic assertions of Congress's constitutional prerogatives made by legislators in the 1970s and the Supreme Court in 1998. But the short-lived experience of the line item veto reveals another lesson. The idea of presidential representation lingers, if not as a foundation, then as a durable critique. It can still be used to badger Congress and to expose its weaknesses. Constitutional formalism has proven useful in defending Congress's prerogatives, but it also highlights how difficult it has been for the "first branch" to effectively recapture its constitutional stature.[126]

Congressional Pushback against
Presidential Economic Policymaking

I think we are interested in permitting Congress to exercise its full responsibility for the development of our economy and meeting all our other national goals.
SENATOR TED KENNEDY (D-MA), 1978[1]

After decades of growth, the American economy stumbled in the 1970s as it faced a plethora of new challenges. "Stagflation" (the combination of high unemployment and high inflation), the energy crisis, a decline in manufacturing, and globalization all combined to call into question the federal government's approach to economic policy.[2] Problems like these, confronting as they did the entire nation, might have seemed well suited to the presidency's claim to represent the national interest and to further bolstering presidential authority in economic management. But this crisis of faith in the American economy occurred at precisely the moment when presidential stewardship itself was being thrown into serious question. That left Congress to wrestle with questions about the institutional arrangements it had set up just a few decades earlier, arrangements that had cemented the role of the presidency as the nation's leading economic policymaker. Presidential authority over both trade and employment policy came under increased scrutiny.

Congress was conflicted. Initially, the scale of the economic challenges facing the nation left legislators poised to grant the presidency new authority over global and domestic economic policy. One way to do that was to renew presidential trade authority, which had expired in 1967 after several previous renewals. In 1973, Congress began to consider a trade bill proposed by Republican president Richard Nixon's administration that would revise policymaking over trade for an even more globally interconnected economy. The proposed legislation would give the president new authority for five years, allowing him to negotiate multilateral agreements with other nations that would address both tariffs and, significantly, nontariff barriers to trade. Offering a minimal concession to the new political climate and growing concerns about presidential power, the president's proposal included a limited role for Congress in the form of a legislative veto, whereby one chamber could vote to disapprove a presidential trade agreement.

Later in the decade, responding to continued economic struggles, Congress considered bills that would have potentially enhanced the president's domestic economic policy authority. First, in 1977, some legislators sought to make the term of the chair of the Board of Governors of the Federal Reserve coterminous with the term of the president. Aligning the president's four-year term in office with the four-year term of the Fed chair, the proposal promised increased presidential influence over the independent Fed. "In recent years," reported the *New York Times*, "economists and political scientists have come to realize how strange and even undemocratic it is that a President, by whose command nuclear holocaust can be unleashed, is powerless vis a vis the Federal Reserve."[3] Second, in 1978, some lawmakers proposed to address unemployment and inflation by increasing the president's responsibilities in proposing economic goals and, significantly, by requiring the Fed to state how its monetary policies would conform with presidential economic objectives.

Together, these changes would have increased the president's influence in economic policy both internationally and domestically. But Congress went in a different direction. Once again, the political context of post-Vietnam, post-Watergate skepticism of presidential representation decisively shaped Congress's actions toward presidential authority. The results varied by policy area.

In foreign affairs, the Nixon administration made a significant concession to Congress to gain reauthorization of presidential trade authority. In the Trade Act of 1974, lawmakers rejected the Nixon administration's proposal for a legislative veto and instead required the affirmative consent of both chambers of Congress. Compared to previous grants of that authority, the legislation marked a "reassertion of Congress" in trade, returning the issue to the legislative agenda.[4] At the same time, however, Congress granted the president substantial trade authority, including the ability both to impose tariffs and to negotiate multilateral agreements affecting tariff and nontariff barriers to trade.[5] This new fast-track system still privileged the president's perspective. It guaranteed a congressional vote on presidential trade proposals and foreclosed the possibility of a Senate filibuster. This both made congressional assent to presidential agreements more likely and recognized that altering nontariff barriers to trade involved changes to domestic law. The legislation also ratified the earlier move by President John Kennedy to place the Office of the Special Trade Representative in the Executive Office of the President, effectively confirming that it would serve as "the negotiating arm of the executive branch." On the whole, Congress's limited pushback indicated the delicacy of trying to reclaim authority in trade, an issue that had morphed into a key tool of presidential foreign policy and one that underscored just how interconnected the US economy was to the rest of the world.[6]

A different institutional outcome resulted from Congress's reconsideration of presidential authority in domestic economic policy. Addressing unemployment and inflation, Congress passed the Full Employment and Balanced Growth Act of 1978, popularly known as Humphrey-Hawkins after its original sponsors, Senator Hubert Humphrey (D-MN) and Representative Augustus Hawkins (D-CA).[7] The act itself is not usually viewed as a significant legislative accomplishment.[8] It left the president's agenda-setting authority from the Employment Act of 1946 in place, and, in fact, it added requirements that the president's Economic Report outline plans to deal with unemployment and inflation. But the final statute otherwise sought to bolster the role of other institutions. Congress set its own economic goals and targets for unemployment and inflation. More significantly, those targets were set as a statutory mandate for the Federal Reserve. With the rising importance of monetary policy over fiscal policy, Congress looked to the Fed—its own institutional agent—as the primary source of policymaking in the public interest. The effect was to diminish presidential influence over short-term domestic economic policy.[9]

What led to Congress's reconsideration of presidential authority in economic policy? And why did the outcomes of the reforms vary between trade and employment policy? Existing accounts of the development of the institutional presidency again cannot fully account for Congress's attempts to reverse course. Explanations pointing to Congress's collective action problem in formulating economic policy would not predict a bipartisan pushback against presidential authority. Partisanship is also insufficient to explain Congress's concerns in both trade and employment policy. Though the new trade legislation was passed during divided government, the emphasis on increasing Congress's role was largely bipartisan, and the final legislation passed with overwhelming majorities.[10] The employment and inflation legislation, passed during unified Democratic government, was similarly bipartisan.[11]

An ideational account connects Congress's earlier creation of the institutional presidency in economic policy with its later reconsideration of presidential authority.[12] New economic challenges prompted Congress's efforts. As one witness testified in hearings on trade, the "dislocations from major economic events," including the "oil crisis" and "price increases," were the proximate cause of the trade legislation.[13] And the unemployment legislation was considered at a time when the nation was, in the words of Council of Economic Advisers (CEA) chairman Charles Schultze, "afflicted with the simultaneous appearance of high unemployment and persistently high levels of inflation."[14] But Congress was coming back to these issues in a political context in which doubts about presidential representation had become pervasive. Questions about whether the president could be counted on to represent the national interest were central to Congress's institutional choices in both laws.

This chapter proceeds as follows. I broadly compare presidential authority in both trade and domestic economic policy. For each policy area, I first chronicle how rising doubts about presidential representation influenced changing perceptions of how much authority the president should have. Second, I consider the extent to which claims of congressional representation and constitutionality gained leverage and influenced the alteration of institutional arrangements. Finally, I briefly consider the broader significance of these changes and their consequences over the ensuing decades.

From Pushback to Fast Track: The Trade Act of 1974

As Congress prepared to consider a renewal of presidential trade authority, the initial presumption was that the president's request would be granted. One journalist predicted that Congress would likely pass a bill mostly "on the lines proposed by the Administration."[15] Unlike previous renewals of that authority, however, President Nixon's "request for a virtually free hand on trade negotiations," observed another journalist, came "amid battles over fund impoundments, executive privilege in the Watergate case, war powers and reorganization."[16] Though the complexity of global trade and the centrality of trade in foreign policy favored presidential authority, and though presidents had lived up to expectations and used their delegated authority to usher in an era of freer trade, legislators' new doubts about presidential representation pulled them in the direction of caution and a fundamental rethinking of how trade agreements should be made. Congress attempted to reconcile these competing impulses in the Trade Act of 1974.

APPLICABILITY: DOUBTING THE PRESIDENT'S NATIONAL PERSPECTIVE

The claim that the president would take a unique national perspective on questions of tariff making was the underlying rationale for presidential trade authority. Officials from the Nixon administration sought to impress on Congress that the president's purported national viewpoint should still be privileged in negotiating and implementing trade agreements. The special representative for trade negotiations, William Eberle, testified that "the President is in the best position to weigh all these factors which bear on the national interest."[17] Referring to the 1930 Smoot-Hawley tariff, Vice President Spiro Agnew charged that the last time Congress had exercised its own authority to negotiate trade agreements, it had produced the "most protectionist tariff measure in our history."[18] Just as in budgeting, Nixon and his administration officials bet that the trope that lawmakers were too parochial to produce an effective policy would win the day.

Outside of the administration, other proponents of presidential trade authority also held that the logic of presidential representation remained true in trade. Testifying for the International Chamber of Commerce, Ian MacGregor stated the assumed relationship between presidential representation and free trade: "The US council trusts the President's authority will be used to continue to liberalize and expand US trading relationships with other nations."[19] Malcolm Lovell, the president of the Rubber Manufacturers Association, argued that presidential trade authority would "serve the national interest well."[20] Likewise, Malcolm Swenson, testifying for the National Building Granite Quarries Associations, posited that the president needed "the power to 'manage' our foreign trade in a way he perceives to be in the Nation's interest."[21]

Yet while these statements counted as support for presidential authority, they also were a stark reminder of just how reliant the whole regime had become on faith in the idea of presidential representation. And in the early 1970s, that faith was at odds with the instincts of many legislators, who were not as willing to trust presidential perceptions as a reliable indicator of national interests. "Under this legislation," contended Representative Bella Abzug (D-NY), "there is no assurance that the President will favor lowered trade barriers. . . . In fact, we have no way of knowing what he will do."[22]

It was in this context that the champions of presidential trade authority asserted that a one-chamber legislative veto was a sufficient safeguard against abuse. "The President can do anything he determines is in the national interest," said a counsel for General Electric, William Kennedy, "so long as he gives you an accounting . . . so long as you have your right to veto."[23] Representative Barber Conable (R-NY) admitted that Congress faced a "rather serious dilemma in the post-Vietnam, post-Watergate era about the extent to which we want to give negotiating authority to the President and have him bind us."[24] But he believed that the legislative veto was a sufficient safeguard. "An elaborate system of congressional review and veto," he argued, "prevents a blank check to the President."[25]

Still, for skeptical legislators, there was good reason to worry about the validity of presidential representation given the design of the proposed trade bill. Though the initial proposal provided Congress some influence over any trade deals through the legislative veto, it also set up a process by which the president could unilaterally raise tariffs on the exports of other nations in retaliation for alleged discriminatory trading practices against US products.[26] Some believed this power could allow the president to favor special interests, reward political friends, and punish political enemies. In a statement on behalf of Japanese American groups concerned with the legislation, Mike Masaoka argued that presidents could no longer be assumed to focus on the national interest:

> The unprecedented revelations of Watergate, with all its multitudinous implications . . . bring into focus . . . the real dangers of entrusting discretionary authorities to the Executive, for such vast authority invites special interest groups and individuals to pressure and intimidate a President to exercise certain of his discretions for selfish gain and not the public good.[27]

Two economics professors, Walter Adams of Michigan State and Joel Dirlam of the University of Rhode Island, also cast doubt on the notion that the president was immune from special interest pressure: "Extreme discretion is left to the President, and this exposes him to special pressures from a politically powerful industry—or campaign contributor—to adopt the measure of import relief the industry prefers."[28] The media echoed these concerns as well. "One can have reservations about giving the President sweeping new powers," noted the *Christian Science Monitor*, as "such powers to act selectively on behalf of certain industries obviously heighten the danger of the administration's being induced to protect those industries in return for political or financial support."[29] While it supported the legislation, the *New York Times* editorial board echoed those concerns, worrying that such presidential trade authority "could be used by a protectionist Administration to defeat the trade liberalization the country has sought for two generations."[30]

Even lawmakers who supported the administration's initial trade bill admitted their uncertainties about the assumption that presidents uniquely favored lower tariffs. Representative Dominick Daniels (D-NJ) supported it reluctantly, expressing concerns about special interest pressures affecting presidents: "What assurance do we have that this or another President will not raise tariffs to harmful levels, as well as use other protectionist powers provided by this bill, in a misguided attempt to protect domestic industry?"[31] This criticism by a Democratic lawmaker of a Republican president was not necessarily surprising. But Republican legislators invoked the same fear. Senator Bob Packwood (R-OR) pointed "to a Congress that has been burned several times because of the Vietnam war."[32] Expressing misgivings about presidential representation, Packwood noted, "I can foresee a President knuckling under to individual pressure . . . from different Members of Congress, different industries, for increases in tariffs that would be a political decision to gain certain benefits in certain States that would not be in the interest of the United States."[33] Moreover, even as he supported it, Representative Charles Whalen (R-OH) admitted that voting in favor of the legislation amounted to "praying that the President of the United States will show enlightenment in his administration by deciding to do all in his power to facilitate free trade, rather than move backward toward restrictions."[34] Just as in budgeting, the equation of Congress with special interests and the president with the national interest had completely broken down.

LEVERAGE: RETHINKING CONSTITUTIONAL RELATIONSHIPS

Along with worries about whether presidents could be trusted to act in the national interest in trade, Congress questioned the entire system through which it had shown deference to presidents in trade over the previous decades. Debates over trade reform saw a revival of opposing ideas—that legislators needed to represent their constituents in determining trade outcomes and that Congress was the branch with constitutional primacy in trade. These claims would exercise a crucial influence in changing the process by which Congress would ratify trade agreements from one that required avoiding a vote of *disapproval* to one that necessitated a vote of *approval.*

Congressional Representation: The People's Branch

For the Nixon administration, providing a legislative veto to Congress allowed for sufficient congressional participation in making trade agreements. The administration admitted that the inclusion of nontariff barriers in trade agreements, in particular, would require more authority from Congress. As the trade representative William Eberle conceded, "with respect to most matters [the president] lacks the authority to implement these agreements on behalf of the United States." "The proposed congressional veto procedure," he argued, "moves from the existing system of granting advance implementing authority to the President on tariff agreements to a closer cooperative relationship between the President and the Congress."[35]

However, lawmakers and others were skeptical that the legislative veto

provided a sufficient way for Congress to meaningfully represent its constituents. "I have some doubts," Representative Al Ullman (D-OR) told Eberle,
"that your proposal involves the Congress to the extent that it should if we
have a true partnership."[36] Calling for an affirmative congressional vote on
any trade deals, Representative Robert Drinan (D-MA) argued that Congress represented the whole nation as well as any president: "Let the President negotiate and then come to us. We can behave with as great a degree
of consideration of the national interest as the President. There is no reason
why this Congress cannot legislate so that we have these affirmative powers of
approval, rejection or modification."[37] Representative James Burke (D-MA)
also advocated requiring positive congressional assent: "we say, 'Why don't
you resubmit this after you have concluded your negotiations and see whether
it meets with the criteria that the representatives of the people in Congress, in
the House and Senate, will approve or disapprove of.'"[38]

Even ordinary citizens argued for increased congressional input on trade
deals. In response to a question on an opinion ballot on whether the president should have greater trade authority, one citizen wrote to Speaker Carl
Albert (D-OK), "I do not think he should have any more power." Trade
agreements should go "only through Congress," who "are there to represent
the people."[39] "I [do] not think one person should make decisions on big
deals like these are," responded another citizen, implicitly criticizing the idea
that a president alone could judge the national interest: "Big deals like these
should be handled by more than one person."[40]

At the same time, however, calls for greater congressional representation
in trade policy were not free of special interest bias, perhaps cautioning legislators about straying too far from presidential authority. Patrick Healy, the
secretary of the National Milk Producers Federation, claimed that granting
too much authority to the president would lead to ignoring the problems
of farmers. "The Members of Congress are responsive to the people in this
country. We can go and talk to our members of Congress," stated Healy. "But
when this [authority] is vested in the President and he has complete control
over the foreign trade," Healy complained, "the farmers of this country are
going to find it very difficult to find anybody to listen to their problems."[41]
And another lawmaker voiced a full-throated defense of congressional parochialism. While Representative John Herman Dent (D-PA) complained
that "to try to discredit [congressional] opposition by the implication that
it is against the national interest is the shoddiest of tactics," he nonetheless
seemed to confirm that charge himself.[42] Pledging fealty to his district's interest above all else, Dent proclaimed, "I would rather disassociate myself from

the whole world if it means one worker in my district losing his American heritage."[43]

Constitutional Authority: Tariffs and Foreign Commerce

If praise for congressional representation carried mixed connotations, Congress's constitutional claim was less ambiguous. Just as in budgeting, Congress could point to its Article I authority over trade and foreign commerce in asserting it should have a greater role in the legislation.

When the initial trade bill, providing only a legislative veto to Congress, was proposed, critics pounced on its grant of power to the president to negotiate agreements affecting tariff and nontariff barriers to trade. "Such an authorization," testified O. R. Strackbein, the president of the Nation-Wide Committee on Import-Export Policy, "would be an abdication of powers conferred on the Congress by the Constitution."[44] Representative Charles Carney (D-OH) argued that the initial bill was in direct opposition to a broader change in American political culture about the appropriate bounds of executive authority: "The American people are literally begging the Congress to reassert its rightful powers under the Constitution. Yet, the bill before us today would further erode the power of Congress and place vast new powers in the hands of the President."[45] "The grant of such power," concurred Representative Elizabeth Holtzman (D-NY), "constitutes an unnecessary and unwise abdication of responsibility by Congress."[46]

Perhaps the most notable critic was Senator Vance Hartke (D-IN), who, along with Representative Burke, had put forth his own alternative legislation that would have lessened presidential authority. "The Constitution," Hartke stressed, "gives plenary power to regulate commerce and foreign trade to the US Congress and not to the President."[47] The aim of the Burke-Hartke bill was to place potential limits on imports and prioritize the protection of American industries.[48] The primary mechanism to do so would be a new Foreign Trade and Investment Commission, a "five-member agency [that] alone would have authority to regulate all imports." As I. W. Abel, the chairman of the Economic Policy Committee of the AFL-CIO, the nation's largest federation of labor unions, explained, the "Foreign Trade and Investment Commission would be responsible for all the trade matters now spread throughout the Government." While protecting American industry and jobs was a priority for supporters of the Burke-Hartke bill, advocates like the AFL-CIO also viewed the bill as being more consistent with Congress's authority under the Constitution: "The Congress has power in the Constitution to regulate interstate and foreign commerce and to pass laws concerning changes in tariffs." Responding to advocates of presidential trade authority, the AFL-CIO argued, "it is time to stop the scare talk aimed at deterring the United States Congress from its right to pass laws in interests of the people of this country. This is a constitutional obligation."[49]

However, the rejection of this alternative revealed the limits to Congress's ability and willingness to roll back presidential authority and reassert its own constitutional claims. Instead, a primary goal for advocates of a greater role for Congress was to change the legislative veto provision to instead require positive congressional assent for presidential trade agreements. "We feel that Congress could much more effectively exercise its constitutional responsibility in this area by strengthening this [legislative veto] provision to require the specific, positive action of Congress on any such agreement," wrote Healy to Congress on behalf of the National Milk Producers Federation. "If such agreements are in the best interests of the nation," as so many proponents of presidential authority promised, "there should be little problem in securing their approval."[50] The chairman of the Bicycle Manufacturers Association, William Hannon, told lawmakers that "Congress must affirm its constitutional obligation to provide guidance in our international trade policy."[51] Most importantly, the Senate Finance Committee chairman Russell Long, the manager of the Senate bill, would embrace the idea that "all trade agreements must be approved by both Houses of Congress."[52]

Fast Track

These assertions of congressional representation and constitutional authority influenced the decisive change in the trade legislation proposed by the Nixon administration. The creation of the fast-track process attempted to reconcile those claims with the complexity of negotiating trade agreements and the reality that trade had increasingly become a tool of foreign policy. The procedure required congressional approval of multilateral trade deals, but through an expedited procedure. The president's perspective would be privileged by forcing Congress to vote up or down on any agreement put before it for consideration. No filibusters or amendments would be allowed. With these stipulations, presidential trade agreements would need positive congressional assent, receiving support from a majority of lawmakers in both the House and the Senate. The act also called for the president to seek more congressional input in formulating agreements to help assure passage in Congress.[53]

The Senate made the initial decision to change the bill, which the House later agreed to. Legislators argued that the alteration made the trade legislation better respect Congress's own constitutional prerogatives. Summarizing the view of the Senate Finance Committee, Senator Abraham Ribicoff (D-CT) stated that senators believed "that the Executive no longer has the sole authority in negotiations. . . . Congress must play a major and continuing role." The bill required "that any new trade agreement entered into by the President which would change domestic Federal law or materially change administrative regulations has to be approved by the Congress before it could take effect." Ribicoff cited constitutional reasoning for this: "To do otherwise would be to reverse the constitutional roles of the legislative and executive branches and would be an abrogation of our legislative responsibilities."[54] Senator Lawton Chiles (D-FL) likewise affirmed that "one of the real strengths of this legislation is that it is not a giveaway—it does not give away the power of the Congress to the Executive."[55]

Outside of Congress, the change to fast track was widely perceived as continuing the trend of Congress attempting to reassert its own authority compared to the president. While noting the significance of the president's trade authority, the *Austin American Statesman* told its readers that "in one respect, however, the Senate cut back sharply on that delegation of power. . . . The Senate bill requires that Congress act one way or the other on such an agreement before it could become effective."[56] The *Hartford Courant* emphasized that the new procedure "greatly expands Congress' role in the trade area."[57] Most revealingly, the White House itself viewed the change from a legislative veto to fast track as a significant concession. "The Administration," explained the *New York Times*, "had much preferred the House bill . . . which provided only that Congress could veto any such agreements."[58]

Still, while the change to require congressional approval marked a significant presidential concession, the design of the legislation also reflected constraints on Congress's ability to rein in its earlier decisions to make the president responsible for tariffs and trade. Decades of presidential tariff making meant that trade was now a central element of foreign policy and the post–World War II political and economic order. The Nixon administration had pressed its own constitutional claim over the issue as part of foreign policy. "The President has his constitutional authority to negotiate trade agreements," Trade Representative Eberle argued. Thus, Congress had long "recognized that international trade matters, particularly negotiations on tariffs, require a greater degree of delegation to the President than do domestic matters."[59] Even lawmakers dubious of presidential power conceded Eberle's point. "I think you can always make an argument in the field of international affairs for more power in the hands of an executive and perhaps even unlimited power," observed Representative Ullman.[60] Senator Ribicoff admitted that the bill was "not designed to cripple or hamper the Executive's ability to negotiate with foreign nations."[61] "I am all for the Congress asserting its proper role," said Representative Jonathan Brewster Bingham (D-NY), "but in this case the Congress cannot possibly do what we want the President to do: The Congress cannot negotiate trade agreements."[62]

In the end, Congress found that it could alter the president's broader authority in tariff making. And it could increase its own role in the trade agreement process. But it could not simply revert to its previous constitutional prerogatives in tariff making.

Congress Looks to the Fed: The Full Employment and Balanced Growth Act of 1978

"The persistence, in the wake of the recession, of unacceptably high levels of both unemployment and inflation makes it clear," declared the *New York Times* in 1976, "that the country needs stronger weapons for balanced growth than were provided in the Employment Act of 1946."[63] The straightforward response would have been to look again to the president, augmenting the "weapons" already at his disposal for setting domestic economic policy. The Employment Act had formalized presidential economic responsibilities; an updated version might have continued that trend toward national planning in the White House.[64]

But rather than enhancing presidential authority, Congress stipulated its own authority over economic policy in the Humphrey-Hawkins Act of 1978, and it looked elsewhere for an institutional surrogate to secure its interests. Congress's pushback against presidential authority in the 1978 law was again uneven. The legislation did build on the Employment Act of 1946, setting new economic goals for the president and underscoring the accountability of the president for the nation's economic performance. But the effort to limit presidential power over the domestic economy was unmistakable and not nearly as compromised as in trade policy. Congress sought to place itself in the driver's seat. It would specify economic goals for the nation and combat stagflation by setting unemployment and inflation targets of its own. In doing so, it built on earlier efforts from the 1974 budget law, which had established the Congressional Budget Office (CBO). The CBO's responsibility for economic forecasting already had begun to diminish the influence of the CEA.[65]

Even more striking than Congress's effort to reclaim power for itself in this domain was its inclination to redirect authority to another institution, the Federal Reserve. The Senate, in particular, exploited the rising importance of monetary policy for combatting inflation in order to emphasize

Congress's control over the Fed's mandate and management of the economy. The 1978 statute included "the establishment of the Fed's first explicit statutory mandate from Congress—one that required the Federal Reserve to secure price stability and maximize employment."[66] This came on the heels of the defeat of an attempt to make the term of the Fed chairman concurrent with that of the president in 1977, as well as Congress's decision to impose a new requirement that the president's choice for Fed chairman receive Senate confirmation. The emphasis on the role of the Federal Reserve in the 1978 law not only "institutionalized a new relationship between Congress and the Fed"; it ratified the Fed's position as the predominant actor in everyday management of the economy.[67]

APPLICABILITY: DOUBTING THE
PRESIDENT'S NATIONAL PERSPECTIVE

Even more than the Employment Act of 1946, the Humphrey-Hawkins Act conceived of presidential power in terms of responsibilities in the service of Congress, the principal decision maker. Congress set unemployment and inflation targets and then expected the president to propose policies aligned with them in the Economic Report. The bill, stated Senator Edward Brooke (R-MA), "places the major responsibility for economic planning upon the President."[68] The chairman of the CEA in Democratic president Jimmy Carter's administration, Charles Schultze, also noted that "the spirit of the bill is that the President has to pay attention to all aspects of the economy."[69] And the co-chairperson of the Full Employment Action Council (FEAC), Coretta Scott King, declared that "the President is required to develop programs to reach the targets contained in the bill."[70] In effect, Congress left the president's agenda-setting authority from the Employment Act in place, but the additional specifications and expectations made it clear that Congress was no longer taking anything for granted.

Skepticism about the merits of the president's and the CEA's purportedly broad perspective in economic policymaking lay just beneath the surface. In fact, one of the act's chief proponents disagreed with other advocates who focused on the role of the president under the law. Leon Keyserling, the former chairman of the CEA under Democratic president Harry Truman, was certainly well acquainted with presidential authority in economic policy. His voice carried weight, then, when he faulted the FEAC, a primary group supporting the legislation, for overemphasizing the authority of the president. Keyserling was upset that a pamphlet published by the FEAC had neglected the authority of Congress. "The complete failure of the pamphlet even to mention the Congress in this connection," wrote Keyserling in a blunt "personal and confidential" letter to the other FEAC co-chairperson, Murray Finley, "is highly damaging because it supports the view of those who incorrectly believe that the Plan would be nothing but an airy exercise by the President and entirely within his discretion to do something about it or do nothing about it. . . . What the pamphlet says is entirely wrong."[71] Keyserling also responded to critics of the legislation who had what he viewed as erroneous understandings of the law's role for the president. "I cannot comprehend at all your criticism to the effect that the sections of the Bill concerned with economic planning . . . continue to allow too much discretionary power in the hands of the President," Keyserling wrote to one detractor: "The Bill necessarily leaves to the Congress what can be done only by the Congress."[72]

Other leading advocates also downplayed the legislation's reliance on presidential judgment. The AFL-CIO stated that the legislation "reflects the lesson learned over the last seven years that Congress cannot simply rely on the good judgment and the good will of the President."[73] Moreover, the sponsors of the 1978 legislation themselves contrasted the 1946 law's reliance on action from the executive branch with the approach outlined in their bill. Representative Hawkins and Senator Muriel Humphrey (D-MN), the widow of former senator Hubert Humphrey who had taken up the legislation while serving in the Senate, explained in a pamphlet that "the 1946 [Employment] Act, in its actual operations thus far, has left to the President and his economic advisers the major determination of employment goals and of acceptable levels of unemployment at given times." But this system of presidential economic stewardship, they contended, was not working. It could not be counted on to realize the nation's economic well-being: "This approach has frequently failed to determine these matters satisfactorily and to achieve optimum and stable growth." Instead, Congress needed to set its own precise economic policy goals. "A Congress which determines how many military planes we should build," they asserted, "can and should also participate more adequately in developing goals and policies which will achieve and maintain full employment in a full economy."[74]

Indeed, beyond again underscoring the president's existing responsibility to submit the Economic Report and stipulating its terms, the act did not move to grant the president any other authority to meet the new economic targets. As a congressional staffer, Nat Semple, explained, the bill depended "almost entirely on congressional action." Semple expressed concern that "the President would be set up as a scapegoat in the event that Congress failed to meet those plans." The FEAC co-chairperson Murray Finley also acknowledged that the president could be made a scapegoat. Although all elected officials might "be held accountable" for such a failure, Finley asserted, he was "sure" that blame "will focus more directly on the President than it will on 435 Congressmen and 100 Senators."[75] Though presidents continued to be held accountable for their economic stewardship and were expected to make policy proposals, the kind of substantial authority they possessed in trade policy was conspicuously absent in the legislation.

LEVERAGE: RETHINKING CONSTITUTIONAL RELATIONSHIPS

In debating domestic economic policy, legislators questioned the assumptions behind the earlier Employment Act of 1946. As they considered whether the president or Congress should set economic goals, lawmakers asserted their own representative claims and responsibilities for outlining the nation's economic policy priorities. Moreover, the decision to have Congress itself set employment and inflation targets was accompanied by a decision to look to the Federal Reserve for action. Legislators underscored that the Fed was Congress's agent in exercising its constitutional authority over monetary policy, and they sought to direct how the Fed would use that authority in the service of congressional economic goals. The net result was a diminishment of presidential authority.

Congressional Representation: Setting Targets

Despite the emphasis of some supporters on the role of the president in the legislation, the Humphrey-Hawkins Act was consciously designed to reassert Congress's own authority. Representative Hawkins stressed that the bill mandated greater congressional involvement in the setting of economic policy than in previous decades. "To those who say that this bill does nothing," Hawkins told his colleagues, "I say if it did nothing more than to have the congressional involvement in the economic policymaking of this Nation, that itself alone would be a step that I think we should applaud and certainly should approve." Hawkins was not content to rely on the president to recommend goals and programs in the Economic Report. Indeed, he complained about past presidents—of both parties—not respecting congressional primacy: "I think it is also true that regardless of what President is in the White House, this Congress is not consulted in policy formulation."[76]

Congress's reassertion of its role in forming overall economic policy took the form of setting unemployment and inflation targets for the nation to meet. Notably, for some legislators, this choice arose from doubts about the assumption that the president would inherently propose more appropriate goals for the nation as a whole than would Congress. For example, in a discussion over whether Congress should set an inflation target itself or allow the president to choose one, Senator Donald Riegle (D-MI) contradicted the notion that the president was better suited to the task. "I do not see any reason to believe that Congress would somehow be more susceptible to political pressures in pulling that percentage in closer than the President of the United States would be," contended Riegle: "The President is not always going to be right."[77] Congress did ultimately choose to set its own inflation target.

Congressional Power and the Federal Reserve

At the time Congress was reconsidering the balance of power between the legislative and executive branches, the role of the Federal Reserve was becoming more salient. The Fed was an "independent" agency positioned outside the regular executive establishment, and as one journalist noted, "For many years . . . Presidents and legislators never thought of the Federal Reserve as a serious rival in formulating economic policy."[78] But because many policymakers increasingly "support the view that monetary policy takes priority over fiscal policy," reported the *New York Times*, "the Federal Reserve's role, thus, has moved from insignificant to critical." As a result, a key question in the late 1970s was whether and how the Fed's actions would be made "consistent with national purpose."[79]

Implicit in that question remained the issue of *who* would get to define the national purpose—the president or Congress? Representative Hawkins complained to legislators that "the President tends to go in one direction, the Congress in another and the Federal Reserve System sometimes in still another."[80] Some sort of unity of purpose, he asserted, was necessary. At first, it appeared that the president would be granted more leverage over the Fed as a way to realize that national purpose. Some House legislators sought to amend the Federal Reserve Reform Act of 1977 along lines that had been suggested by President Carter, attempting to make the term of the chairman of the Board of Governors coterminous with the four-year term of a president.[81]

However, the Senate derailed that effort, instead constructing the Federal Reserve Reform Act of 1977 to reflect greater congressional primacy over the Fed.[82] The Senate removed the proposed provision from the legislation that would have made the Fed chair's term in office coterminous with that of the president. While the House had sought to allow "the President to have his own man as Chairman of the Fed," noted Senator John Tower (R-TX), "I still think the drive of many of us to maintain the independence of the Fed is strong enough that we do not feel this would be a wise move."[83] "The purpose [of the House bill] apparently is to give the President his 'own man' as Chairman of the Fed," echoed Senator Brooke, which went against Congress's preference "to provide monetary authority that is non-political and independent of the White House."[84] "I have opposed making the term of the chairman coterminous for a long time because I felt this would make the Reserve subject to the power of the President directly and explicitly," stressed Senator William Proxmire (D-WI), the chairman of the Senate Committee on Banking, Housing, and Urban Affairs. In fact, contrary to the effort to make the Fed more responsive to the president, the Senate instead made the Fed more responsive to Congress. The new legislation made the president's appointment of the Fed chair subject to Senate confirmation. "This amendment does provide that the confirmation of the chairman of the Federal Reserve Board shall be a function of the Senate for the first time," explained Senator Proxmire: "We have not done that before."[85] Moreover, Proxmire accentuated the point that the Fed was exercising congressional authority: "It is a creature of the Congress. . . . It is our responsibility. We have the money power, and we delegate it to the Federal Reserve Board."[86]

This was the context in which the Humphrey-Hawkins bill was debated in Congress. The earlier Employment Act of 1946 had relied directly on the president and Congress for action, looking to fiscal policy to address employment and economic issues. Monetary policy and the role of the Federal Reserve were never mentioned in that law, which legislators now sought to change.[87] Andrew Biemiller, the legislative director of the AFL-CIO, argued that "one of the greatest deficiencies of the 1946 act was that it did not bring the Federal Reserve Board in any way, shape, form or manner into any coordinated economic policy."[88] Moreover, Senator Proxmire explained that monetary policy had grown in importance since passage of the Employment Act:

> Since 1946, there has also been a change in thinking regarding the importance of monetary policy compared to fiscal policy. Whereas the Employment Act of 1946 looked primarily to the President and the Congress for the conduct of economic policy, today it is clear that monetary policies adopted by the Federal Reserve System can have profound and sometimes decisive effects on our economy.[89]

The final legislation recognized the increased importance of monetary policy and underscored the Fed's responsiveness to Congress. But the initial proposal had again raised the possibility that the independence of the Fed from the president could be compromised. Explaining the goals of an earlier version of the bill, Representative Bruce Vento (D-MN) used strong language that seemed to portend a subordinate status for the Fed to the president in setting economic goals. "The Federal Reserve will be required to say whether its money policies are adequate to support the President's economic targets," proclaimed Vento. "And if they are not," he added, "the Federal Reserve will have to explain why."[90] It was questionable, stated a pamphlet outlining the merits of the proposed full employment legislation, "to take . . . the position that the President of the whole people has no right to take a substantial interest in the monetary policies of the nation."[91]

This apparent threat to the Fed's independence faced opposition. In 1976, a member of the Fed Board of Governors, J. Charles Partee, had expressed concerns over that provision in an earlier version of the Humphrey-Hawkins legislation, noting the stringency of the proposed requirement for the Fed to comment on presidential plans. Partee emphasized Congress's influence over the Fed: "I would point out that Congress has the authority and the right to instruct us. . . . The system is a creature of the Congress."[92] The Fed's position on the legislation, Partee explained, was that "introducing the Executive into the process with his own proposals for monetary policy—creating, in effect, a competition between the President and the Federal Reserve—would be destructive over time." Instead, Partee told legislators, "we would prefer to see the type of relationship strengthened, if you will, between the Congress and the Federal Reserve, rather than between the Executive and the Federal Reserve."[93] In 1978, a Chamber of Commerce economist, Jack Carlson, also expressed suspicion of any "steps [toward] creating subservience of the Federal Reserve Board to the executive branch." Notably, Carlson, who was also a former senior economist for the CEA, also conveyed that the superiority of executive branch wisdom in economic proposals should not be assumed. In his testimony, Carlson admitted that the Fed "was far wiser in its economic policies than we were in the executive branch."[94]

As a result, a number of advocates of the legislation sought to make it clear that the Fed would not have its monetary policy authority encroached on by the president.[95] The final legislation suggested increased coordination of monetary and fiscal policy by having the Fed report to Congress on how its own objectives related to congressional and presidential goals.[96] But the congressional connection to the Fed was the primary emphasis. "These provisions have now been amended considerably," Senator Jacob Javits (R-NY) told his colleagues, "so that now section 108 describes a relationship of comity between the Congress and the Fed in furtherance of the purposes of the act." There was to be "coordination as much as possible" between the Fed Board and the banking committees of each chamber of Congress.[97] The legislation's advocates were clear: "Congress and the Congress only shall determine what action it wants to take, if it seems such action necessary to bring the policies of the Federal Reserve into closer conformity with the objectives of an Act of the Congress itself."[98] Senator Proxmire likewise focused on the Fed's responsiveness to Congress. Legislators would put together "a consistent set of economic goals," which would then be coordinated with the Fed for monetary policy: "The Congress need not and should not make monetary policy, but it must explicitly communicate to the Federal Reserve, where the day-to-day responsibility for monetary policy properly lies, the overall economic goals of national policy."[99]

The adoption of a specific inflation target by Congress—at the expense of the original unemployment goal—also favored the power of the Fed more than that of the president. Like the Employment Act of 1946, the Humphrey-Hawkins legislation had originally sought to primarily address unemployment. Given rising concerns over inflation in the 1970s, however, many legislators sought to make combatting inflation a greater priority. For Representative Hawkins and his allies, this risked derailing the legislation: "An arbitrary inflation goal would be used to postpone action to reach full employment."[100] The Carter administration looked on the effort to specify an inflation target unfavorably, "solidly supporting no inflation target at all," but the administration also confidentially admitted to Representative Hawkins that it "would have a hard time 'fighting like hell'" against it.[101]

The decision to have Congress set the inflation target, rather than delegating that responsibility to the president, punctuated the change in priorities.[102] The Senate, led by Proxmire, altered the legislation to focus on inflation, since "many consider inflation to be our No. 1 domestic economic problem."[103] Moreover, Proxmire argued that Congress, not the president, should set an inflation target for the Fed to reach: "The Banking Committee sees no reason why the establishment of a numerical inflation goal should be delegated to the President. . . . If Congress is competent to establish a goal for reducing unemployment, it should be equally capable of establishing a goal for reducing inflation."[104] The Fed itself, Proxmire noted, was enthusiastic for Congress to set the goal: "The principle of establishing a numerical inflation goal was strongly supported by the Board of Governors of the Federal Reserve System."[105] Senator Muriel Humphrey's effort to stop Congress from setting its own target lost in the Senate.[106]

While the House's version of the legislation had not initially set an inflation goal, Representative Ronald Sarasin (R-CT) praised the Senate change. Significantly, he too connected it to greater congressional direction: "The Senate has added what the House would or could not—a numerical anti-inflation goal." "We were all elected to be responsible to our constituents and to the overall well-being of our country," Sarasin argued, and voting for the measure with an anti-inflation amendment gave Congress "an opportunity to set this country back on productive tracks."[107] By setting its own economic goals and seeking to direct Federal Reserve policy toward those goals, lawmakers both reasserted congressional prerogatives and put another institution to work in meeting their directives.

Constitutional Authority over Monetary Policy

The debate over the Humphrey-Hawkins legislation also continued the general emphasis in the 1970s on Congress explicitly invoking its own constitutional authority as a response to presidentialism. The president of the New York City Council, Paul O'Dwyer, testified about the changing views of the appropriate bounds of presidential and congressional constitutional authority: "Of course, people are more enlightened on their rights today." In prior decades, he contended, presidents "began to acquire more and more power that was never meant by our basic documents. . . . What did that do for us? It finally gave us trouble."[108]

This broader shift in popular understandings of the constitutional roles of the president and Congress was directly connected to Congress's decision to choose its own inflation target. While there had in previous decades been an "enormous increase in Presidential power," the present Congress, Senator Proxmire asserted, was "inclined to be more specific in its guidance" to direct national policy.[109] By emphasizing the role of the Fed, Congress was effectively underscoring its own constitutional authority over monetary policy in the legislation. Decrying "that old myth of independence," Senator Proxmire retold a story stipulating that any Fed chair should "write on your bathroom mirror 'I am a creature of Congress' and look at it every morning." Jack Carlson, the former CEA official who testified for the Chamber of Commerce, acknowledged his point: "No question as far as the Constitution."[110]

Conclusion: An Enduring Distinction

The Trade Act of 1974 and the Full Employment and Balanced Growth Act of 1978 both passed in a political context in which the legitimacy of the idea of presidential representation was under siege. In trade, Congress required the affirmation of both chambers before any multilateral trade agreements negotiated by the president could go into effect. In domestic policy, Congress set its own targets for unemployment and inflation, while strengthening its ties to an increasingly influential Federal Reserve. Both cases were meaningfully influenced by Congress's renewed doubts about the validity of presidential representation, and Congress's pushback altered presidential authority.

From the perspective of the presidency, the outcomes of the Trade Act and the Humphrey-Hawkins Act differed significantly. Presidential influence over trade remained substantial, even with the requirement of congressional assent. By contrast, presidential influence in domestic economic policy was diminished, particularly because of the rising importance of the Fed.

What accounts for this variation in the extent of presidential authority over economic policymaking? The distinction is perhaps best seen as a variation of the classic "two presidencies" thesis, with greater presidential influence over foreign trade than in domestic fiscal and monetary policy.[111] The crucial change was the shift in how tariff making was viewed, no longer as a domestic policy issue but now as one involving foreign affairs. Until the 1930s, tariff rates had been a predominant issue of domestic economic policy and a key point of division in the American party system.[112] With presidents gaining authority over tariffs via the RTAA of 1934 and subsequent statutory renewals by Congress, questions of tariff rates became linked to broader issues of foreign policy and the promotion of an international political and economic order. Part of the significance of this change was that, with tariffs a key component of foreign policy, legislators and other political actors increasingly viewed the issue as being part of the president's perceived authority over foreign affairs under Article II. Congress could and did assert its Article I authority over foreign commerce, but nonetheless, issues of foreign affairs inevitably involved the president. But even on a more practical level, in an increasingly globalized economy in which nations were negotiating multilateral trade deals involving both tariff and nontariff barriers to trade, Congress would alter presidential authority at its own peril.

Conversely, the issues of fiscal and monetary policy considered by the Humphrey-Hawkins Act continued to be perceived as domestic policy, and Congress was more vigorous in asserting its own predominant authority from its sole claim over monetary policy in Article I. With the primary focus of the legislation being on domestic unemployment and inflation issues, the president's perspective did not receive the same deference. Indeed, in contrast to the trade legislation, FEAC co-chairperson Murray Finley asserted that the 1978 legislation would *not* seek to change the legislative process to accommodate presidential authority. The legislation, he explained, conformed with "our American system, when you have separation of the Executive versus Congress," unlike "the parliamentary system."[113] Moreover, as the debates over the legislation made clear, legislators recognized that they were allowing the Fed to exercise power that constitutionally belonged to them.

The power to coin money was one of the essential powers Congress possessed under Article I.

With monetary policy rising in importance, Congress seized an opportunity to exercise its authority through the Fed. Correspondingly, the president and CEA, with roles primarily designed to influence fiscal policy, were left with less meaningful authority. The formation of the CEA had been tied to the purported benefits of the president's national perspective, but now other institutions were asserting their own purported superiority in representing the national interest.[114] Soon the Fed itself would even claim to be the institution best representing the needs of the nation as a whole. As Fed chairman Paul Volcker would tell Congress, "The Federal Reserve is meant to be independent of parochial political interests."[115]

The experience of subsequent presidents in economic management reaffirmed this variation in their influence. While domestic interests can sometimes scuttle efforts at renewal, Congress, for the most part, would consistently look to presidential trade authority via the fast-track process to accomplish trade deals.[116] Using that authority, presidents continued to seek multilateral trade agreements as a tool of foreign policy and as a way to promote overall economic growth, generally acting consistently with the expectations of presidential representation. As Douglas Irwin concludes, "the period since 1934 appears to have been a fairly steady movement in the direction of reducing trade barriers."[117] On the other hand, the Federal Reserve's role became more important over time.[118]

Consider the early experience of Democratic president Bill Clinton. With the congressional passage of the North American Free Trade Agreement (NAFTA) through fast-track trade promotion authority, Clinton achieved a major foreign and economic policy victory and exercised his own influence over Congress.[119] But in domestic economic policy, the limits Clinton faced were immediately made clear to him. As his economic adviser Alan Blinder recounted, "I told President-elect Clinton that, where the economy was concerned, he had just been elected to the *second* most important position in the country—the first was already filled by [Fed chairman] Alan Greenspan."[120] That perception was only solidified during the Great Recession in 2009. With the United States in the midst of a financial crisis, both Democratic president Barack Obama and Congress looked to the Federal Reserve for solutions and expected it to wield significant power.[121]

Republican Donald Trump's presidency threw this variation in presidential power into even sharper relief. Once more, assumptions about how presidents would act in economic policymaking came into question, as Trump's protectionist impulses upended the long-standing assumption that presidents would avoid the purported pathologies of Congress, favoring freer trade and a more international outlook.[122] Trump repeatedly criticized the US trade agreements negotiated by his predecessors, characterizing them as "the worst Trade Deals in world history."[123] After exiting the Trans-Pacific Partnership negotiated by President Obama, Trump also renegotiated one of the preeminent examples of presidential free trade promotion, NAFTA.[124] Moreover, Trump used the delegated authority from previous tariff laws, such as the Trade Expansion Act of 1962 and the Trade Act of 1974, to impose tariffs on goods from many countries.[125] "I want tariffs," Trump told his advisers, "and I want someone to bring me some tariffs."[126] By contrast, Trump's ability to unilaterally affect trade policy did not easily translate into domestic economic policy. Though Trump took credit for a continual stock market rise during the first year of his administration, some pointed to the Fed's policies as being more important. The president "had kind of a free ride in this market and [he had] taken so much credit for [the market's performance]," one analyst noted, "even though so much of it was due to easy-money policies from Janet Yellen and the Fed."[127] Moreover, Trump soon discovered the difficulty of influencing the Federal Reserve's actions on monetary policy, even after he declined to reappoint Yellen and picked Jerome Powell as the new Fed chairman instead.[128] "I'm very unhappy with the Fed," Trump complained after Powell announced interest rate increases. Powell responded with defiance: "Nothing will deter us from what we think is the right thing to do."[129] Echoing Proxmire in 1978, Powell noted, "We're a creature of Congress."[130]

The decades after the 1970s, then, showed the enduring difference that continued after Congress's reconsideration of its earlier institutional adaptations in economic policy. In domestic economic policy, Congress was able to utilize another institutional agent to effectively exercise greater authority on its behalf, taking advantage of the importance of monetary policy and diminishing the relative importance of the president and the CEA. And notably, Congress's constitutional claim to exercise authority over the Fed was unambiguous in Article I. But in trade, Congress's ability to push back against presidential authority was more limited. It was constrained by its own earlier choices, which had made trade an integral part of foreign policy and the global economic order. And Congress was left more exposed to the potential repercussions of a president that had a fundamentally different view of free trade. For even if accountability for the nation's economic performance continues to fall squarely on the shoulders of the president, the president's ability to wield direct influence is decidedly uneven between policy areas.

Congressional Pushback against Presidential Reorganization Authority

As the Members of the Senate are well aware, the whole question of the power of the President to reorganize the executive branch and the role that the Congress must—and will—play in the exercise of that power is one that is fraught with difficulty. For we have only recently ended a period of our history when that power was subject to abuse and the Congress had to fight to preserve its rightful role in our tripartite government.

SENATOR ROBERT BYRD (D-WV), 1977[1]

Reorganization authority was a mainstay of presidential power from the 1930s through the early 1970s.[2] Determining the structure of the executive branch might seem like housekeeping, but for presidents, reorganization meant the chance to exercise authority that otherwise belonged to Congress, and it offered an additional lever of influence and control over their own administrations. Among the many reorganization plans submitted to Congress in those decades, presidents had exercised the authority to establish several institutions, including the Executive Office of the President (EOP) in 1939, the Department of Health, Education, and Welfare in 1953 (today the separate Department of Health and Human Services and Department of Education), the Environmental Protection Agency in 1970, the National Oceanic and Atmospheric Administration in the Department of Commerce in 1970, and the Drug Enforcement Administration in the Department of Justice in 1973. That authority had also been used to reorganize the Bureau of the Budget into the Office of Management and Budget (OMB) in 1970.[3] However, after decades of renewing that authority, Congress began to waver on entrusting presidents with such power in the early 1970s. Amid clashes over budgeting and national security, Congress declined to renew presidential reorganization authority for Republican president Richard Nixon in 1973.

Congress nonetheless appeared poised to return to the trend of the previous decades when a Democrat entered the White House in 1977. Lawmakers in both parties suggested that their sudden doubts about the wisdom of presidential reorganization authority applied only to Nixon personally, not to the presidency itself. The election of Jimmy Carter rekindled the idea that the president would best represent the national interest in achieving a rational reorganization of the executive branch. Carter had promised to make reorganization a central tool of presidential power.[4] It figured prominently in his 1976 campaign: "If you don't want me to reorganize the Federal Government, don't vote for me."[5] Connecting reorganization to presidential representation, Carter used the promise of rational, efficient government to "arouse the support of the people."[6] "The success of his Presidency," noted the *New York Times*, "is therefore likely to be measured to a large extent by his ability to reorganize the Government, and the question of reorganization is almost certain to dominate his dealings with Congress in the years ahead."[7]

Soon legislators reaffirmed their own faith that the president would cut through special interests to better realize the national interest in governmental reorganization. Passing the Reorganization Act of 1977, Congress renewed presidential reorganization authority subject to a one-house legislative veto.[8] Nonetheless, in keeping with a post-Vietnam, post-Watergate context, doubts about the wisdom of presidential representation were expressed in the debates over the statute. One indicator of the force of those doubts was apparent in the law's design, as the 1977 act allowed the president to amend plans submitted to Congress within thirty days or withdraw plans within sixty days. The point of this provision was to give the president more opportunity to alter reorganization proposals to respond to congressional feedback. The provision was a slight diminishment of the extent of presidential reorganization authority, giving Congress another way to register its own input. Rather than legislators being offered a take-it-or-leave-it choice on presidential reorganization proposals, Congress opened the door to a negotiation over the president's plans.[9]

Carter lived up to his promise to utilize that authority. The creation of the Federal Emergency Management Agency (FEMA) in 1978 was accomplished under the provisions of the 1977 law.[10] Even more consequentially, Carter's Reorganization Plan No. 2 helped accomplish what Franklin Roosevelt's Committee on Administrative Management had failed to do: provide the president greater flexibility over executive branch personnel. It reorganized the Civil Service Commission into the Office of Personnel Management and the Merit Systems Protection Board, moves that would quickly be reinforced by Congress's passage of the Civil Service Reform Act of 1978.[11]

Only a few years later, however, presidential reorganization authority was dead. The process still had an Achilles' heel—the legislative veto. In an era of increasingly formalist constitutional reasoning, that provision, allowing one chamber of Congress to reject presidential reorganization plans via a concurrent resolution, was potentially low-hanging fruit. As Congress debated the

1977 statute, some lawmakers had expressed doubts over the constitutional-
ity of the legislative veto, concerns that soon proved prescient. In 1983, the
Supreme Court declared all forms of the legislative veto unconstitutional in
Immigration and Naturalization Service [INS] v. Chadha.

On its own, that decision did not spell the end of presidential reorganization authority. Congress could have reimagined the process by delegating that
authority to the president without a provision for a legislative veto, or it could
have created a process for congressional approval of presidential plans along
the lines of the fast-track procedure in trade policy. Indeed, for a brief moment in 1984, it appeared Congress would opt for that latter approach. Congress passed a reorganization authority in which the president would need
the positive assent of both chambers of Congress for reorganization plans to
go into effect, but, in practice, that reauthorization proved meaningless. The
Senate adjourned after the measure was passed and did not go back into session until after the authority had expired less than two months later.[12] With
the legislative veto invalidated, Congress's lingering doubts about the presidency overcame any desire to find a new solution. Despite consistent presidential requests for it over subsequent decades, Congress stood firm, refusing
to delegate such authority to presidents again.

Why did Congress, which had repeatedly endorsed presidential reorganization authority, reverse course? And how did a Supreme Court decision about
immigration contribute to toppling the system of presidential reorganization
authority? Explanations for the development of the institutional presidency
that emphasize Congress's collective action problem in reorganization—the
difficulty of getting 535 legislators to overcome their own parochial interests
to achieve a rational reorganization of the executive branch—would not predict the sudden end of presidential reorganization authority. Partisanship was
not decisive either. The 1977 act did pass during a unified government, but
the doubts expressed at the time were bipartisan, and the bill commanded
a wide bipartisan margin.[13] Furthermore, while Congress's decision not to
renew presidential reorganization authority after the *Chadha* decision occurred during a period of divided government in the 1980s, the skepticism
that stayed Congress's hand was bipartisan as well. Reorganization authority
was never reenacted even during subsequent periods of unified party control.

Once again, an ideational account links together earlier congressional
choices to establish presidential reorganization authority with later congressional pushback. First, doubts that the president could be counted on to act
as a national steward prompted questions about reorganization authority.
Second, in an era featuring an increasingly formalistic approach to the Constitution, an earlier achievement in institutional adaptability that was cru-

cial to Congress accommodating presidential representation—the legislative veto—became especially vulnerable to challenge.

This chapter proceeds as follows. First, I show how rising doubts about the validity of presidential representation influenced legislators in debating the renewal of reorganization authority. Second, I consider the leverage of opposing claims of congressional representation and constitutionality over subsequent institutional changes. Presidential reorganization authority itself was allowed to expire and was subsequently not renewed, a victim of both the Supreme Court's assessment that the legislative veto was unconstitutional and Congress's subsequent decision that reorganization should remain its own power. However, even in a policy area in which Congress actually rescinded the entirety of the president's authority, Congress still faced challenges in reasserting its own authority in a positive way. In fact, in the face of potential chaos, Congress passed a statute simply ratifying all previously enacted presidential reorganization plans to put them on a firmer legal footing. Finally, I briefly examine the consequences of these changes over subsequent decades for presidential control over the executive branch, demonstrating how presidential reorganization authority has remained a nonstarter even as presidents themselves consistently ask for it.

Applicability: Doubting the President's National Perspective

Whether they supported or opposed the instrument, everyone involved in the debates over presidential reorganization authority recognized that it was linked to the idea of presidential representation. Debates over reorganization in 1977 would once again test the perceived validity of this assumption.

Proponents of renewing that authority echoed their Progressive predecessors. Restating old claims that Congress was too bound to parochial interests and particular bureaus to effectively reorganize the executive branch, they suggested that only the president could accomplish the task. Carter's OMB director Bert Lance reminded Congress that reorganization put "the legislative branch of Government" under "great pressure from interest groups."[14] Senator Abraham Ribicoff (D-CT), who spearheaded the renewal effort in Congress, also bluntly stated that "when you talk about reorganizing the executive branch of the Government, Congress cannot do that job."[15] "The people," asserted Senator Charles Percy (R-IL), "want [the president] to do something to eliminate the duplication, inefficiency, overlapping and the needless cost involved in the hodgepodge that the bureaucracy has become."[16] With Carter's campaign promise from 1976, reorganization also was said to be a mandate from the people: "Renewing this Executive reorganization authority will help rebuild the public's confidence in government, redeem commitments made to the electorate, and prove to the people who have given us their trust that we are ready to make a fresh start."[17]

Notwithstanding these confident pronouncements in the logic of presidential representation, the debates over reorganization revealed underlying cracks in the notion that all presidents could be trusted with such authority. For one thing, supportive legislators openly admitted they had declined to renew the authority for Nixon but stated that they were willing to try again to restore this faith. While Congress "did not renew the authority for President Nixon," noted Ribicoff, "I do think the Congress now wishes to renew this authority for the President of the United States."[18] "Circumstances are different," concurred Senator Percy, "and this seems to be an entirely different President."[19] Percy, a Republican, even suggested that the Democratic president had a mandate for reorganization: "Certainly the urgency of what we are discussing today is really in a sense a commitment to the American people and the basis on which President Carter was elected. . . . It was mandated."[20] But notably, this representational rationale struck a strikingly different note from the usual justifications for reorganization. A plebiscitary justification for reorganization was more associated with Carter as an individual, whereas the traditional understanding of reorganization had conveyed a generalized faith in the presidency, in presidential stewardship as an institutional matter. Ribicoff also revealingly declined to assert the validity of presidential representation overall, only praising his fellow partisan, President Carter. Though "every President since Franklin Roosevelt has had this authority," Ribicoff stressed, "from my own experience with many Presidents, President Carter is the first of the Presidents that I have dealt with who is really serious about reorganization, and wants it to work."[21] In other words, Ribicoff implied, the notion that *all* presidents would be likely to seek rational reorganization plans was historically incorrect. Even for the champions of the 1977 statute, the validity of presidential representation in reorganizing was qualified and conditional.

Other lawmakers expressed their concerns about renewing presidential reorganization authority more forthrightly, pointing to deeper doubts about the presidency in the wake of Vietnam and Watergate. "The memories of the recent past—of Vietnam, Watergate, impoundments, the use and abuse of the veto power—are still very much with us," observed Senator Lee Metcalf (D-MT). For Metcalf, the issue of reorganization was a vital part of Congress's overall goal to reassert its own authority in the constitutional separation of powers: "Would the delegation, once again, of executive reorganization authority to the President be a step in the direction of losing the balance we have worked so hard to achieve?" For Metcalf, the answer was yes.[22] The chairman of the House Government Operations Committee, Jack Brooks (D-TX), outlined the stakes of reorganization in identical terms. "We have lived through a time when we saw what can happen when Congress makes broad delegations of its powers to a President," he explained: "I do not want any President to have the opportunity to abuse our governmental process. . . . Only now are we beginning to restore the balance that should exist between the legislative and executive branches."[23] One lawmaker who opposed a more limited reorganization authority for the president, Representative Bob Walker (R-PA), disputed the validity of presidential representation entirely. Criticizing the notion that "only the President knows what is best in the area of reorganization," Walker proclaimed, "If we cannot be expected to represent the people by doing what is right and what is responsible, then the Constitution has no real meaning."[24]

Leverage: Rethinking Constitutional Relationships

The conventional wisdom that the president was in the best position to reorganize the executive branch had become less tenable, and opposing claims of congressional representation and issues of constitutionality were revived. These claims would exercise a critical influence in a series of events dealing with reorganization and the legislative veto, leading to the ultimate dissolution of presidential reorganization authority.

CONGRESSIONAL REPRESENTATION AND LEGISLATIVE POWER

Though presidential reorganization authority had been in place for decades, lawmakers and others now questioned whether this was an appropriate precedent, pointing to the fact that, when the entirety of American history was considered, presidential reorganization authority was still a relatively new phenomenon. "Determination of the organizational structure of the executive branch is a legislative function," Representative Brooks reminded his colleagues: "Make no mistake about that." "Throughout most of our history the reorganization of the Government has been accomplished through legislation," he noted, and "it was not until the 1930's that we began delegating that authority to the President."[25] Downplaying the idea that other presidents having possessed reorganization authority should serve as a precedent, even for a president of his own party, Brooks argued, "No President should assume that this authority is his automatically because other Presidents had it, and no

Congress should automatically surrender this substantial legislative authority because other Congresses have done so."[26] Similarly, Antonin Scalia, a former assistant attorney general for the Office of Legal Counsel under Republican president Gerald Ford (and a future Supreme Court justice), also criticized the reorganization process for taking away authority from Congress—"the popular branch." Even if congressional representation could be "sometimes embarrassing" and presidential reorganization authority sought "to reduce the impact of lobbying," Scalia held that it did not justify what amounted to "legislation by inattention."[27]

Supporters of renewing reorganization authority also wanted Congress to be more involved. "Renewing the Reorganization Authority is not an open-ended mandate to the President to reorganize the Government on his own," warned Ribicoff. Instead, "Congress should and must be an active participant in the process of formulating and implementing reorganization plans."[28] While noting "all kinds of vested interests" that would oppose reorganization, Senator William Roth (R-DE) cautioned proponents of renewal about the changed ideational context. "We have just gone through a 10-year period [with] a great deal of criticism of the Congress not discharging its responsibility," Roth emphasized, so "even though I support your legislation, I would not want you to think that that gives you a broad mandate to do whatever you think is best, without review, and careful consideration by the Congress."[29]

The form of reorganization authority that Congress passed in 1977 reflected a subtle but significant move to allow Congress another path of influence over reorganization plans. While the law made Congress consider presidential reorganization plans as a whole in deciding whether to disapprove of them, the legislation allowed presidents to amend their plans even after submission to Congress, before legislators would potentially render a verdict. Compared to the reorganization procedure of the previous four decades, this would give Congress an additional constraint on the president and open an avenue for legislative influence over reorganization plans. This was a new and potentially back-and-forth negotiating process.

While the change potentially opened the door to more interest group or agency influence, it was primarily justified as giving Congress more opportunity to participate in the process and as avoiding a presidential monopoly on making proposals.[30] Indeed, the Carter administration itself proposed the provision in order to facilitate its passage by acknowledging legislators' concerns. As Carter noted, the legislation "amends the reorganization plan procedure to permit the President to amend or withdraw a plan within 30 days of the date of transmittal to Congress."[31] Assuring Senator Jacob Javits (R-NY) that congressional authority would be preserved, Senator Ribicoff proclaimed that this new procedure could force the president to amend plans to "comply with the congressional objection."[32] "For the first time in the reorganization authority," Senator Percy declared, the president could be persuaded "to change a provision or two that might be giving Congress trouble." This would provide another way to eliminate a "flawed provision" proposed by the president without sinking "the entire plan."[33] "This new provision," echoed Representative Brooks, "will allow a President to take notice of any objections to or maybe even suggestions for improvements in a plan that might arise in Congress, and act to meet them."[34] Writing to a constituent, Senator Edmund Muskie (D-ME) emphasized that "any reorganization plan that the President submits is subject to review and change by the Congress."[35]

CONSTITUTIONAL CONCERNS: THE LEGISLATIVE VETO

The claim that Congress is responsible for the organization of the executive branch was asserted more vigorously by the late 1970s. But the constitutional issues over the legislative veto would be the proximate cause of the turn away from presidentialism in reorganization. Even more than presidential authority in other policy areas, presidential reorganization authority was especially vulnerable to constitutional criticism because of its reliance on the legislative veto. The mechanism had been invented to make presidential representation safe for Congress and was thus crucial to making reorganization authority work.

The Reorganization Act of 1977

The legislative veto had been a testament to the adaptability of the relationship between the presidency and Congress under the constitutional separation of powers, and the device had many defenders. It reflected the Progressives' pragmatic approach to the formal structure of the government. By the same token, the constitutional justification offered by defenders of the reorganization plan procedure had weaknesses. Supporters of the legislative veto relied on what they construed as silences in the Constitution, which seemed to belie the surety of their assertions. In an opinion about the device, Carter's attorney general, Griffin Bell, admitted that the legislative veto was "a form of Congressional action which is outside the legislative procedures set out in Article I." Rather than claim that the Constitution explicitly authorized a legislative veto procedure, he argued that it did not exclude the possibility: "the statement in Article I, § 7, of the procedural steps to be followed in the enactment of . . . legislation does not exclude other forms of action by

Congress."[36] Similarly, John Harmon, an acting assistant attorney general in the Office of Legal Counsel, relied on assertions that the legislative process prescribed in Article I was not exhaustive. Though "article I, section 7, clause 3 of the Constitution provides that 'every order, resolution, or vote' to which concurrence of both Houses is necessary shall be presented to the President for his approval or veto," he asserted, "Article I, section 7 is not exclusive in the sense that it is not the exclusive means by which Congress can act."[37]

Years before the *Chadha* decision rendered the court's verdict on the matter, some lawmakers were already pointing out this vulnerability using formalist reasoning. In the hearings on the reorganization legislation, Senator Metcalf pointedly contrasted the legislative veto procedure with normal lawmaking under the Constitution. To begin with, Metcalf invoked Article I's original meaning: "Is this what the framers of the Constitution had in mind when they provided that all legislative powers be vested in the Congress?" Answering his own question, he noted that "Article I, section 8 sets forth specific powers for the formulation of government policies by the Congress, and in the last paragraph, it is the legislature that is empowered to make all laws for 'carrying into execution' those policies and any other powers vested by the Constitution in the Government." Metcalf then turned to what authority the president possessed under Article II: "Under article II of the Constitution, the President advises the Congress as to what measures he feels are necessary," and "the burden is on him to get the Congress to consider his proposals." In contrast to this procedure, Metcalf concluded, the reorganization procedure inverted the proper course of the legislative process: "With the President's executive reorganization act approach, this constitutional process would seem to be reversed. . . . The burden of proof is shifted from the President to Senate and House legislators who may oppose his plan."[38]

Other legislators invoked a formalistic critique of the legislative veto in congressional floor debate. Representative John Conyers (D-MI) pointed to both Congress's legislative powers and the presentment clause of the Constitution: "This procedure is unambiguously explained in article I, section 1 of the Constitution which states that 'all legislative powers herein granted shall be vested in a Congress of the United States.' Article I, section 7, further states that bills are passed by the Congress and sent to the President for his approval or disapproval." But the reorganization process "stands traditional procedure upside down." After the experience of delegating authority to the presidency, Conyers declared, "the lawmaking role of Congress should be more fully exercised, not less so."[39] Representative Walker also unambiguously stated his understanding that the reorganization process had lawmaking backward: "Article I, section 7 of the Constitution clearly states that bills are to be passed by Congress and sent to the President for his approval or disapproval."[40] And Representative Brooks argued that "to allow a President to propose and, in effect, pass a law unless Congress vetoes it is to reverse that process and trample on the doctrine of separation of powers."[41]

Legislators were not the only ones expressing these sentiments. In a notable ideological pairing, the conservative Antonin Scalia made the same critiques of the legislative veto as did a variety of Democrats in congressional debate. As a veteran of the Ford administration Justice Department, Scalia held a position that put him into conflict with the Carter Justice Department's verdict on reorganization and the legislative veto. The department was correct, testified Scalia, that "the situation of one-House action is not addressed specifically in article I, section 7." But this constitutional omission, Scalia contended, was "only because it never occurred to the founding fathers that Congress would seek to act with legal effect by one House alone." Responding to the notion that the reorganization process was simply "legislation in reverse," Scalia said that "to let [presidential reorganization plans] take effect through inaction rather than action seems to me not to reverse the process of legislation but to evade it." Instead, Scalia supported Representative Brooks's preferred alternative for reorganization that would require affirmative legislative consent for presidential plans to take effect.[42]

Of course, none of this would have been news to the reformers who built the institutional presidency. The inversion of the formal arrangement and the choice of the legislative veto had been purposeful. But circumstances had changed. The national press commented on these potential constitutional issues as well. A *New York Times* report presciently suggested that "some lawyers believe that there is a danger under the reorganization authority . . . that the restructuring of various agencies could be voided several months or years later by a Supreme Court ruling that the legislative veto procedure was unconstitutional."[43] The *Times* also pointed out that the Carter administration was tying itself into knots trying to defend the reorganization procedure. Like previous administrations, the Carter administration generally held that the legislative veto was unconstitutional. It did not want to make it easy for Congress to overturn its administrative actions. But the Carter administration nonetheless made an explicit exception for reorganization. "By advocating the legislative veto in his reorganization plan," the *Times* noted, "Mr. Carter is placing himself in an awkward position. For, like Presidents before him, he is almost certain to fight Congressional efforts to attach a veto provision to other measures, arguing in those instances using the device is unwise and unconstitutional."[44] Presidential pretensions about the legislative veto were unambiguous: "Most Presidents have opposed legislative vetoes as

unconstitutional except in cases in which they sought extraordinary authority from Congress."[45]

INS v. Chadha *(1983)*

The legislative veto "may be unconstitutional," Representative L. H. Fountain (D-NC) mused during debates over reorganization in 1977, "although I
doubt it. One of these days, that question may be raised."[46] It was only a few
years later that the question came before the Supreme Court. In *Immigration
and Naturalization Service v. Chadha* (1983), the court indicated that it agreed
with the substantial constitutional criticisms that had been lodged against the
legislative veto.

The case addressed a substantive matter that was unrelated to reorganization authority. The Immigration and Naturalization Service had granted
Jagdish Rai Chadha, a foreign exchange student with an expired student
visa, a hardship exemption that would prevent his impending deportation.
However, the House vetoed that decision in 1975. Confounding normal political alliances, both the Reagan Justice Department and the Ralph Nader–
affiliated group Public Citizen pushed the case on Chadha's behalf. For the
Reagan administration, the case represented an opportunity to rid itself of
the legislative veto in other areas of executive power.[47]

In a 7–2 decision, the court struck down the use of one- and two-chamber
legislative vetoes by concurrent resolution as a violation of the presentment
clause. Chief Justice Warren Burger argued that the Constitution provided
only "a single, finely wrought and exhaustively considered procedure" for
legislation, passed by both Houses and agreed to by president. Burger's opinion was joined by five justices: William Brennan, Thurgood Marshall, Harry
Blackmun, John Paul Stevens, and Sandra Day O'Connor. Burger described
the importance of original text, asserting the "profound conviction of the
Framers that the powers conferred on Congress were the powers to be most
carefully circumscribed."[48] Meanwhile, a concurrence with the decision noted
the significant stakes of what the court was deciding. Even as he endorsed the
outcome, Associate Justice Lewis Powell admitted that "the breadth of this
holding gives one pause," since "Congress has included the veto in literally
hundreds of statutes."[49]

Justices Byron White and William Rehnquist dissented. In his dissent,
Justice White lamented that the legislative veto had been an "important if not
indispensable political invention," essentially acknowledging that the device
had potentially departed from constitutional expectations but noting that it
had allowed "the President and Congress to resolve major constitutional and

policy differences." Moreover, Justice White also warned that the court, in making such a decision, had adopted "a profoundly different conception of the Constitution than that held by the Courts which sanctioned the modern administrative state."[50]

Terminating Presidential Reorganization Authority,
Keeping Presidential Reorganizations

The *Chadha* decision had pitted a device invented to accommodate presidential representation in reorganization against claims about the Constitution's original meaning. Formalistic reasoning won the day. Yet on its own, the decision did not necessarily mean the end of presidential reorganization authority. The extended authority from the 1977 law had expired in 1981, but the choice over whether to devise a new procedure for reorganization remained in the hands of Congress.[51]

Legislators had already made it clear that the loss of a legislative veto would be a problem. The legislative veto had been vital to congressional willingness to trust, but check, that the president would act in the national interest in reorganization. Senator Percy, for example, had explained in 1977 that the legislative veto was what made him comfortable with buying into the notion of presidential authority: "We always have the right of veto, and in the legislation we will be working out, the Congress can act, and I think the Republic will be protected. But I lean in the direction of giving the President the authority to take the initiative."[52] This viewpoint was further echoed in the aftermath of the *Chadha* decision. The scope of changes that could be accomplished through presidential reorganization plans, observed Representative Elliott Levitas (D-GA), was significant: "Now, when a reorganization plan comes in, it results in the repeal of laws, the rewriting of new laws, the shifting of personnel and functions—it is a massive change." The legislative veto, he stressed, was the crucial protection: "it was considered simpler to let the President propose it," but "if Congress didn't like it, they could say, 'no.'"[53] Indeed, while Congress generally allowed presidential proposals to go into effect, it had exercised the legislative veto to reject many such plans over previous decades.[54]

The court's decision to take away the safeguard of the legislative veto made relying on presidential representation seem more dubious. Skepticism of the president's purportedly more rationalistic approach to reorganization that was voiced in scholarship made its way into congressional hearings. In an ironic twist, political scientists—the profession that had been responsible for promulgating faith in presidential stewardship—increasingly concurred with legislators who were suspicious of the concept. Louis Fisher and Ronald Moe summed up these doubts, admitting that, "like most students of government, we had long assumed that the president's reorganization authority served the interests of both branches." Reformers who had been "hostile towards Congress" had believed that "the reorganization plan method is attractive" because the president could "outmaneuver" agency or interest group resistance and "propose what is 'right.'" But now, acknowledged Fisher and Moe, they "doubted [their] preconceptions."[55] In his testimony before Congress, Fisher elaborated on the point, noting the contrast to the "attitude back in the 1930's [that] was one of distrust of Congress, that you had to take Congress out of the picture because Congress would not support any reasonable proposal."[56]

With the legislative veto out of the question, Congress ultimately chose not to reauthorize presidential reorganization authority. It could have chosen otherwise. For example, in 1977, Scalia had argued that a congressional delegation of reorganization authority to the presidency that was *not* subject to legislative veto would be constitutional.[57] But Congress was not willing to countenance giving any presidents even greater authority in reorganization than they had previously possessed. Another possibility that might have taken hold was creating a process like fast track. In 1984, Representative Brooks had introduced a bill to require a joint resolution of both chambers of Congress to approve presidential reorganization plans. But while Congress adopted that measure, this procedure was in effect for less than two months. And with the Senate having adjourned for the duration of the time in which the authority was valid, there was no opportunity for the president to even attempt to utilize it. The authority soon expired, at the end of 1984.[58]

For many observers, the decline of presidential reorganization authority seemed to promise a corresponding resurgence of congressional power. Unlike in other policy areas in which the demise of the legislative veto had diminished congressional power, this change was viewed as a serious setback for the presidency in reorganization.[59] Some legislators expressed their expectation that the outcome would benefit Congress as an institution. "On many occasions in recent years," said Representative Brooks, "I have argued the dubious constitutionality of the legislative veto procedure. . . . I feel that the decision was proper as a matter of constitutional law."[60] "The *Chadha* decision negates not one of the authorities granted Congress in article I of the Constitution," said Representative John Dingell (D-MI).[61] He expected Congress's role would be strengthened as a result: "Quite honestly, the result will be, I think, then, a Congress which will be strengthened in relation to the other branches, but it will be strengthened because we do what we can do under the Constitution, we do what we should do under the Constitution and we do it in a vigorous and proper and sensible way."[62] "In the long run," agreed Representative Joe Moakley (D-MA), "the Congress will be strengthened in relation to the President, the bureaucracy, and the courts."[63]

With the president losing reorganization authority, that authority certainly belonged only to Congress. But Congress quickly discovered its own limitations. In the aftermath of the court's decision, it was initially unclear whether previous reorganization plans that had been "agreed to" by Congress—through the absence of any congressional disapproval—would still be considered valid. The issue was one of severability: would those reorganization plans have been accepted by legislators anyway, even without the legislative veto procedure?[64]

Given this uncertainty, Congress worried about the potential instability in government if all the reorganization plans of the previous decades were found to be unconstitutional as a result of their being enacted through an invalid process. Referring to Justice White's opinion, Representative Claude Pepper (D-FL) opined that "the Court just rather cavalierly . . . declared unconstitutional more statutes than had been invalidated by the courts in the history of the country with one sweep, with all kinds of various situations." Even Representative Brooks—who agreed with the constitutional reasoning behind the decision—worried that "it would disrupt the entire framework of Government," imploring his colleagues that it would be "just absolute foolishness . . . to allow that to happen."[65]

This was not a Congress eager to reexamine the wisdom and rationale behind presidential choices made through the reorganization plans of the previous decades to alter the executive branch structure and vest functions in different secretaries and officers in the executive branch.[66] Instead, it was a Congress panicked at the thought of wreaking chaos. Both Republicans and Democrats expressed similar urgency. "Past reorganization plans must remain in effect in order to ensure an orderly and effective government," stressed Representative Frank Horton (R-NY). "Enactment of this legislation," argued Representative Brooks, "is essential to ensure that the authority of agencies affected by past reorganization plans is not disrupted." Even more pointedly, Representative Levitas complained, "The train wreck of government which the Supreme Court created in that case, in which they demonstrated a rather abysmal ignorance of our system of government, has left a great mess to be cleaned up now."[67]

To head off any potential for the court to evaluate the constitutionality of all the presidential reorganization plans enacted through a process only now deemed to be illegitimate, Congress undertook a quick fix. In one brief but sweeping law, legislators ratified all the previously enacted presidential reorganization plans. The long title of the 1984 statute captured the essence of its purpose: "An Act to Prevent Disruption of the Structure and Functioning of the Government by Ratifying All Reorganization Plans as a Matter of Law."[68] This put the structure of the executive branch on a sounder statutory basis. It also effectively ratified some of the transfers of functions to different executive branch officers, particularly to cabinet secretaries, that presidents had undertaken. And in fact, one result was that some limited reorganization authorities were left in the hands of a few cabinet secretaries for potential use *within* their own departments, even as presidents lost their broader authority.[69]

Legislators realized that it was better to live with the transformation in the executive branch structure that presidents had already undertaken, and to that extent, the institutional reinvention of the previous decades had made an indelible mark. But Congress also decided to largely halt that kind of adaptation, choosing not to grant presidents leeway to reorganize the broader executive branch structure in the future.

Conclusion: Ideas and Presidential Control over Administration

The reorganization process adopted in 1939 had excluded claims and reforms associated with the unitary executive theory in order to ensure passage. To make presidential representation palatable to Congress, the legislative veto—a device of debated constitutionality—had been utilized, becoming a feature of the subsequent renewals of presidential reorganization authority. By contrast, the unitary executive theory, which Congress had rejected in the 1930s, would have required adopting a particular reading of the meaning of Article II. The full implications of Congress's choice to accommodate presidential representation through the invention of the legislative veto emerged in the 1980s with the *Chadha* decision. Indeed, it had always been possible that the Supreme Court would reject the legislative veto as unconstitutional if given the chance.

It was not a coincidence that conservative insurgents in the 1970s and 1980s began to express new interest in the unitary executive theory.[70] At a time when it was pushing the politics of originalism, the Reagan administration sought to secure its control of the executive branch in constitutional claims about the president's executive power under Article II. Despite its implications for reorganization authority, Republican president Ronald Reagan's attorney general, William French Smith, had notably praised the *Chadha* decision as "a return to our moorings."[71] The lesson was clear: presidential control over the executive branch needed another basis on which to rest.[72]

But the unitary theory did not reach to the power of reorganization. It promised greater control over the *personnel* and *policymaking* of the administration, but it could not help presidents regain authority to *restructure* the administration as a whole. Promises to reorganize the executive branch continued unabated, but now they were routinely left unfulfilled. In the words of one journalist, such a promise became one of the "three lame stories" the press covers during every presidency.[73] The unitary executive theory could demand responsiveness from actors within the executive branch, but it had little bearing on Congress. Determining the general institutional arrangements of the executive branch remained the prerogative of legislators.[74] In effect, the return to formalism severed a significant government capacity and thwarted further institutional adaptation.

In an era of formalist reasoning and sweeping assertions of unitary claims, it is telling that presidents have still reached for claims of presidential representation in their quest to regain some form of reorganization authority from Congress. Critiques of congressional representation and bureaucratic self-interest are a staple of these requests. Calling for a "permanent reorganization authority," the George W. Bush administration argued, "The protection of turf and jurisdiction should no longer stand in the way of more effective government."[75] Reprising earlier rationales behind reorganization authority, Barack Obama also equated Congress with special interest influence: "congressional committees fought to protect their turf and lobbyists fought to keep things the way they were because they were the only ones who could navigate the confusion." By contrast, he made a vow of stewardship: "I will only use this authority for reforms that result in more efficiency, better service, and a leaner Government."[76] His successor, Donald Trump, promised a "very special" reorganization to make the executive branch "efficient, effective, and accountable to the people."[77]

The consistent logic offered by presidents as different as Bush, Obama, and Trump suggests that presidential reorganization authority remains reliant on presidential representation as a rationale. Inherent in any delegation of that authority is the perception that Congress is itself incapable of overcoming special interests to efficiently reorganize the executive branch and that only the president can meet the challenge. But Congress still has to buy that claim, and given legislators' reticence to create an alternative reorganization process in recent decades, presidents who continue to promise reorganizations that would adapt the executive branch to changing national needs are now only grasping at straws. The idea of the unitary executive may promise presidents greater executive control, but insofar as institutional adaptability is concerned, it has proven to be no substitute for presidential representation.

Congressional Pushback against Presidential National Security Authority

> Our constitutional system requires confidence that the Congress will act as responsibly as any President in the national interest. Even more significantly, it assumes that the national interest can best be defined and acted upon when both the President and the Congress are required to come to an understanding as to what is that national interest.
>
> SENATOR JACOB JAVITS (R-NY), 1973[1]

As the Vietnam War escalated in 1966, an American named Robert Goetz wrote a letter to then House majority leader Carl Albert (D-OK). "The unleashing of a powerful war machine (or of one missile!) is too formidable and irrevocable to be entrusted to the fallible judgment of any one man," argued Goetz: "Deliberation and dialogue are of the essence. In the interests of national safety, Article 2, Section 2 of the Constitution should be amended to relieve the President of his responsibilities as commander in chief."[2] "Your views on this matter are appreciated," Albert wrote succinctly in reply, no doubt viewing the proposal as absurd.[3]

Whatever the wisdom of Goetz's proposed course of action, his letter proved perceptive of changes underway in American politics. First, in criticizing a reliance on individual judgment over collective judgment, Goetz recognized an ongoing shift in the ideational foundations of the presidency. The idea of presidential representation—that the president alone could better represent the national interest than members of Congress collectively—was now viewed as naïve. Second, while the proposition of a constitutional amendment to eliminate the president's role as commander in chief was farfetched, Goetz correctly recognized that the president's Article II authority stipulating this responsibility would pose an enormous obstacle to any potential congressional pushback against presidential supremacy in national security policy.

Of all the policy areas in which Congress sought to curb presidential authority in the 1970s, perhaps none attracted as much popular attention and passion as war powers. Tackling this issue area before any other, the reform efforts were "the earliest conspicuous symbol of the congressional resurgence."[4] The widespread dissatisfaction with the Vietnam conflict augured the possibility of Congress reversing the decades-long shift toward greater presidential control over national security policy. In its efforts to institutionalize coordination and collective responsibility for national security in the executive branch in the National Security Act of 1947, Congress had also affirmed the president's authority as commander in chief and primacy over the national security apparatus. Seemingly adding to that authority, Republican president Richard Nixon achieved an overwhelming victory in the 1972 presidential election, bolstering his claim to represent the nation. Yet a critical mass of legislators from both parties was poised in 1973 to reassert congressional primacy in declaring war and to demarcate the bounds of unilateral presidential military actions. The effort marked Congress's attempt "to grapple with the president for leadership of the national security state."[5]

Passed over Nixon's veto, the War Powers Resolution (WPR) of 1973 was symptomatic of a decisive turn against the idea of presidential representation. Lawmakers and other political actors argued that presidents no longer could be trusted to act in the national interest, claimed that the collective membership of Congress better represented the people than an individual president, and asserted that Congress possessed unquestionable authority and primacy in national security decisions over war under Article I of the Constitution. Though the WPR might have appeared to be a partisan measure because of its passage during divided government, the resolution passed with substantial bipartisan majorities.[6] Key congressional Republicans were among the most vigorous proponents of seeking to limit presidential authority. Senator Jacob Javits (R-NY), a primary WPR sponsor, spoke for many when he emphasized that the conflict was over institutional authority rather than partisanship: "This is a struggle, between the Congress and the President. This President—whom I helped to elect, and I am not a bit bashful about it nor do I feel sorry about it at all because he was the best man for the job under all the circumstances which we faced in the last election in my judgment—but nevertheless, his concept of the Presidency is different from mine, and, I think, from a majority of the Congress."[7]

The immediate reason Congress began to doubt the wisdom of presidential judgment and reconsider its own institutional capacity was the debacle in Vietnam. As the war's unpopularity grew, many lawmakers had ample opportunity to hear from their constituents and respond to their concerns. By the time the new war powers legislation passed, one poll found that 80 percent of Americans supported the reform.[8] But whether responding based on electoral self-interest or for more idealistic reasons, these legislators viewed Vietnam as a symptom of a deeper institutional problem, and they sought to address the issue on those terms. "Motivation for this bill," stated Representative James Hanley (D-NY), "stems from the controversial Vietnam war which unfortunately divided the American people . . . and justifiably so produced overwhelming public demand that the Congress reassert itself in the all-important matter of war and peace."[9] "'No more Vietnams' should be our objective," stressed Representative Spark Matsunaga (D-HI) more directly.[10] Several events in the conflict, including Nixon's ground invasion of Cambodia in 1970, the aerial invasion of Laos in 1971, and the renewed bombing of North Vietnam, contributed to a perception that presidents had become unconstrained in war making.[11] In 1971, Congress had also repealed the 1964 Gulf of Tonkin Resolution that had been the basis for the Vietnam conflict, eliminating any legislative sanction for continued American actions and underscoring that the conflict had become a presidential war.[12]

Congress was also reacting to several decades of its own authority diminishing. Democratic president Harry Truman had undertaken the Korean conflict without a formal declaration of war in 1950.[13] Invoking both Korea and Vietnam, Representative Claude Pepper (D-FL) explained that Congress's efforts were necessary "after the trauma of two wars in less than 25 years in which this country sustained casualties of several hundred thousands and spent several hundreds of billions of dollars and suffered a dangerous division of the country without a declaration of war by the Congress."[14] The passage of the WPR, reported the *New York Times*, "was not so much a vote against Mr. Nixon as it was a Congressional protest against the powers of the Presidency as they had been interpreted by Mr. Nixon and his predecessors over the past 30 years."[15]

Far from achieving its lofty aims, however, the WPR codified in statute a presidential right to initiate conflicts.[16] The new empowerment was embedded in the qualifications. In addition to obliging the president to notify Congress within forty-eight hours of any military actions being undertaken, the final version of the resolution, in a compromise between the House and Senate, sought to require the president to terminate a commitment of military forces within sixty days unless that commitment received specific authorization by Congress. An extension of thirty days would be granted if the president stated that it was militarily necessary for the safe removal of troops. The statute also provided Congress the ability to disapprove any presidential military actions and to require the removal of military forces through a concurrent resolution of both chambers.[17] Thus, though the measure was meant to constrain the president's ability to undertake military conflicts without congressional authorization, the WPR essentially gave the president a blank check for up to ninety days to initiate war and then to dare Congress to respond.[18] On top of that, the legislative veto in the resolution was viewed as constitutionally questionable, since a concurrent resolution would not be subject to a presidential veto. As we have seen in chapter 9, the legislative veto was later overturned by the Supreme Court in *INS v. Chadha* (1983). While the WPR itself was not amended to reflect that outcome, legislators in 1983 passed a separate provision to specify that Congress could seek to disapprove of a president's military actions via a joint resolution, which would be subject to presidential approval and require a two-thirds majority to overcome a potential presidential veto.[19]

What accounts for the discrepancy between the intent behind the WPR and the legislative outcome? Remarks prepared by Senator Javits for a lecture at Princeton in 1970 offer one initial hint. The speech began with a challenge to the wisdom of presidential authority. "The implication that the Presidency is beyond the power of Congress to check in the exercise of war powers raises a constitutional danger," argued Javits: "It could leave the nation solely dependent on the good judgment and benign intent of the incumbent President." "While we have had a high standard for eminence in the Presidency throughout our history," Javits warned, "experience has shown that our liberties require firmer institutional safeguards if they are to survive." However, Javits then admitted a problem. While the president's war powers had grown over time, Javits viewed them as stemming from the president's constitutional duty as commander in chief. Though "the Presidents have developed the Commander-in-Chief function in novel and vastly expanded ways never contemplated in the Constitution," Javits stated, "there was an historical logic behind this turn of events and even today I know of no Senator who questions the need for vigorous, vigilant and decisive exercise of the Commander-in-Chief function."[20] Thus, even as Javits questioned presidential authority, he rooted it in a claim different from the idea of presidential representation, one that appeared more resilient.

Just as in other policy areas in the 1970s, Congress reconsidered the president's authority in national security in the face of growing doubts about the validity of presidential representation. Accompanying assertions of congressional representation and constitutionality were also central to Congress's attempt to curtail presidential power. But the extent to which Congress could push back on presidential authority in war differed from the congressional pushback in other policy areas. In some areas, such as budgeting, this pushback against institutional arrangements that had relied on an assumption of presidential stewardship proved significant. The difference was hinted at in trade policy, which, having changed its complexion from domestic to foreign policy, still favored the president's initiative. Presidential authority in national security proved comparatively resilient as well. Like trade, it involved an issue of foreign policy, which naturally favored the presidency. But more significantly, presidential authority on issues of national security did not need to rely on presidential representation for legitimacy. As the debates over the earlier National Security Act of 1947 had shown, this authority was rooted in Congress's perceptions of the meaning of Article II's commander in chief clause.[21] Congress's recognition of that alternative conception, grounded in the Constitution, had a constraining influence on congressional efforts to restrict presidential war making.

This chapter proceeds as follows. First, I show that rising doubts about the validity of presidential representation were repeatedly invoked by lawmakers as they sought to limit presidential authority in war making. Second, I examine the extent to which opposing claims of congressional authority had influence over the WPR. Accompanying their skepticism of presidential representation were lawmakers' arguments both that Congress was institutionally superior in determining the national interest through its collective deliberation and that the legislature had primacy in war making under Article I. However, as I demonstrate, congressional perceptions of the president's authority as commander in chief were cited even by proponents of the WPR as a constraining influence and affected key choices in the design of the final legislation. Finally, I conclude by briefly considering the long-term impact of the WPR since the 1970s and its implications for understanding the role of ideas in supporting presidential power.

Applicability: Doubting the President's National Perspective

Not all legislators were ready to discard the idea of presidential representation. Some attempted to use it to defend presidential power over war making. Referring to President Nixon's overwhelming reelection victory in 1972, Senator John Tower (R-TX) invoked both a plebiscitary and a stewardship justification of the president's representative role. The American people, Tower held, had signaled both their mandate for Nixon's policies and their broader trust in his ability to represent the national interest. By seeking to pass the war powers bill, Congress was "flying in the teeth of the mandate conferred by the American people on the President." "The principal issue in the campaign was foreign policy," Tower argued, and voters had "expressed at the ballot box their confidence in his ability to formulate and implement a foreign policy that is in the best interest of the United States."[22]

Despite such defenses, a consistent theme emerged in debates over war powers: an individual president's judgment could not be counted on to determine the national interest. That assertion struck at the core of presidential representation, which held that the president alone was fully focused on the national interest by virtue of his national constituency.

One exchange between two Democratic legislators captured the stakes of that sentiment. Representative L. H. Fountain (D-NC) outlined the connection between growing presidential power and American faith in presidential representation: "We happen to be a people who will accede to the President's exceeding his power if he ends up doing the right thing, or ends up acting in the best interests of the country." For the legislation's primary sponsor, Representative Clement Zablocki (D-WI), this was precisely the problem. Zablocki's response to Fountain made it clear that he did not trust presidents to discern the national interest correctly: "What happens when he does the wrong thing? That is what bothers me." "Then we all take the consequences," Fountain acknowledged.[23]

Among the most notable legislators invoking doubts about presidential stewardship was the Senate majority leader, Mike Mansfield (D-MT). Issues of war "must be decided not alone by the President," he argued, but instead should include the deliberative judgment of "the men and women in the Congress who answer directly to the people."[24] As a Democratic congressional leader, Mansfield had made a statement that would seem like a predictable and strategic critique to lodge against a Republican president. But Mansfield's sentiment matched his rationale from a decade earlier when his fellow Democrat Lyndon Johnson had been president. In a confidential memo to Johnson in 1964, Mansfield had disputed that LBJ's decision to increase American involvement in Vietnam reflected the national interest. "We are already on the verge of turning a war in Vietnam which is still primarily a Vietnamese responsibility into an American war to be paid for primarily with American lives," he lamented: "I see no national interest at this time which would justify that plunge and I most emphatically do not recommend it."[25] Johnson ignored Mansfield's plea. Mansfield's view that the president's judgment alone could not be counted on to adequately determine the national interest came from painful experience.

The notion that decisions over war were too significant to be left to the president alone was a bipartisan one. "It is the people who should decide this course, through their elected representatives," opined Senator Herman Talmadge (D-GA), as "the decision is too great for one man to make alone."[26] Legislators did not shy away from expressing that sentiment even when it put them into conflict with their copartisan colleagues. Testifying as a witness in the House hearings on the legislation, the bill's Senate sponsor, Senator Javits, criticized a fellow Republican, Senator Barry Goldwater (R-AZ), for continuing to invoke the trope of presidential representation as a justification for presidential war power. Javits quoted Goldwater, who had stated, "I have more confidence in the judgment of the one man who is the President of the United States than in the judgment of the 535 men in the Congress." This type of thinking—"probably the classic statement on this subject"—was the crux of the issue, Javits explained: "that is what it gets down to. Do we succumb to that or do we not[?]" For Javits, the temptation to yield to that line of argument needed to be resisted, as the nation could no longer "assume that one man alone knows the national interest."[27]

Lawmakers also invoked the Vietnam experience to make a slightly different criticism of presidential war making. For some legislators, the identification of a war with the president alone weakened the nation's resolve to undertake the necessary effort. Republican arguments to this effect were especially notable with Richard Nixon in office. "The Vietnam war literally brought this country to its knees," argued Senator Javits, because it was viewed as "essentially a Presidential war."[28] The severe political division in the country, Representative Paul Findley (R-IL) affirmed, was due to presidential action: "Much of the polarization, the dissension and the downright frustration that this country suffered during the Vietnam conflict can be attributed to the fact that Congress was ignored by a series of Presidents."[29] Senator Pete Domenici (R-NM) argued that wars that were identified solely with presidents would not reflect or attract the popular support necessary for success: "God forbid that we should ever have another war of aggression, but if ever such should occur, it should not be 'Kennedy's war' or 'Johnson's war' or 'Nixon's war' but rather an 'American involvement.'" "We have learned the hard way," Domenici emphasized, "that when the American people through their elected Representatives do not share in a decision to go to war, they do not bring to it their full support and sense of personal obligation. The spirit of patriotism is absent."[30] In effect, these Republicans argued that presidential wars would divide the nation, damaging the national interest in the process.

Leverage: Rethinking Constitutional Relationships

As they questioned the validity of presidential representation, lawmakers asserted the superiority of congressional representation and stressed the constitutional authority that belonged to Congress. Both claims were applied to efforts to curtail presidential power over war and to delineate the boundaries of that authority. But these claims also ran into an obstacle, limited by legislators' perceptions of the president's authority as commander in chief. To a significant extent, the form that the WPR took turned on lawmakers trying to deal with what they viewed as a tension within the Constitution itself—

the power to declare war granted to Congress in Article I versus the role of commander in chief specified for the president in Article II—and attempting to reconcile that tension with the practical demands of twentieth-century national security. The end result was a statute that implicitly accepted presidential initiative in committing the nation to military action, even as it sought to increase congressional input and evaluation of those decisions.

CONGRESSIONAL REPRESENTATION:
THE PEOPLE'S BRANCH

In the debates over war powers, Congress asserted its own standing in representing the nation. For legislators who supported curbing presidential authority, decisions over war and peace required the participation of the branch closest to the people. Perhaps unsurprisingly, congressional Democrats claimed to be the superior representatives of the people during a Republican presidency. "Who is most accountable to the people?" Senator Joseph Montoya (D-NM) asked rhetorically. The answer was Congress: "the direct representatives of the people."[31] Only "Congress, as the representative of the people," stated Representative B. F. Sisk (D-CA), "should determine whether or not an international situation is the type of hostility of necessity or emergency in which our troops should be engaged."[32] "With the war powers bill," Senator Lawton Chiles (D-FL) proclaimed, "we put the dog of war back on the people's leash, where it can only be turned loose through the people's representatives."[33] The legislation, wrote Senator Edmund Muskie (D-ME) to a constituent, would prevent "another open-ended situation" from continuing "without the concurrence of the Congress, through which the American people speak."[34]

Democratic criticism of a Republican president's ability to represent the national will was to be expected. More notable, then, was that the same rationale was echoed by Republican legislators. For these Republicans, proclaiming the representative superiority of Congress was a curious move from a partisan standpoint. In effect, they were concurring that a Congress controlled by Democrats better reflected the will of the people than did the Republican president. Senator Charles Percy (R-IL) enthused that the war powers bill could prevent the president from going against the will of the people: "adherence to the provisions of the War Powers Act could save Presidents from undertaking military adventures contrary to the wishes and interests of the American people."[35] While Representative Bud Shuster (R-PA) stated that he broadly supported the foreign policy of the Nixon administration, he too contrasted the representative character of Congress with that of the president.

For Shuster, presidents had too much of a bias toward military action, one that often came at the expense of ordinary people: "Unfortunately, history tells us that most rulers, whether they be called Presidents, kings, or princes, are better warmakers than peacemakers." Therefore, Congress's voice needed to count for more in decisions over war: "It is the people who bleed and die, and what affects the lives of the people should be decided by the representatives of the people."[36] As Senator Javits also argued, Americans had "just learned the hard way that wars cannot be successfully fought except with the consent of the people and with their support." Thus, the importance of the measure was "giving the broad representation of the people in the Congress a voice" in war making.[37]

Complementing their claims of speaking for the people, legislators also took more direct aim at presidential representation by claiming that Congress was needed to collectively determine the national interest in war.[38] While Congress might not be "infallible in its wisdom," noted the Senate majority whip, Robert Byrd (D-WV), "the collective best judgment of the Nation's elected leaders" would be "the Nation's one best hope of following the right course of action."[39] "Our founding fathers were careful not to give to one man the authority and responsibility for taking us into war," wrote one citizen to Speaker Carl Albert in 1972. Rather, they had wanted the responsibility of deciding on war to be subject to "the composite judgment of the men of the Congress."[40] Moreover, legislators also argued that the national interest would be served by making any American commitment to military action more credible to adversaries through congressional support. Javits saw congressional involvement, rather than simply relying on the president, as a way to "raise the credibility of the American commitment because, when the Nation speaks, it will speak with one voice."[41] Representative Ogden Reid (D-NY) asserted that a congressionally declared war would "carry more weight overseas than a unilateral act of a President which is not necessarily supported by the people." In the context of the Cold War, he further posited that "the Soviets . . . are fully sensitive, for instance, to the distinction between a broad national mandate and a decision that does not imply broad support."[42]

CONSTITUTIONAL AUTHORITY: CONGRESS'S POWER TO DECLARE WAR

Supporters of the war powers legislation argued that Congress was restoring its appropriate constitutional role in war making, pointing to Congress's authority under Article I to declare war. They did not seek to justify Congress's efforts as a departure but characterized the legislation as a return to the Constitution's original meaning. While opponents of that effort, such as Senator Goldwater, claimed proponents "were trying to amend the Constitution," Senator Javits alleged quite the opposite: "We are restoring the Constitution."[43] "The record is clear," asserted Senator Thomas Eagleton (D-MO), "that those in attendance at the Constitutional Convention were surprised and dismayed at the suggestion that the President be given power to make decisions which might result in offensive military action."[44] The "purpose of the bill," argued Representative Michael Harrington (D-MA), was "to fulfill— not to alter, amend or adjust—the intent of the framers of the Constitution," which in "Article I, section 8 . . . clearly vests the authority to initiate war in the Congress."[45] "I was a cosponsor of the War Powers bill," wrote Senator Muskie to one citizen, "because I strongly believe that the power to decide when and whether our country will go to war should reside in the Congress, as our Constitution originally intended."[46] "Your bills merely seek to restore the original design," Harvard law professor Raoul Berger testified to the House: "It cannot be unconstitutional to go back to the Constitution."[47]

Just as supporters of the legislation characterized themselves as returning to the Constitution's original meaning, they also portrayed the constitutional reasoning of the Nixon administration as decidedly nonoriginalist. The "overtowering bulk of the warmaking power was lodged in Congress," Berger testified to the Senate: "The apologists [for presidential power] depend on extra-constitutional, post-1787 self-serving statements or actions by the President [and] not on the Constitution, not on anything that was said by a Framer."[48] Perhaps the most notable critic on that score was the chairman of the Senate Foreign Relations Committee, Senator J. William Fulbright (D-AR). In 1961, Fulbright had championed the notion that only the president could "rise above parochialism" and alleged that the president was "hobbled" by the Constitution's restrictions.[49] Now, however, Fulbright mocked the Nixon administration for holding that any action it took would be consistent with the Constitution's original meaning. He asserted that the administration claimed the right "to interpret the Constitution as we see fit" and "therefore do as we please, confident in the knowledge that such was the intent of the Founding Fathers."[50] Significantly, Fulbright's concerns did not just arise out of partisanship, and he did not seek to hold only the Republican administration accountable. Emphasizing that his motives were institutional, Fulbright pointed the finger at previous Democratic presidents as well, stating that "many of us feel the previous administrations . . . departed from the Constitution. This one didn't initiate it." Thus, Fulbright characterized the war powers bill as "an effort to kind of remind the country and the people that the Constitution still stands."[51]

The most notable assertion of the Constitution's original meaning came as Congress considered overriding Nixon's veto of the war powers legislation. In his veto message, Nixon cited both his understanding of the national interest and his view that the legislation was unconstitutional: "the restrictions which this resolution would impose upon the authority of the President are both unconstitutional and dangerous to the best interests of our Nation."[52] Not only did many of Nixon's fellow congressional Republicans defy their party leader to vote to override that veto; they did so by asserting that their position was the more accurate understanding of the Constitution. Bucking his party leader, Representative John Anderson (R-IL) argued that "the time has clearly come for the Congress to squarely confront the question of 'whose power is the war power' and recognize the central role the Founding Fathers intended for the Congress to play in this vital area."[53] Representative Findley pointedly asked his colleagues, "Do we believe in the balance of powers intended by the Founding Fathers?"[54] And the Republican champion of the legislation, Senator Javits, emphasized that "the Constitution lays upon the Congress, unmistakably, the responsibility of deciding whether or not the state of our Nation should be changed from peace to war."[55]

CONSTITUTIONAL AUTHORITY:
THE PRESIDENT AS COMMANDER IN CHIEF

The focus of lawmakers reasserting Congress's power over declaring war on the Constitution's original meaning had obvious strategic utility given the text of Article I. It was a firm base from which to push back on the president's claim to represent the national interest. Not only could reformers dispute that pretention; they could paint it as less legitimate than Congress's constitutional claim. But even as the language of constitutional formalism appeared to open up the opportunity for Congress to reassert itself against the presidency, it simultaneously hemmed that effort in, foreclosing bolder pushback. Prioritizing constitutional clauses meant that lawmakers had to deal with the meaning of the president's responsibility as commander in chief. And while the meaning of that role was contested by both proponents and opponents of the legislation, the fact that the debate took place on those terms at all proved consequential in shaping the legislation.

The Nixon administration and other defenders of presidential power offered expansive readings of the meaning of the commander in chief clause in their efforts to oppose the war powers legislation.[56] Foreshadowing some of the most ambitious constitutional claims of the George W. Bush administration decades later, Charles Brower, an acting legal adviser at the State Department, argued to lawmakers that "the President's authority [in war making] rests on his general authority under article II of the Constitution."[57] Offering a warning that presidential leadership in foreign policy was needed for global stability, Representative Jack Kemp (R-NY) also made a sweeping claim about the president's constitutional authority over foreign policy. "Shorn of the power to act decisively," he argued, "the Presidency and the foreign policy he constitutionally directs would be incapable of playing their crucial, stabilizing roles in the world."[58]

A more interesting view of the president's authority came from another Republican, Senator Tower. Paying homage to the changed ideational context in which presidential authority was being reconsidered, Tower conceded that Congress needed to reassert itself in policymaking: "We are guilty of having delegated away our power and responsibility and authority to the President." But Tower drew a distinction between domestic and foreign policy. Congress's role in granting power to the president, he argued, had "been largely in the domestic field over which the Congress should establish policy." By contrast, Tower asserted that presidential authority over foreign affairs was envisioned by the Constitution: "when we get to the historic field where everyone who is a scholar of the American system of Government realizes that [by] the constitutional processes . . . this is a field in which the executive branch should be preeminent."[59] Passage of the WPR, Tower alleged, would be "undermining the historic and constitutional role of the President of the United States as the principal spokesman and negotiator for our Nation in the field of diplomatic relations."[60]

Another argument that presaged the later claims of the George W. Bush administration downplayed the meaning of the Article I clause giving the legislature authority to "declare war."[61] In his congressional testimony, Brower argued that the framers of the Constitution had explicitly chosen to ensure that the president would have war making authority absent a congressional declaration of war:

> You may recall that the provision in the Constitution giving Congress the power to declare war was actually changed from a previous draft before the Committee on Detail in the Constitutional Convention. That previous draft would have given Congress the power to make war, and the explanation for the change from 'make war' to 'declare war,' I believe the precise language was the President must have the authority to repel sudden attacks. . . . So it is quite clear that the Founding Fathers had very much in their minds that the military forces of the United States would be employed in serious hostilities in the absence of a declaration of war.[62]

Officials from the Nixon administration were not the only ones pointing to the significance of that change as evidence of the framers' purported intent. "When the framers of our Constitution narrowed the authority of Congress by substituting 'declare' for 'make' in the declaration of war clause," Representative Kemp posited, "they clearly understood that there had been and might continue to be many instances in which hostilities would occur with no declaration of war."[63]

Some even downplayed the notion that declaring war had any practical significance at all. Senator Goldwater's reasoning was instructive. While Goldwater was concerned that the war powers measure would restrain the president's "constitutional powers of national defense," he did observe that the president's war power was not unrestricted, arguing that the president "cannot begin a war of conquest of another's territory." But Goldwater's focus still prioritized determining the meaning of the Article II role of commander in chief, and it sidelined the Article I power of Congress to declare war. "The declaration," Senator Goldwater argued, "had come to mean no more than a formal notice to the world and to one's own people that an already existing state of war was officially acknowledged."[64]

These ambitious readings of the commander in chief clause were criticized by other legislators and political actors. "The Constitution says nothing whatever about the President's initiating [war]," asserted Senator Javits: "A President is Commander in Chief, period. . . . It is what is read into those words that have caused this doctrine to be erected for over 200 years."[65] Former executive branch officials also attacked that broad view of presidential authority. Arthur Schlesinger Jr.—the author of *The Imperial Presidency* and a former member of the Kennedy administration—ridiculed the "self-serving pronouncements by members of the executive branch." Those expansive readings of the commander in chief clause, he contended, "cannot be afforded the status of constitutional gospel."[66] A former assistant secretary of defense for international security affairs under LBJ, Paul Warnke, also tried to draw a distinction between the role of commander in chief and the extent of the power that role implied. While "the President's authority as Commander in Chief puts him in charge of combat operations during such war and enables him to take emergency actions to protect American security," Warnke wrote, it "cannot be read to give him the right to carry on an air war in a civil conflict in a tiny country on the other side of the world."[67]

Few lawmakers embraced any overpowering vision of the commander in chief authority. Senator Javits even complained "that Presidents have tended to see their role, as Commander in Chief conducting a war, as the decisive power of the Presidency."[68] Nonetheless, even many of the chief advocates of the war powers measure did perceive the president's Article II authority as constraining their efforts. Underscoring the difficulty they faced in rolling back presidential authority in the realm of national security, proponents of that effort openly worried about the constitutional issues they were addressing. Writing to a New Hampshire constituent, Senator Thomas McIntyre (D-NH) emphasized that "the war powers of the respective branches of government have been set by the Constitution. No law could stand which contravenes this."[69] "I think we are in a weak position if, indeed, the constitutional question is not adequately resolved," Representative Zablocki admitted.[70] While he agreed with the goal of the war powers bill, Representative Pete du Pont (R-DE) expressed the need for caution in dealing with a "sensitive area" of the president's "constitutional prerogatives." In response, Senator Javits conceded that the president would retain significant authority regardless of the war powers legislation: "No one is trying to denude the President of authority. . . . I want to make that very clear. The President will still have a great deal of power."[71] Senator Fulbright worried that Congress might preserve too much presidential power that had been "established by tradition" only, but he nonetheless also expressed deference to the president as commander in chief: "I do not believe that in any substantial way at all it encroaches upon the prerogatives of the commander in chief, the President."[72]

In fact, deference to the president's authority under Article II was widely expressed in congressional floor debate. "In no sense," stated Senator Percy, "would any Member of this body wish to take away the prerogative of the Commander in Chief from the standpoint of protecting the best interests of this country."[73] Senator Javits acknowledged that the president's strong claim over national security was accommodated under the war powers legislation: "The President is left with his true, preexisting constitutional authority as Commander in Chief to deploy the forces of the United States, assuming he can get the Congress to raise the forces and to finance them."[74] Affirming that "as Commander in Chief of military forces the President has immense power," Representative Findley pledged, "This legislation does not diminish 1 ounce of that vast power. The power is inherent in his position as Commander in Chief."[75] Coming from Republicans, these statements might have appeared to simply be cover for preserving the authority of a president from their own party. But congressional Democrats also echoed the same understanding of the legislation. Senator Hubert Humphrey (D-MN), another notable critic of presidential war powers, stated that the bill would not "cripple the President in his role as Commander in Chief and in his role as chief spokesman of the Nation in matters of foreign policy."[76]

The difference that Congress faced in pushing back against presidential power in national security, as opposed to other policy areas like budgeting, was made especially vivid in the behavior of Senator Sam Ervin (D-NC). At the same time that Congress was considering the war powers legislation, Ervin took the role as a leading critic of presidential budgeting. He expressed doubts about the validity of presidential representation, and he helped lead the charge to create a separate congressional budget process and augment Congress's analytical capacity with the establishment of the Congressional Budget Office. Indeed, Ervin also led the Senate's inquiry into the Watergate scandal. But in the debates over the president's authority in national security, Ervin took the opposite side. Despite a scandal-ridden president from the other party holding office, the Democratic senator supported Nixon's "sound" veto of the war powers bill. The basis was different, turning on the authority of the commander in chief. As Ervin argued, "It is the constitutional power and the constitutional duty of the President, without any declaration of war and without any action by Congress, to defend this country against invasion." The war powers bill, complained Ervin, "in effect, says that the President cannot exercise his constitutional power and cannot perform his constitutional duty for more than 60 days without the consent of Congress." Ervin believed Congress was usurping the president's constitutional authority: "It says that the President cannot be the Commander in Chief of the Army and the Navy when the United States is attacked for more than 60 days and that at the end of 60 days, Congress assumes that role."[77] In attacking the president's authority in budgeting, but coming to the opposite conclusion with national security at the same time, Ervin underscored that the issues transcended partisanship and, instead, turned on different ideas about presidential authority.

DEFINITION OR DISCRETION?

Congressional concerns about the president's constitutional authority influenced the central choice in the design of the final war powers legislation. This was a change to avoid specifying under what circumstances presidents could use force on their own without congressional approval. Legislators had taken varied positions on the extent to which the president's authority should be privileged. For defenders of presidential power who took the most expansive reading of the role of commander in chief, no restrictions on the president's authority could be imposed by Congress. For the most vigorous proponents of legislative authority, Congress could specify in the statute the only possible circumstances that would justify the president taking military action without separate congressional authorization.

In considering the House and Senate versions of the legislation, lawmakers were faced with a choice over whether to define acceptable circumstances for a president to take unilateral military actions or whether to leave such decisions to the executive's discretion. In the end, they settled on a choice that did not endorse the most ambitious understandings of the commander in chief clause. But they also deferred to that conception of presidential authority in allowing the president flexibility to act for any reason and then calling on Congress to subsequently evaluate the action.[78]

The Senate version of the war powers legislation had specified when the president could act alone. It offered three exceptions for presidential action without congressional authorization: an attack on the continental United States, an attack on US forces legally deployed abroad, and missions to rescue American nationals.[79] But lawmakers in the House doubted the wisdom of this course.[80] Representative David Dennis (R-IN), for example, argued that those categories "are inherent constitutional rights on the part of the Executive."[81]

The clearest statement of the rationale behind the House's alternative approach came from the sponsor of the legislation, Representative Zablocki. Describing "the most important" difference between the Senate and House bills as being "related to the question of Presidential authority," Zablocki noted that "the Senate bill defined the President's authority in warmaking and sought to mandate the circumstances under which he could act." By contrast, "the House resolution did not attempt such a definition or mandate, on the grounds that to do so was constitutionally questionable and from a practical standpoint unwise." The final bill set a purported time limit on the engagement of troops at sixty days, which could be "extended for up to 30 additional days if the President certifies in writing to the Congress that unavoidable military necessity respecting the safety of the troops required their continued use." The key justification for the House's approach, Zablocki stressed, was to avoid infringing on what proponents of the legislation viewed as the president's authority as commander in chief: "the House conferees believe that 60 days is ample time to permit the President to act in a national emergency under his powers as Commander in Chief." The legislation thus did not "encroach upon the legitimate authority of the President as Commander in Chief."[82]

Zablocki did assert Congress's claims against the president in touting the legislative veto provision as an additional safeguard against presidential abuse. But the court's decision that legislative vetoes were constitutionally invalid in 1983 made the House's choice to avoid specifying circumstances that much more consequential. By consciously choosing to give the president more discretion, Congress had granted legitimacy to a broader reading of the president's national security authority under Article II.[83]

Several other choices also spoke to the limits of Congress's pushback against presidential authority. In 1969, then senator Charles Goodell (R-NY) had attempted to pass a bill to require a withdrawal of forces from Vietnam by withholding funds. Such a precedent, with Congress wielding its power of the purse, might have contributed to the development of stronger congressional alternatives to deal with presidential war power. But many proponents of reform, such as Javits, were not comfortable with that step.[84] As Javits later explained, "the fund-cutoff remedy" would be "a clumsy, blunt and obsolescent tool." Moreover, Javits contended that this method would still be an option for Congress to pursue, regardless of whether the war powers legislation specified a process for the threatened withholding of funds.[85] Another option had been a substitute amendment introduced by Representative Dennis. That alternative would have required not only approval of the president's action within ninety days but continued reauthorizations of the commitment of military forces every six months. In effect, Congress's power to declare war would be invoked multiple times in any long conflict, and the intent of the legislation was to prevent a drawn-out military involvement without reconsideration of its wisdom. But the House rejected that proposal.[86]

PRESIDENTIAL WAR BY STATUTE

The concerns of legislators not to intrude on the president's constitutional authority as commander in chief led to a measure that arguably codified greater presidential authority over war in statute. This was certainly how many political observers understood the outcome at the time. Perhaps most revealingly, even opponents of the bill who held the broadest view of what the commander in chief clause implied for presidential power admitted that they believed the war powers legislation expanded the president's authority in statute. Though he would vote against the legislation, the House minority leader, Gerald Ford (R-MI), believed there was "some validity to the argument that the President's war authority is expanded by the conference report."[87] Senator Goldwater, while complaining that the legislation unconstitutionally intruded on presidential prerogatives, still opined that "this conference report . . . I could probably actually vote for, because it gives the President even broader powers than the authors of the original bill thought they were correcting." In response, one of the chief critics of the legislation, Senator Eagleton, who believed the bill gave too much authority to the president, accentuated what Goldwater had just stated: "Did I correctly hear the Senator say that in some respects he even considered voting for the measure, because this bill as presently drafted gives the President greater powers to wage one-man war than he had before?"[88]

Eagleton had been one of the original and most ardent supporters of the effort to restrict presidential war powers. In the end, however, he voted against the final measure. Senator Eagleton's preference had been for the earlier Senate bill, which had specified the circumstances in which the president could act alone and otherwise required affirmative congressional assent.[89] Having lost that battle, Eagleton understood the significance of the final version of the war powers legislation in terms similar to the strongest defenders of the president's authority as commander in chief. He believed that the WPR enshrined a presidential initiative for war making in statute. While Congress's override of Nixon's veto was being "acclaimed as an 'historic recapture' of the Congressional prerogative to declare war," Eagleton lamented that "the opposite is true." "After struggling for three years to re-establish its primacy in the war-making area," Eagleton explained, "Congress has now legally relegated itself—unconstitutionally, in my opinion—to the secondary role it has sadly and mistakenly accepted in the contemporary era." By allowing the president to unilaterally make war for up to ninety days without requiring affirmative congressional consent, "the President assumes the inherent right to initiate war. . . . Congress has now provided a legal basis for the President's erroneous claim."[90]

Other lawmakers agreed with Eagleton's assessment. The "major flaw" in the measure, said Representative Robert Bauman (R-MD), was that "it does not require the Congress to pass judgment, one way or the other, on any military initiatives in which the President may involve US Armed Forces." A "tacit veto" was provided in the legislation, since "if Congress [did] not act within 60 days of the military action in question, the President must call it to a halt." However, "such a scheme" was "inadequate" and would offer "more than ample opportunity for abuse by any President."[91] Even as he supported the bill, Senator Mark Hatfield (R-OR) admitted it was "not totally satisfactory to me," as "there is still a wide degree of Executive discretion and latitude that many find questionable."[92]

Some of the critics of the final measure changed their minds about voting for it after Nixon's veto. Two New York Democrats were an example. Representative Bella Abzug (D-NY) fretted that the legislation would do "exactly the reverse of what we set out to do; that is, to prevent the President, any President, from usurping the power of Congress to declare war."[93] Representative Elizabeth Holtzman (D-NY) similarly complained that the way to "reassert the rights and responsibilities of Congress" was not "implicitly to grant to the

President—as this bill does—the power to commence and conduct a war."[94] But both congresswomen decided to vote to override the president, thinking that it was worth passing and, perhaps, deciding that inflicting defeat on a Republican president was enough to tip the scales.[95] Senator Eagleton did not join them. In a despairing address to lawmakers in the Senate during the override debate, Eagleton argued that the bill "will haunt us every time in the future an American boy dies somewhere in the world in a Presidentially initiated war. The blood of those young men will be ours because we are giving away the authority that sends them to die, and we are giving up the greatest responsibility that the Constitution gives to the Congress—the power to declare war."[96]

Conclusion: Developmental versus Constitutional Claims

The War Powers Resolution of 1973 demonstrated the limitations of congressional efforts to challenge presidential war powers and national security authority. The political context in which reform was considered had been promising. As the debates over the legislation showed, congressional skepticism of the president's claim to represent the national interest was widespread and stemmed from deep discontent over the behavior of multiple presidents of previous decades. Rooted in that frustration, lawmakers asserted that deliberation by legislators, on behalf of the people, would be better than relying only on the president to determine the national interest. At the same time, legislators asserted a constitutional claim to preeminence in war making, pointing to Congress's Article I authority.

But unlike other policy areas, such as budgeting, presidential authority over national security had not rested on the idea of presidential representation. Instead, it was reliant on the idea that the role as commander in chief from Article II conferred on the president inherent national security authority. While doubts about the validity of presidential representation were strong enough to lead to a reckoning in Congress over the president's authority over national security, the commander in chief clause constrained even advocates of the WPR in their pursuit of reform. "If nothing else, the uncertain, tortured history of the legislation demonstrates that the President as Commander-in-Chief still has formidable war-making powers," summed up the *New York Times*: "At most the legislation may make future Presidents somewhat more cautious and deliberative in committing American forces, and more inclined to consult with Congress on his decision."[97] The president's preeminence in war and in leading the national security state endured. In Keith Whittington's summation, "the unwillingness of Congress to question the foundation of the imperial presidency—the postwar national security state—limited the effect" of its pushback.[98] The increased prominence of the position of national security adviser in the presidential foreign policy of the 1970s—with Henry Kissinger and Zbigniew Brzezinski supplanting the influence of the Senate-confirmed secretaries of state for Presidents Nixon and Jimmy Carter—seemed to mock Congress's involvement in the national security state, underscoring the durability of presidential authority. Furthermore, even Congress's strong impulse to assert its own authority to determine the national interest in the early 1970s was tenuous over the longer term. The importance of military spending to the districts and states of so many lawmakers would be another consistent force curbing the desire of legislators to reconsider the national security state.[99]

The WPR's passage did put presidents on notice that Congress would be less deferential to presidential actions in national security going forward. Congressional leaders would expect to be consulted about major military actions, and Congress would often adopt a more "antagonistic stance" and skepticism of presidential policies.[100] Presidents can certainly be influenced by Congress directly or indirectly in considering their decisions. In particular, the partisan composition of Congress relative to the president can impact whether presidents undertake major military ventures.[101] For conflicts that are likely to be long and large in scope, presidents generally seek congressional approval, though they still do not admit that they constitutionally need to do so. Furthermore, the president's actions and justifications in national security policy are also subject to ever-increasing media and public scrutiny.[102]

But on the whole, presidential actions in subsequent decades have underscored the substantial limitations of the WPR. As contemporary critics of the legislation had feared, presidents have tended to act unilaterally for short-term conflicts of more a limited scope, citing their role as commander in chief and authority over foreign policy.[103] Consider a few examples. In 1983, the US military operations in Grenada under Republican president Ronald Reagan were completed within sixty days, so congressional authorization was not pursued.[104] Similarly, under Republican president George H. W. Bush, the brief US intervention in Panama in 1989–90 was not authorized by Congress.[105] Several actions by Democratic president Bill Clinton in the 1990s, including air strikes in Bosnia and the US role in the war in Yugoslavia, were undertaken without congressional approval.[106]

Even in cases where presidents have sought and received congressional authorization, they have still taken care to stress their own constitutional authority. Congress authorized the Gulf War in 1991, but George H. W. Bush emphasized the importance of his own constitutional authority as well.[107] In the wake of the 9/11 attacks in 2001, Congress passed the sweeping Authorization for Use of Military Force of 2001 to support action against those who were responsible for the attacks, which was quickly used for military action in Afghanistan, and it also subsequently authorized the war in Iraq. But Republican president George W. Bush went beyond these authorizations and pursued a variety of expansive executive powers in national security, asserting the right to preemptive war and authorizing the use of military tribunals.[108]

The growing unpopularity of the Iraq War seemed poised to lead to a different approach for Democratic president Barack Obama, Bush's successor. In reaction to the perceived overreach of the Bush administration, Obama had pledged to reestablish some limits on presidential authority and deference to Congress. With its intervention in Libya in 2011, however, the Obama administration argued that the US actions did not constitute a participation in hostilities and were not covered by the WPR. The rise in US reliance on drone strikes during his administration also occurred without congressional authorization.[109]

More recently, Republican president Donald Trump acted to protect his authority as commander in chief even in the face of renewed congressional pushback. In directing missile strikes in Syria, the administration argued that Trump had acted "as commander-in-chief to protect vital national interests."[110] Trump ventured a bolder move in authorizing a strike that killed a top Iranian leader. Renouncing that action for risking a wider conflict, and angry that the president had not conferred with Congress in advance, concerned legislators mounted a challenge to the president's authority. And indeed, had the WPR's provision for a legislative veto via concurrent resolution remained operable, Congress might have been able to force the president's hand. But as it was, Trump was able to veto the House and Senate's joint resolution of disapproval, and Congress was unable to override it. Notably, the president justified his veto on constitutional grounds: "the Constitution recognizes that the president must be able to anticipate our adversaries' next moves and take swift and decisive action in response."[111]

The commander in chief clause has served as an alternative basis for the national security authority of the institutional presidency. What that clause means and how much authority it actually bestows on presidents remain disputed. But while the developmental claim of presidential representation proved vulnerable to critiques, the commander in chief clause has remained comparatively resilient. This has a significant implication for institutional adaptability in America, suggesting that ideas that can claim roots in the Constitution—however dubious some interpretations of them may be—are a more durable basis for presidential power. For better or worse, it appears presidents have grasped this lesson.

Conclusion: Ideas and the Politics of Adaptability

The twentieth-century shift toward presidential government was a remarkable achievement, a veritable reinvention of the American Constitution. The whole story is counterintuitive. It turns out that Congress was the prime mover in the creation of the "modern presidency." Members of Congress legislated presidential power in statute, addressing many of the most consequential policy domains of the federal government. Moreover, legislators were not forced to do this; they chose to do it. Supported and prodded by other political entrepreneurs, lawmakers made their choices plain in the design of those statutes, proceeding in one domain after another on the basis of the perceived validity, indeed the superiority, of presidential representation.

At bottom, this is a story that demonstrates the centrality of ideas in political development. The idea of presidential representation was promoted by early twentieth-century Progressive reformers who derided legislators as too parochial to meet national challenges. More remarkably, it was members of the very institution that the Progressives scorned who embraced the logic of presidential representation and, to a substantial degree, effected the transformation they had sought. The idea stood at the center of a larger constitutional critique, and that itself had consequences down the line. Just as surely as the critique gave presidential representation its transformative punch, it also proved to be a vulnerability for reforms resting on that idea. When Congress's second thoughts about its earlier creation prompted efforts to put things right again, legislators found that there were no easy or straightforward paths back to the original setup. The great adaptation had narrowed the range of future options, leaving interbranch relations seemingly askew and entrapped.[1]

From Pragmatism to Formalism

Legislators institutionalized presidential leadership in a series of statutes. Despite their enactment in three different decades, the Budget and Accounting Act of 1921, Reciprocal Trade Agreements Act of 1934, Reorganization Act of 1939, and Employment Act of 1946 all shared the same premise: that the president, chosen by the nation as a whole, is the institutional actor best positioned to represent the national interest. In budgeting and employment, Congress gave the president agenda-setting authority, privileging the president's position in policymaking in order to help guide legislators to focus on the national interest. The Bureau of the Budget and Council of Economic Advisers gave the president corresponding organizational capacity and expertise. In reorganization and trade, Congress went even further. Reorganization authority inverted the legislative process. It put even more weight on presidential proposals to reorganize the executive branch by allowing them to go into effect unless Congress rejected them. The creation of the Executive Office of the President was an immediate consequence of that law. And presidential trade authority cut Congress out of the loop entirely, allowing presidents to negotiate bilateral agreements with other nations to reduce tariffs that were not subject to congressional approval.

Not all elements of this new, institutional presidency relied on presidential representation as a design assumption. To be sure, Congress had the same objective in mind when it bolstered the president's role in the domain of national security, but there, the president's preexisting authority under the Constitution seemed to legislators to determine much of what could be done. The National Security Act of 1947 created new resources to support the president in the executive branch, aiming to improve the government's ability to take a holistic perspective on national security. The president's authority as commander in chief functioned as an alternative premise supporting that part of the institutional presidency.

Congress reconsidered its choices during the 1970s and 1980s in a series of statutes addressing the same policy areas, including the War Powers Resolution of 1973, Congressional Budget and Impoundment Control Act of 1974, Trade Act of 1974, Reorganization Act of 1977, and Full Employment and Balanced Growth Act of 1978. Lawmakers now saw presidential government less as a great achievement of constitutional reinvention and more as a threat to the basic governing framework. In the wake of Vietnam and Watergate, the reliance on presidential representation, tantamount to political common sense in those earlier decades, became a cautionary tale of misplaced trust and naïveté. Institutional reinvention became suspect; constitutional restoration became the order of the day. It was no coincidence that the declining faith in presidential representation was associated with calls for a return to the allocation of powers and institutional arrangements set up by the Constitution. Those arrangements had been what the reform project associated with presidential representation had set out to repudiate and replace.

Efforts to reassert legislative power and congressional claims to national representation exposed the extent to which presidential authority had been contingent on the perceived validity of presidential representation. Congress no longer was content to simply privilege presidential agenda setting in budgeting; it created its own budget process and asserted its primacy in setting national priorities. The Congressional Budget Office ensured that legislators had their own organizational capacity and expertise to rival that of the president. In economic policy, the president still would propose an annual Economic Report, but Congress took charge of declaring its preferred targets for unemployment and inflation and looked to the Federal Reserve to serve as its agent in advancing the interests of the nation in everyday economic management. Presidential reorganization authority was undone first by the Supreme Court's ruling that the legislative veto was constitutionally invalid, and then by legislators' unwillingness to renew the president's power. Even in trade, an issue bound up with foreign affairs, Congress ensured that it would have the ability to approve of multilateral trade agreements through the new fast-track process.

And yet while Congress reconsidered its earlier choices—while it increased its own power relative to the presidency and diminished some of the president's powers in the legislative realm—it was also constrained by its own earlier reinvention. In budgeting and domestic economic policy, Congress found it easier to layer yet another set of institutional arrangements over presidential authority, as opposed to pulling back that authority altogether. In other areas, presidential authority had alternative claims it could rest on. Presidential national security authority, in particular, was more durable, with lawmakers again deferring to the president's constitutional role as commander in chief in the War Powers Resolution of 1973. In trade, the fast-track process also continued to privilege the president's perspective. This was partly a recognition that tariffs had become an issue of foreign affairs, which naturally favored presidential authority, but it was also a realization that congressional primacy in trade would be difficult to restore in an increasingly globalized economy. And though Congress ultimately chose not to grant presidents reorganization authority in the aftermath of the court's ruling in *INS v. Chadha* (1983), legislators recognized that wholesale reconsideration of the transformations already wrought by presidents through that process over the previous fifty years was impractical. Thus, in a single statute, Congress ratified all previously accepted presidential reorganization plans, endorsing the actions of former presidents even as it declined to extend such authority to future presidents.

The agencies that Congress had created in the executive branch that made up the institutional presidency—the Office of Management and Budget, Executive Office of the President, Council of Economic Advisers, and National Security Council—all endured. The OMB and EOP, in particular, not only retained their importance but were utilized further in presidential efforts to exert control over the executive branch. The OMB's practice of regulatory review in its Office of Information and Regulatory Affairs (OIRA) became one of the primary powers of the presidency.

Furthermore, even in policy areas in which Congress reasserted its own authority, that proved to be no guarantee of effectiveness. The debacle of the congressional budget process and the resurgence of calls for a presidential line item veto were testaments to the limitations of the congressional restoration in that realm. The congressional resurgence did not restore "balance" or produce a new equilibrium. Instead, it left the legitimacy of both institutions in limbo. One of the chief critics of the presidency appeared chastened about the prospects of congressional primacy by the end of the 1970s. The retired senator J. William Fulbright (D-AR) affirmed that "an assertive Congress" had been "a necessary corrective" to presidential abuses, but he had soured on congressional government going forward: "In a time, such as the present, when Congress is asserting its prerogatives aggressively, but without a commensurate demonstration of public responsibility, there is much to be said for a revival of presidential leadership."[2]

The fundamental consequences of the idea of presidential representation are, then, still very much with us, even if some presidential authority was pared back. Presidents are still expected to play a major role in the legislative process, and they can all draw on the resources, information, and expertise of the various components of the Executive Office of the President. As significant as Congress's reconsideration of presidential authority was, it did not displace the presidency from the center of American government in the name of reclaiming its own status as the "first branch." What it did was to rob the modern presidency of its original rationale.

Indeed, the more profound effect of Congress's skepticism of presidential representation was to change the terms of debate by which power between the legislative and executive branches would be contested. Legislators had reembraced the separation of powers as a way to push back against the presidency and restore congressional authority. Adaptability and institutional experimentation gave way to an interest in formality and a sense of constitutional constraint. But it soon became clear that the new emphasis on formalism could also serve as a vehicle for the presidency to regain its footing. Advocates of presidentialism would lean into the resurgence in formalist reasoning to read an even more expansive view of presidential power into the Constitution. While Congress pulled back from its endorsement of the presidency as the nation's chief *representative*, presidents would turn inward, pushing their constitutional authority as chief *executive* to the limit.

Securing the Executive Power

Critics of presidential power turned to formalism in the 1970s, and advocates of a robust presidency responded in kind. Recognizing that the authority of the office was less secure in the wake of Vietnam and Watergate, they looked to head off potential challenges to the legitimacy of presidential power by embracing a strict understanding of the separation of powers. And as battles over policy increasingly moved to the administrative realm, a new kind of presidentialism emerged.

For conservatives, the new idea was one they claimed to be an old one: the unitary executive theory.[3] Champions of this idea viewed it as a constitutional claim, focusing on the vesting clause of Article II: "The executive Power shall be vested in a President of the United States of America." The inference drawn from that vesting clause was, in Justice Antonin Scalia's words, that Article II vests "*all* of the executive power" in the president.[4] While reforms associated with such expansive claims about the executive power were rejected by Congress during battles over reorganization in the late 1930s, the idea was resurrected and elaborated on within conservative legal circles and pushed into the national consciousness.[5]

Though both ideas have been used as justifications for the president's removal power, the institutional implications of unitary theory are distinct from those associated with presidential stewardship. Presidential representation is associated with allowing the president's purported superior national perspective to have a more significant role in legislating. It seeks to guide lawmakers to better outcomes in the national interest. The idea anticipates bridging the separation of powers. By contrast, unitary theory envisions the president having personal, hierarchical control over the executive branch.[6] It embraces a strict reading of the separation of powers, and it draws on growing conservative and populist distrust of the bureaucracy.

The primary institutional audiences for each idea outside of the executive branch are also distinct. The main audience for presidential representation proved to be members of Congress, who built the institutional presidency through a series of statutes. For the more formalistic claim of the unitary executive theory, the principal audience outside of the executive branch has been the judiciary. Presidents and executive branch officials themselves may instinctively act in ways that are consistent with the theory, but the most ambitious readings of the president possessing all the executive power look to the Supreme Court to overturn existing institutional structures of the administrative state created by Congress. The aim of that idea has been to achieve a series of decisions that would steadily put the administrative state under more direct presidential control.

That goal has been repeatedly expressed and expounded from the 1970s onward, pushed forward by the conservative legal movement and elaborated on by some of the most notable Republican promulgators of presidential control over administration.[7] Consider a few examples. In 1972, President Nixon's domestic policy adviser, John Ehrlichman, wrote in a memo to OMB director Caspar Weinberger, "I'm for whatever will strengthen the President's hand vs. the bureaucracy."[8] A more constitutional gloss was added to this presidentialist instinct in the Reagan administration. Speaking to the Federal Bar Association in 1985, Attorney General Edwin Meese complained that "the real law making power in Washington is wielded neither by the Congress or the President, but by relatively anonymous members of the federal agencies." The remedy, Meese posited, was to look to the framers and restore the proper separation of powers: "to borrow the theme of a currently popular movie, the most effective means of increasing responsibility may be to go 'Back to the Future', to recapture a proper sense of how the Framers of the Constitution intended the federal systems to work." The framers had "carefully enumerated the powers and responsibilities" of each branch, including vesting "the executive power *solely* in the President."[9] In a draft of what would be an undelivered speech in 1989, Dick Cheney also wrote of the need for a greater emphasis on the separation of powers going forward: "We would do well, therefore, to reinvigorate the Framers' understanding of the separation of powers as we head toward the 21st century."[10] From serving as chief of staff in the Ford administration after Watergate, to spearheading the minority report in Congress defending the Reagan administration in the Iran-Contra affair, to his role as secretary of defense in the George H. W. Bush administration, and finally as vice president in the George W. Bush administration, Cheney was one of the chief actors in resurrecting presidential power after Watergate.

Unitary theory emerged as a conservative idea, but the embrace of some of its implications was not limited to only Republican administrations or officials.[11] Just as presidential representation was invoked by reformers in both parties in the early twentieth century, presidents and their defenders in both parties grew enamored with the attractiveness of governing through administration from the 1970s onward. Democratic presidents differed from Republican incumbents in generally avoiding invoking the theory as constitutional doctrine, but they shared the instinct to exercise greater control over the executive branch. In the area of regulatory review, for example, presidents increased their influence over agency rule making, gaining greater leverage over domestic policymaking within the executive branch and enhancing their ability to govern without Congress.[12] Elena Kagan, the Clinton administration veteran who went on to serve as President Barack Obama's solicitor general before being appointed to the Supreme Court, famously declared that "an era of presidential administration has arrived."[13] Moreover, even those who did not adopt unitary theory as constitutional doctrine seemed to concede the attractiveness of the theory on constitutional grounds. As Lawrence Lessig and Cass Sunstein wrote, "If we are to translate [the framers'] structural choices into current conditions, we may conclude that a largely hierarchical executive branch is the best way of keeping faith with the original plan."[14]

Presidentialists did not entirely jettison the idea of presidential representation in focusing on executive power, but the claim was utilized for new institutional purposes. Whether promoting the "unitary executive" or "presidential administration," advocates subsumed that claim within those ideas as an additional normative justification for their implications. Effective accountability in the executive branch to the national electorate, they asserted, was ensured by the president. Since "the President has a national constituency," Kagan contended, "he is likely to consider, in setting the direction of administrative policy on an ongoing basis, the preferences of the general public, rather than merely parochial interests."[15] The leading academic proponent of unitary theory, Steven Calabresi, argued that "the President is our only constitutional backstop against the redistributive collective action problem."[16]

Yet even as the new emphasis on presidential control over the executive branch sought to draw on the notion of presidential stewardship, invocations of that claim had a stronger plebiscitary basis. Kagan herself noted the significance of the "advent of what has become known as the permanent presidential campaign" to presidential control over administration.[17] For the unitarian Calabresi, the connection between the executive power and a plebiscitary vision was more explicit, based on the relationship between presidents and their political base: "Representing as he does a national electoral college majority, the President at least has an incentive to steer national resources toward the 51% of the nation that last supported him (and that might support him again), thereby mitigating the bad distributional incentives faced by members of Congress."[18] More than a vision of stewardship, the understanding of presidential representation joined to unitary theory was, in practice, a plebiscitary and partisan one. Each president would be elected by his or her supporters to pursue his or her own mandate for change through administration. The unitary vision of presidential representation was one that would turn the executive branch into a political arm of the presidential party.[19]

Still, while unitary theory mixes a constitutional claim with a plebiscitary justification, it is the constitutional claim that was meant to be the key to securing presidential power against challenges to its legitimacy.[20] And notably, not all unitarians view the justification of presidential representation as helpful. Some unitary proponents have instead argued that the questionable validity of presidential representation on stewardship grounds has undermined the principal justification behind the theory. As Jide Nzelibe has suggested, "under the winner-take-all system of our electoral college, the president will often have an incentive to cater to a narrower geographic and population constituency than that of the median member of Congress."[21] The implication, for Nzelibe, is that "since there are otherwise reasonable functional arguments for vesting control of the administrative state in the President, proponents of the unitary President should abandon the weak and potentially harmful nationalist justification."[22]

The utility of unitary theory's distinctiveness from presidential representation as a constitutional claim was underscored by the Supreme Court's decision in 2020 that the Consumer Financial Protection Bureau's structure of a single director insulated from presidential removal was unconstitutional. In his opinion for the court, Chief Justice John Roberts coupled presidential representation to the president's administrative control: "Only the President (along with the Vice President) is elected by the entire Nation. And the President's political accountability is enhanced by the solitary nature of the Executive Branch, which provides 'a single object for the jealousy and watchfulness of the people.'" But while he cited presidential representation, Roberts left no doubt that the formalist claim was the primary justification for the decision: "We hold that the CFPB's leadership by a single individual removable only for inefficiency, neglect, or malfeasance violates the separation of powers. . . . Article II provides that '[t]he executive Power shall be vested in a President.' . . . The entire 'executive Power' belongs to the President alone."[23] The CFPB decision has been only the most obvious sign that the formalistic claims about the president's control over the executive branch have gained a foothold in the judiciary. By articulating an underlying idea with a gloss of constitutional plausibility, unitarians have presented a starker challenge to those who seek to question the appropriate bounds of presidential control over the executive branch. This idea may prove more difficult to dislodge.

What the idea offers in practice amounts to a system of "makeshift presidentialism."[24] Unitary theory leads to policy whiplash from one incumbent to the next. In the face of political polarization and legislative gridlock, presidents often act unilaterally, proclaiming the fierce urgency of the moment to justify policy interventions. They seek to demonstrate vitality even in the face of political and institutional resistance. "America's policy state," surmise Karen Orren and Stephen Skowronek, "relies for its operations on the perilous presidentialism of catch-me-if-you-can."[25] Presidents may dare Congress and the courts to challenge them, and they may each have a greater capacity for independent action. But presidents simultaneously find that their achievements are contingent and unstable, subject to the backlash of citizens and the whims of the subsequent occupant of the office.[26] With their role as chief representative diminished, their ability to enact durable reforms is compromised.

Constitutionalizing Presidential Representation

Restoring—and *securing*—a more reliable form of political leadership is the objective of another set of reformers.

It is revealing that two of the leading proponents of presidential representation today have settled on a constitutional solution to the dilemmas of effective governance. William Howell and Terry Moe have sought to shift the discussion of executive power back to legislative leadership, only now, keeping with the shift from pragmatism to formalism, they propose a constitutional amendment to secure presidential agenda-setting authority. Like their Progressive predecessors, they view presidential representation in terms of stewardship, asserting that presidents have a relatively more encompassing view of policymaking than legislators do. But they forthrightly acknowledge the restrictions and boundaries that Congress and the Constitution present for this particular vision of presidential power. The Progressives "were partially successful at creating a more modern form of government" that was "led by a more powerful president." And the institutional presidency became "the president's prime means of trying to impose coherent order, and make coherent policy." Nonetheless, that reinvention did not change the written Constitution itself: "the fundamentals of the original constitutional system remained intact."[27]

This gives their proposal its implicit rationale: it seeks to *constitutionalize* the idea of presidential representation. Howell and Moe set out to tap what they see as the benefits of the president's broader national perspective while making national leadership less reliant on the contingent political legitimacy of the idea. Perceptions of presidential representation are subject to change over time. This proposal would lock it in, insulating presidential steward-ship from the vulnerabilities it has previously faced. Bucking the reaction against presidential leadership that took hold with the Trump presidency, Howell and Moe indict the Congress and argue that Trump's election itself was a symptom of a lack of effective government. As they see it, it has been Congress's failure to address the nation's challenges that has led voters to look to populist candidates. By turning to the unfinished work of the old solution and securing presidential power in the legislative realm, they seek to force Congress to consider coherent programs targeted to address major problems such as health care, budget deficits, inequality, and climate change.

Notable too is that Howell and Moe do not seek to enhance presidential power across the board. Rather, they propose "to selectively harness and *use* the presidency to social advantage, not to simply boost its power." While re-viving presidential representation as the primary underlying idea of the pres-idency, they would also jettison the idea of a unitary executive. In their view, presidents have too little constitutional authority over legislative agenda set-ting and too much authority over the executive branch. As a balance to privi-leging the president's national perspective in crafting policy, they would limit presidential authority to control law enforcement and intelligence agencies, eliminate the pardon power, and require transparency about an individual president's business interests. In this way, they argue, the greatest benefit would be extracted from the presidential office with the least risk.[28] Other scholars increasingly echo this concern about presidential control over ad-ministration, and some also envision formally securing the standing of the administrative state via constitutional amendment.[29]

Undertaking reforms of the magnitude of the Howell and Moe proposal would be a tall order, challenging two ideational developments. First, the pro-posal seeks to double down on stewardship in the wake of the damage Presi-dent Trump inflicted on the legitimacy of that idea.[30] Second, in questioning presidential control over elements of the administration, the proposal takes on the primary idea supporting presidential authority in recent decades, an idea promoted by defenders of presidential power who have sought in other ways to provide executive power with a more durable ideational foundation. Whatever the merits of the reform and the steep challenges to its enactment, this combination of stewardship and formalism is a novel reformulation and an ironic testament to the Progressives' pragmatic vision for the presidency.

Diagnosis before Prognosis

Ideas have the capacity to shape and reshape American political development, and explanations discount them at their own peril. Ideas lie at the center of our system's fabled adaptability. Designing or reformulating institutional arrangements inherently involves uncertainty, making the choices involved highly susceptible to the assumptions of political actors about how different reforms will work in practice.

Those assumptions then become embedded in our understandings of the institutions themselves. They are standards of judgment applied not only to institutional performance but to broader questions of legitimacy. A more foundational question is implicit. How do political actors come to the ideas that they apply to questions of institutional design in the first place? While the sheer range of potential influences on political actors may seem endless, this study suggests that one starting point would be to focus on perceptions of system failure and the impulse to repudiate the existing state of affairs. The authority to rearrange institutions on new ideational foundations starts with a thoroughgoing repudiation of the idea that came before.[31]

The history of the idea of presidential representation and the ongoing battles over the unitary executive theory both suggest that repudiation is an inherent part of institutional adaptability. When established understandings seem to be leading us astray, ideas that promise to disrupt and dislodge them are more likely to gain the traction needed to remake politics and rearrange political authority. When the primary criticism in American government was that members of Congress were too localistic, the presidency benefited from an idea that promised a cure. When the main concern of Americans became presidents acting contrary to the national interest, Congress more directly asserted its purported representative superiority and constitutional primacy. The unitary executive theory arose in part because of critiques of what was perceived as an unaccountable administrative state. In the aftermath of the Trump presidency, it remains to be seen what responses might arise from doubts about the unitary executive theory and presidential administration.

Renouncing the existing political order does not preordain what ideas may next become influential. Discrediting existing institutions and ideas only opens up the opportunity for new or reformulated ideas to emerge and wield influence. It is up to political and ideational entrepreneurs to offer ideas that respond to what has been discredited, to connect problems to solutions, and to generate a modicum of consensus about what is to be done. At the moment, there seems to be a general agreement that we have a problem with our institutional arrangements, but thinking about what to do about it is all over the map.[32]

That raises the sobering prospect that our past experience with institutional adaptation may have gotten the better of us. It seems to have left us with contradictory lessons and an ideational free-for-all. The intellectual class has been on so many different sides of the problem of institutional adaptation that our thinking about it is now beginning to spin in circles. First, constitutional rigidity was the problem, and a pragmatic embrace of presidentialism was the solution. Then pragmatism became the problem, and a return to constitutional formalism was the solution. Now, unitarians have pushed formalism in the presidency to the limit, while some seek to turn away from formalism and others suggest we change course again by formalizing pragmatic adaptation via constitutional amendment. Debates over institutional reform are rich and fierce, but for all that, the absence of a shared diagnosis is conspicuous. Ideas about what to do are proliferating, but they lack traction without a common carrier. Our history tells us that ideas matter most when intellectuals have their act together sufficiently to present a coherent path forward. If we have lost that capacity, we may be in real trouble. For any of our ideas of institutional reform to become "more powerful than is commonly understood," they must be able to pivot off of a shared indictment of what has gone wrong with American government.[33]

Acknowledgments

This book began as a hypothesis hastily scribbled down in a notebook during Stephen Skowronek's American Political Development graduate seminar at Yale during the spring 2015 semester. Throughout writing it, I have been the fortunate recipient of generous insights, advice, and support from many mentors, scholars, friends, and family.

Above all, I am indebted to Stephen Skowronek, whose mentorship has made this book possible. Its scope is a testament to his encouragement to take my interest in the importance of the idea of presidential representation to American political development and make a broader statement about the relationship between ideas and institutional change. Steve's ideas, advice, probing questions, and careful readings have immeasurably improved the book, and his feedback remained indispensable from beginning to end. He served as my primary sounding board during revisions, suggested a decisive title alteration, and offered comments in the last weeks of writing that led to too many improvements to count. Working with Steve and Desmond King on our book *Phantoms of a Beleaguered Republic* also has yielded insights that substantially enriched this project.

David Mayhew's guidance, support, and continuous encouragement have been invaluable throughout this project and my academic career. Like many others, I have benefited from David's encyclopedic historical knowledge and perspective on Congress and the presidency. On one occasion, a single comment from him prompted me to suddenly envision the structure of the second half of the book. David was also the first person to inform me of the phrase "American political development" when I was preparing to apply to graduate school—a critical juncture, in retrospect. Frequent conversations with him about research, current events, or Yankee baseball have always been highlights of my experience at Yale.

Jacob Hacker has provided valuable advice and mentorship throughout this project. On many occasions, he pointed out strengths in my argument I had not recognized myself. This book's focus on comparisons in institutional change across different areas of policymaking is reflective of his influence on my thinking and interests. Moreover, he has also been a crucial supporter of my professional development.

Working with the University of Chicago Press has been a rewarding experience. I am especially indebted to Susan Herbst for her keen interest in this project. Susan's exceptional guidance and advice on both the work's substance and its overall framing proved immensely helpful. Larry Jacobs also provided helpful feedback that particularly improved the introduction. I am deeply grateful to Chuck Myers for his interest in the project and helpful feedback, and I appreciate the guidance and efforts of Chuck, Alicia Sparrow, Noor Shawaf, Holly Smith, Caterina MacLean, and Jenni Fry throughout the publication process. Kathleen Kageff expertly assisted in copyediting. Furthermore, I appreciate the work of three anonymous reviewers, whose advice and critiques improved the manuscript significantly.

In January 2020, the Yale Institution for Social and Policy Studies, under Jacob Hacker's leadership, generously sponsored a book manuscript workshop for this project. I am profoundly grateful to William Howell, Wendy Schiller, and Daniel Carpenter for serving as commentators for that workshop. Their detailed comments on every aspect of this manuscript, and their collective feedback in conversation with each other, were vital to making this a better book in every way. In addition to his comments at the manuscript workshop, Will has, more generally, gone above and beyond to offer his support for and feedback on this project. His interest in presidential representation has enhanced my understanding of the institutional implications associated with the idea. Will has pushed me to think through when political actors might be transcending their self-interest and, in particular, prodded me toward a critical improvement in my argument about Congress's reaction to presidential authority in the 1970s. At the conference, Susan Herbst, Stephen Skowronek, David Mayhew, Limor Peer, Ian Turner, Christina Kinane, Noah Rosenblum, Brendan Shanahan, Benjamin Waldman, Annabelle Hutchinson, and Jack Greenberg all provided helpful comments and great conversations in response to points raised by Will, Wendy, and Dan. I also especially thank Pam LaMonaca for expertly organizing all aspects of the manuscript workshop. From providing me (and my books) with office space in ISPS to engaging in conversations about politics and UConn Huskies basketball,

Pam has been a crucial source of moral support throughout the writing of this book.

Two centers at Yale have provided wonderful intellectual homes as I've revised this book. I gratefully acknowledge support for this project from the Yale Center for the Study of Representative Institutions at the Whitney and Betty MacMillan Center for International and Area Studies and the Policy Lab at the Institution for Social and Policy Studies. The YCRI's codirector Steven Smith has been a source of ideas, support, and conversations about Yankee baseball for years. Serving as Steven's teaching fellow for his Lincoln course furthered my interest in the role of ideas in political history. In addition, Steven's discussion of Bolingbroke's concept of the "Patriot King" during his Statesmanship seminar in the fall 2014 semester undoubtedly served as an initial inspiration to me for this project. At ISPS, my two officemates for a few years, Torey McMurdo and Annabelle Hutchinson, have been supportive colleagues and wonderful friends. Their feedback anticipated some of the biggest challenges the manuscript would face early on and vastly improved my ability to respond to them. Numerous conversations with Jack Greenberg and Benjamin Waldman have also challenged and improved my thinking about the presidency. Pam Greene arranged multiple presentations for me to the American politics faculty and students, and she also set up travel for one of my favorite archival trips to Montana. Furthermore, I have benefited from the feedback of Bruce Ackerman, Greg Huber, Matthew Graham, Sophie Jacobson, Patrick O'Brien, Cleo O'Brien-Udry, Lilla Orr, Lauren Pinson, Gwen Prowse, Naomi Scheinerman, Ian Turner, and Jen Wu.

Outside of Yale, I have been fortunate to receive support from many other scholars of the presidency, Congress, American political development, and American political thought. Mark Zachary Taylor has offered substantial feedback on this project over the past few years. His suggestions early on about how to better frame the role of ideas in political change proved crucial. George Krause gave me helpful feedback for my chapters on budget reform and provided great insights on communicating historical research to a broader political science audience. On that front, Ruth Bloch Rubin also generously provided advice about how this research speaks to scholars of Congress and about the process of writing a book heavily based on historical sources and archival materials. Calvin TerBeek provided excellent feedback on various chapters, and our now long-running dialogue about the role of ideas in American political development has improved many aspects of the manuscript. Noah Rosenblum's shared interest in the development of the institutional presidency has led us to some great conversations and has significantly improved my understanding of executive reorganization. Daphna

Renan's thought-provoking comments provided me with some key insights about ideas and political change and, in particular, about the relationship between presidential representation and the unitary executive theory. Jeremy Bailey, Susan McWilliams Barndt, and George Thomas generously supported my attendance at the 2019 American Political Thought conference at Claremont McKenna College and, more generally, provided both great feedback and stimulating conversations about the connection between political thought and political development. I have further benefited from conversations with and feedback from David Bateman, Richard Bensel, Richard Beth, Terri Bimes, Jordan Cash, Catherine Baylin Duryea, Stephen Engel, Connor Ewing, Paul Frymer, Sean Gailmard, Michael Genovese, Lisa Gilson, William Greene, Gary Jacobson, Scott James, Jeff Jenkins, Nancy Kassop, Burdett Loomis, Mark Major, Isaac Martin, Gillian Metzger, Joshua Miller, Curt Nichols, Shannon Bow O'Brien, Justin Craig Peck, James Pfiffner, Andrew Reeves, David Brian Robertson, Andrew Rudalevige, Robert Saldin, Elizabeth Sanders, Eric Schickler, Reuel Schiller, Amy Semet, Rogers Smith, Sharece Thrower, and Joseph Warren.

I am grateful to have received several grants to support my travels for archival research from the Dirksen Congressional Center, the Yale Center for the Study of American Politics, the Carl Albert Center at the University of Oklahoma, the UCLA Library, and the Dole Institute at the University of Kansas. Mike Crespin and Chuck Finocchiaro generously provided me the opportunity both to undertake archival research at the Carl Albert Center and to present my work there; Kay Blunck helped facilitate logistics of my trip; and Rachel Henson and J. A. Pryse helped provide a great research experience in the archives. Audrey Coleman and Sarah D'Antonio Gard made my experience at the Dole Institute highly productive and gave me the opportunity to partake in a number of events during my visit. Teresa Johnson facilitated my visit to the Manuscripts Division of the Department of Special Collections at UCLA. I have also been assisted in my archival work by many other amazing archivists and librarians, particularly Brenda Burk at the Special Collections and Archives at Clemson University, Ted Jackson at the Booth Family Center for Special Collections at Georgetown, Amy Purcell at the Archives and Special Collections of Ekstrom Library at the University of Louisville, Hannah Soukup at the Archives and Special Collections of the Maureen and Mike Mansfield Library at the University of Montana, Leigh McWhite at the Archives and Special Collections of the J. D. Williams Library at the University of Mississippi, Caitlin Lampman at the Edmund S. Muskie Archives and Special Collections Library at Bates College, Mylinda Woodward at the Milne Archives and Special Collections at the University of New

Hampshire, and Brian Nelson Burford at the New Hampshire Division of Archives and Records Management. I also was helped by many of the archivists and librarians during research at the Rauner Special Collections Library at Dartmouth College, the Wilson Library at the University of North Carolina, the Manuscript Division at the Library of Congress, and both Manuscripts and Archives and the Sterling Memorial Library at Yale University. Geoffrey Stark at the Special Collections of the University of Arkansas Libraries also provided a crucial document in response to my inquiry.

Two chapters have been adapted from previous articles. Chapter 3 is adapted from "The 'Proper Organs' for Presidential Representation: A Fresh Look at the Budget and Accounting Act of 1921," *Journal of Policy History* 31, no. 1 (January 2019): 1–41; it is used here with the permission of Cambridge University Press. Donald Critchlow and the *Journal of Policy History* reviewers also provided substantial feedback that improved that portion of the project. Chapter 5 is adapted from "The Foundations of the Modern Presidency: Presidential Representation, the Unitary Executive Theory, and the Reorganization Act of 1939," *Presidential Studies Quarterly* 49, no. 1 (March 2019): 185–203; it is used here with the permission of Wiley-Blackwell and the Center for the Study of the Presidency and Congress. And I am grateful to Richard Ellis for being interested in that paper and for encouraging me to pursue it as an article.

All this guidance and support has improved this project in numerous ways. Whatever errors remain are, of course, my own.

My interest in political science stems from my amazing undergraduate experience at the University of Connecticut in the Department of Political Science and the Honors Program. In multiple courses and then as my senior thesis adviser, Ronald Schurin furthered my interest in presidential history and allowed me to explore the role of ideas in presidential foreign policy, a project that I now see led to the interests in this book. Shayla Nunnally greatly enhanced my interest in Congress during her course that accompanied our Washington, DC, internship program. Virginia Hettinger is the model of college teaching and academic advising, and her exceptional support and valuable advice guided me into graduate school. Vincent Moscardelli's course American Political Leadership spurred my interest in the notion of executive representation. Jeffrey Ladewig's course on the presidency and Congress introduced me to two things that later proved critical to making this book possible: (1) Stephen Skowronek's theory of political time and (2) the importance of the Budget and Accounting Act of 1921. The late Lynne Goodstein, as director of the Honors Program, was the first person to suggest I might want to go into academia, and she persuaded me to teach as a course facilitator during my sophomore year. Jessamy Hoffmann and Rebecca Gates provided excellent training in teaching and academic mentorship and many life lessons along the way.

As I begin as assistant professor of political science at Vanderbilt University, I hope to live up to the example of all of these amazing educators and to pay forward the extraordinary mentorship I've received at UConn and at Yale.

My wife, Laura Hatchman, has been my best friend and partner, all the way back to our days at UConn. She is a family medicine doctor who also majored in history, giving her a unique perspective on this project. Laura has pushed me to clarify my arguments and ensure that the big picture stays in focus. Her combination of kindness, patience, humor, pointed feedback, and prods to writing have both improved this book and put the entire process into appropriate perspective. It is a joy to go through life together. Laura's wonderful parents, Jeff and Diane Hatchman, have also been a great source of support.

Finally, my parents, Betsy and John B. Dearborn, instilled in me the importance of education and gave me the confidence that I could pursue such a goal as a PhD. They have indulged my interests in politics and history from a young age. Their support and encouragement have lifted me up throughout my life and made this work possible, and I dedicate this book to them.

Notes

Preface

1. Robert A. Nisbet, *The Present Age: Progress and Anarchy in Modern America* (New York: Harper and Row, 1988), 77.

2. Donald J. Trump, "Remarks in New York City Accepting Election as the 45th President of the United States," November 9, 2016, *The American Presidency Project*, https://www.presidency.ucsb.edu/documents/remarks-new-york-city-accepting-election-the-45th-president-the-united-states.

3. John Sides, Michael Tesler, and Lynn Vavreck, *Identity Crisis: The 2016 Presidential Campaign and the Battle for the Meaning of America* (Princeton, NJ: Princeton University Press, 2018).

4. Bob Woodward, *Fear: Trump in the White House* (New York: Simon and Schuster, 2018), 46.

5. Dan Roberts, "Clinton and Obama Lead Calls for Unity as US braces for Trump Presidency," *Guardian*, November 9, 2016, https://www.theguardian.com/us-news/2016/nov/09/trump-victory-obama-clinton-unity.

6. Hillary Clinton, "Remarks in New York City Conceding the 2016 Presidential Election," November 9, 2016, *The American Presidency Project*, https://www.presidency.ucsb.edu/documents/remarks-new-york-city-conceding-the-2016-presidential-election.

7. Barack Obama, "Remarks on the 2016 Presidential Election," November 9, 2016, *The American Presidency Project*, https://www.presidency.ucsb.edu/documents/remarks-the-2016-presidential-election.

8. Peter Baker, "For Trump, a Year of Reinventing the Presidency," *New York Times*, December 31, 2017, https://www.nytimes.com/2017/12/31/us/politics/trump-reinventing-presidency.html.

9. Sean Wilentz, "They Were Bad: He May Be Worse," *New York Times*, January 20, 2018, https://www.nytimes.com/2018/01/20/opinion/sunday/trump-bad-presidents-history.html.

10. "Full Transcript: Jeff Flake's Speech on the Senate Floor," *New York Times*, October 24, 2017, https://www.nytimes.com/2017/10/24/us/politics/jeff-flake-transcript-senate-speech.html.

11. John D. Dingell, "My Last Words for America," *Washington Post*, February 9, 2019, https://www.washingtonpost.com/opinions/john-dingell-my-last-words-for-america/2019/02/08/99220186-2bd3-11e9-984d-9b8fba003e81_story.html.

12. Thomas S. Langston, *With Reverence and Contempt: How Americans Think about Their President* (Baltimore: Johns Hopkins University Press, 1995), 32.

13. George W. Bush, "Remarks at a Bush-Cheney Reception in New York City," June 23, 2003, *The American Presidency Project*, https://www.presidency.ucsb.edu/documents/remarks -bush-cheney-reception-new-york-city.

14. Tina Daunt, "Obama on Letterman: The President Represents the Whole Country," *Hollywood Reporter*, September 18, 2012, https://www.hollywoodreporter.com/news/obama -letterman-romney-fundraiser-371387.

15. Brian Bennett, "'My Whole Life Is a Bet': Inside President Trump's Gamble on an Un-tested Re-election Strategy," *Time*, June 20, 2019, https://time.com/longform/donald-trump -2020/.

16. Joseph Biden, "Address Accepting the Democratic Presidential Nomination in Wilming-ton, Delaware," August 20, 2020, *The American Presidency Project*, https://www.presidency.ucsb .edu/documents/address-accepting-the-democratic-presidential-nomination-wilmington -delaware.

17. Jeffrey Goldberg, "James Mattis Denounces President Trump, Describes Him as a Threat to the Constitution," *Atlantic*, June 3, 2020, https://www.theatlantic.com/politics/archive/ 2020/06/james-mattis-denounces-trump-protests-militarization/612640/.

18. Kathryn Watson, "John Kelly Agrees with Mattis and Says Nation Needs to Choose Lead-ers More Wisely," *CBS News*, June 5, 2020, https://www.cbsnews.com/news/john-kelly-trump -military-force-agrees-with-mattis/.

19. Peter Baker and Maggie Haberman, "As Protests and Violence Spill Over, Trump Shrinks Back," *New York Times*, May 31, 2020, https://www.nytimes.com/2020/05/31/us/politics/ trump-protests-george-floyd.html.

20. Joseph Biden, "Address in Wilmington, Delaware Accepting Election as the 46th Presi-dent of the United States," November 7, 2020, *The American Presidency Project*, https://www .presidency.ucsb.edu/documents/address-wilmington-delaware-accepting-election-the-46th -president-the-united-states.

21. "The Decency Agenda," *New York Times*, December 5, 2020, https://www.nytimes.com/ 2020/12/05/opinion/sunday/joe-biden-presidency-style.html.

22. "Parochial Congress," *Hartford Courant*, April 7, 1934, 10. Reprinted from the *Boston Herald*.

23. John Dickerson, "The Hardest Job in the World," *Atlantic*, May 2018, https://www .theatlantic.com/magazine/archive/2018/05/a-broken-office/556883/.

24. "Fix America's National Emergencies Law: And Not Just Because of Trump," *New York Times*, March 5, 2019, https://www.nytimes.com/2019/03/05/opinion/trump-national -emergency.html.

25. Elizabeth Goitein, "The Alarming Scope of the President's Emergency Powers," *Atlantic*, January/February 2019, https://www.theatlantic.com/magazine/archive/2019/01/presidential -emergency-powers/576418/.

26. "'I Am a Tariff Man,'" *Wall Street Journal*, December 4, 2018, https://www.wsj.com/ articles/i-am-a-tariff-man-1543965558.

27. Burgess Everett, "Republicans Gobsmacked by Trump's Tariffs," *Politico*, May 31, 2018, https://www.politico.com/story/2018/05/31/trump-tariffs-canada-mexico-republican -response-615479.

28. John Bolton, "John Bolton: The Scandal of Trump's China Policy," *Wall Street Journal*,

June 17, 2020, https://www.wsj.com/articles/john-bolton-the-scandal-of-trumps-china-policy-11592419564.

Chapter One

1. David R. Mayhew, *Congress: The Electoral Connection* (New Haven, CT: Yale University Press, 1974), 169; R. Douglas Arnold, *The Logic of Congressional Action* (New Haven, CT: Yale University Press, 1990), 3–4.

2. Terri Bimes and Quinn Mulroy, "The Rise and Decline of Presidential Populism," *Studies in American Political Development* 18, no. 2 (Fall 2004): 136–59, at 140.

3. On constitutional adaptability, see Stephen Skowronek and Karen Orren, "The Adaptability Paradox: Constitutional Resilience and Principles of Good Government in Twenty-First-Century America," *Perspectives on Politics* 18, no. 2 (June 2020): 354–69.

4. William G. Howell, with David Milton Brent, *Thinking about the Presidency: The Primacy of Power* (Princeton, NJ: Princeton University Press, 2013).

5. Richard E. Neustadt, *Presidential Power: The Politics of Leadership* (New York: Wiley, 1960); Terry M. Moe, "The Politicized Presidency," in *New Directions in American Politics*, ed. John E. Chubb and Paul E. Peterson (Washington, DC: Brookings Institution, 1985), 235–71; Kenneth R. Mayer, *With the Stroke of a Pen: Executive Orders and Presidential Power* (Princeton, NJ: Princeton University Press, 2001); Andrew Rudalevige, *Managing the President's Program: Presidential Leadership and Legislative Policy Formulation* (Princeton, NJ: Princeton University Press, 2002); William G. Howell, *Power without Persuasion: The Politics of Direct Presidential Action* (Princeton, NJ: Princeton University Press, 2003); Daniel Galvin and Colleen Shogan, "Presidential Politicization and Centralization across the Modern-Traditional Divide," *Polity* 36, no. 3 (April 2004): 477–504; Fang-Yi Chiou and Lawrence S. Rothenberg, *The Enigma of Presidential Power: Parties, Policies, and Strategic Uses of Unilateral Action* (New York: Cambridge University Press, 2017); Dino P. Christenson and Douglas L. Kriner, *The Myth of the Imperial Presidency: How Public Opinion Checks the Unilateral Executive* (Chicago: University of Chicago Press, 2020).

6. James L. Sundquist, *The Decline and Resurgence of Congress* (Washington, DC: Brookings Institution, 1981), 155.

7. Sean Gailmard and John W. Patty, *Learning While Governing: Expertise and Accountability in the Executive Branch* (Chicago: University of Chicago Press, 2013), 167–68.

8. John P. Burke, *The Institutional Presidency* (Baltimore: Johns Hopkins University Press, 1992).

9. Alexander Hamilton, "The Federalist No. 70" [March 15, 1788], in Alexander Hamilton, James Madison, and John Jay, *The Federalist*, ed. Terence Ball (New York: Cambridge University Press, 2003), 341.

10. Jeffrey K. Tulis, *The Rhetorical Presidency* (Princeton, NJ: Princeton University Press, 1987); Julia R. Azari and Jennifer K. Smith, "Unwritten Rules: Information Institutions in Established Democracies," *Perspectives on Politics* 10, no. 1 (March 2012): 37–55, at 48. On layering, see James Mahoney and Kathleen Thelen, "A Theory of Gradual Institutional Change," in *Explaining Institutional Change: Ambiguity, Agency, and Power*, ed. James Mahoney and Kathleen Thelen (New York: Cambridge University Press, 2010), 1–37. The laws creating the institutional presidency are an example of the development of the presidential office in "secular time," which is the emergent structure of greater resources and presidential independence, as opposed to the

recurrent structures of political authority in "political time." Stephen Skowronek, *The Politics Presidents Make: Leadership from John Adams to Bill Clinton* (Cambridge, MA: Belknap Press of Harvard University Press, 1997), 30.

11. Sundquist, *Decline and Resurgence*, 156–60. See also Samuel Haber, *Efficiency and Uplift: Scientific Management in the Progressive Era, 1890–1920* (Chicago: University of Chicago Press, 1964), ch. 6; David Epstein and Sharyn O'Halloran, *Delegating Powers: A Transaction Cost Politics Approach to Policy Making under Separate Powers* (New York: Cambridge University Press, 1999).

12. Gailmard and Patty, *Learning While Governing*, 223.

13. David R. Mayhew, *Divided We Govern: Party Control, Lawmaking, and Investigations, 1946–2002*, 2nd ed. (New Haven, CT: Yale University Press, 2005); Sarah A. Binder, "The Dynamics of Legislative Gridlock, 1947–1996," *American Political Science Review* 93, no. 3 (September 1999): 519–33.

14. Alan M. Jacobs, "Process Tracing the Effects of Ideas," in *Process Tracing: From Metaphor to Analytic Tool*, ed. Andrew Bennett and Jeffrey T. Checkel (New York: Cambridge University Press, 2014), 41–73, at 41.

15. Kathy B. Smith, "The Representative Role of the President," *Presidential Studies Quarterly* 11, no. 2 (Spring 1981): 203–13; Anne Norton, *Republic of Signs: Liberal Theory and American Popular Culture* (Chicago: University of Chicago Press, 1993), ch. 3; Gary L. Gregg II, *The Presidential Republic: Executive Representation and Deliberative Democracy* (Lanham, MD: Rowman and Littlefield, 1997).

16. Jeremy D. Bailey, *The Idea of Presidential Representation: An Intellectual and Political History* (Lawrence: University Press of Kansas, 2019).

17. Bernard Manin, *The Principles of Representative Government* (New York: Cambridge University Press, 1997), 219; Matthew Soberg Shugart and Stephan Haggard, "Institutions and Public Policy in Presidential Systems," in *Presidents, Parliaments, and Policy*, ed. Stephan Haggard and Mathew D. McCubbins (New York: Cambridge University Press, 2001), 64–102, at 64; Bailey, *Idea of Presidential Representation*, 40–41, 102.

18. Juan J. Linz, "Presidential or Parliamentary Democracy: Does It Make a Difference?," in *The Failure of Presidential Democracy: Comparative Perspectives*, ed. Juan J. Linz and Arturo Valenzuela (Baltimore: Johns Hopkins University Press, 1994), 3–90, at 7. See also Willmoore Kendall, "The Two Majorities," *Midwest Journal of Political Science* 4, no. 4 (November 1960): 317–35.

19. *Congressional Record*, 74th Congress, 2nd Session (April 17, 1936), 5637.

20. Barry R. Weingast, Kenneth A. Shepsle, and Christopher Johnsen, "The Political Economy of Benefits and Costs: A Neoclassical Approach to Distributive Politics," *Journal of Political Economy* 89, no. 4 (August 1981): 642–64, at 657.

21. Terry M. Moe and Scott A. Wilson, "Presidents and the Politics of Structure," *Law and Contemporary Problems* 57, no. 2 (Spring 1994): 1–44, at 11. See also David E. Lewis, *Presidents and the Politics of Agency Design: Political Insulation in the United States Government Bureaucracy, 1946–1997* (Stanford, CA: Stanford University Press, 2003); Michael A. Bailey, Judith Goldstein, and Barry R. Weingast, "The Institutional Roots of American Trade Policy: Politics, Coalitions, and International Trade," *World Politics* 49, no. 3 (April 1997): 309–38, at 326; Sharyn O'Halloran, *Politics, Process, and American Trade Policy* (Ann Arbor: University of Michigan Press, 1994), 5; Amy B. Zegart, *Flawed by Design: The Evolution of the CIA, JCS, and NSC* (Stanford, CA: Stanford University Press, 1999), 8.

22. B. Dan Wood, *The Myth of Presidential Representation* (New York: Cambridge University Press, 2009). See also Barry Edwards, "Does the Presidency Moderate the President?," *Presidential Studies Quarterly* 47, no. 1 (March 2017): 5–26; Bruce Miroff, *Presidents on Political Ground: Leaders in Action and What They Face* (Lawrence: University Press of Kansas, 2016), ch. 3; Jeffrey E. Cohen, *Presidential Leadership in Public Opinion: Causes and Consequences* (New York: Cambridge University Press, 2015), ch. 5; Julia Azari, *Delivering the People's Message: The Changing Politics of the Presidential Mandate* (Ithaca, NY: Cornell University Press, 2014); Jesse H. Rhodes, "Party Polarization and the Ascendance of Bipartisan Posturing as a Dominant Strategy in Presidential Rhetoric," *Presidential Studies Quarterly* 44, no. 1 (March 2014): 120–42; Matthew Eshbaugh-Soha and Brandon Rottinghaus, "Presidential Position Taking and the Puzzle of Representation," *Presidential Studies Quarterly* 43, no. 1 (March 2013): 1–15.

23. Historically, Electoral College coalitional considerations also influenced Democratic presidents' positions on regulatory policy. Scott C. James, *Presidents, Parties, and the State: A Party System Perspective on Democratic Regulatory Choice, 1884–1936* (New York: Cambridge University Press, 2000).

24. Douglas L. Kriner and Andrew Reeves, *The Particularistic President: Executive Branch Politics and Political Inequality* (New York: Cambridge University Press, 2015); Douglas L. Kriner and Andrew Reeves, "Presidential Particularism in Disaster Declarations and Military Base Closures," *Presidential Studies Quarterly* 45, no. 4 (December 2015): 679–702. See also David Karol, "Does Constituency Size Affect Elected Officials' Trade Policy Preferences?," *Journal of Politics* 69, no. 2 (May 2007): 483–94; Kenneth S. Lowande, Jeffrey A. Jenkins, and Andrew J. Clarke, "Presidential Particularism and US Trade Politics," *Political Science Research and Methods* 6, no. 2 (April 2018): 265–81; Christopher R. Berry, Barry C. Burden, and William G. Howell, "The President and the Distribution of Federal Spending," *American Political Science Review* 104, no. 4 (November 2010): 783–99.

25. John Hudak, *Presidential Pork: White House Influence over the Distribution of Federal Grants* (Washington, DC: Brookings Institution Press, 2014).

26. James N. Druckman and Lawrence R. Jacobs, *Who Governs? Presidents, Public Opinion, and Manipulation* (Chicago: University of Chicago Press, 2015). See also John Griffin and Brian Newman, "The Presidency and Political Equality," *Congress and the Presidency* 43, no. 3 (2016): 352–76; Martin Gilens, *Affluence and Influence: Economic Inequality and Political Power in America* (New York: Russell Sage Foundation; Princeton, NJ: Princeton University Press, 2012); Jacob S. Hacker and Paul Pierson, "Presidents and the Political Economy: The Coalitional Foundations of Presidential Power," *Presidential Studies Quarterly* 42, no. 1 (March 2012): 101–31; Larry M. Bartels, *Unequal Democracy: The Political Economy of the New Gilded Age* (New York: Russell Sage Foundation; Princeton, NJ: Princeton University Press, 2008).

27. Elizabeth Sanders, *Roots of Reform: Farmers, Workers, and the American State, 1877–1917* (Chicago: University of Chicago Press, 1999), 395.

28. On distributive policies in the Senate, see Frances E. Lee and Bruce I. Oppenheimer, *Sizing Up the Senate: The Unequal Consequences of Equal Representation* (Chicago: University of Chicago Press, 1999); Frances E. Lee, "Senate Representation and Coalition Building in Distributive Politics," *American Political Science Review* 94, no. 1 (March 2000): 59–72. On intelligence oversight, see Amy B. Zegart, "The Domestic Politics of Irrational Intelligence Oversight," *Political Science Quarterly* 126, no. 1 (Spring 2011): 1–25. On localistic incentives and military spending, see Rebecca U. Thorpe, *The American Warfare State: The Domestic Politics of Military Spending* (Chicago: University of Chicago Press, 2014).

29. David R. Mayhew, "Congress as a Handler of Challenges: The Historical Record," *Studies in American Political Development* 29, no. 2 (October 2015): 185–212.

30. Alex Keena and Misty Knight-Finley, "Governed by Experience: Political Careers and Party Loyalty in the Senate," *Congress and the Presidency* 45, no. 1 (2018): 20–40.

31. William G. Howell and Terry M. Moe, *Relic: How Our Constitution Undermines Effective Government and Why We Need a More Powerful Presidency* (New York: Basic Books, 2016), ch. 3; William G. Howell, Saul P. Jackman, and Jon C. Rogowski, *The Wartime President: Executive Influence and the Nationalizing Politics of Threat* (Chicago: University of Chicago Press, 2013).

32. Kriner and Reeves, *Particularistic President*, 20.

33. Daphna Renan, "The President's Two Bodies," *Columbia Law Review* 120, no. 5 (June 2020): 1119–214, at 1145–52.

34. Josh Chafetz, *Congress's Constitution: Legislative Authority and the Separation of Powers* (New Haven, CT: Yale University Press, 2017), 18.

35. Richard J. Ellis and Stephen Kirk, "Presidential Mandates in the Nineteenth Century: Conceptual Change and Institutional Development," *Studies in American Political Development* 9, no. 1 (Spring 1995): 117–86; Jeremy D. Bailey, *Thomas Jefferson and Executive Power* (New York: Cambridge University Press, 2007), 9–10; Marc Stears, *Demanding Democracy: American Radicals in Search of a New Politics* (Princeton, NJ: Princeton University Press, 2010), ch. 1; J. Bailey, *Idea of Presidential Representation*, ch. 1.

36. Eric Nelson, *The Royalist Revolution: Monarchy and the American Founding* (Cambridge, MA: Belknap Press of Harvard University Press, 2014), 12–13.

37. Ralph Ketcham, *Presidents above Party: The First American Presidency, 1789–1829* (Chapel Hill: University of North Carolina Press, 1984).

38. Susan Herbst also points out that even the concept of "public opinion" can have changing meanings over time and become associated with different "rhetorical purposes." Susan Herbst, *Numbered Voices: How Opinion Polling Has Shaped American Politics* (Chicago: University of Chicago Press, 1993), 46.

39. James Madison, "The Federalist No. 49" [February 2, 1788], in *The Federalist*, 247.

40. The connection between representation and legislation became firmly established especially in the early 1500s in England. G. R. Elton, ed., *The Tudor Constitution: Documents and Commentary*, 2nd ed. (Cambridge: Cambridge University Press, 1982), 236–40. American political culture had developed a strong emphasis on the necessity of local representation based on colonial experience with the British Parliament. John Phillip Reid, *The Concept of Representation in the Age of the American Revolution* (Chicago: University of Chicago Press, 1989), 28–30, 82–85, 129–36.

41. David Brian Robertson, *The Original Compromise: What the Constitution's Framers Were Really Thinking* (New York: Oxford University Press, 2013), chs. 9–10; Karen Orren and Stephen Skowronek, *The Policy State: An American Predicament* (Cambridge, MA: Harvard University Press, 2017), 123–25. The Electoral College compromise that was reached in the Constitutional Convention also arose out of disputes between larger and smaller states. J. Bailey, *Idea of Presidential Representation*, 35–41.

42. Michael Lind, "The Out-of-Control Presidency," *New Republic*, August 14, 1995, 18–23, at 20.

43. Nelson, *Royalist Revolution*.

44. Gordon S. Wood, *The Creation of the American Republic, 1776–1787* (Chapel Hill: University of North Carolina Press, 1969), 139; J. Bailey, *Idea of Presidential Representation*, 22.

45. Anthony King, *The Founding Fathers v. the People: Paradoxes of American Democracy* (Cambridge, MA: Harvard University Press, 2012), 49–50; J. Bailey, *Idea of Presidential Representation*, 33–34.

46. James Madison, "The Federalist No. 63" [March 1, 1788], in *The Federalist*, 309. Emphasis in original.

47. J. Bailey, *Idea of Presidential Representation*, 31–32.

48. Bruce Ackerman, *The Failure of the Founding Fathers: Jefferson, Marshall, and the Rise of Presidential Democracy* (Cambridge, MA: Belknap Press of Harvard University Press, 2005); J. Bailey, *Idea of Presidential Representation*, ch. 2. See also Robert A. Dahl, "The Myth of the Presidential Mandate," *Political Science Quarterly* 105, no. 3 (Autumn 1990): 355–72.

49. Abraham Lincoln, "Fourth Annual Message," December 6, 1864, *The American Presidency Project*, https://www.presidency.ucsb.edu/documents/fourth-annual-message-8; Ellis and Kirk, "Presidential Mandates." For an account that focuses on the continued partisan differences over the notion of a mandate during this period, see J. Bailey, *Idea of Presidential Representation*, 74–79.

50. Robert V. Remini, *Andrew Jackson and the Bank War: A Study in the Growth of Presidential Power* (New York: W. W. Norton, 1967).

51. Andrew Jackson, "Veto Message [of the Reauthorization of Bank of the United States]," July 10, 1832, *The American Presidency Project*, https://www.presidency.ucsb.edu/documents/veto-message-the-re-authorization-bank-the-united-states.

52. Andrew Jackson, "Message Read to the Cabinet on Removal of the Public Deposits," September 18, 1833, *The American Presidency Project*, https://www.presidency.ucsb.edu/documents/message-read-the-cabinet-removal-the-public-deposits.

53. Andrew Jackson, "Message to the Senate Protesting Censure Resolution," April 15, 1834, *The American Presidency Project*, https://www.presidency.ucsb.edu/documents/message-the-senate-protesting-censure-resolution.

54. J. Bailey, *Idea of Presidential Representation*, 58.

55. Howell and Moe, *Relic*, xvi.

56. Looking comparatively, presidents' legislative powers might include the package veto, partial veto, exclusive introduction of legislation, budgetary initiation, and proposal of referenda. See Matthew Soberg Shugart and John M. Carey, *Presidents and Assemblies: Constitutional Design and Electoral Dynamics* (New York: Cambridge University Press, 1992), 150, table 8.1.

57. On the historical variation in presidents' control over the executive branch, see Patrick R. O'Brien, "A Theoretical Critique of the Unitary Executive Framework: Rethinking the First-Mover Advantage, Collective-Action Advantage, and Informational Advantage," *Presidential Studies Quarterly* 47, no. 1 (March 2017): 169–85.

58. James W. Ceaser, *Presidential Selection: Theory and Development* (Princeton, NJ: Princeton University Press, 1979), 185. See also Sidney M. Milkis, "The Presidency and American Political Development: The Advent—and Illusion—of an Executive-Centered Democracy," in *The Oxford Handbook of American Political Development*, ed. Richard Valelly, Suzanne Mettler, and Robert Lieberman (New York: Oxford University Press, 2016), 286–308.

59. J. Bailey, *Idea of Presidential Representation*, 2, 9.

60. Andrew Bennett and Jeffrey T. Checkel, "Process Tracing: From Philosophical Roots to Best Practices," in *Process Tracing*, ed. Bennett and Checkel, 3–37.

61. John Gerring, *Case Study Research: Principles and Practices* (New York: Cambridge University Press, 2007).

62. Stephen Skowronek, John A. Dearborn, and Desmond King, *Phantoms of a Beleaguered Republic: The Deep State and the Unitary Executive* (New York: Oxford University Press, 2021).

Chapter Two

1. John Dickinson, "Democratic Realities and Democratic Dogma," *American Political Science Review* 24, no. 2 (May 1930): 283–309, at 284.

2. Walter Lippmann, *Drift and Mastery: An Attempt to Diagnose the Current Unrest* (New York: Mitchell Kennerley, 1914), 270.

3. John Maynard Keynes, *The General Theory of Employment, Interest, and Money* (London: Macmillan, 1936), 383.

4. See, for example, Anthony Giddens, "Marx, Weber, and the Development of Capitalism," *Sociology* 4, no. 3 (September 1970): 289–310; Michael Löwy, "Weber against Marx? The Polemic with Historical Materialism in the Protestant Ethic," *Science and Society* 53, no. 1 (Spring 1989): 71–83; Jonathan Eastwood, "The Role of Ideas in Weber's Theory of Interests," *Critical Review* 17, nos. 1–2 (2005): 89–100; Mark Gould, "Marx and Weber and the Logic of Historical Explanation: The Rise of Machine Capitalism," *Journal of Classical Sociology* 16, no. 4 (2016): 321–48.

5. Karl Marx, *A Contribution to the Critique of Political Economy*, trans. N. I. Stone (Chicago: Charles H. Kerr, 1904), 11–12. See also Karl Marx, *Capital: A Critical Analysis of Capitalist Production*, ed. [Friedrich] Engels, trans. Samuel Moore and Edward Aveling (New York: Appleton, 1889).

6. H. H. Gerth and C. Wright Mills, "Intellectual Orientations," in *From Max Weber: Essays in Sociology*, ed. H. H. Gerth and C. Wright Mills (New York: Oxford University Press, 1946), 45–74, at 46–47, 61–65.

7. Max Weber, "The Protestant Sects and the Spirit of Capitalism," in *From Max Weber*, ed. Gerth and Mills, 302–22, at 309. See also Max Weber, *The Protestant Ethic and the Spirit of Capitalism*, trans. Talcott Parsons (New York: Charles Scribner's Sons, 1930).

8. Quoted in Gerth and Mills, "Intellectual Orientations," 64.

9. See, for example, Judith Goldstein and Robert O. Keohane, "Ideas and Foreign Policy: An Analytical Framework," in *Ideas and Foreign Policy: Beliefs, Institutions, and Political Change*, ed. Judith Goldstein and Robert O. Keohane (Ithaca, NY: Cornell University Press, 1993), 3–30; Barry R. Weingast, "A Rational Choice Perspective on the Role of Ideas: Shared Belief Systems and State Sovereignty in International Cooperation," *Politics and Society* 23, no. 4 (December 1995): 449–64; Albert S. Yee, "Thick Rationality and the Missing 'Brute Fact': The Limits of Rationalist Incorporations of Norms and Ideas," *Journal of Politics* 59, no. 4 (November 1997): 1001–39; John L. Campbell, "Ideas, Politics, and Public Policy," *Annual Review of Sociology* 28 (2002): 21–38; Mark Blyth, "Structures Do Not Come with an Instruction Sheet: Interests, Ideas, and Progress in Political Science," *Perspectives on Politics* 1, no. 4 (December 2003): 695–706.

10. Judith Goldstein, *Ideas, Interests, and American Trade Policy* (Ithaca, NY: Cornell University Press, 1993), xi; Alexander Wendt, *Social Theory of International Politics* (New York: Cambridge University Press, 1999), 117. For both authors, these statements are part of their critiques of rational choice theory.

11. Daniel Béland and Robert Henry Cox, "Introduction," in *Ideas and Politics in Social Science Research*, ed. Daniel Béland and Robert Henry Cox (New York: Oxford University Press, 2011), 3–22, at 3.

12. Peter A. Hall, "Introduction," in *The Political Power of Economic Ideas: Keynesianism across Nations*, ed. Peter A. Hall (Princeton, NJ: Princeton University Press, 1989), 3–26, at 4.

13. Jal Mehta, "The Varied Roles of Ideas in Politics: From 'Whether' to 'How,'" in *Ideas and Politics in Social Science Research*, ed. Béland and Cox, 23–46, at 25.

14. Béland and Cox, "Introduction," 3.

15. Verlan Lewis, *Ideas of Power: The Politics of American Party Ideology Development* (New York: Cambridge University Press, 2019), xiv.

16. Suzanne Mettler and Richard Valelly, "Introduction: The Distinctiveness and Necessity of American Political Development," in *Oxford Handbook of American Political Development*, ed. Richard Valelly, Suzanne Mettler, and Robert Lieberman (New York: Oxford University Press, 2016), 1–23, at 6.

17. George Thomas, "Political Thought and Political Development," *American Political Thought* 3, no. 1 (Spring 2014): 114–25, at 123.

18. Louis Hartz, *The Liberal Tradition in America: An Interpretation of American Political Thought since the Revolution* (New York: Harcourt, Brace, 1955); J. David Greenstone, *The Lincoln Persuasion: Remaking American Liberalism* (Princeton, NJ: Princeton University Press, 1993); Rogers M. Smith, *Civic Ideals: Conflicting Visions of Citizenship in US History* (New Haven, CT: Yale University Press, 1997).

19. Karen Orren and Stephen Skowronek, *The Search for American Political Development* (New York: Cambridge University Press, 2004), 83.

20. Karen Orren and Stephen Skowronek, "Have We Abandoned a 'Constitutional Perspective' on American Political Development?," *Review of Politics* 73, no. 2 (Spring 2011): 295–99, at 298.

21. Mark Blyth, *Great Transformations: Economic Ideas and Institutional Change in the Twentieth Century* (New York: Cambridge University Press, 2002), ch. 2. See also Martha Derthick and Paul J. Quirk, *The Politics of Deregulation* (Washington, DC: Brookings Institution, 1985).

22. Rogers M. Smith, "Ideas and the Spiral of Politics: The Place of American Political Thought in American Political Development," *American Political Thought* 3, no. 1 (Spring 2014): 126–36, at 126, 130–32.

23. Orren and Skowronek, *Search*, 123.

24. Rogers M. Smith, "Which Comes First, the Ideas or the Institutions?," in *Rethinking Political Institutions: The Art of the State*, ed. Ian Shapiro, Stephen Skowronek, and Daniel Galvin (New York: New York University Press, 2006), 91–113, at 95.

25. Alan M. Jacobs, "Process Tracing the Effects of Ideas," in *Process Tracing: From Metaphor to Analytic Tool*, ed. Andrew Bennett and Jeffrey T. Checkel (New York: Cambridge University Press, 2014), 41–73, at 48–49.

26. Vivien A. Schmidt, "Discursive Institutionalism: The Explanatory Power of Ideas and Discourse," *Annual Review of Political Science* 11 (2008): 303–26.

27. Stephen Skowronek, "The Reassociation of Ideas and Purposes: Racism, Liberalism, and the American Political Tradition," *American Political Science Review* 100, no. 3 (August 2006): 385–401.

28. For example, Ken Kersch documents the widespread rise of arguments for constitutional restoration in the conservative movement. Ken I. Kersch, *Conservatives and the Constitution: Imagining Constitutional Restoration in the Heyday of American Liberalism* (New York: Cambridge University Press, 2019).

29. Robert C. Lieberman, "Ideas, Institutions, and Political Order: Explaining Political Change," *American Political Science Review* 96, no. 4 (December 2002): 697–712, at 709.

30. Lewis, *Ideas of Power*, 25.

31. Jacobs, "Process Tracing the Effects of Ideas," 48–49.

32. James W. Ceaser, *Nature and History in American Political Development: A Debate* (Cambridge, MA: Harvard University Press, 2006), 5; Sidney M. Milkis, "Ideas, Institutions, and the New Deal Constitutional Order," *American Political Thought* 3, no. 1 (Spring 2014): 167–76, at 167.

33. Mehta, "Varied Roles," 45–46.

34. George Thomas, *The Founders and the Idea of a National University: Constituting the American Mind* (New York: Cambridge University Press, 2015).

35. David A. Bateman, "Transatlantic Anxieties: Democracy and Diversity in Nineteenth-Century Discourse," *Studies in American Political Development* 33, no. 2 (October 2019): 133–77.

36. Chloe N. Thurston, *At the Boundaries of Homeownership: Credit, Discrimination, and the American State* (New York: Cambridge University Press, 2018), 26, 102, 125.

37. Paul Frymer, *Building an American Empire: The Era of Territorial and Political Expansion* (Princeton, NJ: Princeton University Press, 2017), 281.

38. John A. Dearborn, "American Imperial Development," *Journal of Politics* 81, no. 2 (April 2019): e44–e49.

39. Richard J. Ellis and Stephen Kirk, "Presidential Mandates in the Nineteenth Century: Conceptual Change and Institutional Development," *Studies in American Political Development* 9, no. 1 (Spring 1995): 117–86, at 137–44.

40. Aaron L. Friedberg, *In the Shadow of the Garrison State: America's Anti-statism and Its Cold War Grand Strategy* (Princeton, NJ: Princeton University Press, 2000).

41. Goldstein and Keohane, "Ideas and Foreign Policy," 12.

42. Gerald Berk, *Louis D. Brandeis and the Making of Regulated Competition, 1900–1932* (New York: Cambridge University Press, 2009).

43. Daphna Renan, "Presidential Norms and Article II," *Harvard Law Review* 131, no. 8 (June 2018): 2187–82, at 2207–15; Stephen Skowronek, John A. Dearborn, and Desmond King, *Phantoms of a Beleaguered Republic: The Deep State and the Unitary Executive* (New York: Oxford University Press, 2021), 78–79.

44. Daniel P. Carpenter, *The Forging of Bureaucratic Autonomy: Reputations, Networks, and Policy Innovation in Executive Agencies, 1862–1928* (Princeton, NJ: Princeton University Press, 2001), 13. See also Daniel Carpenter, *Reputation and Power: Organizational Image and Pharmaceutical Regulation at the FDA* (Princeton, NJ: Princeton University Press, 2010).

45. Colin D. Moore, *American Imperialism and the State, 1893–1921* (New York: Cambridge University Press, 2017), 29.

46. Robert C. Lieberman, *Shaping Race Policy: The United States in Comparative Perspective* (Princeton, NJ: Princeton University Press, 2005), 11. See also Desmond S. King and Rogers M. Smith, "'Without Regard to Race': Critical Ideational Development in Modern American Politics," *Journal of Politics* 76, no. 4 (July 2014): 958–71.

47. Anthony Sparacino, "Compassionate Conservatism in the Spiral of Politics," *American Political Thought* 7, no. 3 (Summer 2018): 480–513.

48. Blyth, *Great Transformations*, 37–38.

49. Elvin Lim, "Political Thought, Political Development, and America's Two Foundings,"

American Political Thought 3, no. 1 (Spring 2014): 146–56; Jeffrey K. Tulis and Nicole Mellow, *Legacies of Losing in American Politics* (Chicago: University of Chicago Press, 2018), ch. 2. For an account of how the meaning of impeachment has become legalized and layered over traditional constitutional understandings of impeachment, see Allen C. Sumrall, "Incongruous Ideas of Impeachment: 'Impeachable Offenses' and the Constitutional Order," *Presidential Studies Quarterly* 50, no. 4 (December 2020): 948–67.

50. Howard Gillman, "The Collapse of Constitutional Originalism and the Rise of the Notion of the 'Living Constitution' in the Course of American State-Building," *Studies in American Political Development* 11, no. 2 (Fall 1997): 191–247, at 194.

51. Stephen Skowronek, *The Politics Presidents Make: Leadership from John Adams to Bill Clinton* (Cambridge, MA: Belknap Press of Harvard University Press, 1997), 37.

52. Karen Orren, "Ideas and Institutions," *Polity* 28, no. 1 (Autumn 1995): 97–101, at 98; Smith, "Which Comes First, the Ideas or the Institutions?," 98.

53. Lieberman, "Ideas, Institutions, and Political Order," 697.

54. Sparacino, "Compassionate Conservatism," 507.

55. Paul Pierson, *Politics in Time: History, Institutions, and Social Analysis* (Princeton, NJ: Princeton University Press, 2004), ch. 4.

56. Samuel P. Huntington, *American Politics: The Promise of Disharmony* (Cambridge, MA: Belknap Press of Harvard University Press, 1981), 3, 85.

57. Hugh Heclo, "OMB and the Presidency—the Problem of 'Neutral Competence,'" *National Interest* 38 (Winter 1975): 80–99; Terry M. Moe, "The Politicized Presidency," in *The New Direction in American Politics*, ed. John E. Chubb and Paul E. Peterson (Washington, DC: Brookings Institution, 1985), 144–61.

58. Rogers M. Smith, "Beyond Tocqueville, Myrdal, and Hartz: The Multiple Traditions in America," *American Political Science Review* 87, no. 3 (September 1993): 549–66.

59. Tulis and Mellow, *Legacies of Losing*, chs. 2–4.

60. Anne Norton, *Republic of Signs: Liberal Theory and American Popular Culture* (Chicago: University of Chicago Press, 1993), 1. On "settled" versus "unsettled" models of cultural influence, see Ann Swidler, "Culture in Action: Symbols and Strategies," *American Sociological Review* 51, no. 2 (April 1986): 273–86.

Part One

1. Henry Jones Ford, *The Rise and Growth of American Politics: A Sketch of Constitutional Development* (New York: Macmillan, 1898), 214–15.

2. On changes to presidential selection procedures, see James W. Ceaser, *Presidential Selection: Theory and Development* (Princeton, NJ: Princeton University Press, 1979); Jeremy D. Bailey, *The Idea of Presidential Representation: An Intellectual and Political History* (Lawrence: University Press of Kansas, 2019).

3. Jeffrey K. Tulis, *The Rhetorical Presidency* (Princeton, NJ: Princeton University Press, 1987), chs. 4–5; Victoria A. Farrar-Myers, *Scripted for Change: The Institutionalization of the American Presidency* (College Station: Texas A&M University Press, 2007).

4. George C. Herring, *From Colony to Superpower: US Foreign Relations since 1776* (New York: Oxford University Press, 2008), chs. 8–10.

5. Richard E. Neustadt, "The Presidential 'Hundred Days': An Overview," *Presidential Studies Quarterly* 31, no. 1 (March 2001): 121–25.

6. Keith E. Whittington and Daniel P. Carpenter, "Executive Power in American Institutional Development," *Perspectives on Politics* 1, no. 3 (September 2003): 495–513.

7. For a more skeptical view of the transformation associated with the Progressives' view of presidential representation, see Bailey, *Idea of Presidential Representation*, ch. 3.

8. Frederick Jackson Turner, *The Frontier in American History* (New York: Henry Holt, 1920); Marc Stears, *Progressives, Pluralists, and the Problems of the State: Ideologies of Reform in the United States and Britain, 1909–1926* (Oxford: Oxford University Press, 2002), ch. 2; Marc Stears, *Demanding Democracy: American Radicals in Search of a New Politics* (Princeton, NJ: Princeton University Press, 2010), ch. 1; Jackson Lears, *Rebirth of a Nation: The Making of Modern America, 1877–1920* (New York: Harper, 2009).

9. William Allen White, *The Old Order Changeth: A View of American Democracy* (New York: Macmillan, 1910), 250.

10. Christopher Capozzola, *Uncle Sam Wants You: World War I and the Making of the Modern American Citizen* (New York: Oxford University Press, 2008); J. Kevin Corder and Christina Wolbrecht, *Counting Women's Ballots: Female Voters from Suffrage through the New Deal* (New York: Cambridge University Press, 2016), 3.

11. White, *Old Order Changeth*, 247–48.

12. Albert Shaw, *Political Problems of American Development* (New York: Columbia University Press, 1907), 1.

13. Sidney M. Milkis and Daniel J. Tichenor, *Rivalry and Reform: Presidents, Social Movements, and the Transformation of American Politics* (Chicago: University of Chicago Press, 2019), ch. 3; Thomas C. Leonard, *Illiberal Reformers: Race, Eugenics, and American Economics in the Progressive Era* (Princeton, NJ: Princeton University Press, 2016).

14. Herbert Croly, *The Promise of American Life* (New York: Macmillan, 1909), 270.

15. Frank Buffington Vrooman, *The New Politics* (New York: Oxford University Press, 1911), 191.

16. Walter E. Weyl, *The New Democracy: An Essay on Certain Political and Economic Tendencies in the United States* (New York: Macmillan, 1912), 314.

17. Jane Addams, *Democracy and Social Ethics* (New York: Macmillan, 1902), 256.

18. Edward Elliot, *American Government and Majority Rule: A Study in American Political Development* (Princeton, NJ: Princeton University Press, 1916), 141–42. On Senate representation prior to the Seventeenth Amendment, see Wendy J. Schiller and Charles Stewart III, *Electing the Senate: Indirect Democracy before the Seventeenth Amendment* (Princeton, NJ: Princeton University Press, 2015).

19. Woodrow Wilson, *Congressional Government: A Study in American Politics* (Boston: Houghton Mifflin, 1885), 280.

20. Croly, *Promise of American Life*, 69.

21. Arthur Twining Hadley, *Standards of Public Morality* (New York: Macmillan, 1907), 117.

22. Herbert Croly, *Progressive Democracy* (New York: Macmillan, 1914), 355.

23. Saladin M. Ambar, *How Governors Built the Modern American Presidency* (Philadelphia: University of Pennsylvania Press, 2012), chs. 1–3.

24. Mary Parker Follett, *The New State: Group Organization the Solution of Popular Government* (New York: Longmans, Green, 1918), 178.

25. "Speech of Hon. Charles E. Hughes, While Candidate for Governor of the State of New York, Delivered at Bethel A.M.E. Church, New York City, on November 4, 1906, Hon.

Charles W. Anderson, Presiding," November 4, 1906, Microfilm, Reel 136, Charles Evans Hughes Papers, Manuscript Division, Library of Congress, Washington, DC.

26. Theodore Roosevelt, *An Autobiography* (New York: Macmillan, 1913), 357.

27. Grover Cleveland, *The Independence of the Executive* (Princeton, NJ: Princeton University Press, 1913), 9–11.

28. William Howard Taft, *Representative Government in the United States* (New York: New York University Press, 1921), 34.

29. Harry S. Truman, "Informal Remarks in Washington," June 10, 1948, *The American Presidency Project*, https://www.presidency.ucsb.edu/documents/informal-remarks-washington.

30. James Bryce, *The American Commonwealth*, vol. 1, rev. ed. (New York: Macmillan, 1910), 67.

31. Nicholas Murray Butler, *The American as He Is* (New York: Macmillan, 1908), 25.

32. Simeon E. Baldwin, *Modern Political Institutions* (Boston: Little, Brown, 1898), 109.

33. Nicholas Murray Butler, *True or False Democracy* (New York: Macmillan, 1907), 35.

34. Simeon E. Baldwin, *The Relations of Education to Citizenship* (New Haven, CT: Yale University Press, 1912), 85.

35. Jeremiah W. Jenks, *Principles of Politics from the Viewpoint of the American Citizen* (New York: Columbia University Press, 1909), 111.

36. Samuel W. McCall, *The Business of Congress* (New York: Columbia University Press, 1911), 188.

37. Woodrow Wilson, *Constitutional Government in the United States* (New York: Columbia University Press, 1908), 203, 68. Wilson's speech in 1907 was part of a lecture series sponsored by the George Blumenthal Foundation. See also Daniel D. Stid, *The President as Statesman: Woodrow Wilson and the Constitution* (Lawrence: University Press of Kansas, 1998); John A. Dearborn, "The 'Two Mr. Wilsons': Party Government, Personal Leadership, and Woodrow Wilson's Political Thought," *Congress and the Presidency* 47, no. 1 (2020): 32–61.

38. Charles E. Hughes, "Some Aspects of Our Democracy," *Harvard Graduates' Magazine* 19, no. 73 (September 1910): 1–10, at 7.

39. John Corbin, "Harding Will Try to Regain Lost Leadership of Nation," *New York Times*, April 15, 1923, 3, 6.

40. Aaron Hardy Ulm, "Shall Cabinet Members Sit in Congress?," *Dearborn Independent*, August 12, 1922, 2. Emphasis in original.

41. "Let the President Lead!," *Atlanta Constitution*, June 1, 1932, 6. Reprinted from *Kansas City Star*.

42. Quoted in Henry Jones Ford, *The Cost of Our National Government: A Study in Political Pathology* (New York: Columbia University Press, 1910), 113.

43. "Pro Bono Publico," *Outlook*, November 27, 1909, 646.

44. Harold Zink, *A Survey of American Government* (New York: Macmillan, 1948), 251.

45. Wilfred E. Binkley and Malcolm C. Moos, *A Grammar of American Politics: The National Government* (New York: Alfred A. Knopf, 1949), 328.

46. Sinclair Lewis, *It Can't Happen Here* (Garden City, NY: Doubleday, Doran, 1935), 119.

47. Allen Drury, *Advise and Consent* (London: Collins, 1959), 401.

48. Henry L. Stimson and McGeorge Bundy, *On Active Service in Peace and War* (New York: Harper and Brothers, 1948), ch. 3.

49. "Outline No. 2" for Speech before Law Academy of Philadelphia, May 1913, c, Microfilm

183, Box U130, Series HM52, Henry Lewis Stimson Papers, Manuscripts and Archives, Sterling Memorial Library, Yale University, New Haven, CT.

50. "Initiative and Responsibility of the Executive: A Remedy for Inefficient Legislation," Address before Law Academy of Philadelphia, May 27, 1913, 5, 11, Microfilm 153, 158, Box U130, HM 52, Stimson Papers. Emphasis in original.

51. "Initiative and Responsibility of the Executive," 7, 25–27, Microfilm 155, 173–75, Box U130, Series HM 52, Stimson Papers. On the tension between institutionalizing presidential leadership and the individual officeholder, see Daphna Renan, "The President's Two Bodies," *Columbia Law Review* 120, no. 5 (June 2020): 1119–214.

52. "Outline No. 2," f, Microfilm 186, Box U130, Series HM 52, Stimson Papers; Material for Speech, "Divided Responsibility in Government," May 1913, Microfilm 202, Box U130, Series HM52, Stimson Papers.

53. Ford, *Rise and Growth*, 215. See also Stephen Skowronek, "Henry Jones Ford on the Development of American Institutions," *PS: Political Science and Politics* 32, no. 2 (June 1999): 233–34.

54. "Initiative and Responsibility of the Executive," 23, Microfilm 170, Box U130, Series HM 52, Stimson Papers.

55. Walter Lippmann, "The President's Return," *Today and Tomorrow*, December 21, 1943, in *The Essential Lippmann: A Political Philosophy for Liberal Democracy*, ed. Clinton Rossiter and James Lare (New York: Random House, 1963), 284.

56. Harold J. Laski, *The American Presidency: An Interpretation* (New York: Harper and Brothers, 1940), 20.

57. William Franklin Willoughby, *The Problem of a National Budget* (New York: D. Appleton, 1918), 63.

58. E. Pendleton Herring, *Public Administration and the Public Interest* (New York: McGraw-Hill, 1936), 384.

59. Arthur Twining Hadley, *The Education of the American Citizen* (New York: Charles Scribner's Sons, 1901), 79.

60. "Initiative and Responsibility of the Executive," 1, Microfilm 149, Box U130, Series HM 52, Stimson Papers.

61. Lyman Abbott, *America in the Making* (New Haven, CT: Yale University Press, 1911), 94–95.

62. George H. Sabine, "What Is the Matter with Representative Government?," *North American Review* 213, no. 786 (May 1921): 587–97, at 589.

63. Ford, *Rise and Growth*, 278–79. The subject of changing the relationship between the presidency and Congress even made its way into Ford's political science classes. For example, his fall 1913 exam asked, "[James] Bryce says that in our system of government 'there can be little effective responsibility for legislation.' What grounds does he give for that opinion[?]" "Princeton University, Mid-term Test, Politics 405," November 11, 1913, Folder 12, Box 1, Ford Family Papers, Manuscripts Division, Department of Rare Books and Special Collections, Princeton University Library, Princeton, NJ.

64. John W. Burgess, *Political Science and Comparative Constitutional Law*, vol. 2 (Boston: Ginn, 1890), 254.

65. Gamaliel Bradford, *The Lesson of Popular Government*, vol. 1 (New York: Macmillan, 1899), 367.

66. Letter from Gamaliel Bradford to Charles Evans Hughes, June 30, 1910, 1, Microfilm, Reel 3, Hughes Papers.

67. "Initiative and Responsibility of the Executive," 21, Microfilm 168, Box U130, Series HM 52, Stimson Papers.

68. Ulm, "Shall Cabinet Members Sit in Congress?"

69. Charles A. Beard, "The Living Constitution," *Annals of the American Academy of Political and Social Science* 185 (May 1936): 29–34; M. J. C. Vile, *Constitutionalism and the Separation of Powers* (Oxford: Oxford University Press, 1967); Howard Gillman, "The Collapse of Constitutional Originalism and the Rise of the Notion of the 'Living Constitution' in the Course of American State-Building," *Studies in American Political Development* 11, no. 2 (Fall 1997): 191–247. See also Calvin TerBeek, "The Search for an Anchor: Living Constitutionalism from the Progressives to Trump," *Law and Social Inquiry*, forthcoming.

70. James T. Young, "The Relation of the Executive to the Legislative Power," *Proceedings of the American Political Science Association* 1 (1904): 47–54, at 53.

71. Howard Lee McBain, *The Living Constitution: A Consideration of the Realities and Legends of Our Fundamental Law* (New York: Workers Education Bureau Press, 1927), 115. For an analysis of an alternative view of formalism during this period, see Andrea S. Katz, "The Lost Promise of Progressive Formalism," *Texas Law Review* 99, no. 4 (March 2021): 679–742.

72. Ford, *Rise and Growth*, 292–93.

Chapter Three

1. Edward A. Fitzpatrick, *Budget Making in a Democracy: A New View of the Budget* (New York: Macmillan, 1918), viii. Emphasis in original.

2. James L. Sundquist, *The Decline and Resurgence of Congress* (Washington, DC: Brookings Institution, 1981), 39.

3. F. W. Maitland, *The Constitutional History of England: A Course of Lectures Delivered* (Cambridge: Cambridge University Press, 1908), 67–68, 95–96; J. C. Holt, *Magna Carta*, 2nd ed. (New York: Cambridge University Press, 1992), 34–35, 43–45; 321–22; 398–400; 404–5; G. R. Elton, ed., *The Tudor Constitution: Documents and Commentary*, 2nd ed. (Cambridge: Cambridge University Press, 1982), 43, 233, 248, 309.

4. Louis Fisher, *Defending Congress and the Constitution* (Lawrence: University Press of Kansas, 2011), 199–200; David Brian Robertson, *The Original Compromise: What the Constitution's Framers Were Really Thinking* (New York: Oxford University Press, 2013), 107–9.

5. "1920 Campaign," 1920, Folder "Speech File, Mar. 1920–[1920]," Box 110, Hanna-McCormick Family Papers, Manuscript Division, Library of Congress, Washington, DC.

6. Warren G. Harding, "Address Accepting the Republican Presidential Nomination," June 12, 1920, *The American Presidency Project*, https://www.presidency.ucsb.edu/documents/address-accepting-the-republican-presidential-nomination-2.

7. Sundquist, *Decline and Resurgence*, 39–44.

8. Sean Gailmard and John W. Patty, *Learning While Governing: Expertise and Accountability in the Executive Branch* (Chicago: University of Chicago Press, 2013), 184–92.

9. "For more than a century, Congress received what was called a 'Book of Estimates': an uncoordinated pile of agency budget requests from executive agencies." Fisher, *Defending Congress*, 199.

10. The Senate bill passed without a recorded vote. *Congressional Record*, 67th Congress, 1st Session (April 26, 1921), 662. The House bill passed 344–9 (with 76 not voting). *Congressional Record*, 67th Congress, 1st Session (May 5, 1921), 1092–93. The Senate passed the conference report without a recorded vote. *Congressional Record*, 67th Congress, 1st Session (May 26, 1921), 1783. The House passed the conference report 335–3 (with 92 not voting). *Congressional Record*, 67th Congress, 1st Session (May 27, 1921), 1859.

11. For example, consider that budget reform after the Civil War involved centralizing through the Appropriations Committee, rather than involving the president. Louis Fisher, *Presidential Spending Power* (Princeton, NJ: Princeton University Press, 1975), 19–21.

12. For the influence of Taylorism and scientific management on politics, see Samuel Haber, *Efficiency and Uplift: Scientific Management in the Progressive Era, 1890–1920* (Chicago: University of Chicago Press, 1964), ch 6.

13. Henry Jones Ford, *The Rise and Growth of American Politics: A Sketch of Constitutional Development* (New York: Macmillan, 1898), 215.

14. Henry Jones Ford, *The Cost of Our National Government: A Study in Political Pathology* (New York: Columbia University Press, 1910), 63.

15. Fitzpatrick, *Budget Making*, viii. Emphasis in original.

16. Haber, *Efficiency and Uplift*, ix.

17. F. Scott Fitzgerald, "The Curious Case of Benjamin Button," in *Tales of the Jazz Age* (New York: Charles Scribner's Sons, 1922), 192–224, at 221.

18. Peri E. Arnold, *Making the Managerial Presidency: Comprehensive Reorganization Planning, 1905–1996*, 2nd ed. (Lawrence: University Press of Kansas, 1998), 17–20. Struggles over the structure of the bureaucracy were also cloaked in the language of efficiency. Stephen Skowronek, *Building a New American State: The Expansion of National Administrative Capacities, 1877–1920* (New York: Cambridge University Press, 1982), 177–78.

19. Jonathan Kahn, *Budgeting Democracy: State Building and Citizenship in America, 1890–1928* (Ithaca, NY: Cornell University Press, 1997), 5.

20. Charles Wallace Collins, *A Plan for a National Budget System*, 65th Congress, 2nd Session, House Document No. 1006 (Washington, DC: Government Printing Office, 1918), 16.

21. William Bennett Munro, *The Government of the United States: National, State, and Local* (New York: Macmillan, 1919), 305.

22. Both quoted in Ford, *Cost*, 3.

23. Roy T. Meyers and Irene S. Rubin, "The Executive Budget in the Federal Government: The First Century and Beyond," *Public Administration Review* 71, no. 3 (May/June 2011): 334–44, at 335.

24. Fitzpatrick, *Budget Making*, 38, 44. Emphasis in original.

25. Frederick A. Cleveland, "How We Have Been Getting Along without a Budget," *Proceedings of the American Political Science Association* 9 (1912): 47–67, at 47, 61.

26. Ford, *Cost*, 45.

27. "Political Pathology," *New York Times*, May 21, 1911, 310.

28. William Howard Taft, *Our Chief Magistrate and His Powers* (New York: Columbia University Press, 1916), 6.

29. President's Commission on Economy and Efficiency (PCEE), *The Need for a National Budget*, 62nd Congress, 2nd Session, House Document No. 854 (Washington, DC: Government Printing Office, 1912), 141. Emphasis in original.

30. Institute for Government Research (IGR), *A National Budget System: The Most Impor-*

tant of All Governmental Reconstruction Measures (Washington, DC: Institute for Government Research, 1919), 2.

31. "Critical Analysis of H.R. 9783 Sixty-Sixth Congress First Session—The So-Called Good Budget Bill," 1919, 1, Folder "General Correspondence, Nov. 18–Dec. 1919," Box 6, Hanna-McCormick Family Papers. Though its authorship is not stated, the memo belonged to Senator McCormick.

32. *Congressional Record*, 66th Congress, 2nd Session (May 29, 1920), 7955.

33. *Congressional Record*, 67th Congress, 1st Session (May 27, 1921), 1854.

34. Leonard D. White, *The Federalists: A Study in Administrative History* (New York: Macmillan, 1948), 118–19, 58; Leonard D. White, *The Jeffersonians: A Study in Administrative History* (New York: Macmillan, 1951), 140–42.

35. Leonard D. White, *The Jacksonians: A Study in Administrative History* (New York: Macmillan, 1954), 39–47; Leonard D. White, *The Republican Era, 1869–1901: A Study in Administrative History* (New York: Macmillan, 1958, 66–67, 97–98.

36. For example, Democratic president James Polk sought to direct the attention of the cabinet to budget estimates. Fisher, *Presidential Spending Power*, 15–19.

37. White, *Republican Era*, 61–65; Fisher, *Presidential Spending Power*, 19–21.

38. Collins, *Plan for a National Budget System*, chart 1, p. 16.

39. Charles H. Stewart, *Budget Reform Politics: The Design of the Appropriations Process in the House of Representatives* (New York: Cambridge University Press, 1989), 191–96.

40. Letter from Champ Clark to Swagar Sherley, October 25, 1915, Folder "Congressional Correspondence 1914–1915," Box 8, Subseries 3, Series IV, J. Swagar Sherley Papers, Archives and Special Collections, Ekstrom Library, University of Louisville, Louisville, KY.

41. Joseph G. Cannon, *The National Budget*, 66th Congress, 1st Session, House Document No. 264 (Washington, DC: Government Printing Office, 1919), 29.

42. Untitled Speech, May 1921, 8–9, Folder "Speech File, May 1921–[1921]," Box 110, Hanna-McCormick Family Papers.

43. *National Budget System*, Hearings before the Select Committee on the Budget, House of Representatives, 66th Congress, 1st Session (Washington, DC, 1919), 539; William Franklin Willoughby, *The Movement for Budgetary Reform in the States* (New York: D. Appleton, 1918); Frederick A. Cleveland and Arthur Eugene Buck, *The Budget and Responsible Government* (New York: Macmillan, 1920), 124.

44. William Howard Taft, "Second Annual Message," December 6, 1910, *The American Presidency Project*, https://www.presidency.ucsb.edu/documents/second-annual-message-17.

45. Letter from William Howard Taft to Horace D. Taft, December 12, 1910, 110847, Reel 125, Series 3, William H. Taft Papers, Manuscript Division, Library of Congress, Washington, DC.

46. Arnold, *Making the Managerial Presidency*, 26–39. Joining Cleveland were William Willoughby, Merritt Chance, Frank Goodnow, Walter Warwick, and Harvey Chase.

47. "Wilson for Economy Board," *New York Times*, April 5, 1913, 3.

48. Fisher, *Presidential Spending Power*, 32. See also Woodrow Wilson, "The Study of Administration," *Political Science Quarterly* 2, no. 2 (June 1887): 197–222.

49. "I am very glad, indeed," wrote Wilson to Sherley, "to have the material you so thoughtfully send [*sic*] me about the budget and shall look forward with real pleasure to reading it." Letter from Woodrow Wilson to Swagar Sherley, August 24, 1912, Folder "Congressional Correspondence 1911–1913," Box 8, Subseries 3, Series IV, Sherley Papers.

50. Skowronek, *Building a New American State*, 175.

51. Taft, *Our Chief Magistrate*, 64–65.

52. Charles Wallace Collins, *The National Budget System and American Finance* (New York: Macmillan, 1917), 136.

53. Cleveland and Buck, *Budget and Responsible Government*, 123.

54. "Republican Party Platform of 1912," June 18, 1912, *The American Presidency Project*, https://www.presidency.ucsb.edu/documents/republican-party-platform-1912; "1912 Democratic Party Platform," June 25, 1912, *The American Presidency Project*, https://www.presidency.ucsb.edu/documents/1912-democratic-party-platform. The Progressive Party called for a "readjustment of the business methods" of government. "Progressive Party Platform of 1912," November 5, 1912, *The American Presidency Project*, https://www.presidency.ucsb.edu/documents/progressive-party-platform-1912.

55. "Democratic Party Platform of 1916," June 14, 1916, *The American Presidency Project*, https://www.presidency.ucsb.edu/documents/1916-democratic-party-platform; "Republican Party Platform of 1916," June 7, 1916, *The American Presidency Project*, https://www.presidency.ucsb.edu/documents/republican-party-platform-1916.

56. Quoted in Collins, *National Budget System and American Finance*, 143.

57. Stewart, *Budget Reform Politics*, 198.

58. *Congressional Record*, 66th Congress, 1st Session (October 17, 1919), 7083.

59. Fisher, *Presidential Spending Power*, 31–34; Stewart, *Budget Reform Politics*, 233; Kahn, *Budgeting Democracy*, 166.

60. The Democratic platform also sought to prevent a budget increase by Congress "except by a two-thirds vote." "Democratic Party Platform of 1920," June 28, 1920, *The American Presidency Project*, https://www.presidency.ucsb.edu/documents/1920-democratic-party-platform.

61. "Republican Party Platform of 1920," June 8, 1920, *The American Presidency Project*, https://www.presidency.ucsb.edu/documents/republican-party-platform-1920.

62. Warren G. Harding, "Business in Government and the Problem of Governmental Reorganization for Greater Efficiency," *Proceedings of the Academy of Political Science in the City of New York* 9, no. 3 (July 1921): 99–103, at 102.

63. "House Passes Bill for Budget Bureau," *New York Times*, May 6, 1921, 15.

64. *National Budget System*, Conference Report to accompany S. 1084, 67th Congress, 1st Session, House Report No. 96 (May 25, 1921), 10.

65. Budget and Accounting Act, 1921 (P.L. 67-13, 42 Stat. 20, June 10, 1921).

66. PCEE, *Need for a National Budget*, 7–8.

67. PCEE, 138.

68. PCEE, 141.

69. IGR, *National Budget System*, 2.

70. William Franklin Willoughby, *The Problem of a National Budget* (New York: D. Appleton, 1918), 62–67.

71. *Congressional Record*, 62nd Congress, 1st Session (June 15, 1911), 2106–7.

72. Letter from William H. Allen to Swagar Sherley, November 6, 1918, Folder "Congressional Correspondence Sept–December 1918," Box 8, Subseries 3, Series IV, Sherley Papers.

73. *National Budget System*, Hearings, 396–97.

74. *National Budget System*, 391.

75. *National Budget System*, 503.

76. *National Budget System*, 534.

77. *National Budget System*, 641.

78. Letter from Henry L. Stimson to Leonard Wood, October 3, 1919, Microfilm 197, Box U53, Series HM52, Henry Lewis Stimson Papers, Manuscripts and Archives, Sterling Memorial Library, Yale University, New Haven, CT.

79. *National Budget System*, Hearings, 570–71, 586.

80. Letter from Henry L. Stimson to James W. Good, October 9, 1919, Microfilm 242, Box U53, Series HM52, Stimson Papers.

81. *Congressional Record*, 66th Congress, 1st Session (October 17, 1919), 7087.

82. *Congressional Record*, 66th Congress, 1st Session (October 17, 1919), 7092–93.

83. *Congressional Record*, 66th Congress, 1st Session (October 18, 1919), 7130.

84. *Congressional Record*, 67th Congress, 1st Session (April 26, 1921), 660.

85. Representative James Frear (R-WI) advocated for a joint committee in Congress that would be able to add amendments to *reduce* presidential budget requests by a simple majority, but would be able to *increase* requests only with the support of a two-thirds supermajority of the committee. Frederick Cleveland and Arthur Buck argued that presidents would be better "held accountable to the people" with such a stronger agenda-setting power, and in their disappointment at its rejection, they criticized the main proposal (H.R. 1021) as "essentially a well-camouflaged *legislative budget* device." Though their criticism underscored the limits Congress would impose on reform, it understated the significance of the main proposal. Cleveland and Buck, *Budget and Responsible Government*, 359–60, 363, 373–74.

86. *Message of the President of the United States Submitting for the Consideration of the Congress a Budget with Supporting Memoranda and Reports*, 62nd Congress, 3rd Session, Senate Document No. 1113 (February 26, 1913), appendix 2, "The Need for the Organization of a Bureau of Central Administrative Control," 191, 194, 195, 200.

87. Willoughby, *Problem of a National Budget*, 132.

88. Willoughby, 135.

89. IGR, *National Budget System*, 7.

90. Willoughby, *Problem of a National Budget*, 34–35.

91. *National Budget System*, Hearings, 79–80.

92. *National Budget System*, 86.

93. *National Budget System*, 380.

94. *National Budget System*, 641.

95. *National Budget System*, 345.

96. *National Budget System*, 654, 672–73.

97. *National Budget System*, Report to Accompany H.R. 9783, 66th Congress, 2nd Session, Senate Report No. 524 (April 13, 1920), 1–2.

98. *Congressional Record*, 66th Congress, 1st Session (October 17, 1919), 7089.

99. *Congressional Record*, 67th Congress, 1st Session (May 27, 1921), 1854–56.

100. *Congressional Record*, 67th Congress, 1st Session (May 27, 1921), 1857.

101. Cleveland and Buck, *Budget and Responsible Government*, 359–60; Lucius Wilmerding Jr., *The Spending Power: A History of the Efforts of Congress to Control Expenditures* (New Haven, CT: Yale University Press, 1943), ch. 12.

102. *National Budget System*, Hearings, 480.

103. *National Budget System*, 97.

104. *National Budget System*, 543.

105. *National Budget System*, Conference Report to Accompany H.R. 9783, 66th Congress, 2nd Session, House Report No. 1044 (May 26, 1920), 5.

106. Fisher, *Presidential Spending Power*, 35.

107. Skowronek, *Building a New American State*, 206.

108. Fisher, *Defending Congress*, 199–200.

109. James Madison, "The Federalist No. 58" [February 20, 1788], in Alexander Hamilton, James Madison, and John Jay, *The Federalist*, ed. Terence Ball (New York: Cambridge University Press, 2003), 284–85.

110. Fisher, *Defending Congress*, 201.

111. Ford, *Cost*, 9, 11, 15.

112. PCEE, *Need for a National Budget*, 10.

113. As Representative Good noted, the president was "the only official who is designated by the Constitution to give Congress, from time to time, information on the state of the Union." *Congressional Record*, 67th Congress, 1st Session (May 27, 1921), 1854.

114. PCEE, *Need for a National Budget*, 140.

115. Arnold, *Making the Managerial Presidency*, 39–40.

116. *National Budget System*, Hearings, 621.

117. Thus, the commission was limited to only Cleveland, Warwick, and Chance. Arnold, *Making the Managerial Presidency*, 41.

118. Haber, *Efficiency and Uplift*, 114.

119. Cleveland and Buck, *Budget and Responsible Government*, 342.

120. "Taft Insistent, Orders a Budget," *New York Times*, September 20, 1912, 7.

121. "Taft Will Submit Budget to Congress," *New York Times*, September 29, 1912, 7; Arnold, *Making the Managerial Presidency*, 45–48.

122. Fisher, *Presidential Spending Power*, 31; Arnold, *Making the Managerial Presidency*, 49.

123. Stewart, *Budget Reform Politics*, 182.

124. Stewart, 191–96.

125. "Now Favor Budget, with House Control," *New York Times*, November 30, 1912, 5.

126. *Congressional Record*, 62nd Congress, 3rd Session (February 28, 1913), 4349–50.

127. Letter from Unknown to Swagar Sherley, May 3, 1913, Folder "Congressional Correspondence, 1911–1913," Box 8, Subseries 3, Series IV, Sherley Papers.

128. Kahn, *Budgeting Democracy*, 167–75. On the origins of the IGR, see Donald T. Critchlow, *The Brookings Institution, 1916–1952: Expertise and the Public Interest in a Democratic Society* (DeKalb: Northern Illinois University Press, 1985), ch. 2.

129. Willoughby, *Problem of a National Budget*, 145, 66.

130. IGR, *National Budget System*, 12. On "strategic preferences," see Jacob S. Hacker and Paul Pierson, "Business Power and Social Policy: Employers and the Formation of the American Welfare State," *Politics and Society* 30, no. 2 (June 2002): 277–325.

131. Cannon, *National Budget*, 28–29.

132. *National Budget System*, Hearings, 165–66. On the National Budget Committee, see Jesse Tarbert, "Corporate Lessons for Public Governance: The Origins and Activities of the National Budget Committee, 1919–1923," *Seattle University Law Review* 42, no. 2 (2019): 565–89.

133. *National Budget System*, Hearings, 304.

134. In 1939, Franklin Roosevelt would transfer BOB to the new Executive Office of the President under the authority of the Reorganization Act of 1939.

135. Peri E. Arnold, *Remaking the Presidency: Roosevelt, Taft, and Wilson, 1901–1916* (Lawrence: University Press of Kansas, 2009).

136. F. Scott Fitzgerald, *The Vegetable, or From President to Postman* (New York: Charles Scribner's Sons, 1923), 71.

137. Arnold, *Making the Managerial Presidency*, 54.

138. Warren G. Harding, "Address of the President," *Addresses of the President of the United States and the Director of the Bureau of the Budget at the Second Semiannual Meeting of the Business Organization of Government* (Washington, DC: Government Printing Office, 1922), 8, 4.

139. Charles G. Dawes, *The First Year of the Budget of the United States* (New York: Harper and Brothers, 1923), 2.

140. Dawes, 115.

141. Dawes, x; Arnold, *Making the Managerial Presidency*, 55.

142. Warren G. Harding, "Address of the President," *Addresses of the President of the United States and the Director of the Bureau of the Budget at the Fourth Regular Meeting of the Business Organization of Government* (Washington, DC: Government Printing Office, 1923), 5.

143. Warren G. Harding, "Address of the President," *Addresses of the President of the United States and the Director of the Bureau of the Budget at the Fifth Regular Meeting of the Business Organization of Government* (Washington, DC: Government Printing Office, 1923), 4.

144. Calvin Coolidge, "Address of the President," *Addresses of the President of the United States and the Director of the Bureau of the Budget at the Sixth Regular Meeting of the Business Organization of the Government* (Washington, DC: Government Printing Office, 1924), 4.

145. Richard E. Neustadt, "Presidency and Legislation: The Growth of Central Clearance," *American Political Science Review* 48, no. 3 (September 1954): 641–71. See also George A. Krause and Roger Qiyuan Jin, "Organizational Design and Its Consequences for Administrative Reform: Historical Lessons from the US Budget and Accounting Act of 1921," *Governance* 33, no. 2 (April 2020): 365–84.

146. Iwan Morgan, *The Age of Deficits: Presidents and Unbalanced Budgets from Jimmy Carter to George W. Bush* (Lawrence: University Press of Kansas, 2009), ch. 1.

147. Max Beloff, *The American Federal Government* (London: Oxford University Press, 1959), 78.

148. Herbert Emmerich, *Federal Organization and Administrative Management* (Tuscaloosa: University of Alabama Press, 1971), 40−41.

Chapter Four

1. Walter Lippmann, *The Method of Freedom* (New York: Macmillan, 1934), 85.

2. See, for example, John V. Kane, "Control, Accountability, and Constraints: Rethinking Perceptions of Presidential Responsibility for the Economy," *Presidential Studies Quarterly* 46, no. 2 (June 2016): 335−64.

3. Richard Franklin Bensel, *Sectionalism and American Political Development, 1880−1980* (Madison: University of Wisconsin Press, 1984).

4. Sean Gailmard and John W. Patty, *Learning While Governing: Expertise and Accountability in the Executive Branch* (Chicago: University of Chicago Press, 2013), 202−3.

5. The five Republican senators were Arthur Capper (R-KS), James Couzens (R-MI), George Norris (R-NE), Peter Norbeck (R-SD), and Robert La Follette Jr. (R-WI), who was then organizing a new Progressive Party in Wisconsin. The House bill passed 274−111 (with 47 not voting). *Congressional Record*, 73rd Congress, 2nd Session (March 29, 1934), 5808. The Senate

bill passed 57–33 (with 6 not voting). *Congressional Record*, 73rd Congress, 2nd Session (June 4, 1934), 10395. The House accepted the Senate's amended bill 154–53, making conference unnecessary. *Congressional Record*, 73rd Congress, 2nd Session (June 6, 1934), 10636.

6. The Senate bill passed 71–10 (with 15 not voting). *Congressional Record*, 79th Congress, 1st Session (September 28, 1945), 9153. The House bill passed 255–126 (with 50 not voting). *Congressional Record*, 79th Congress, 1st Session (December 14, 1945), 12095. The House passed the conference report 322–84 (with 23 not voting). *Congressional Record*, 79th Congress, 2nd Session (February 6, 1946), 986. The Senate passed the conference report without a recorded vote. *Congressional Record*, 79th Congress, 2nd Session (February 8, 1946), 1144.

7. An Act to Amend the Tariff Act of 1930 (P.L. 73-316, 48 Stat. 943, June 12, 1934).

8. Stephen Haggard, "The Institutional Foundations of Hegemony: Explaining the Reciprocal Trade Agreements Act of 1934," *International Organization* 42, no. 1 (Winter 1988): 91–119; Sharyn O'Halloran, *Politics, Process, and American Trade Policy* (Ann Arbor: University of Michigan Press, 1994), 182.

9. James L. Sundquist, *The Decline and Resurgence of Congress* (Washington, DC: Brookings Institution, 1981), 99.

10. Richard Franklin Bensel, *The Political Economy of American Industrialization, 1877–1900* (New York: Cambridge University Press, 2000), ch. 7.

11. Benjamin O. Fordham, "Protectionist Empire: Trade, Tariffs, and United States Foreign Policy, 1890–1914," *Studies in American Political Development* 31, no. 2 (October 2017): 170–92.

12. Tariff Act of 1930 (P.L. 71-361, 46 Stat. 590, March 13, 1930); E. E. Schattschneider, *Politics, Pressures and the Tariff: A Study of Free Private Enterprise in Pressure Politics, as Shown in the 1929–1930 Revision of the Tariff* (New York: Prentice-Hall, 1935); Douglas A. Irwin, *Clashing over Commerce: A History of US Trade Policy* (Chicago: University of Chicago Press, 2017), 371. However, the act had one innovation of significance for the presidency. It allowed the president, under its flexibility provision, to raise tariff rates on goods if he received such a recommendation after an investigation by the Tariff Commission.

13. Irwin, *Clashing over Commerce*, ch. 9.

14. "Mr. Roosevelt and World Trade," *New Republic*, April 19, 1933, 268.

15. Franklin D. Roosevelt, *Looking Forward* (New York: John Day, 1933), ch. 10.

16. Cordell Hull, *Memoirs*, vol. 1 (New York: Macmillan, 1948), ch. 26.

17. Franklin D. Roosevelt, "Message to Congress Requesting Authority Regarding Foreign Trade," March 2, 1934, *The American Presidency Project*, https://www.presidency.ucsb.edu/documents/message-congress-requesting-authority-regarding-foreign-trade.

18. Some in Roosevelt's "Brain Trust" had wanted "to give the President the power to fix tariff duties for all time, and thereby take the tariff out of politics." "Roosevelt Decides to Ask for Tariff Powers Now: Plans Reciprocal Deals," *New York Times*, March 1, 1934, 1, 4. Hull had wanted a multilateral effort but felt that bilateral agreements would be more politically realistic. Hull, *Memoirs*, 1:356.

19. Michael J. Hiscox, "The Magic Bullet? The RTAA, Institutional Reform, and Trade Liberalization," *International Organization* 53, no. 4 (Autumn 1999): 669–98, at 677. See also Michael J. Gilligan, *Empowering Exporters: Reciprocity, Delegation, and Collective Action in American Trade Policy* (Ann Arbor: University of Michigan Press, 1997), 5, 54.

20. Judith Goldstein, *Ideas, Interests, and American Trade Policy* (Ithaca, NY: Cornell University Press, 1993), 141–46; Michael A. Bailey, Judith Goldstein, and Barry R. Weingast, "The Institutional Roots of American Trade Policy: Politics, Coalitions, and International Trade,"

World Politics 49, no. 3 (April 1997): 309–38; Karen E. Schnietz, "The Institutional Foundation of US Trade Policy: Revisiting Explanations for the 1934 Reciprocal Trade Agreements Act," *Journal of Policy History* 12, no. 4 (October 2000): 417–44.

21. "Senator Byrd Praises Roosevelt's Proposal," *Washington Post*, March 4, 1934, 5.

22. *Reciprocal Trade Agreements*, Hearings before the Committee on Finance, United States Senate, 73rd Congress, 2nd Session (Washington, DC: Government Printing Office, 1934), 396.

23. *Reciprocal Trade Agreements*, Hearings before the Committee on Ways and Means, House of Representatives, 73rd Congress, 2nd Session (Washington, DC: Government Printing Office, 1934), 118.

24. "Tariff Board Head Backs Reciprocity," *New York Times*, March 10, 1934, 19.

25. *Reciprocal Trade Agreements*, Hearings before the Committee on Ways and Means, 118.

26. *Reciprocal Trade Agreements*, 72.

27. *Congressional Record*, 73rd Congress, 2nd Session (March 23, 1934), 5260.

28. *Congressional Record*, 73rd Congress, 2nd Session (March 23, 1934), 5275–77.

29. *Congressional Record*, 73rd Congress, 2nd Session (May 17, 1934), 8997–98.

30. *Congressional Record*, 73rd Congress, 2nd Session (June 4, 1934), 10379.

31. *Congressional Record*, 73rd Congress, 2nd Session (March 23, 1934), 5264.

32. *Congressional Record*, 73rd Congress, 2nd Session (June 6, 1934), 10630.

33. *Congressional Record*, 73rd Congress, 2nd Session (May 17, 1934), 8994. For the original address, see William McKinley, "President McKinley's Last Public Utterance to the People in Buffalo, New York," September 5, 1901, *The American Presidency Project*, https://www.presidency .ucsb.edu/documents/president-mckinleys-last-public-utterance-the-people-buffalo-new -york.

34. O'Halloran, *Politics, Process, and American Trade Policy*, 85.

35. Irwin, *Clashing over Commerce*, 423.

36. *Reciprocal Trade Agreements*, Hearings before the Committee on Ways and Means, 11.

37. *Reciprocal Trade Agreements*, 33.

38. *Reciprocal Trade Agreements*, 47.

39. *Reciprocal Trade Agreements*, 365, 358. See also Francis Bowes Sayre, *The Way Forward: The American Trade Agreements Program* (New York: Macmillan, 1939), 41–42.

40. *Congressional Record*, 73rd Congress, 2nd Session (March 23, 1934), 5256, 5259.

41. *Congressional Record*, 73rd Congress, 2nd Session (June 4, 1934), 10375.

42. Arthur Krock, "In Washington: Stimson's Speech on Tariff Upsets Republican Senators," *New York Times*, May 1, 1934, 22.

43. Henry L. Stimson, "Are the Powers of the President Improving the American Government?," typed copy of article from *Congressional Digest*, November 1933, Microfilm 637, Box U133, Series HM52, Henry Lewis Stimson Papers, Manuscripts and Archives, Sterling Memorial Library, Yale University, New Haven, CT.

44. "Text of Stimson's Radio Speech for Changes in the Tariff," *New York Times*, April 30, 1934, 8.

45. Letter from Henry L. Stimson to C. Bascom Slemp, May 1, 1934, Microfilm 52, Box U87, Series HM52, Stimson Papers.

46. Letter from Morgan J. O'Brien to Henry L. Stimson, May 1, 1934, Microfilm 44, Box U87, Series HM52, Stimson Papers.

47. Letter from Francis B. Sayre, to Henry L. Stimson, May 1, 1934, Microfilm 45, Box U87, Series HM52, Stimson Papers.

48. *Congressional Record*, 73rd Congress, 2nd Session (May 17, 1934), 8992.

49. *Reciprocal Trade Agreements*, Hearings before the Committee on Finance, 147.

50. The House rejected an amendment from Representative Treadway to require Congress to positively assent to presidentially negotiated agreements. It also declined to adopt a similar follow-up amendment from Representative Charles Bakewell (R-CT) to allow Congress to veto negotiated bilateral agreements within one year from the time they would come into force. *Congressional Record*, 73rd Congress, 2nd Session (March 29, 1934), 5802, 5807. Two Senate amendments regarding congressional approval or disapproval also failed. One would have given Congress, in essence, a legislative veto; presidential bilateral agreements would need to avoid the disapproval of Congress. Another would have required Congress to positively affirm the president's agreements. *Congressional Record*, 73rd Congress, 2nd Session (June 4, 1934), 10372–73, 10381–82, 10386.

51. *Congressional Record*, 73rd Congress, 2nd Session (March 29, 1934), 5799.

52. *Reciprocal Trade Agreements*, Hearings before the Committee on Ways and Means, 370.

53. *Congressional Record*, 73rd Congress, 2nd Session (May 17, 1934), 8989.

54. Not convinced that the three-year duration of the trade authority was a safeguard, Representative Emanuel Celler (D-NY) offered an amendment to limit the duration of trade agreements themselves to five years from the date of the proposed law's enactment. But the amendment was rejected by the House. *Congressional Record*, 73rd Congress, 2nd Session (March 29, 1934), 5800–5801. A Senate amendment to limit the duration of any bilateral agreements themselves to six months after the end of the three-year period of the law was likewise rejected. *Congressional Record*, 73rd Congress, 2nd Session (June 4, 1934), 10387.

55. *Reciprocal Trade Agreements*, Hearings before the Committee on Ways and Means, 77.

56. *Reciprocal Trade Agreements*, Hearings before the Committee on Finance, 392.

57. *Congressional Record*, 73rd Congress, 2nd Session (March 23, 1934), 5277.

58. *Congressional Record*, 73rd Congress, 2nd Session (June 4, 1934), 10395.

59. *Reciprocal Trade Agreements*, Hearings before the Committee on Ways and Means, 402.

60. *Reciprocal Trade Agreements*, Hearings before the Committee on Finance, 19–20.

61. *Congressional Record*, 73rd Congress, 2nd Session (May 17, 1934), 8990.

62. *Congressional Record*, 73rd Congress, 2nd Session (June 6, 1934), 10629.

63. *Congressional Record*, 73rd Congress, 2nd Session (March 27, 1934), 5549–50.

64. *Reciprocal Trade Agreements*, Hearings before the Committee on Ways and Means, 31.

65. *Reciprocal Trade Agreements*, 53.

66. *Congressional Record*, 73rd Congress, 2nd Session (May 17, 1934), 9012, 9016.

67. *Reciprocal Trade Agreements*, Hearings before the Committee on Finance, 315.

68. *Reciprocal Trade Agreements*, 290, 288.

69. Letter from E. Kent Hubbard to Allen T. Treadway, in *Congressional Record*, 73rd Congress, 2nd Session (March 23, 1934), 5269.

70. Letter from William H. Cliff to Robert L. Doughton, with "Resolution, Passed at a Meeting of the Board of Directors of the Home Market Club," March 14, 1934, Folder 315, Box 8, Robert Lee Doughton Papers, Southern Historical Collection, Wilson Library, University of North Carolina, Chapel Hill.

71. *Reciprocal Trade Agreements*, Hearings before the Committee on Ways and Means, 257.

72. For example, Representative Francis Condon (D-RI) had attempted to require the president to assure Congress no industries would be destroyed by negotiated agreements. *Congressional Record*, 73rd Congress, 2nd Session (March 29, 1934), 5798.

73. *Congressional Record*, 73rd Congress, 2nd Session (June 4, 1934), 10360.

74. *Reciprocal Trade Agreements*, Hearings before the Committee on Ways and Means, 430.

75. *Reciprocal Trade Agreements*, 5.

76. Hull, *Memoirs*, 1:354.

77. *Congressional Record*, 73rd Congress, 2nd Session (March 23, 1934), 5258.

78. *Congressional Record*, 73rd Congress, 2nd Session (March 23, 1934), 5262.

79. *Reciprocal Trade Agreements*, Hearings before the Committee on Ways and Means, 16, 18.

80. *Reciprocal Trade Agreements*, 354–55.

81. *Congressional Record*, 73rd Congress, 2nd Session (May 17, 1934), 8995.

82. Letter from W. E. Stewart to Robert L. Doughton, March 28, 1934, Folder 327, Box 9, Doughton Papers.

83. *Reciprocal Trade Agreements*, Hearings before the Committee on Ways and Means, 15–16.

84. *Congressional Record*, 73rd Congress, 2nd Session (March 27, 1934), 5532.

85. *Congressional Record*, 73rd Congress, 2nd Session (May 17, 1934), 9007–8.

86. *Congressional Record*, 73rd Congress, 2nd Session (March 29, 1934), 5803, 5802, 5805.

87. *Congressional Record*, 73rd Congress, 2nd Session (June 4, 1934), 10360.

88. *Congressional Record*, 73rd Congress, 2nd Session (May 17, 1934), 8992.

89. *Congressional Record*, 73rd Congress, 2nd Session (March 23, 1934), 5271.

90. *Congressional Record*, 73rd Congress, 2nd Session (March 23, 1934), 5270.

91. *Congressional Record*, 73rd Congress, 2nd Session (March 28, 1934), 5668.

92. *Reciprocal Trade Agreements*, Hearings before the Committee on Ways and Means, 79.

93. *Congressional Record*, 73rd Congress, 2nd Session (June 4, 1934), 10360.

94. *Congressional Record*, 73rd Congress, 2nd Session (June 4, 1934), 10378.

95. "The Republicans and the Tariff," *Hartford Courant*, March 6, 1934, 10.

96. Employment Act of 1946 (P.L. 79-304, 60 Stat. 23, February 20, 1946).

97. See, for example, Alvin H. Hansen, *After the War—Full Employment* (Washington, DC: National Resources Planning Board, 1942).

98. John Maynard Keynes, *The General Theory of Employment, Interest, and Money* (London: Macmillan, 1936); William H. Beveridge, *Full Employment in a Free Society* (London: George Allen and Unwin, 1944); Franklin D. Roosevelt, "State of the Union Message to Congress," January 11, 1944, *The American Presidency Project*, https://www.presidency.ucsb.edu/documents/state-the-union-message-congress; Franklin D. Roosevelt, "Address at Soldiers' Field, Chicago, Illinois," October 28, 1944, *The American Presidency Project*, https://www.presidency.ucsb.edu/documents/address-soldiers-field-chicago-illinois; Henry A. Wallace, *Sixty Million Jobs* (New York: Simon and Schuster, 1945).

99. F. A. Hayek, *The Road to Serfdom* (Chicago: University of Chicago Press, 1944); Stephen Kemp Bailey, *Congress Makes a Law: The Story Behind the Employment Act of 1946* (New York: Columbia University Press, 1950), 55.

100. Margaret Weir, *Politics and Jobs: The Boundaries of Employment Policy in the United States* (Princeton, NJ: Princeton University Press, 1993), ch. 2; Alan Brinkley, *The End of Reform: New Deal Liberalism in Recession and War* (New York: Alfred A. Knopf, 1995), 245–64.

101. *Congressional Record*, 79th Congress, 2nd Session (February 8, 1946), 1141–42.

102. Eric Schickler, *Disjointed Pluralism: Institutional Innovation and the Development of the US Congress* (Princeton, NJ: Princeton University Press, 2001), ch. 4.

103. Philip W. Warken, "A History of the National Resources Planning Board," PhD diss., Ohio State University, 1969, 246.

104. Administrative Procedure Act (P.L. 79-404, 60 Stat. 237, June 11, 1946); Legislative Reorganization Act of 1946 (P.L. 79-601, 60 Stat. 812, August 2, 1946).

105. Roger H. Davidson, "The Advent of the Modern Congress: The Legislative Reorganization Act of 1946," *Legislative Studies Quarterly* 15, no. 3 (August 1990): 357–73; Schickler, *Disjointed Pluralism*, 141–50; David H. Rosenbloom, "'Whose Bureaucracy Is This, Anyway?': Congress' 1946 Answer," *PS: Political Science and Politics* 34, no. 4 (December 2001): 773–77.

106. Karen Orren and Stephen Skowronek, *The Policy State: An American Predicament* (Cambridge, MA: Harvard University Press, 2017), 108–9.

107. *Congressional Record*, 79th Congress, 2nd Session (February 8, 1946), 1142.

108. *Full Employment Act of 1945*, Hearings before a Subcommittee of the Committee on Banking and Currency, United States Senate, 79th Congress, 1st Session (Washington, DC: Government Printing Office, 1945), 62.

109. *Congressional Record*, 79th Congress, 2nd Session (February 6, 1946), 980.

110. *Full Employment Act of 1945*, Hearings before the Committee on Expenditures in the Executive Departments, House of Representatives, 79th Congress, 1st Session (Washington, DC: Government Printing Office, 1945), 1003.

111. *Full Employment Act of 1945*, Hearings before a Subcommittee of the Committee on Banking and Currency, 797.

112. Sundquist, *Decline and Resurgence*, 63.

113. Letter from Kenneth B. Murdock and Eleanor E. Murdock to Senator Charles W. Tobey, August 1, 1945, Folder 34, Box 38, Charles W. Tobey Papers, Rauner Special Collections Library, Dartmouth College, Hanover, NH.

114. *Congressional Record*, 79th Congress, 1st Session (January 22, 1945), 377–78.

115. Bernice Kandel, *Jobs for 60 Million* (Union for Democratic Action, 1945 [pamphlet]), 7.

116. Letter from George E. Outland to Mike Mansfield, September 14, 1945, with "Basic Principles of the Full Employment Bill," 3, Folder 5, Box 20, Series II, Mike Mansfield Papers, Archives and Special Collections, Maureen and Mike Mansfield Library, University of Montana, Missoula.

117. *Congressional Record*, 79th Congress, 1st Session (January 22, 1945), 382.

118. "Address by Honorable James E. Murray, United States Senator (Montana)," September 25, 1945, 22, Folder 15, Box 950, Series III, James E. Murray Papers, Archives and Special Collections, Maureen and Mike Mansfield Library, University of Montana, Missoula.

119. *Full Employment Act of 1945*, Hearings before a Subcommittee of the Committee on Banking and Currency, 4.

120. "Address by Senator Robert F. Wagner of New York at the Roosevelt-Truman-Wagner Victory Dinner of the Democratic County Committee of the County of New York, Commodore Hotel," February 17, 1945, 4, Folder 58, Box SF 104, Robert F. Wagner Papers, Booth Family Center for Special Collections, Georgetown University Library, Georgetown University, Washington, DC.

121. *Congressional Record*, 79th Congress, 1st Session (September 28, 1945), 9121.

122. *Full Employment Act of 1945*, Hearings before a Subcommittee of the Committee on Banking and Currency, 238.

123. *Full Employment Act of 1945*, Hearings before the Committee on Expenditures, 1000.

124. *Full Employment Act of 1945*, Hearings before a Subcommittee of the Committee on Banking and Currency, 863.

125. *Full Employment Act of 1945*, Hearings before the Committee on Expenditures, 341.

126. *Full Employment Act of 1945*, 59.

127. *Full Employment Act of 1945*, 65.

128. *Full Employment Act of 1945*, 60.

129. *Full Employment Act of 1945*, 63.

130. *Full Employment Act of 1945*, 61.

131. *Full Employment Act of 1945*, 101.

132. *Full Employment Act of 1945*, 213–14.

133. *Congressional Record*, 79th Congress, 1st Session (December 13, 1945), 11973.

134. *Congressional Record*, 79th Congress, 1st Session (December 14, 1945), 12078.

135. S. Bailey, *Congress Makes a Law*, 167.

136. *Congressional Record*, 79th Congress, 2nd Session (February 6, 1946), 980.

137. *Congressional Record*, 79th Congress, 2nd Session (February 8, 1946), 1136.

138. *Congressional Record*, 79th Congress, 2nd Session (February 8, 1946), 1141.

139. *Full Employment Act of 1945*, Hearings before a Subcommittee of the Committee on Banking and Currency, 25.

140. *Congressional Record*, 79th Congress, 1st Session (January 22, 1945), 379–80.

141. Harry S. Truman, "Statement by the President upon Signing the Employment Act," February 20, 1946, *The American Presidency Project*, https://www.presidency.ucsb.edu/documents/statement-the-president-upon-signing-the-employment-act.

142. Harry S. Truman, "Special Message to the Congress: The President's First Economic Report," January 8, 1947, *The American Presidency Project*, https://www.presidency.ucsb.edu/documents/special-message-the-congress-the-presidents-first-economic-report.

143. *Congressional Record*, 79th Congress, 1st Session (January 22, 1945), 379.

144. *Full Employment Act of 1945*, Hearings before a Subcommittee of the Committee on Banking and Currency, 238.

145. *Full Employment Act of 1945*, 862.

146. *Full Employment Act of 1945*, Hearings before the Committee on Expenditures, 594.

147. *Full Employment Act of 1945*, 1104.

148. *Congressional Record*, 79th Congress, 1st Session (December 14, 1945), 12068.

149. *Congressional Record*, 79th Congress, 1st Session (December 13, 1945), 11978.

150. *Congressional Record*, 79th Congress, 1st Session (December 13, 1945), 12011.

151. *Congressional Record*, 79th Congress, 1st Session (December 14, 1945), 12066.

152. *Congressional Record*, 79th Congress, 1st Session (December 14, 1945), 12074.

153. Sundquist, *Decline and Resurgence*, 66.

154. S. Bailey, *Congress Makes a Law*, 170–71.

155. *Congressional Record*, 79th Congress, 2nd Session (February 6, 1946), 980.

156. *Congressional Record*, 79th Congress, 2nd Session (February 8, 1946), 1142.

157. *Congressional Record*, 79th Congress, 2nd Session (February 8, 1946), 1138.

158. 60 Stat. 24 § 4(a).

159. Edwin G. Nourse, *Economics in the Public Service: Administrative Aspects of the Employment Act* (New York: Harcourt, Brace, 1953), 92. The three members chosen for the CEA by Truman in July 1946 were Chairman Edwin Nourse, Leon Keyserling, and John Davidson Clark. Harry S. Truman, *Memoirs*, vol. 1, *Year of Decisions* (Garden City, NY: Doubleday, 1955), 491–94.

160. Gailmard and Patty, *Learning While Governing*, 202–3.

161. *Congressional Record*, 79th Congress, 2nd Session (February 8, 1946), 1143–44.

162. S. Bailey, *Congress Makes a Law*, 52–53.

163. *Congressional Record*, 79th Congress, 1st Session (January 22, 1945), 379.

164. Nourse, *Economics in the Public Service*, 458.

165. *Congressional Record*, 79th Congress, 2nd Session (February 8, 1946), 1144.

166. *Congressional Record*, 79th Congress, 2nd Session (February 6, 1946), 980.

167. *Full Employment Act of 1945*, Hearings before the Committee on Expenditures, 612.

168. *Full Employment Act of 1945*, 817.

169. *Congressional Record*, 79th Congress, 1st Session (December 13, 1945), 12006–7.

170. *Full Employment Act of 1945*, Hearings before the Committee on Expenditures, 1067.

171. David R. Mayhew, *The Imprint of Congress* (New Haven, CT: Yale University Press, 2017), 68.

172. Irwin, *Clashing over Commerce*, 413. See also Grace Beckett, *The Reciprocal Trade Agreements Program* (New York: Columbia University Press, 1941).

173. Letter from Franklin D. Roosevelt to Pat Harrison, March 14, 1939, with enclosed Letter from Sumner Welles to President and Letter from Cordell Hull to Pat Harrison, March 13, 1939, 8–9, Folder "President's Letters, 1914–1941," Box 78, Pat Harrison Collection, Archives and Special Collections, J. D. Williams Library, University of Mississippi, Oxford.

174. Letter from Sumner Welles to Marguerite A. LeHand, March 16, 1939, with enclosed statement "Dictated by Secretary Hull over the Telephone from Florida," March 15, 1939, Folder "President's Letters, 1914–1941," Box 78, Harrison Collection.

175. Irwin, *Clashing over Commerce*, 455, 483–84, 527–28.

176. Trade Expansion Act of 1962 (P.L. 87-794, 76 Stat. 872, October 11, 1962); John F. Kennedy, "Executive Order 11075—Administration of the Trade Expansion Act of 1962," January 15, 1963, *The American Presidency Project*, https://www.presidency.ucsb.edu/documents/executive-order-11075-administration-the-trade-expansion-act-1962.

177. J. Bradford DeLong, "Keynesianism, Pennsylvania Avenue Style: Some Economic Consequences of the Employment Act of 1946," *Journal of Economic Perspectives* 10, no. 3 (Summer 1996): 41–53, at 51, 46.

178. Hugh S. Norton, *The Employment Act and the Council of Economic Advisers, 1946–1976* (Columbia: University of South Carolina Press, 1977), chs. 4–5, 10; Murray Weidenbaum, "The Employment Act of 1946: A Half Century of Presidential Policymaking," *Presidential Studies Quarterly* 26, no. 3 (Summer 1996): 880–86.

179. Robert A. Pastor, *Congress and the Politics of US Foreign Economic Policy* (Berkeley: University of California Press, 1980), 93.

Chapter Five

1. Lewis Meriam, "Part I: An Analysis of the Problem," in *Reorganization of the National Government: What Does It Involve?*, ed. Lewis Meriam and Laurence F. Schmeckebier (Washington, DC: Brookings Institution, 1939), 9–177, at 117.

2. J. David Alvis, Jeremy D. Bailey, and F. Flagg Taylor IV, *The Contested Removal Power, 1789–2010* (Lawrence: University Press of Kansas, 2013).

3. Stephen Skowronek, "The Conservative Insurgency and Presidential Power: A Developmental Perspective on the Unitary Executive," *Harvard Law Review* 122, no. 8 (June 2009): 2070–103; Stephen Skowronek, John A. Dearborn, and Desmond King, *Phantoms of a Beleaguered Republic: The Deep State and the Unitary Executive* (New York: Oxford University Press, 2021), ch. 3.

4. Steven G. Calabresi and Christopher S. Yoo, *The Unitary Executive: Presidential Power from Washington to Bush* (New Haven, CT: Yale University Press, 2008).

5. William G. Howell and Terry M. Moe, *Relic: How Our Constitution Undermines Effective Government and Why We Need a More Powerful Presidency* (New York: Basic Books, 2016).

6. Richard Polenberg, *Reorganizing Roosevelt's Government: The Controversy over Executive Reorganization, 1936–1939* (Cambridge, MA: Harvard University Press, 1966), 3; Jesse Tarbert, "The Quest to Bring 'Business Efficiency' to the Federal Executive: Herbert Hoover, Franklin Roosevelt, and the Civil Service Reformers in the Late 1920s," *Journal of Policy History* 31, no. 4 (October 2019): 512–32.

7. Louis Brownlow, *A Passion for Anonymity: The Autobiography of Louis Brownlow, Second Half* (Chicago: University of Chicago Press, 1958), 392.

8. Reorganization Act of 1939 (P.L. 76-19, 53 Stat. 561, April 3, 1939).

9. James L. Sundquist, *The Decline and Resurgence of Congress* (Washington, DC: Brookings Institution, 1981), 50–54; Sean Gailmard and John W. Patty, *Learning While Governing: Expertise and Accountability in the Executive Branch* (Chicago: University of Chicago Press, 2013), 197–204.

10. The House bill passed 246–153 (with 34 not voting). *Congressional Record*, 76th Congress, 1st Session (March 8, 1939), 2504. The Senate bill passed 63–23 (with 10 not voting). *Congressional Record*, 76th Congress, 1st Session (March 22, 1939), 3105. The Senate agreed to the conference report without a recorded vote. *Congressional Record*, 76th Congress, 1st Session (March 28, 1939), 3400. The House also agreed to the conference report without a recorded vote. *Congressional Record*, 76th Congress, 1st Session (March 29, 1939), 3469.

11. David R. Mayhew, "The Defeat of Roosevelt's Administrative Reorganization Bill: A Study of the 75th Congress at Work" (unpublished manuscript, Harvard University, 1959), https://works.bepress.com/david-mayhew/80/.

12. Stephen Skowronek, "Franklin Roosevelt and the Modern Presidency," *Studies in American Political Development* 6, no. 2 (Fall 1992): 322–58; Sidney M. Milkis, *The President and the Parties: The Transformation of the American Party System since the New Deal* (New York: Oxford University Press, 1993), chs. 5–6; Matthew J. Dickinson, *Bitter Harvest: FDR, Presidential Power, and the Growth of the Presidential Branch* (New York: Cambridge University Press, 1997), chs. 2–3; Peri E. Arnold, *Making the Managerial Presidency: Comprehensive Reorganization Planning, 1905–1996*, 2nd ed. (Lawrence: University Press of Kansas, 1998), ch. 4; Richard J. Ellis, *The Development of the American Presidency* (New York: Routledge, 2012), 277–81.

13. Brownlow, *Passion for Anonymity*, 346; Polenberg, *Reorganizing Roosevelt's Government*, 31–36.

14. President's Committee on Administrative Management (PCAM), *Report of the Committee with Studies of Administrative Management in the Federal Government*, 74th Congress, 2nd Session (Washington, DC: Government Printing Office, 1937), 4, 52.

15. PCAM, *Report*, 10–11; Noah A. Rosenblum, "The Antifascist Roots of Presidential Administration," *Columbia Law Review*, forthcoming.

16. *Humphrey's Executor v. United States* 295 U.S. 602 (1935). See also Hiroshi Okayama, *Judicializing the Administrative State: The Rise of the Independent Regulatory Commissions in the United States, 1883–1937* (New York: Routledge, 2019), ch. 5.

17. PCAM, *Report*, 31.

18. Franklin D. Roosevelt, "Message of the President of the United States," in PCAM, iv.

19. PCAM, 40.

20. PCAM, 24.

21. PCAM, 21; Rosenblum, "Antifascist Roots of Presidential Administration."

22. *Investigation of the Executive Agencies of the Government*, Preliminary Report of the Select Committee to Investigate the Executive Agencies of the Government, 75th Congress, 1st Session, Senate Report No. 1275 (Washington, DC: Government Printing Office, 1937) ("the Brookings report," in text), 18.

23. *Investigation of the Executive Agencies of the Government*, 8.

24. Jessica Korn, *The Power of Separation: American Constitutionalism and the Myth of the Legislative Veto* (Princeton, NJ: Princeton University Press, 1996), 5.

25. Arnold, *Making the Managerial Presidency*, 81−84.

26. *Congressional Record*, 72nd Congress, 2nd Session (February 11, 1933), 3903.

27. *Congressional Record*, 72nd Congress, 2nd Session (January 26, 1933), 2588.

28. Franklin D. Roosevelt, *Looking Forward* (New York: John Day, 1933), 88.

29. Louis Brownlow, *The President and the Presidency* (Chicago: Public Administration Service, 1949), 19.

30. Charles Edward Merriam, *A History of American Political Theories* (New York: Macmillan, 1903), 178−81.

31. Charles Edward Merriam, *American Political Ideas: Studies in the Development of American Political Thought, 1865−1917* (New York: Macmillan, 1920), 127. For a comparison of Merriam's views of administration to those of other contemporary reformers, see Benjamin I. Waldman, "Reimagining the Administrative State: James Landis and the Lost Progressive Alternative," University of Cambridge, working paper.

32. PCAM, *Report*, 1.

33. Roosevelt, "Message," in PCAM, iii.

34. PCAM, 53.

35. *Investigation of the Executive Agencies of the Government*, Preliminary Report, 2.

36. *Investigation of the Executive Agencies of the Government*, 18.

37. *Investigation of the Executive Agencies of the Government*, 22.

38. Meriam, "Part I: An Analysis of the Problem," 117−18.

39. "Reorganization Jitters," *New Republic*, April 6, 1938, 263.

40. "Reorganization," *New York Times*, March 1, 1938, 20.

41. Arthur Krock, "Reorganization Shaped for a Better Reception," *New York Times*, December 11, 1938, 87.

42. "Government Reorganization Speech, Station W.O.L.," February 13, 1938, 1, Folder 20, Box 3, Series 9, James F. Byrnes Papers, Special Collections and Archives, Clemson University, Clemson, SC.

43. *Reorganization of the Government Agencies*, Hearings before the Select Committee on Government Organization, United States Senate, 75th Congress, 1st Session (Washington, DC: Government Printing Office, 1937), 87−88.

44. *Congressional Record*, 76th Congress, 1st Session (March 7, 1939), 2395.

45. Quoted in *Appendix to the Congressional Record*, 76th Congress, 1st Session (February 27, 1939), 708.

46. Memo, Sunday, 2 p.m., February 7, 1937, Folder 274, Box 7, Lindsay C. Warren Papers, Southern Historical Collection, Special Collections, Wilson Library, University of North Carolina, Chapel Hill.

47. Letter from Lindsay C. Warren to William Bragaw, March 11, 1939, Folder 318-A, Box 9, Warren Papers.

48. Some legislators also opposed the creation of a Department of Welfare. Polenberg, *Reorganizing Roosevelt's Government*, 148–49, 166.

49. Letter from A. N. Back to James F. Byrnes, December 15, 1937, Folder 6, Box 50, Series 2, Byrnes Papers.

50. Telegram from Grace Babcock to Lindsay C. Warren, April 6, 1938, Folder 305-J, Box 8, Warren Papers.

51. Polenberg, *Reorganizing Roosevelt's Government*, 185.

52. Henry B. Hogue, "Presidential Reorganization Authority: History, Recent Initiatives, and Options for Congress," Report R42852, *Congressional Research Service*, December 11, 2012, 12–13.

53. Calabresi and Yoo, *Unitary Executive*, 295.

54. PCAM, *Report*, 40.

55. PCAM, 53.

56. Alvis, Bailey, and Taylor, *Contested Removal Power*, ch. 5. On how PCAM departed from the earlier Progressive vision by embracing the separation of powers, see Rosenblum, "Antifascist Roots of Presidential Administration."

57. Letter from A. L. Reed to Lindsay C. Warren, February 20, 1937, Folder 276, Box 7, Warren Papers.

58. Letter from C. A. Cannon to Lindsay C. Warren, April 23, 1937, Folder 283, Box 7, Warren Papers.

59. Letter from Joseph Daniels to Lindsay C. Warren, April 8, 1938, Folder 305-J, Box 8, Warren Papers.

60. Polenberg, *Reorganizing Roosevelt's Government*, 23.

61. PCAM, *Report*, 22.

62. PCAM, 24, 23.

63. PCAM, 24–25.

64. PCAM, 21.

65. *Investigation of the Executive Agencies of the Government*, Preliminary Report, 9.

66. Polenberg, *Reorganizing Roosevelt's Government*, 39.

67. *Reorganization of the Executive Departments*, Hearings before the Joint Committee on Government Organization, 75th Congress, 1st Session (Washington, DC: Government Printing Office, 1937), 283–84, 277.

68. *Reorganization of the Executive Departments*, 8, 11.

69. *Reorganization of the Executive Departments*, 14, 223, 251, 266.

70. Senator Byrd's amendment was defeated 36–47. The reorganization bill of Senator Byrnes passed the Senate 49–42 in March 1938. The bill sought to establish a Department of Welfare. Polenberg, *Reorganizing Roosevelt's Government*, 138–43.

71. Polenberg, 185.

72. PCAM, *Report*, 32.

73. PCAM, 36.

74. PCAM, 33.

75. Hogue, "Presidential Reorganization Authority," 10–11.

76. *Reorganization of the Executive Departments*, Hearings, 131.

77. Meriam, "Part I: An Analysis of the Problem," 16.

78. Meriam, 177.

79. *Reorganization of the Executive Departments*, Hearings, 89.

80. *Reorganization of the Executive Departments*, 91.

81. *Reorganization of the Government Agencies*, Hearings, 40.

82. "Suggested Outline of Points in Support Bill with Particular Reference to the Wheeler Amendment," Memorandum from Joseph P. Harris to James F. Byrnes, March 17, 1939, 4, Folder 8, Box 50, Series 2, Byrnes Papers.

83. *Reorganization of the Executive Departments*, Hearings, 91–92.

84. *Reorganization of the Government Agencies*, Hearings, 56–57.

85. *Congressional Record*, 75th Congress, 3rd Session (March 3, 1938), 2741.

86. The amendment lost 39–43. Polenberg, *Reorganizing Roosevelt's Government*, 130–31.

87. Polenberg, 130–31.

88. *Reorganization of Executive Departments*, Address by Hon. James F. Byrnes, March 27, 1938 (Washington, DC: Government Printing Office, 1938), 5, Folder 21, Box 3, Series 9, Byrnes Papers.

89. The amendment passed 151–113. Polenberg, *Reorganizing Roosevelt's Government*, 168–69.

90. Franklin D. Roosevelt, "Letter on the Reorganization Bill," March 29, 1938, *The American Presidency Project*, https://www.presidency.ucsb.edu/documents/letter-the-reorganization-bill.

91. *Congressional Record*, 75th Congress, 3rd Session (April 8, 1938), 5122.

92. Letter from Lindsay C. Warren to A. B. Houtz, April 2, 1938, Folder 305-E, Box 8, Warren Papers.

93. *Congressional Record*, 75th Congress, 3rd Session (April 8, 1938), 5123; "Reorganization Measure Killed When House Votes to Recommit 204–196," *Hartford Courant*, April 9, 1938, 1–2.

94. "New Bill in House for Reorganizing on Roosevelt Plan," *New York Times*, February 24, 1939, 1, 8.

95. Brownlow, *Passion for Anonymity*, 413–14.

96. The amendment failed 139–176. *Congressional Record*, 76th Congress, 1st Session (March 8, 1939), 2500–2501.

97. "Suggested Outline of Points in Support Bill with Particular Reference to the Wheeler Amendment," Memorandum, 1, Folder 8, Box 50, Series 2, Byrnes Papers.

98. The amendment was rejected 193–209. Polenberg, *Reorganizing Roosevelt's Government*, 186–87.

99. *Congressional Record*, 76th Congress, 1st Session (March 8, 1939), 2500.

100. The law also gave the president the ability to hire new administrative assistants.

101. Karen Orren and Stephen Skowronek, *The Policy State: An American Predicament* (Cambridge, MA: Harvard University Press, 2017), 114.

102. Skowronek, "Franklin Roosevelt and the Modern Presidency."

103. Franklin D. Roosevelt, "Annual Message to Congress," January 6, 1937, *The American Presidency Project*, https://www.presidency.ucsb.edu/documents/annual-message-congress-1.

104. Merriam, *American Political Ideas*, 220.

105. Luther Gulick, "Politics, Administration, and the 'New Deal,'" *Annals of the Academy of Political and Social Science* 169 (September 1933): 55–66, at 66.

106. Quoted in Milkis, *President and the Parties*, 109.

107. Arthur Krock, "The President Discusses His Political Philosophy," *New York Times*, February 28, 1937, 1, 33.

108. Letter from J. L. Carson to James F. Byrnes, February 19, 1937, Folder 4, Box 3, Series 2, Byrnes Papers.

109. PCAM, *Report*, 31.

110. *Congressional Record*, 75th Congress, 3rd Session (March 3, 1938), 2738–39.

111. Revealingly, even the critic Josiah Bailey admitted that Congress's parochialism prevented an effective executive branch reorganization, as lawmakers feared paying a "price on election day" if they went against agencies that were able to reach "into our States and districts." *Congressional Record*, 75th Congress, 3rd Session (March 3, 1938), 2740, 2746.

112. Roosevelt, "Letter on the Reorganization Bill."

113. *Congressional Record*, 75th Congress, 3rd Session (April 8, 1938), 5114–15.

114. Telegram from E. H. P. Ward to Lindsay C. Warren, April 2, 1938, Folder 305-E, Box 8, Warren Papers.

115. Postcard from Waldo P. Clement to Lindsay C. Warren, April 5, 1938, Folder 305-I, Box 8, Warren Papers.

116. *Congressional Record*, 75th Congress, 3rd Session (April 8, 1938), 5121; Polenberg, *Reorganizing Roosevelt's Government*, 164–65.

117. *Congressional Record*, 76th Congress, 1st Session (March 7, 1939), 2396.

118. *Congressional Record*, 76th Congress, 1st Session (March 7, 1939), 2403.

119. Meriam, "Part I: An Analysis of the Problem," 175.

120. *Reorganization of the Executive Departments*, Hearings, 171, 173.

121. Letter from Lindsay C. Warren to Homer Peele, March 25, 1939, Folder 320-A, Box 9, Warren Papers.

122. Hogue, "Presidential Reorganization Authority," 14.

123. Franklin D. Roosevelt, "Message to the Congress on the Reorganization Act," April 25, 1939, *The American Presidency Project*, https://www.presidency.ucsb.edu/documents/message-congress-the-reorganization-act.

124. Louis Brownlow, "A General View," *Public Administration Review* 1, no. 2 (Winter 1941): 101–5, at 103–4, 101.

125. Luther Gulick, "Conclusion," *Public Administration Review* 1, no. 2 (Winter 1941): 138–40, at 139.

126. PCAM, *Report*, 17.

127. *Reorganization of the Executive Departments*, Hearings, 283.

128. Harold D. Smith, "The Bureau of the Budget," *Public Administration Review* 1, no. 2 (Winter 1941): 106–15, at 114–15. See also Richard E. Neustadt, "Presidency and Legislation: The Growth of Central Clearance," *American Political Science Review* 48, no. 3 (September 1954): 641–71.

129. Brownlow, *President and the Presidency*, 107. The other initial EOP agency, the National Resources Planning Board, was short-lived owing to its abolition by conservatives in Congress in 1943, but its emphasis on long-term planning remained in EOP, especially in the Council of Economic Advisers established under the Employment Act of 1946.

130. Orren and Skowronek, *Policy State*, 108.

131. Clinton Rossiter, *The American Presidency* (New York: Harcourt, Brace, 1956), 104.

132. Hogue, "Presidential Reorganization Authority," 4.

Chapter Six

1. *National Defense Establishment (Unification of the Armed Services)*, Hearings before the Committee on Armed Services, Part 3, United States Senate, 80th Congress, 1st Session (Washington, DC: Government Printing Office, 1947), 564.

2. Commission on Organization of the Executive Branch of the Government, *Foreign Affairs: A Report to the Congress* (Washington, DC: Government Printing Office, 1949), 10.

3. Stephen Skowronek, John A. Dearborn, and Desmond King, *Phantoms of a Beleaguered Republic: The Deep State and the Unitary Executive* (New York: Oxford University Press, 2021), 129–31.

4. National Security Act of 1947 (P.L. 80-253, 61 Stat. 495, September 18, 1947); National Security Amendments of 1949 (P.L. 81-216, 63 Stat. 578, August 10, 1949); Mark R. Shulman, "The Progressive Era Origins of the National Security Act," *Dickinson Law Review* 104, no. 2 (Winter 2000): 289–330.

5. Douglas T. Stuart, *Creating the National Security State: A History of the Law that Transformed America* (Princeton, NJ: Princeton University Press, 2008), ch. 2.

6. Amy B. Zegart, *Flawed by Design: The Evolution of the CIA, JCS, and NSC* (Stanford, CA: Stanford University Press, 1999), 75.

7. Paul Y. Hammond, *Organizing for Defense: The American Military Establishment in the Twentieth Century* (Princeton, NJ: Princeton University Press, 1961); Demetrios Caraley, *The Politics of Military Unification: A Study of Conflict and the Policy Process* (New York: Columbia University Press, 1966); Michael J. Hogan, *A Cross of Iron: Harry S. Truman and the Origins of the National Security State, 1945–1954* (New York: Cambridge University Press, 1998); Zegart, *Flawed by Design*; Aaron L. Friedberg, *In the Shadow of the Garrison State: America's Anti-statism and Its Cold War Grand Strategy* (Princeton, NJ: Princeton University Press, 2000); Stuart, *Creating*; Robert P. Saldin, *War, the American State, and Politics since 1898* (New York: Cambridge University Press, 2011), chs. 4–5; Stephen M. Griffin, *Long Wars and the Constitution* (Cambridge, MA: Harvard University Press, 2013), chs. 2–3.

8. Stuart, *Creating*, 7, 79, 94.

9. *National Defense Establishment (Unification of the Armed Services)*, Hearings before the Committee on Armed Services, Part 2, United States Senate, 80th Congress, 1st Session (Washington, DC: Government Printing Office, 1947), 460.

10. *Congressional Record*, 80th Congress, 1st Session (July 9, 1947), 8527; *Congressional Record*, 80th Congress, 1st Session (July 19, 1947), 9457; *Congressional Record*, 80th Congress, 1st Session (July 24, 1947), 9923; *Congressional Record*, 80th Congress, 1st Session (July 25, 1947), 10198.

11. *Congressional Record*, 81st Congress, 1st Session (July 28, 1949), 10349. The House vote on the conference bill was 356 yes, 7 no, and 69 not voting. *Congressional Record*, 81st Congress, 1st Session (August 2, 1949), 10610.

12. Sean Gailmard and John W. Patty, *Learning While Governing: Expertise and Accountability in the Executive Branch* (Chicago: University of Chicago Press, 2013), 215–21.

13. *National Defense Establishment (Unification of the Armed Services)*, Hearings before the Committee on Armed Services, Part 1, United States Senate, 80th Congress, 1st Session (Washington, DC: Government Printing Office, 1947), 44.

14. Jeremy D. Bailey, *The Idea of Presidential Representation: An Intellectual and Political History* (Lawrence: University Press of Kansas, 2019), 133–34.

15. Stuart, *Creating*, 2.

16. Hogan, *Cross of Iron*, 2.

17. Walter Lippmann, "Today and Tomorrow: If Only," *Washington Post*, January 2, 1947, 7.

18. "For the National Defense," *New York Times*, March 9, 1947, E8.

19. Quoted in Hogan, *Cross of Iron*, 53.

20. *National Defense Establishment (Unification of the Armed Services)*, Hearings before the Committee on Armed Services, Part 1, 23.

21. "Address by US Senator Styles Bridges (R) N.H. before the New Hampshire Organized Reserved Corps, the Hotel Carpenter," September 23, 1947, File 68–69, Styles Bridges Papers, New Hampshire Division of Archives and Records Management, Concord.

22. *National Defense Establishment (Unification of the Armed Services)*, Hearings before the Committee on Armed Services, Part 3, 504.

23. *Congressional Record*, 80th Congress, 1st Session (July 19, 1947), 9409.

24. Stuart, *Creating*, 5–6, 27–42.

25. E. Pendleton Herring, *Group Representation before Congress* (Baltimore: Johns Hopkins University Press, 1929), 242.

26. E. Pendleton Herring, *Public Administration and the Public Interest* (New York: McGraw-Hill, 1936), 6–7, 15.

27. Herring did caution, however, that "presidential policy, however 'pure' in motivation, must mean the promotion of certain interests at the expense of others." Pendleton Herring, *Presidential Leadership: The Political Relations of Congress and the Chief Executive* (New York: Rinehart, 1940), 2–3, 9.

28. Herring, 18.

29. Herring, 20.

30. Pendleton Herring, "IV. Executive-Legislative Responsibilities," *American Political Science Review* 38, no. 6 (December 1944): 1153–65, at 1163, 1160.

31. Herring, *Public Administration and the Public Interest*, 384.

32. *Congressional Record*, 80th Congress, 1st Session (July 9, 1947), 8499.

33. *Congressional Record*, 80th Congress, 1st Session (July 9, 1947), 8504.

34. *National Defense Establishment (Unification of the Armed Services)*, Hearings before the Committee on Armed Services, Part 3, 634.

35. Harold Koh even goes so far as to argue that, by placing decisions about national security under the more unified control of the executive, the new "system was designed to be personally managed by a strong plebiscitary president with the support of a bureaucratic institutional presidency." Harold Hongju Koh, *The National Security Constitution: Sharing Power after the Iran-Contra Affair* (New Haven, CT: Yale University Press, 1990), 102.

36. As Stephen Griffin argues, "the Constitution can influence policy even when it is not enforced by the courts," particularly on issues of national security and war. Griffin, *Long Wars*, 4.

37. Franklin D. Roosevelt, "Press Conference," December 20, 1940, *The American Presidency Project*, https://www.presidency.ucsb.edu/documents/press-conference-4.

38. Pendleton Herring, *The Impact of War: Our American Democracy under Arms* (New York: Farrar and Rinehart, 1941), 163.

39. *Congressional Record*, 80th Congress, 1st Session (July 9, 1947), 8498.

40. *Congressional Record*, 80th Congress, 1st Session (July 19, 1947), 9397.

41. *Congressional Record*, 80th Congress, 1st Session (July 25, 1947), 10198.

42. Hammond, *Organizing for Defense*, 85; Stuart, *Creating*, 77.

43. Zegart, *Flawed by Design*, 58–60.

44. Stuart, *Creating*, ch. 3.

45. Stuart, 81–84.

46. Zegart, *Flawed by Design*, 58–60.

47. Hanson W. Baldwin, "Merger Fight Near End," *New York Times*, May 29, 1946, 10.

48. Stuart, *Creating*, ch. 4.

49. *Unification of the War and Navy Departments and Postwar Organization for National Security*, Report to Hon. James Forrestal, Secretary of the Navy, United States Senate, Committee on Naval Affairs, 79th Congress, 1st Session (Washington, DC: Government Printing Office, 1945), 3.

50. Sidney Shalett, "A Truman Victory," *New York Times*, January 17, 1947, 1–2.

51. Sidney Shalett, "Truman Asks Vote on Service Merger," *New York Times*, February 27, 1947, 1, 10.

52. Harry S. Truman, "Special Message to the Congress Recommending the Establishment of a Department of National Defense," December 19, 1945, *The American Presidency Project*, https://www.presidency.ucsb.edu/documents/special-message-the-congress-recommending -the-establishment-department-national-defense.

53. *National Defense Establishment (Unification of the Armed Services)*, Hearings before the Committee on Armed Services, Part 3, 533.

54. *National Defense Establishment (Unification of the Armed Services)*, Hearings before the Committee on Armed Services, Part 1, 57.

55. *National Defense Establishment (Unification of the Armed Services)*, 90–91, 99.

56. *Congressional Record*, 80th Congress, 1st Session (July 9, 1947), 8504.

57. *Congressional Record*, 80th Congress, 1st Session (July 19, 1947), 9407.

58. *National Defense Establishment (Unification of the Armed Services)*, Hearings before the Committee on Armed Services, Part 1, 113.

59. *National Defense Establishment (Unification of the Armed Services)*, Hearings before the Committee on Armed Services, Part 2, 458; "Army-Navy Merger Backed by Stimson," *New York Times*, May 5, 1947, 14.

60. Truman, "Special Message," December 19, 1945.

61. *Congressional Record*, 80th Congress, 1st Session (July 7, 1947), 8297.

62. *Congressional Record*, 80th Congress, 1st Session (July 9, 1947), 8501.

63. *National Defense Establishment (Unification of the Armed Services)*, Hearings before the Committee on Armed Services, Part 1, 211–14.

64. *National Defense Establishment (Unification of the Armed Services)*, 23, 29.

65. Harry S. Truman, "Special Message to the Congress on Reorganization of the National Military Establishment," March 5, 1949, *The American Presidency Project*, https://www .presidency.ucsb.edu/documents/special-message-the-congress-reorganization-the-national -military-establishment.

66. Stuart, *Creating*, 192–93, 196.

67. *Congressional Record*, 81st Congress, 1st Session (August 2, 1949), 10597–98; Stuart, *Creating*, 202.

68. Zegart, *Flawed by Design*, 55.

69. Lindsay Rogers, "Making a Democratic Government Effective in Crisis," *Proceedings of the Academy of Political Science* 19, no. 3 (May 1941): 66–75, at 74.

70. Stuart, *Creating*, ch. 4.

71. *Unification*, Report, 5.

72. *Unification*, 5.

73. *Unification*, 7.

74. *National Defense Establishment (Unification of the Armed Services)*, Hearings before the Committee on Armed Services, Part 1, 25.

75. *National Defense Establishment (Unification of the Armed Services)*, 55–56.

76. *National Defense Establishment (Unification of the Armed Services)*, 116.

77. *National Defense Establishment (Unification of the Armed Services)*, Hearings before the Committee on Armed Services, Part 2, 458.

78. *National Defense Establishment (Unification of the Armed Services)*, Hearings before the Committee on Armed Services, Part 3, 499.

79. Stuart, *Creating*, 134–36. See also Zegart, *Flawed by Design*, chs. 6–7.

80. *National Defense Establishment (Unification of the Armed Services)*, Hearings before the Committee on Armed Services, Part 3, 567.

81. *National Defense Establishment (Unification of the Armed Services)*, 507.

82. *National Defense Establishment (Unification of the Armed Services)*, 694.

83. *Congressional Record*, 80th Congress, 1st Session (July 9, 1947), 8520, 8518.

84. *Congressional Record*, 80th Congress, 1st Session (July 9, 1947), 8496.

85. "Eisenhower, Spaatz and Nimitz Call on the United States to Retain Its Strength," *New York Times*, August 30, 1947, 4.

86. Arthur Krock, "An Integrated Security System at Last," *New York Times*, September 19, 1947, 22.

87. Hammond, *Organizing for Defense*, 232–33.

88. *National Defense Establishment (Unification of the Armed Services)*, Hearings before the Committee on Armed Services, Part 3, 564.

89. Zegart, *Flawed by Design*, 79, 98–100; Stuart, *Creating*, 131.

90. Harry S. Truman, *Memoirs*, vol. 2, *Years of Trial and Hope* (Garden City, NY: Doubleday, 1956), 60.

91. Stuart, *Creating*, 233.

92. *Congressional Record*, 80th Congress, 1st Session (July 9, 1947), 8520.

93. Truman, "Special Message," March 5, 1949; Stuart, *Creating*, 237.

94. Hogan, *Cross of Iron*, 3; Zegart, *Flawed by Design*, 79–80; Stuart, *Creating*, 237.

95. Zegart, *Flawed by Design*, ch. 2.

96. Truman, *Memoirs*, 2:60.

97. Zegart, *Flawed by Design*, 10–11.

98. Anna Kasten Nelson, "The 'Top of Policy Hill': President Eisenhower and the National Security Council," *Diplomatic History* 7, no. 4 (October 1983): 307–26; Stuart, *Creating*, 241–42.

99. Robert Cutler, "The Development of the National Security Council," *Foreign Affairs* 34 (April 1956): 441–58, at 441–42.

100. Hogan, *Cross of Iron*, 370.

101. James L. Sundquist, *The Decline and Resurgence of Congress* (Washington, DC: Brookings Institution, 1981), 107.

102. Mariah Zeisberg, *War Powers: The Politics of Constitutional Authority* (Princeton, NJ: Princeton University Press, 2013).

103. Commission on Organization of the Executive Branch of the Government, *Foreign Affairs*, 5.

104. Quoted in Zegart, *Flawed by Design*, 28. See also Louis Fisher, "Presidential Inherent Power: The 'Sole Organ' Doctrine," *Presidential Studies Quarterly* 37, no. 1 (March 2007): 139–52.

105. *U.S. v. Curtiss-Wright Export Corp.*, 299 U.S. 304, 328 (1936) (Sutherland, J., opinion of the Court). Sutherland had written about the role of the president as commander in chief: "Whatever war powers he possesses under the Constitution—that is, without legislative authority—he has, not because he is President, but because he is Commander in Chief." George Sutherland, *Constitutional Power and World Affairs* (New York: Columbia University Press, 1919), 73. See also Jordan T. Cash, "George Sutherland and the Contextualization of Executive Power," *American Political Thought* 9, no. 1 (Winter 2020): 50–84.

106. Hogan, *Cross of Iron*, 35.

107. *Unification*, Report, 36; Stuart, *Creating*, 77.

108. *National Defense Establishment (Unification of the Armed Services)*, Hearings before the Committee on Armed Services, Part 2, 451.

109. *National Defense Establishment (Unification of the Armed Services)*, Hearings before the Committee on Armed Services, Part 1, 133, 147.

110. *National Defense Establishment (Unification of the Armed Services)*, 100.

111. *Congressional Record*, 80th Congress, 1st Session (July 9, 1947), 8497.

112. *Congressional Record*, 80th Congress, 1st Session (July 19, 1947), 9430.

113. Hogan, *Cross of Iron*, 32–37.

114. *Unification*, Report, 7–8.

115. Zegart, *Flawed by Design*, 94–95; Stuart, *Creating*, 129.

116. Stuart, *Creating*, 104–5.

117. *Congressional Record*, 80th Congress, 1st Session (July 19, 1947), 9431, 9456.

118. Stuart, *Creating*, 130.

119. *National Defense Establishment (Unification of the Armed Services)*, Hearings before the Committee on Armed Services, Part 2, 351.

120. *National Defense Establishment (Unification of the Armed Services)*, Hearings before the Committee on Armed Services, Part 1, 63.

121. *National Defense Establishment (Unification of the Armed Services)*, 92.

122. *Congressional Record*, 80th Congress, 1st Session (July 9, 1947), 8497.

123. William S. White, "War Plans Ready for an Emergency, Nimitz Testifies," *New York Times*, March 27, 1947, 1, 6.

124. *Congressional Record*, 80th Congress, 1st Session (July 7, 1947), 8297.

125. *Congressional Record*, 80th Congress, 1st Session (July 7, 1947), 8311–12.

126. *Congressional Record*, 80th Congress, 1st Session (July 19, 1947), 9414–15.

127. *Congressional Record*, 81st Congress, 1st Session (August 2, 1949), 10598; Stuart, *Creating*, 199–201.

128. *Congressional Record*, 81st Congress, 1st Session (July 28, 1949), 10347.

129. *Congressional Record*, 81st Congress, 1st Session (August 2, 1949), 10599; Stuart, *Creating*, 202.

130. *Congressional Record*, 81st Congress, 1st Session (May 24, 1949), 6711–12.

131. Sarah Burns, *The Politics of War Powers: The Theory and History of Presidential Unilateralism* (Lawrence: University Press of Kansas, 2019), ch. 8.

132. Stuart, *Creating*, 266–67.

Part Two

1. Jeffrey Hart, "The Presidency: Shifting Conservative Perspectives?," *National Review*, November 22, 1974, 1351–55, at 1352.

2. Jeffrey K. Tulis, *The Rhetorical Presidency* (Princeton, NJ: Princeton University Press, 1987).

3. Franklin D. Roosevelt, "Message to Congress on the Reorganization Act," April 25, 1939, *The American Presidency Project*, https://www.presidency.ucsb.edu/documents/message-congress-the-reorganization-act; Dwight D. Eisenhower, "Special Message to Congress Transmitting Reorganization Plan of 1953 Creating the Department of Health, Education, and Welfare," March 12, 1953, *The American Presidency Project*, https://www.presidency.ucsb.edu/documents/special-message-the-congress-transmitting-reorganization-plan-1953-creating-the-department; Richard Nixon, "Special Message to the Congress about Reorganization Plans to Establish the Environmental Protection Agency and the National Oceanic and Atmosphere Administration," July 9, 1970, *The American Presidency Project*, https://www.presidency.ucsb.edu/documents/special-message-the-congress-about-reorganization-plans-establish-the-environmental.

4. Karen E. Schnietz, "The Institutional Foundation of US Trade Policy: Revisiting Explanations for the 1934 Reciprocal Trade Agreements Act," *Journal of Policy History* 12, no. 4 (October 2000): 417–44.

5. Richard E. Neustadt, "The Presidency at Mid-century," *Law and Contemporary Problems* 21, no. 4 (Autumn 1956): 609–45, at 611. See also Richard E. Neustadt, "Presidency and Legislation: Planning the President's Program," *American Political Science Review* 49, no. 4 (December 1955): 980–1021; Andrew Rudalevige, *Managing the President's Program: Presidential Leadership and Legislative Policy Formulation* (Princeton, NJ: Princeton University Press, 2002), ch. 3.

6. "Text of Senator Kennedy's Speech on Presidency at National Press Club Luncheon," *New York Times*, January 15, 1960, 14.

7. James L. Sundquist, *The Decline and Resurgence of Congress* (Washington, DC: Brookings Institution, 1981).

8. Kevin M. Kruse and Julian E. Zelizer, *Fault Lines: A History of the United States since 1974* (New York: W. W. Norton, 2019), 7.

9. Stephen Skowronek and Karen Orren, "The Adaptability Paradox: Constitutional Resilience and Principles of Good Government in Twenty-First Century America," *Perspectives on Politics* 18, no. 2 (June 2020): 354–69, at 359.

10. Sidney M. Milkis and Daniel J. Tichenor, *Rivalry and Reform: Presidents, Social Movements, and the Transformation of American Politics* (Chicago: University of Chicago Press, 2019), ch. 4.

11. Philip Shabecoff, "Presidency Is Found Weaker under Ford," *New York Times*, March 28, 1976, 1, 44. See also Bruce Miroff, "After Consensus: The Dilemmas of Contemporary American Leadership; A 1979 View," *Presidential Studies Quarterly* 11, no. 3 (Summer 1981): 411–23; Kruse and Zelizer, *Fault Lines*, ch. 1.

12. Pierre Rosanvallon, *Good Government: Democracy beyond Elections*, trans. Malcolm DeBevoise (Cambridge, MA: Harvard University Press, 2018), chs. 14–15.

13. Stephen Skowronek, "Presidency and American Political Development: A Third Look," *Presidential Studies Quarterly* 32, no. 4 (December 2002): 743–52, at 744; Keith E. Whittington, *Constitutional Construction: Divided Power and Constitutional Meaning* (Cambridge, MA: Harvard University Press, 1999), 162.

14. Richard E. Neustadt, *Presidential Power: The Politics of Leadership* (New York: Wiley, 1960), 175. Emphasis in original.

15. Samuel P. Huntington, "The United States," in Michel Crozier, Samuel P. Huntington, and Joji Watanuki, *The Crisis of Democracy: Report on the Governability of Democracies to the Trilateral Commission* (New York: New York University Press, 1975), 59–118, at 93–94.

16. Theodore J. Lowi, *The End of Liberalism: The Second Republic of the United States*, 2nd ed. (New York: W. W. Norton, 1979), 52.

17. Thomas E. Cronin, "A Resurgent Congress and the Imperial Presidency," *Political Science Quarterly* 95, no. 2 (Summer 1980): 209–37, at 237.

18. Neal B. Freeman, "Track-Covering," *National Review*, May 24, 1974, 603–4, at 603.

19. "The Congress and America's Future," Address by Congressman Charles McC. Mathias Jr. at the Third Rocky Mountain Assembly, Brigham Young University, September 8, 1965, in *The Congress and America's Future*, Report of the Third Rocky Mountain Assembly, Brigham Young University, Provo, Utah, September 8–10, 1965, 6–7, 10, Folder 6, Box 153, Subseries 3, Series 2, Robert J. Dole House of Representatives Papers, 1960–69, Robert and Elizabeth Dole Archive and Special Collections, Robert J. Dole Institute of Politics, University of Kansas, Lawrence.

20. Letter from Edmund S. Muskie to Ronald L. Stanley, June 14, 1973, Folder 10, Box 1587, Subseries A9, Series V, Edmund S. Muskie Papers, Edmund S. Muskie Archives and Special Collections Library, Bates College, Lewiston, ME.

21. "National Goals and National Consensus," Pre-recorded speech before the Summer Cubberly Conference, Stanford University, July 28, 1961, 7–8, Folder 8, Box 20, Series 72, J. William Fulbright Papers, Special Collections, University of Arkansas Libraries, Fayetteville.

22. David R. Mayhew, *America's Congress: Actions in the Public Sphere; James Madison through Newt Gingrich* (New Haven, CT: Yale University Press, 2000), 64, table 2.5.

23. J. William Fulbright, *The Arrogance of Power* (New York: Random House, 1966), 54.

24. *Impoundment of Appropriated Funds by the President*, Joint Hearings before the Ad Hoc Subcommittee on Impoundment of Funds of the Committee on Government Operations and the Subcommittee on Separation of Powers of the Committee on the Judiciary, United States Senate, 93rd Congress, 1st Session (Washington, DC: Government Printing Office, 1973), 240.

25. Donovan quoted in "The Crack in the Constitution," *Time*, January 15, 1973, 12–17, at 12–13.

26. Congressional Research Service, *Resolved: That the Powers of the Presidency Should Be Curtailed; A Collection of Excerpts and Bibliography Relating to the Intercollegiate Debate Topic, 1974–75*, 93rd Congress, 2nd Session, House Document No. 93-273 (Washington, DC: Government Printing Office, 1974), 266.

27. Letter from Jeffrey E. Jacobs to Edmund S. Muskie, April 10, 1973, Folder 6, Box 1596, Subseries A9, Series V, Muskie Papers.

28. Letter from Thomas E. Woodman to Norris Cotton, November 16, 1973, Folder 96c, Box 19, Series 4, Norris Cotton Papers, Milne Archives and Special Collections, University of New Hampshire, Durham.

29. Letter from William Gadon to Thomas J. McIntyre, October 22, 1973, 1, Folder 35, Box 135, Thomas J. McIntyre Papers, Milne Archives and Special Collections, University of New Hampshire, Durham.

30. Letter from Rose H. Mahar to Thomas J. McIntyre, October 24, 1973, Folder 39, Box 173, McIntyre Papers.

31. Letter from Osgood Nichols to Ronald A. Sarasin, cc: Norris Cotton, December 7, 1973, Folder 96c, Box 19, Series 4, Cotton Papers.

32. Letter from Frances P. Brady to Bob Dole, September 1973, Folder 15, Box 316, Series 4, Robert J. Dole Senate Papers—Constituent Relations, 1969–96, Robert and Elizabeth Dole Archive and Special Collections, Robert J. Dole Institute of Politics, University of Kansas, Lawrence.

33. Letter from Richard A. Biscorner to Thomas J. McIntyre, October 1973, Folder 35, Box 173, McIntyre Papers.

34. Richard F. Fenno Jr., "US House Members in Their Constituencies: An Exploration," *American Political Science Review* 71, no. 3 (September 1977): 883–917, at 917.

35. Ronald Reagan, "Address on Behalf of Senator Barry Goldwater: 'A Time for Choosing,'" October 27, 1964, *The American Presidency Project*, https://www.presidency.ucsb.edu/documents/address-behalf-senator-barry-goldwater-time-for-choosing.

36. Arthur M. Schlesinger Jr., *The Imperial Presidency* (Boston: Houghton Mifflin, 1973), viii. Emphasis in original.

37. "The Constitution on Powers," *New York Times*, March 5, 1973, 20.

38. Skowronek and Orren, "Adaptability Paradox," 359. See also Bryan D. Jones, Sean M. Theriault, and Michelle Whyman, *The Great Broadening: How the Vast Expansion of the Policymaking Agenda Transformed American Politics* (Chicago: University of Chicago Press, 2019).

39. David E. Rosenbaum, "The Framers Would Not Recognize Congress," *New York Times*, May 2, 1976, E4.

40. David Mayhew, *Congress: The Electoral Connection* (New Haven, CT: Yale University Press, 1974), 104.

41. Frances E. Lee, *Insecure Majorities: Congress and the Perpetual Campaign* (Chicago: University of Chicago Press, 2016).

42. Frances E. Lee, *Beyond Ideology: Politics, Principles, and Partisanship in the US Senate* (Chicago: University of Chicago Press, 2009), ch. 4.

43. Colleen J. Shogan, "The President's State of the Union Address: Tradition, Function, and Policy Implications," Report R40132, *Congressional Research Service*, January 16, 2015, 12–14; Charles Zug and Connor M. Ewing, "What Happened to the State of the Union Address? Originally, It Helped the President and Congress Deliberate," *Washington Post*, Monkey Cage, January 30, 2018, https://www.washingtonpost.com/news/monkey-cage/wp/2018/01/30/what-happened-to-the-state-of-the-union-address-originally-it-helped-the-president-and-congress-deliberate/.

44. Nolan McCarty, *Polarization: What Everyone Needs to Know* (New York: Oxford University Press, 2019), ch. 5.

45. Sam Rosenfeld, *The Polarizers: Postwar Architects of Our Partisan Era* (Chicago: University of Chicago Press, 2018), 79, 83.

46. Rosenfeld, 186.

47. Susan Herbst, "The Rhetorical Presidency and the Contemporary Media Environment," *Critical Review* 19, nos. 2–3 (2007): 335–43.

48. Brian Newman and Emerson Siegle, "The Polarized Presidency: Depth and Breadth of Public Partisanship," *Presidential Studies Quarterly* 40, no. 2 (June 2010): 342–63; Julia R. Azari, *Delivering the People's Message: The Changing Politics of the Presidential Mandate* (Ithaca, NY: Cornell University Press, 2014).

49. Jeremy D. Bailey, *The Idea of Presidential Representation: An Intellectual and Political History* (Lawrence: University Press of Kansas, 2019), ch. 5.

50. Gary C. Jacobson, *Presidents and Parties in the Public Mind* (Chicago: University of Chicago Press, 2019).

51. J. David Alvis, Jeremy D. Bailey, and F. Flagg Taylor IV, *The Contested Removal Power, 1789–2010* (Lawrence: University Press of Kansas, 2013), 187.

52. Stephen Skowronek, "The Conservative Insurgency and Presidential Power: A Developmental Perspective on the Unitary Executive," *Harvard Law Review* 122, no. 8 (June 2009): 2070–103.

53. Elena Kagan, "Presidential Administration," *Harvard Law Review* 114, no. 8 (June 2001): 2245–385.

54. Stephen Skowronek, John A. Dearborn, and Desmond King, *Phantoms of a Beleaguered Republic: The Deep State and the Unitary Executive* (New York: Oxford University Press, 2021), ch. 3.

55. Peter Baker, "A President of the People or a President of His People?," *New York Times*, April 16, 2019, https://www.nytimes.com/2019/04/16/us/politics/trump-presidency-base.html.

Chapter Seven

1. *Improving Congressional Budget Control*, Hearings before the Joint Study Committee on Budget Control, 93rd Congress, 1st Session (Washington, DC: Government Printing Office, 1973), 80.

2. Roger H. Davidson, "The Advent of the Modern Congress: The Legislative Reorganization Act of 1946," *Legislative Studies Quarterly* 15, no. 3 (August 1990): 357–73; Andrew Rudalevige, *Managing the President's Program: Presidential Leadership and Legislative Policy Formulation* (Princeton, NJ: Princeton University Press, 2002), ch. 3; George A. Krause and Roger Qiyuan Jin, "Organizational Design and Its Consequences for Administrative Reform: Historical Lessons from the US Budget and Accounting Act of 1921," *Governance* 33, no. 2 (April 2020): 365–84.

3. Peri E. Arnold, *Making the Managerial Presidency: Comprehensive Reorganization Planning, 1905–1996*, 2nd ed. (Lawrence: University Press of Kansas, 1998), 298.

4. Richard Nixon, "Message to the Congress Transmitting Reorganization Plan 2 of 1970," March 12, 1970, *The American Presidency Project*, https://www.presidency.ucsb.edu/documents/message-the-congress-transmitting-reorganization-plan-2-1970.

5. Hugh Heclo, "OMB and the Presidency—the Problem of 'Neutral Competence,'" *National Interest* 38 (Winter 1975): 80–99; Richard P. Nathan, *The Plot That Failed: Nixon and the Administrative Presidency* (New York: John Wiley and Sons, 1975), chs. 3–4; Terry M. Moe, "The Politicized Presidency," in *The New Direction in American Politics*, ed. John E. Chubb and Paul E. Peterson (Washington, DC: Brookings Institution, 1985), 235–71.

6. "In the fiscal year just ended, President Nixon impounded $18 billion, or roughly 7 per cent of the total budget, most of it in the environmental and social welfare programs." "No Item Veto," *New York Times*, July 24, 1973, 34. See also James P. Pfiffner, *The President, the Budget, and Congress: Impoundment and the 1974 Budget Act* (Boulder, CO: Westview, 1979); Keith E. Whittington, *Constitutional Construction: Divided Power and Constitutional Meaning* (Cambridge, MA: Harvard University Press, 1999), 162–63.

7. On Congress reacting to Nixon's assertion of presidential authority, see Eric Schickler,

Disjointed Pluralism: Institutional Innovation and the Development of the US Congress (Princeton, NJ: Princeton University Press, 2001), ch. 5.

8. Congressional Budget and Impoundment Control Act of 1974 (P.L. 93-344, 88 Stat. 297, July 12, 1974).

9. Arthur M. Schlesinger Jr., *The Imperial Presidency* (Boston: Houghton Mifflin, 1973), 397–98; Louis Fisher, *Presidential Spending Power* (Princeton, NJ: Princeton University Press, 1975), 48–51; Larry Berman, *The Office of Management and Budget and the Presidency, 1921–1979* (Princeton, NJ: Princeton University Press, 1979), ch. 5; James L. Sundquist, *The Decline and Resurgence of Congress* (Washington, DC: Brookings Institution, 1981), ch. 8.

10. Sundquist, *Decline and Resurgence*, 156–60; Samuel Haber, *Efficiency and Uplift: Scientific Management in the Progressive Era, 1890–1920* (Chicago: University of Chicago Press, 1964), ch. 6.

11. Sean Gailmard and John W. Patty, *Learning While Governing: Expertise and Accountability in the Executive Branch* (Chicago: University of Chicago Press, 2013), ch. 6.

12. The House passed its version of budget reform 386–23 (with 24 not voting) in December 1973. *Congressional Record*, 93rd Congress, 1st Session (December 5, 1973), 39739. The Senate passed its version of budget reform 80–0 (with 20 not voting) in March 1974. *Congressional Record*, 93rd Congress, 2nd Session (March 22, 1974), 7937–38. In June 1974, the conference bill passed the House 401–6 (with 26 not voting) and the Senate 75–0 (with 25 not voting). *Congressional Record*, 93rd Congress, 2nd Session (June 18, 1974), 19698; *Congressional Record*, 93rd Congress, 2nd Session (June 21, 1974), 20500.

13. "Congress Gains Wide Budget Role," *New York Times*, July 13, 1974, 6.

14. Richard Nixon, "The President's News Conference," January 31, 1973, *The American Presidency Project*, https://www.presidency.ucsb.edu/documents/the-presidents-news-conference-86.

15. *Impoundment of Appropriated Funds by the President*, Joint Hearings before the Ad Hoc Subcommittee on Impoundment of Funds of the Committee on Government Operations and the Subcommittee on Separation of Powers of the Committee on the Judiciary, United States Senate, 93rd Congress, 1st Session (Washington, DC: Government Printing Office, 1973), 363.

16. Letter from Roy L. Ash to Mike Mansfield, September 26, 1973, Folder 7, Box 84, Series XXII, Mike Mansfield Papers, Archives and Special Collections, Maureen and Mike Mansfield Library, University of Montana, Missoula.

17. *Improving Congressional Budget Control*, Hearings, 36.

18. *Impoundment of Appropriated Funds by the President*, Joint Hearings, 247–48.

19. *Improving Congressional Budget Control*, Hearings, 123.

20. Hugh Scott, "The Case for Impoundment," *New York Times*, May 25, 1973, 35.

21. *Impoundment of Appropriated Funds by the President*, Joint Hearings, 170.

22. *Congressional Record*, 93rd Congress, 2nd Session (June 18, 1974), 19677.

23. Letter from Thomas J. McIntyre to R. C. Summe, March 20, 1973, 1, Folder 30, Box 133, Thomas J. McIntyre Papers, Milne Archives and Special Collections, University of New Hampshire, Durham.

24. *Impoundment of Appropriated Funds by the President*, Joint Hearings, 240.

25. *Impoundment of Appropriated Funds by the President*, 240, 358.

26. *Impoundment of Appropriated Funds by the President*, 482.

27. Untitled Document, containing Questions to Speaker and Answers, 1973, 7, Folder 26,

Box 179, Series 7, Carl Albert Collection, Carl Albert Congressional Center and Political Collections, University of Oklahoma, Norman.

28. *Impoundment of Appropriated Funds by the President*, Joint Hearings, 469.

29. *Improving Congressional Budget Control*, Hearings, 37.

30. Arthur D. Little, Inc., *Management Study of the US Congress*, Report Commissioned by NBC News for the Special Report "Congress Needs Help," Broadcast on the NBC Television Network, 10:00–11:00 p.m. EST, Wednesday, November 24, 1965, 15–16, 30–31, Folder 6, Box 153, Subseries 3, Series 2, Robert J. Dole House of Representatives Papers, 1960–69, Robert and Elizabeth Dole Archive and Special Collections, Robert J. Dole Institute of Politics, University of Kansas, Lawrence.

31. Whittington, *Constitutional Construction*, 166, 171.

32. *Congressional Record*, 93rd Congress, 2nd Session (March 19, 1974), 7172.

33. *Improving Congressional Budget Control*, Hearings, 157.

34. *Improving Congressional Budget Control*, 121.

35. *Improving Congressional Budget Control*, 43–44, 49.

36. Letter from Edmund S. Muskie to John Hale, January 18, 1973, Folder 11, Box 1587, Subseries A9, Series V, Edmund S. Muskie Papers, Edmund S. Muskie Archives and Special Collections Library, Bates College, Lewiston, ME.

37. Letter from Russell B. Long to Mike Mansfield, May 1, 1973, Folder 7, Box 84, Series XXII, Mansfield Papers.

38. Letter from Thomas F. Eagleton to Mike Mansfield, April 11, 1973, Folder 7, Box 84, Series XXII, Mansfield Papers.

39. *Improving Congressional Budget Control*, Hearings, 21.

40. "Budget Revolution," *New York Times*, June 7, 1974, 34.

41. Tom Wicker, "Impounding and Implying," *New York Times*, February 8, 1973, 43.

42. *Impoundment of Appropriated Funds by the President*, Joint Hearings, 27.

43. *Congressional Record*, 93rd Congress, 2nd Session (March 19, 1974), 7147.

44. "Minutes of the Senate Democratic Conference," July 18, 1974, 2, Folder 2, Box 86, Series XXII, Mansfield Papers.

45. *Improving Congressional Budget Control*, Hearings, 218.

46. *Congressional Record*, 93rd Congress, 1st Session (December 5, 1973), 39735.

47. *Congressional Record*, 93rd Congress, 2nd Session (March 19, 1974), 7144.

48. *Impoundment of Appropriated Funds by the President*, Joint Hearings, 20.

49. *Congressional Record*, 93rd Congress, 1st Session (December 5, 1973), 39735.

50. Letter from Edmund S. Muskie to Ann Wagg, January 9, 1973, Folder 11, Box 1587, Subseries A9, Series V, Muskie Papers.

51. Letter from Sam J. Ervin Jr. to Mike Mansfield, April 17, 1973, Folder 7, Box 84, Series XXII, Mansfield Papers.

52. Letter from Harrison A. Williams Jr. to Mike Mansfield, April 19, 1973, Folder 7, Box 84, Series XXII, Mansfield Papers.

53. "The Case for Congress," *New York Times*, March 18, 1973, 214.

54. "Elderly Stage Protest on Steps of Capitol," *New York Times*, June 8, 1973, 10.

55. *Improving Congressional Budget Control*, Hearings, 133.

56. *Improving Congressional Budget Control*, 4.

57. Letter from Joseph W. Barr to Carl Albert, May 3, 1973, Folder 6, Box 179, Series 7, Albert Collection.

58. James M. Naughton, "Senate Panel Backs Curb on Impounding of Funds," *New York Times*, April 4, 1973, 30.

59. Whittington, *Constitutional Construction*, 170.

60. *Improving Congressional Budget Control*, Hearings, 85.

61. *Improving Congressional Budget Control*, 329.

62. *Improving Congressional Budget Control*, 137.

63. *Congressional Record*, 93rd Congress, 1st Session (December 5, 1973), 39733.

64. *Congressional Record*, 93rd Congress, 1st Session (December 5, 1973), 39697.

65. "Charges and Answers to Democratic Study Group Special Report on the Recommendations of the Joint Study Committee on Budget Control," undated, 9, Folder 6, Box 179, Series 7, Albert Collection.

66. *Congressional Record*, 93rd Congress, 1st Session (December 5, 1973), 39731.

67. *Congressional Record*, 93rd Congress, 1st Session (December 5, 1973), 39733.

68. *Improving Congressional Budget Control*, Hearings, 267.

69. *Congressional Record*, 93rd Congress, 1st Session (December 5, 1973), 39730.

70. *Congressional Record*, 93rd Congress, 1st Session (December 5, 1973), 39729.

71. *Congressional Record*, 93rd Congress, 1st Session (December 5, 1973), 39728.

72. *Improving Congressional Budget Control*, Hearings, 329.

73. *Improving Congressional Budget Control*, 22.

74. *Improving Congressional Budget Control*, 40.

75. *Improving Congressional Budget Control*, 10.

76. Memorandum to Members of the Senate Budget Committee from Edmund S. Muskie, August 22, 1974, 4, Folder 16, Box 52, Subseries C, Series V, Muskie Papers.

77. Letter from Bella S. Abzug to Carl Albert, July 24, 1974, Folder 28, Box 179, Series 7, Albert Collection.

78. *Congressional Record*, 93rd Congress, 2nd Session (March 19, 1974), 7145.

79. Schickler, *Disjointed Pluralism*, 193.

80. *Improving Congressional Budget Control*, Hearings, 42.

81. *Improving Congressional Budget Control*, 73.

82. *Improving Congressional Budget Control*, 331.

83. *Improving Congressional Budget Control*, 242.

84. *Congressional Record*, 93rd Congress, 2nd Session (March 19, 1974), 7152.

85. *Improving Congressional Budget Control*, Hearings, 132.

86. P.L. 93-250, 88 Stat. 11, March 2, 1974.

87. Marjorie Hunter, "House Backs Curb on Budget Aides," *New York Times*, May 2, 1973, 13. See also James M. Naughton, "The Congress: Now It's in a Mood for a Real Fight," *New York Times*, January 28, 1973, 3; James Naughton, "Test for Congress: Struggle over the Power of the Purse," *New York Times*, February 11, 1973, 205; Tom Wicker, "'Life-Size' Presidents," *New York Times*, September 18, 1973, 43; Fisher, *Presidential Spending Power*, 51–55.

88. *Congressional Record*, 93rd Congress, 1st Session (January 4, 1973), 212–13.

89. *Improving Congressional Budget Control*, Hearings, 242.

90. Letter from Edmund S. Muskie to Mary Ridlen, February 15, 1973, Folder 11, Box 1587, Subseries A9, Series V, Muskie Papers.

91. *Confirmation of the Director and Deputy Director of the Office of Management and Budget*, Hearings before a Subcommittee of the Committee on Government Operations, House of Representatives, 93rd Congress, 1st Session (Washington, DC: Government Printing Office, 1973), 8.

92. *Confirmation of the Director and Deputy Director of the Office of Management and Budget*, 2.

93. *Confirmation of the Director and Deputy Director of the Office of Management and Budget*, 26.

94. *Congressional Record*, 93rd Congress, 1st Session (January 4, 1973), 212.

95. *Confirmation of the Director and Deputy Director of the Office of Management and Budget*, Hearings, 2.

96. *Confirmation of the Director and Deputy Director of the Office of Management and Budget*, 26.

97. Ronald Reagan, "Executive Order 12291—Federal Regulation," February 17, 1981, *The American Presidency Project*, https://www.presidency.ucsb.edu/documents/executive-order-12291-federal-regulation; Andrew Rudalevige, "Beyond Structure and Process: The Early Institutionalization of Regulatory Review," *Journal of Policy History* 30, no. 4 (October 2018): 577–608.

98. Josh Chafetz, *Congress's Constitution: Legislative Authority and the Separation of Powers* (New Haven, CT: Yale University Press, 2017), 63–64.

99. Patrick O'Brien, "Maximizing Control: First-Year Presidents and the Appointment and Agenda-Setting Powers," in *Crucible: The President's First Year*, ed. Michael Nelson, Jeffrey L. Chidester, and Stefanie Georgakis Abbott (Charlottesville: University of Virginia Press, 2018), 250–55, at 250. See also Philip Joyce, "Evaluating the Impact of the Congressional Budget Office at Middle Age," *Congress and the Presidency* 43, no. 3 (2016): 279–99.

100. Quoted in O'Brien, "Maximizing Control," 250.

101. Iwan Morgan, *The Age of Deficits: Presidents and Unbalanced Budgets from Jimmy Carter to George W. Bush* (Lawrence: University Press of Kansas, 2009), 83–85, 95. See also, David A. Stockman, *The Triumph of Politics: How the Reagan Revolution Failed* (New York: Harper and Row, 1986), 97–99.

102. Allen Schick, *The Federal Budget: Politics, Policy, Process*, rev. ed. (Washington, DC: Brookings Institution, 2000), 92.

103. Morgan, *Age of Deficits*, 157.

104. Memorandum, "Government Operations vs. Budget Committee," from Al From to Edmund S. Muskie, April 12, 1974, 1, Folder 31, Box 53, Subseries C, Series V, Muskie Papers.

105. *Congressional Record*, 93rd Congress, 2nd Session (June 18, 1974), 19685.

106. Between the late 1970s and February 2019, only four regular appropriations bills were passed on time. James V. Saturno, "Federal Funding Gaps: A Brief Overview," Report RS20348, *Congressional Research Service*, February 4, 2019, 1.

107. Molly E. Reynolds, "This Is Why the Congressional Budget Process is Broken," Monkey Cage, *Washington Post*, October 26, 2017, https://www.washingtonpost.com/news/monkey-cage/wp/2017/10/27/this-is-why-the-congressional-budget-process-is-broken/.

108. *Line-Item Veto*, Joint Hearing before the Committee on Government Reform and Oversight, House of Representatives, and the Committee on Governmental Affairs, United States Senate, 104th Congress, 1st Session (Washington, DC: Government Printing Office, 1995), 14.

109. "Selected Dole Quotations, Line Item Veto," April 23, 1987, Folder 21, Box 161, Subseries 6, Series 8, Robert J. Dole Presidential Campaign Papers, 1988–96, Robert and Elizabeth Dole Archive and Special Collections, Robert J. Dole Institute of Politics, University of Kansas, Lawrence.

110. Letter from John McCain to Bob Dole, March 12, 1993, Folder 4, Box 303, Series 10, Rob-

ert J. Dole Senate Papers—Personal/Political Files, 1969–96, Robert and Elizabeth Dole Archive and Special Collections, Robert J. Dole Institute of Politics, University of Kansas, Lawrence.

111. Line Item Veto Act of 1996 (P.L. 104-130, 110 Stat. 1200, April 9, 1996).

112. *Congressional Record*, 104th Congress, 1st Session (March 20, 1995), 8340.

113. *Congressional Record*, 104th Congress, 2nd Session (March 27, 1996), 6555.

114. *Congressional Record*, 104th Congress, 2nd Session (March 27, 1996), 6554.

115. William J. Clinton, "Remarks on Signing the Line Item Veto Act and an Exchange with Reporters," April 9, 1996, *The American Presidency Project*, https://www.presidency.ucsb.edu/documents/remarks-signing-the-line-item-veto-act-and-exchange-with-reporters.

116. *Congressional Record*, 104th Congress, 2nd Session (March 27, 1996), 6551.

117. *The Line-Item Veto: A Constitutional Approach*, Hearing before the Subcommittee on the Constitution, Federalism, and Property Rights of the Committee on the Judiciary, United States Senate, 104th Congress, 1st Session (Washington, DC: Government Printing Office, 1996 [1995]), 6, 16.

118. *Line-Item Veto*, Joint Hearing, 62.

119. *Line-Item Veto: A Constitutional Approach*, Hearing. The conference report passed 69–31 in the Senate and 328–91 in the House (with 12 not voting). *Congressional Record*, 104th Congress, 2nd Session (March 27, 1996), 6568–69; *Congressional Record*, 104th Congress, 2nd Session (March 28, 1996), 6940.

120. *Congressional Record*, 104th Congress, 2nd Session (March 27, 1996), 6504.

121. *Line-Item Veto*, Joint Hearing, 45.

122. *Clinton v. City of New York*, 524 U.S. 417, 438–39 (1998) (Stevens, J., opinion of the Court).

123. Robert Pear, "Spending at Issue," *New York Times*, June 26, 1998, A1, A16.

124. *Line-Item Veto Constitutional Issues*, Hearing before the Committee on the Budget, House of Representatives, 109th Congress, 2nd Session (Washington, DC: Government Printing Office, 2006).

125. Sarah Ferris and Jennifer Scholtes, "Trump Scales Back Request for Stiff Budget Cuts," *Politico*, February 11, 2018, https://www.politico.com/story/2018/02/11/trump-budget-cuts-domestic-programs-403636.

126. "Congress is not doing its constitutionally required job of controlling the purse strings of the federal government." James A. Thurber, "The Dynamics and Dysfunction of the Congressional Budget Process: From Inception to Deadlock," in *Congress Reconsidered*, 10th ed., ed. Lawrence C. Dodd and Bruce I. Oppenheimer (Thousand Oaks, CA: CQ Press, 2012), 319–45, at 319.

Chapter Eight

1. *Congressional Record*, 95th Congress, 2nd Session (October 13, 1978), 36737.

2. Kevin M. Kruse and Julian E. Zelizer, *Fault Lines: A History of the United States since 1974* (New York: W. W. Norton, 2019), 26–34.

3. Jonas Prager, "The Fed Wasn't Always Independent," *New York Times*, October 30, 1977, 134.

4. Louis Fisher, *Constitutional Conflicts between Congress and the President*, 4th ed. (Lawrence: University Press of Kansas, 1997), 92. See also Susan Ariel Aaronson, "Who Decides? Congress and the Debate over Trade Policy in 1934 and 1974," Council on Foreign Relations,

November 17, 1999, https://www.cfr.org/report/who-decides-congress-and-debate-over-trade
-policy-1934-and-1974.

5. Trade Act of 1974 (P.L. 93-618, 88 Stat. 1978, January 3, 1975).

6. Douglas A. Irwin, *Clashing over Commerce: A History of US Trade Policy* (Chicago: University of Chicago Press, 2017), 549–55, quoted at 554.

7. Full Employment and Balanced Growth Act of 1978 (P.L. 95-523, 92 Stat. 1887, October 27, 1978).

8. For an argument against conceiving of the law as insignificant, see Patrick Andelic, "'The Old Economic Rules No Longer Apply': The National Planning Idea and the Humphrey-Hawkins Full Employment Act, 1974–1978," *Journal of Policy History* 31, no. 1 (January 2019): 72–100.

9. Allan H. Meltzer, *A History of the Federal Reserve*, vol. 2, book 2, *1970–1986* (Chicago: University of Chicago Press, 2009), 985–92; Sarah Binder and Mark Spindel, *The Myth of Independence: How Congress Governs the Federal Reserve* (Princeton, NJ: Princeton University Press, 2017), ch. 6; Patrick O'Brien, "Maximizing Control: First-Year Presidents and the Appointment and Agenda-Setting Powers," in *Crucible: The President's First Year*, ed. Michael Nelson, Jeffrey L. Chidester, and Stefanie Georgakis Abbott (Charlottesville: University of Virginia Press, 2018), 250–55, at 250.

10. The House passed its version of trade reform, containing a legislative veto, 272–140 (with 20 not voting). *Congressional Record*, 93rd Congress, 1st Session (December 11, 1973), 40813. The Senate bill, devising the fast-track process, passed 77–4 (with 19 not voting). *Congressional Record*, 93rd Congress, 2nd Session (December 13, 1974), 39858. The conference report passed the Senate 72–4 (with 23 not voting) and passed the House 323–36 (with 75 not voting). *Congressional Record*, 93rd Congress, 2nd Session (December 20, 1974), 41652, 41807.

11. The House bill passed 257–152 (with 25 not voting). *Congressional Record*, 95th Congress, 2nd Session (March 16, 1978), 7345. The Senate bill passed 70–19 (with 11 not voting). *Congressional Record*, 95th Congress, 2nd Session (October 13, 1978), 36808. The House then assented to the Senate amendments to the legislation. *Congressional Record*, 95th Congress, 2nd Session (October 14, 1978), 38609.

12. For another perspective on the relationship between ideas and institutions in trade policy, see Judith Goldstein, "Ideas, Institutions, and American Trade Policy," *International Organization* 42, no. 1 (Winter 1988): 179–217.

13. Testimony of the Executive Director of the Council on International Economic Policy, Peter Flanigan. *The Trade Reform Act of 1973*, Hearings before the Committee on Finance, United States Senate, 93rd Congress, 2nd Session, Part 1 (Washington, DC: Government Printing Office, 1974), 170.

14. *Full Employment and Balanced Growth Act, Part 2*, Hearings before the Subcommittee on Employment Opportunities of the Committee on Education and Labor, House of Representatives, 95th Congress, 2nd Session (Washington, DC: Government Printing Office, 1978), 200.

15. Brendan Jones, "US Trade Policy Faces an Airing in Congress," *New York Times*, July 5, 1973, 43, 45.

16. Robert C. Toth, "Nixon Asks Trade Negotiating Powers," *Los Angeles Times*, April 11, 1973, 1, 22.

17. *Trade Reform*, Hearings before the Committee on Ways and Means, House of Representatives, 93rd Congress, 1st Session, Part 2 of 15 (Washington, DC: Government Printing Office, 1973), 356.

18. "Agnew Asks Broad Presidential Powers for Foreign Trade," *Chicago Tribune*, June 13, 1973, C9.

19. *Trade Reform*, Hearings before the Committee on Ways and Means, House of Representatives, 93rd Congress, 1st Session, Part 3 of 15 (Washington, DC: Government Printing Office, 1973), 938.

20. *The Trade Reform Act of 1973*, Hearings before the Committee on Finance, United States Senate, 93rd Congress, 2nd Session, Part 5 (Washington, DC: Government Printing Office, 1974), 1881.

21. *Trade Reform*, Hearings before the Committee on Ways and Means, House of Representatives, 93rd Congress, 1st Session, Part 10 of 15 (Washington, DC: Government Printing Office, 1973), 3162.

22. *Congressional Record*, 93rd Congress, 1st Session (December 11, 1973), 40807.

23. *The Trade Reform Act of 1973*, Hearings before the Committee on Finance, United States Senate, 93rd Congress, 2nd Session, Part 4 (Washington, DC: Government Printing Office, 1974), 1676.

24. *Trade Reform*, Hearings before the Committee on Ways and Means, House of Representatives, 93rd Congress, 1st Session, Part 7 of 15 (Washington, DC: Government Printing Office, 1973), 2050.

25. *Congressional Record*, 93rd Congress, 1st Session (December 11, 1973), 40777.

26. Under Section 301, a US exporter could petition the US trade representative for an investigation into discriminatory foreign trading practices. If no negotiated settlement were reached, the president could raise tariffs as a reprisal. Irwin, *Clashing over Commerce*, 554.

27. *Trade Reform*, Hearings before the Committee on Ways and Means, House of Representatives, 93rd Congress, 1st Session, Part 5 of 15 (Washington, DC: Government Printing Office, 1973), 1533.

28. *Trade Reform*, Hearings before the Committee on Ways and Means, House of Representatives, 93rd Congress, 1st Session, Part 4 of 15 (Washington, DC: Government Printing Office, 1973), 1166.

29. "The President and Trade Power," *Christian Science Monitor*, April 12, 1973, 22.

30. "Vital Trade Reform," *New York Times*, December 9, 1974, 34.

31. *Congressional Record*, 93rd Congress, 1st Session (December 11, 1973), 40783.

32. *Trade Reform Act of 1973*, Hearings before the Committee on Finance, Part 1, 246.

33. *The Trade Reform Act of 1973*, Hearings before the Committee on Finance, United States Senate, 93rd Congress, 2nd Session, Part 3 (Washington, DC: Government Printing Office, 1974), 743.

34. *Congressional Record*, 93rd Congress, 1st Session (December 11, 1973), 40774–76.

35. *Trade Reform*, Hearings before the Committee on Ways and Means, Part 2, 344, 346.

36. *Trade Reform*, 385.

37. *Trade Reform*, Hearings before the Committee on Ways and Means, House of Representatives, 93rd Congress, 1st Session, Part 14 of 15 (Washington, DC: Government Printing Office, 1973), 5157.

38. *Trade Reform*, Hearings before the Committee on Ways and Means, House of Representatives, 93rd Congress, 1st Session, Part 1 of 15 (Washington, DC: Government Printing Office, 1973), 189.

39. Opinion Ballot Letter from W. B. Thompson to Carl Albert, 1973, Folder 11, Box 176,

Series 7, Carl Albert Collection, Carl Albert Congressional Center and Political Collections, University of Oklahoma, Norman.

40. Opinion Ballot Letter from Earl A. Haggard to Carl Albert, 1973, Folder 11, Box 176, Series 7, Albert Collection.

41. *Trade Reform*, Hearings before the Committee on Ways and Means, House of Representatives, 93rd Congress, 1st Session, Part 13 of 15 (Washington, DC: Government Printing Office, 1973), 4355.

42. *Congressional Record*, 93rd Congress, 1st Session (December 11, 1973), 40781.

43. *Congressional Record*, 1st Session (December 11, 1973), 40769.

44. *Trade Reform*, Hearings before the Committee on Ways and Means, Part 3, 919.

45. *Congressional Record*, 93rd Congress, 1st Session (December 11, 1973), 40782.

46. *Congressional Record*, 93rd Congress, 1st Session (December 11, 1973), 40804.

47. *Congressional Record*, 93rd Congress, 2nd Session (December 13, 1974), 39758.

48. Irwin, *Clashing over Commerce*, 540.

49. *Trade Reform*, Hearings before the Committee on Ways and Means, Part 4, 1255, 1225, 1230–31, 1244.

50. *Trade Reform Act of 1973*, Hearings before the Committee on Finance, Part 3, 986.

51. *Trade Reform*, Hearings before the Committee on Ways and Means, House of Representatives, 93rd Congress, 1st Session, Part 6 of 15 (Washington, DC: Government Printing Office, 1973), 1894.

52. *Congressional Record*, 93rd Congress, 2nd Session (December 20, 1974), 41637.

53. Irwin, *Clashing over Commerce*, 551.

54. *Congressional Record*, 93rd Congress, 2nd Session (December 13, 1974), 39755.

55. *Congressional Record*, 93rd Congress, 2nd Session (December 20, 1974), 41641.

56. "Trade Bill Gets Preliminary Okay by Panel," *Austin American Statesman*, September 23, 1974, 6.

57. "Amendments May Drag Down Broad Foreign Trade Bill," *Hartford Courant*, November 21, 1974, 1.

58. "Trade Bill Moves toward Approval," *New York Times*, December 20, 1974, 55, 57.

59. *Trade Reform*, Hearings before the Committee on Ways and Means, Part 2, 344.

60. *Trade Reform*, Hearings before the Committee on Ways and Means, Part 1, 184.

61. *Congressional Record*, 93rd Congress, 2nd Session (December 13, 1974), 39755.

62. *Congressional Record*, 93rd Congress, 1st Session (December 11, 1973), 40786.

63. "Full Employment . . . ," *New York Times*, March 19, 1976, 31.

64. Andelic, "'Old Economic Rules No Longer Apply.'"

65. Iwan Morgan, *The Age of Deficits: Presidents and Unbalanced Budgets from Jimmy Carter to George W. Bush* (Lawrence: University of Kansas Press, 2009), 69.

66. Binder and Spindel, *Myth of Independence*, 23.

67. Binder and Spindel, 171–72. See also O'Brien, "Maximizing Control," 250–51.

68. *Full Employment and Balanced Growth Act of 1978*, Joint Hearing before the Committee on Human Resources and the Committee on Banking, Housing, and Urban Affairs, United States Senate, 95th Congress, 2nd Session, Part 1 (Washington, DC: Government Printing Office, 1978), 160.

69. *Full Employment and Balanced Growth Act, Part 2*, Hearings, 211.

70. *Full Employment and Balanced Growth Act, Part 1*, Hearings before the Subcommittee on

Employment Opportunities of the Committee on Education and Labor, House of Representatives, 95th Congress, 2nd Session (Washington, DC: Government Printing Office, 1978), 2.

71. Letter from Leon H. Keyserling to Murray H. Finley, March 21, 1977, 1, Folder "Dr. Keyserling," Box 83, Augustus F. Hawkins Papers, Manuscripts Division, Department of Special Collections, UCLA Library, Los Angeles, CA.

72. Letter from Leon H. Keyserling to Leon Shull, March 21, 1977, 4, Folder "Dr. Keyserling," Box 83, Hawkins Papers.

73. AFL-CIO Press Release, "Text of an Address by AFL-CIO Secretary-Treasurer Lane Kirkland at a Labor Education Advancement Program Meeting of the National Urban League at the Four Ambassadors Hotel, Miami Beach Florida," May 13, 1976, 4, Folder "Organizational Endorsers," Box 35, Hawkins Papers.

74. "Goals for Full Employment and How to Achieve Them under the 'Full Employment and Balanced Growth Act of 1978' (S. 50 and H.R. 50)," A Clarification of the Basic Issues by Senator Muriel Humphrey and Representative Augustus F. Hawkins, February 1978, 59, Box 82, Hawkins Papers.

75. *Full Employment and Balanced Growth Act, Part 1*, Hearings, 84.

76. *Congressional Record*, 95th Congress, 2nd Session (October 14, 1978), 38606.

77. *Congressional Record*, 95th Congress, 2nd Session (October 13, 1978), 36476.

78. Paul Lewis, "The Federal Reserve, and How It Grew," *New York Times*, March 13, 1977, 155.

79. Prager, "Fed Wasn't Always Independent."

80. Augustus F. Hawkins, Dear Colleague Letter, July 23, 1976, Folder "Dear Colleague, H.R. 50, 7/23/76," Box 35, Hawkins Papers.

81. Jimmy Carter, "An Economic Position Paper for Now and Tomorrow," April 22, 1976, in *The Presidential Campaign 1976*, vol. 1, part 1, *Jimmy Carter* (Washington, DC: Government Printing Office, 1978), 141–48, at 145.

82. Federal Reserve Reform Act of 1977 (P.L. 95-188, 91 Stat. 1387, November 16, 1977); Binder and Spindel, *Myth of Independence*, 182–85.

83. *Congressional Record*, 95th Congress, 1st Session (November 1, 1977), 36203.

84. *Congressional Record*, 95th Congress, 1st Session (November 1, 1977), 36204.

85. *Congressional Record*, 95th Congress, 1st Session (November 1, 1977), 36203.

86. *Congressional Record*, 95th Congress, 1st Session (November 1, 1977), 36203; Binder and Spindel, *Myth of Independence*, 185.

87. Binder and Spindel, *Myth of Independence*, 149.

88. *Full Employment and Balanced Growth Act, Part 1*, Hearings, 48.

89. *Congressional Record*, 95th Congress, 2nd Session (October 10, 1978), 35359.

90. *Congressional Record*, 95th Congress, 2nd Session (March 8, 1978), 6103.

91. "Goals for Full Employment and How to Achieve Them under the 'Full Employment and Balanced Growth Act of 1978' (S. 50 and H.R. 50)," Clarification, 52.

92. *Full Employment and Balanced Growth Act of 1976*, Hearings before the Subcommittee on Manpower, Compensation, and Health and Safety of the Committee on Education and Labor, House of Representatives, 94th Congress, 2nd Session (Washington, DC: Government Printing Office, 1976), 205.

93. *Full Employment and Balanced Growth Act of 1976*, 216.

94. *Full Employment and Balanced Growth Act, Part 1*, Hearings, 88, 109.

95. Meltzer, *History of the Federal Reserve*, vol. 2, book 2, 989–90.

96. *Congressional Record*, 95th Congress, 2nd Session (October 13, 1978), 38607.

97. *Congressional Record*, 95th Congress, 2nd Session (October 10, 1978), 35364.

98. "What Does the Bill Do about the Federal Reserve Board?," undated, "Fact Sheets" section of "Humphrey-Hawkins Notebook," Box 103, Hawkins Papers.

99. *Full Employment and Balanced Growth Act of 1978*, Joint Hearing, 157.

100. "Coalition Voices Objection against Proxmire Amendment to Humphrey Hawkins Full Employment Bill," Press Release, June 5, 1978, 1, Folder "Press Release, January Thru June, 1978," Box 60, Hawkins Papers.

101. "Confidential Notes on Issues Related to Inflation Targets," February 2, 1978, Folder "Inflation Arguments," Box 83, Hawkins Papers.

102. Binder and Spindel, *Myth of Independence*, 178.

103. *Congressional Record*, 95th Congress, 2nd Session (October 10, 1978), 35359.

104. *Congressional Record*, 95th Congress, 2nd Session (October 10, 1978), 35362.

105. *Congressional Record*, 95th Congress, 2nd Session (October 10, 1978), 35361.

106. Humphrey's amendment to not specify an inflation target was defeated 41–45 (with 12 not voting). *Congressional Record*, 95th Congress, 2nd Session (October 13, 1978), 36785.

107. *Congressional Record*, 95th Congress, 2nd Session (October 14, 1978), 38608.

108. *Full Employment and Balanced Growth Act of 1976*, Hearings, 403.

109. *Congressional Record*, 95th Congress, 2nd Session (October 10, 1978), 35359.

110. *Full Employment and Balanced Growth Act of 1978*, Hearings before the Committee on Banking, Housing, and Urban Affairs, United States Senate, 95th Congress, 2nd Session (Washington, DC: Government Printing Office, 1978), 168.

111. Aaron Wildavsky, "The Two Presidencies," *Trans-Action* 4 (December 1966): 7–14; Brandice Canes-Wrone, William G. Howell, and David E. Lewis, "Toward a Broader Understanding of Presidential Power: A Reevaluation of the Two Presidencies Thesis," *Journal of Politics* 70, no. 1 (January 2008): 1–16.

112. Richard Franklin Bensel, *The Political Economy of American Industrialization, 1877–1900* (New York: Cambridge University Press, 2000), ch. 7.

113. *Full Employment and Balanced Growth Act, Part 1*, Hearings, 85.

114. David Naveh, "The Political Role of Academic Advisers: The Case of the US President's Council of Economic Advisers, 1946–1976," *Presidential Studies Quarterly* 11, no. 4 (Fall 1981): 492–510, at 492.

115. Quoted in Binder and Spindel, *Myth of Independence*, 199.

116. Richard S. Conley, "Derailing Presidential Fast-Track Authority: The Impact of Constituency Pressures and Political Ideology on Trade Policy in Congress," *Political Research Quarterly* 52, no. 4 (December 1999): 785–99.

117. Irwin, *Clashing over Commerce*, 690. See also Brandon Rottinghaus and Elvin Lim, "Proclaiming Trade Policy: 'Delegated Unilateral Powers' and the Limits on Presidential Unilateral Enactment of Trade Policy," *American Politics Research* 37, no. 6 (November 2009): 1003–23.

118. Lawrence R. Jacobs and Desmond King, *Fed Power: How Finance Wins* (New York: Oxford University Press, 2016).

119. Irwin, *Clashing over Commerce*, 625–44.

120. Quoted in O'Brien, "Maximizing Control," 251.

121. Meltzer, *History of the Federal Reserve*, vol. 2, book 2, 1243–56.

122. Irwin, *Clashing over Commerce*, 690.

123. @realDonaldTrump, July 5, 2017, 7:14 a.m., Twitter, https://twitter.com/realDonald Trump/status/882558219285131265.

124. Peter Baker, "Trump Abandons Trans-Pacific Partnership, Obama's Signature Trade Deal," *New York Times*, January 23, 2017, https://www.nytimes.com/2017/01/23/us/politics/tpp -trump-trade-nafta.html; Adam Behsudi, Alexander Panetta, and Doug Palmer, "US Reaches Trade Deal with Canada and Mexico, Providing Trump a Crucial Win," *Politico*, September 30, 2018, https://www.politico.com/story/2018/09/30/nafta-trade-canada-819081.

125. Ana Swanson, "White House to Impose Metal Tariffs on E.U., Canada and Mexico," *New York Times*, May 31, 2018, https://www.nytimes.com/2018/05/31/us/politics/trump -aluminum-steel-tariffs.html; Ben White, Nancy Cook, Andrew Restuccia, and Doug Palmer, "Trump's Trade War Was Decades in the Making," *Politico*, July 9, 2018, https://www.politico .com/story/2018/07/09/trump-trade-war-china-tariffs-702292.

126. Jonathan Swan, "Exclusive: Trump Vents in Oval Office, 'I Want Tariffs. Bring Me Some Tariffs!," *Axios*, August 27, 2017, https://www.axios.com/exclusive-trump-vents-in-oval-office -i-want-tariffs-bring-me-some-tariffs-1513305111-5cba21a2-6438-429a-9377-30f6c4cf2e9e .html.

127. Ben White, "'The President Clearly Set Himself Up': Trump's Stock Market Miscalculation," *Politico*, February 5, 2018, https://www.politico.com/story/2018/02/05/trump-stock -market-down-324880.

128. On Trump's frustration with the Federal Reserve, see Stephen Skowronek, John A. Dearborn, and Desmond King, *Phantoms of a Beleaguered Republic: The Deep State and the Unitary Executive* (New York: Oxford University Press, 2021), 160–64.

129. Victoria Guida, "Trump: Fed Is 'Biggest Risk' to US Economy," *Politico*, October 23, 2018, https://www.politico.com/story/2018/10/23/trump-fed-biggest-risk-economy-884242; Matt Egan, "Why Jerome Powell's Quiet Show of Defiance against Trump and Wall Street Is So Important," *CNN Business*, December 20, 2018, https://www.cnn.com/2018/12/20/business/ powell-fed-trump-markets/index.html.

130. "Full Transcript: Fed Chair Jerome Powell's 60 Minutes Interview on Economic Recovery from the Coronavirus Pandemic," *CBS News*, May 17, 2020, https://www.cbsnews.com/ news/full-transcript-fed-chair-jerome-powell-60-minutes-interview-economic-recovery-from -coronavirus-pandemic/.

Chapter Nine

1. *Congressional Record*, 95th Congress, 1st Session (March 3, 1977), 6151.

2. Congress had changed the form of reorganization authority even when renewing it— switching from a two-chamber to a one-chamber legislative veto (1949) and forbidding the president from creating new departments (an authority granted by the 1949 act) (1964). Louis Fisher and Ronald C. Moe, "Presidential Reorganization Authority: Is It Worth the Cost?," *Political Science Quarterly* 96, no. 2 (Summer 1981): 301–18, at 311–12.

3. Henry B. Hogue, "Presidential Reorganization Authority: History, Recent Initiatives, and Options for Congress," Report R42852, *Congressional Research Service*, December 11, 2012, 25–26.

4. Peri E. Arnold, *Making the Managerial Presidency: Comprehensive Reorganization Planning, 1905–1996*, 2nd ed. (Lawrence: University Press of Kansas, 1998), ch. 10.

5. Quoted in Martin Tolchin, "Grappling with the Monster of Bureaucracy," *New York Times*, July 23, 1978, E2.

6. Quoted in Arnold, *Making the Managerial Presidency*, 303.

7. David E. Rosenbaum, "Congress May Give Carter Power to Reorganize but Balk at Its Use," *New York Times*, January 31, 1977, 12.

8. Reorganization Act of 1977 (P.L. 95-17, 91 Stat. 29, April 6, 1977).

9. Additionally, the law did not allow the president to create or abolish cabinet departments or statutory functions but did allow the president to "propose plans to abolish, transfer, consolidate or modify existing bodies within departments and agencies." Charles Mohr, "President Signs Bill to Permit Government Reorganization: First Effort Will Be His Own Office," *New York Times*, April 7, 1977, 17. See also Fisher and Moe, "Presidential Reorganization Authority," 311–12; Hogue, "Presidential Reorganization Authority," 28.

10. Hogue, "Presidential Reorganization Authority," 28.

11. Jimmy Carter, "Federal Civil Service Reorganization Message to the Congress Transmitting Reorganization Plan No. 2 of 1978," May 23, 1978, *The American Presidency Project*, https://www.presidency.ucsb.edu/documents/federal-civil-service-reorganization-message-the-congress-transmitting-reorganization-plan; Civil Service Reform Act of 1978 (P.L. 95-454, 92 Stat. 1111, October 13, 1978).

12. Hogue, "Presidential Reorganization Authority," 30–31.

13. The Senate bill passed 94–0 (with 6 not voting). *Congressional Record*, 95th Congress, 1st Session (March 3, 1977), 6153. The House bill passed 395–22 (with 15 not voting). *Congressional Record*, 95th Congress, 1st Session (March 29, 1977), 9366. The Senate voted to concur with the House bill and its amendments and agreed to the bill without a recorded vote. *Congressional Record*, 95th Congress, 1st Session (March 31, 1977), 9773.

14. *To Renew the Reorganization Authority*, Hearing before the Committee on Government Operations, United States Senate, 95th Congress, 1st Session (Washington, DC: Government Printing Office, 1977), 28.

15. *To Renew the Reorganization Authority*, 1.

16. *To Renew the Reorganization Authority*, 2.

17. Jimmy Carter, "Reorganization Plan Authority Message to the Congress Transmitting Proposed Legislation," February 4, 1977, *The American Presidency Project*, https://www.presidency.ucsb.edu/documents/reorganization-plan-authority-message-the-congress-transmitting-proposed-legislation.

18. *To Renew the Reorganization Authority*, Hearing, 2.

19. *To Renew the Reorganization Authority*, 4.

20. *To Renew the Reorganization Authority*, 2.

21. *To Renew the Reorganization Authority*, 1–2.

22. *To Renew the Reorganization Authority*, 5.

23. "Brooks Enters Reorganization Bill," *Galveston Daily News*, February 5, 1977, 1-A.

24. *Congressional Record*, 95th Congress, 1st Session (March 29, 1977), 9350.

25. *Congressional Record*, 95th Congress, 1st Session (March 29, 1977), 9344.

26. Quoted in David E. Rosenbaum, "Rep. Brooks Assails Reorganization Plan," *New York Times*, March 2, 1977, 22.

27. *To Renew the Reorganization Authority*, Hearing, 44.

28. *Congressional Record*, 95th Congress, 1st Session (March 3, 1977), 6145.

29. *To Renew the Reorganization Authority*, Hearing, 37.

30. Fisher and Moe, "Presidential Reorganization Authority," 312.

31. Jimmy Carter, "Reorganization Plan Authority Letter to the Speaker of the House and

the President of the Senate," February 4, 1977, *The American Presidency Project*, https://www
.presidency.ucsb.edu /documents /reorganization-plan-authority-letter-the-speaker-the-house
-and-the-president-the-senate.

32. *To Renew the Reorganization Authority*, Hearing, 20.

33. *Congressional Record*, 95th Congress, 1st Session (March 3, 1977), 6146.

34. *Congressional Record*, 95th Congress, 1st Session (March 29, 1977), 9344.

35. Letter from Edmund S. Muskie to Paul H. Enman, March 25, 1977, Folder 2, Box 2107,
Subseries A11, Series V, Edmund S. Muskie Papers, Edmund S. Muskie Archives and Special
Collections Library, Bates College, Lewiston, ME.

36. Letter from Griffin B. Bell, Attorney General, to President Jimmy Carter, January 31,
1977, quoted in *To Renew the Reorganization Authority*, Hearing, 11.

37. *To Renew the Reorganization Authority*, 13.

38. *To Renew the Reorganization Authority*, 4–5.

39. *Congressional Record*, 95th Congress, 1st Session (March 29, 1977), 9330.

40. *Congressional Record*, 95th Congress, 1st Session (March 29, 1977), 9350.

41. *Congressional Record*, 95th Congress, 1st Session (March 29, 1977), 9344.

42. *To Renew the Reorganization Authority*, Hearing, 41, 44–46.

43. Rosenbaum, "Congress May Give Carter Power to Reorganize but Balk at Its Use," 12.

44. David E. Rosenbaum, "A Fashionable but Troubling Device: Veto by Congress," *New
York Times*, February 27, 1977, 135.

45. Martin Tolchin, "Hoover Was First to Let Congress Veto President," *New York Times*,
June 24, 1983, B4.

46. *Congressional Record*, 95th Congress, 1st Session (March 29, 1977), 9346.

47. Lena Williams, "Faces behind Famous Cases," *New York Times*, June 19, 1985, C1; Jessica
Korn, *The Power of Separation: American Constitutionalism and the Myth of the Legislative Veto*
(Princeton, NJ: Princeton University Press, 1996), ch. 3.

48. *Immigration and Naturalization Service v. Chadha* 462 U.S. 919, 947 (1983) (Burger, C. J.,
opinion of the Court).

49. *Immigration and Naturalization Service v. Chadha* 462 U.S. 919, 959–60 (1983) (Powell, J., concurring).

50. *Immigration and Naturalization Service v. Chadha* 462 U.S. 919, 972, 1002 (1983) (White,
J., dissenting). See also E. Donald Elliott, "INS v. Chadha: The Administrative Constitution, the
Constitution, and the Legislative Veto," *Supreme Court Review* (1983): 125–76.

51. Arnold, *Making the Managerial Presidency*, 302.

52. *To Renew the Reorganization Authority*, Hearing, 4.

53. *Legislative Veto after Chadha*, Hearings before the Committee on Rules, House of Representatives, 98th Congress, 2nd Session (Washington, DC: Government Printing Office, 1984), 643.

54. Hogue, "Presidential Reorganization Authority," 4.

55. Fisher and Moe, "Presidential Reorganization Authority," 301, 310.

56. *Legislative Veto after Chadha*, Hearings, 647. See also James G. March and Johan P.
Olson, "Organizing Political Life: What Administrative Reorganization Tells Us about Government," *American Political Science Review* 77, no. 2 (June 1983): 281–96.

57. *To Renew the Reorganization Authority*, Hearing, 44.

58. Hogue, "Presidential Reorganization Authority," 30–31.

59. Korn, *Power of Separation*, ch. 3.

60. *Legislative Veto after Chadha*, Hearings, 311.

61. *Legislative Veto after Chadha*, 8.

62. *Legislative Veto after Chadha*, 10.

63. *Legislative Veto after Chadha*, 32.

64. Richard B. Smith and Guy M. Struve, "Aftershocks of the Fall of the Legislative Veto," *American Bar Association Journal* 69, no. 9 (September 1983): 1258–62.

65. *Legislative Veto after Chadha*, Hearings, 314.

66. *Ratification of Reorganization Plans*, Hearing before a Subcommittee of the Committee on Government Operations, House of Representatives, 98th Congress, 2nd Session (Washington, DC: Government Printing Office, 1985 [1984]), 27, chart 2.

67. *Congressional Record*, 98th Congress, 2nd Session (October 1, 1984), 28059–60.

68. P.L. 98-532; 98 Stat. 2705; *Congressional Record*, 98th Congress, 2nd Session (October 1, 1984), 28059; Hogue, "Presidential Reorganization Authority," 31.

69. *Ratification of Reorganization Plans*, Hearing, 27, chart 2. For example, ratifying Reorganization Plan No. 2 of 1953 meant that the secretary of agriculture retained authority for reorganizations within the Department of Agriculture. Dwight D. Eisenhower, "Special Message to the Congress Transmitting Reorganization Plan 2 of 1953 concerning the Department of Agriculture," March 25, 1953, *The American Presidency Project*, https://www.presidency.ucsb.edu/documents/special-message-the-congress-transmitting-reorganization-plan-2-1953-concerning-the.

70. Stephen Skowronek, "The Conservative Insurgency and Presidential Power: A Developmental Perspective on the Unitary Executive," *Harvard Law Review* 122, no. 8 (June 2009): 2070–103.

71. William French Smith, "Congress: No Loss in Ruling by Court," *New York Times*, July 12, 1983, A21.

72. Steven G. Calabresi and Christopher S. Yoo, *The Unitary Executive: Presidential Power from Washington to Bush* (New Haven, CT: Yale University Press, 2008).

73. Jack Schafer, "The Three Lame Stories the Press Writes about Every President," *Politico Magazine*, March 27, 2017, http://www.politico.com/magazine/story/2017/03/the-three-lame-stories-the-press-writes-about-every-president-214960.

74. On occasion, Congress delegated specific reorganization authority to department secretaries for use within individual departments. One case was in the Homeland Security Act of 2002, creating the Department of Homeland Security. Henry B. Hogue, "Executive Branch Reorganization," Report R44909, *Congressional Research Service*, August 3, 2017, 8.

75. *Fiscal Year 2003*, Budget of the US Government (Washington, DC: Government Printing Office, 2002), 52.

76. Barack Obama, "Remarks on Government Reform," January 13, 2012, *The American Presidency Project*, https://www.presidency.ucsb.edu/documents/remarks-government-reform.

77. Donald J. Trump, "Remarks on Signing an Executive Order on a Comprehensive Plan for Reorganizing the Executive Branch," March 13, 2017, *The American Presidency Project*, https://www.presidency.ucsb.edu/documents/remarks-signing-executive-order-comprehensive-plan-for-reorganizing-the-executive-branch.

Chapter Ten

1. *War Powers*, Hearings before the Subcommittee on National Security Policy and Scientific Developments of the Committee on Foreign Affairs, House of Representatives, 93rd Congress, 1st Session (Washington, DC: Government Printing Office, 1973), 7.

2. Letter from Robert J. Goetz to Carl Albert, January 1966, Folder 89, Box 89, Series 7, Carl Albert Collection, Carl Albert Congressional Center and Political Collections, University of Oklahoma, Norman.

3. Letter from Carl Albert to Robert J. Goetz, January 22, 1966, Folder 89, Box 89, Series 7, Albert Collection.

4. James L. Sundquist, *The Decline and Resurgence of Congress* (Washington, DC: Brookings Institution, 1981), 238.

5. Keith E. Whittington, *Constitutional Construction: Divided Power and Constitutional Meaning* (Cambridge, MA: Harvard University Press, 1999), 176. See also Louis Fisher, *Presidential War Power*, 3rd ed. (Lawrence: University Press of Kansas, 2013), ch. 6; Mariah Zeisberg, *War Powers: The Politics of Constitutional Authority* (Princeton, NJ: Princeton University Press, 2013).

6. The House version passed 244–170 (with 19 not voting). *Congressional Record*, 93rd Congress, 1st Session (July 18, 1973), 24707. The Senate version passed 72–18 (with 10 not voting). *Congressional Record*, 93rd Congress, 1st Session (July 20, 1973), 25119. The Senate passed the conference report 75–20 (with 5 not voting). *Congressional Record*, 93rd Congress, 1st Session (October 10, 1973), 33569. The House passed the conference report 238–123 (with 73 not voting). *Congressional Record*, 93rd Congress, 1st Session (October 12, 1973), 33873–74. When President Nixon vetoed that report, the House had been three votes short of the required two-thirds majority necessary for a veto override. Richard L. Madden, "Nixon Vetoes a Bill to Cut War Power of the Presidency," *New York Times*, October 25, 1973, 1, 5. Obtaining the necessary two-thirds majority, the House successfully overrode Nixon's veto 284–135 (with 14 not voting), and the Senate overrode the veto 75–18 (with 7 not voting). *Congressional Record*, 93rd Congress, 1st Session (November 7, 1973), 36221–22, 36198.

7. *War Powers*, Hearings, 11–12.

8. "80% in Poll Back War-Powers Curb," *New York Times*, November 18, 1973, 8.

9. *Congressional Record*, 93rd Congress, 1st Session (November 7, 1973), 36205.

10. *War Powers*, Hearings, 98.

11. Arthur Schlesinger Jr., "Presidential War: 'See If You Can Fix Any Limit to His Power,'" *New York Times*, January 7, 1973, 310–11, 324, 326, 328, 330. As early as 1966, Senator J. William Fulbright (D-AR) held hearings questioning the Johnson administration over the Gulf of Tonkin Resolution. Sundquist, *Decline and Resurgence*, 241–45.

12. *War Powers*, Hearings, 30.

13. Sundquist, *Decline and Resurgence*, 107.

14. *Congressional Record*, 93rd Congress, 1st Session (November 7, 1973), 36206.

15. John W. Finney, "On the Big One, Congress Stood Up to Be Counted," *New York Times*, November 11, 1973, 228.

16. Sarah Burns, *The Politics of War Powers: The Theory and History of Presidential Unilateralism* (Lawrence: University Press of Kansas, 2019), 156–57, 179–80.

17. War Powers Resolution of 1973 (P.L. 93-148, 87 Stat. 555, November 7, 1973); Whittington, *Constitutional Construction*, 183–84.

18. Louis Fisher and David Gray Adler, "The War Powers Resolution: Time to Say Goodbye," *Political Science Quarterly* 113, no. 1 (Spring 1998): 1–20; Whittington, *Constitutional Construction*, 184.

19. P.L. 98-164, 97 Stat. 1062 § 1013 (November 22, 1983); Louis Fisher, "Legislative Vetoes after *Chadha*," Report RS22132, *Congressional Research Service*, May 2, 2005, 2.

20. Letter from Jacob K. Javits to Robert Dole, December 7, 1970, with enclosed lecture,

"Who Makes War?," Woodrow Wilson School of Public and International Affairs, Princeton University, December 8, 1970, 3, Folder 15, Box 632, Series 6, Robert J. Dole Senate Papers— Legislative Relations, 1969–96, Robert and Elizabeth Dole Archive and Special Collections, Robert J. Dole Institute of Politics, University of Kansas, Lawrence.

21. Sean Gailmard and John W. Patty, *Learning While Governing: Expertise and Accountability in the Executive Branch* (Chicago: University of Chicago Press, 2013), 215–21.

22. *Congressional Record*, 93rd Congress, 1st Session (July 20, 1973), 25090–91.

23. *War Powers*, Hearings, 155.

24. "State of the Congress—1974," February 1, 1974, 5, Folder 47, Box 49, Series XXI, Mike Mansfield Papers, Archives and Special Collections, Maureen and Mike Mansfield Library, University of Montana, Missoula.

25. Memo from Mike Mansfield to the President on the Viet Namese Situation, January 6, 1964, 3, Folder 6, Box 97, Series XXII, Mansfield Papers.

26. *Congressional Record*, 93rd Congress, 1st Session (July 20, 1973), 25109.

27. *War Powers*, Hearings, 9–10.

28. *Congressional Record*, 93rd Congress, 1st Session (November 7, 1973), 36187.

29. *Congressional Record*, 93rd Congress, 1st Session (November 7, 1973), 36203.

30. *Congressional Record*, 93rd Congress, 1st Session (July 20, 1973), 25105.

31. *Congressional Record*, 93rd Congress, 1st Session (July 18, 1973), 24549–50.

32. *Congressional Record*, 93rd Congress, 1st Session (July 18, 1973), 24667.

33. *Congressional Record*, 93rd Congress, 1st Session (November 7, 1973), 36194.

34. Letter from Edmund S. Muskie to Clifton R. Mahan, December 6, 1973, Folder 4, Box 1596, Subseries A9, Series V, Edmund S. Muskie Papers, Edmund S. Muskie Archives and Special Collections Library, Bates College, Lewiston, ME.

35. *Congressional Record*, 93rd Congress, 1st Session (November 7, 1973), 36194.

36. *Congressional Record*, 93rd Congress, 1st Session (November 7, 1973), 36205.

37. *Congressional Record*, 93rd Congress, 1st Session (November 7, 1973), 36187.

38. Whittington, *Constitutional Construction*, 178.

39. *Congressional Record*, 93rd Congress, 1st Session (July 20, 1973), 25112.

40. Letter from Harry A. Blachman to Carl Albert, April 12, 1972, Folder 13, Box 131, Series 7, Albert Collection.

41. *War Powers*, Hearings, 14–15.

42. *Congressional Record*, 93rd Congress, 1st Session (November 7, 1973), 36211.

43. *War Powers*, Hearings, 13.

44. *War Powers*, 31.

45. *War Powers*, 124, 123.

46. Letter from Edmund S. Muskie to Cindy Harrell, October 31, 1973, Folder 6, Box 1599, Subseries A9, Series V, Muskie Papers.

47. *War Powers*, Hearings, 211.

48. *War Powers Legislation, 1973*, Hearings before the Committee on Foreign Relations, United States Senate, 93rd Congress, 1st Session (Washington, DC: Government Printing Office, 1973), 7–8.

49. "National Goals and National Consensus," Pre-recorded speech before the Summer Cubberly Conference, Stanford University, July 28, 1961, 7–8, Folder 8, Box 20, Series 72, J. William Fulbright Papers, Special Collections, University of Arkansas Libraries, Fayetteville.

50. *War Powers Legislation, 1973*, Hearings, 1.

51. *War Powers Legislation, 1973*, 64.

52. Richard Nixon, "Veto of the War Powers Resolution," October 24, 1973, *The American Presidency Project*, https://www.presidency.ucsb.edu/documents/veto-the-war-powers-resolution.

53. *Congressional Record*, 93rd Congress, 1st Session (November 7, 1973), 36216.

54. *Congressional Record*, 93rd Congress, 1st Session (November 7, 1973), 36202.

55. *Congressional Record*, 93rd Congress, 1st Session (November 7, 1973), 36187.

56. Whittington, *Constitutional Construction*, 179.

57. *War Powers Legislation, 1973*, Hearings, 100; Whittington, *Constitutional Construction*, 181.

58. *Congressional Record*, 93rd Congress, 1st Session (November 7, 1973), 36210.

59. *Congressional Record*, 93rd Congress, 1st Session (November 7, 1973), 36179.

60. *Congressional Record*, 93rd Congress, 1st Session (November 7, 1973), 36195.

61. John Yoo, *The Powers of War and Peace: The Constitution and Foreign Affairs after 9/11* (Chicago: University of Chicago Press, 2005).

62. *War Powers*, Hearings, 143–44.

63. *Congressional Record*, 93rd Congress, 1st Session (October 12, 1973), 33865.

64. *War Powers*, Hearings, 296–97.

65. *Congressional Record*, 93rd Congress, 1st Session (October 10, 1973), 33550.

66. *War Powers*, Hearings, 171. Arthur Schlesinger Jr., *The Imperial Presidency* (Boston: Houghton Mifflin, 1973).

67. Paul C. Warnke, "The Dread Responsibility," *New York Times*, May 20, 1973, 223.

68. *War Powers*, Hearings, 5.

69. Letter from Thomas J. McIntyre to Frederick T. Ernst, June 21, 1972, Folder 3, Box 77B, Thomas J. McIntyre Papers, Milne Archives and Special Collections, University of New Hampshire, Durham.

70. *War Powers*, Hearings, 12.

71. *War Powers*, 21–22.

72. *Congressional Record*, 93rd Congress, 1st Session (October 10, 1973), 33548.

73. *Congressional Record*, 93rd Congress, 1st Session (November 7, 1973), 36193.

74. *Congressional Record*, 93rd Congress, 1st Session (November 7, 1973), 36188.

75. *Congressional Record*, 93rd Congress, 1st Session (October 12, 1973), 33861.

76. *Congressional Record*, 93rd Congress, 1st Session (November 7, 1973), 36190.

77. *Congressional Record*, 93rd Congress, 1st Session (November 7, 1973), 36195.

78. Fisher and Adler, "War Powers Resolution," 3.

79. *War Powers*, Hearings, 32–36; *Congressional Record*, 93rd Congress, 1st Session (November 7, 1973), 36177.

80. Sundquist, *Decline and Resurgence*, 258.

81. *War Powers*, Hearings, 115.

82. *Congressional Record*, 93rd Congress, 1st Session (October 12, 1973), 33859.

83. Whittington, *Constitutional Construction*, 184.

84. Finney, "On the Big One, Congress Stood Up to Be Counted," 228.

85. *War Powers*, Hearings, 5.

86. The amendment failed 166–250. Richard L. Madden, "House Passes Bill to Curb President's War Powers," *New York Times*, July 19, 1973, 1, 5.

87. *Congressional Record*, 93rd Congress, 1st Session (October 12, 1973), 33867.

88. *Congressional Record*, 93rd Congress, 1st Session (October 10, 1973), 33553.

89. *War Powers*, Hearings, 32–36; *Congressional Record*, 93rd Congress, 1st Session (November 7, 1973), 36177; Sundquist, *Decline and Resurgence*, 258.

90. Thomas F. Eagleton, "A Dangerous Law," *New York Times*, December 3, 1973, 39.

91. *Congressional Record*, 93rd Congress, 1st Session (November 7, 1973), 36214.

92. *Congressional Record*, 93rd Congress, 1st Session (November 7, 1973), 36196.

93. *Congressional Record*, 93rd Congress, 1st Session (October 12, 1973), 33870.

94. Elizabeth Holtzman, "The War Powers," *New York Times*, August 3, 1973, 31.

95. Richard L. Madden, "House and Senate Override Veto by Nixon on Curb of War Powers: Backers of Bill Win 3-Year Fight," *New York Times*, November 8, 1973, 1, 20.

96. *Congressional Record*, 93rd Congress, 1st Session (November 7, 1973), 36178.

97. Finney, "On the Big One, Congress Stood Up to Be Counted," 228.

98. Whittington, *Constitutional Construction*, 184.

99. Rebecca U. Thorpe, *The American Warfare State: The Domestic Politics of Military Spending* (Chicago: University of Chicago Press, 2014).

100. Whittington, *Constitutional Construction*, 185.

101. William G. Howell and Jon C. Pevehouse, *While Dangers Gather: Congressional Checks on Presidential War Powers* (Princeton, NJ: Princeton University Press, 2007).

102. Jack Goldsmith, *Power and Constraint: The Accountable Presidency after 9/11* (New York: W. W. Norton, 2012), ch. 7.

103. Fisher, *Presidential War Power*, ch. 7.

104. Fisher, 161–63. "Since Lebanon and Grenada, presidents have interpreted the War Powers Act as affirmative authorization to employ military force for at least sixty days without permission." Thorpe, *American Warfare State*, 140.

105. Fisher, *Presidential War Power*, 165–68.

106. Fisher, ch. 8.

107. Fisher, 168–73.

108. Andrew Rudalevige, *The New Imperial Presidency: Renewing Presidential Power after Watergate* (Ann Arbor: University of Michigan Press, 2005), chs. 7–8; Fisher, *Presidential War Power*, ch. 9.

109. Bruce Ackerman, "Legal Acrobatics, Illegal War," *New York* Times, June 20, 2011, https://www.nytimes.com/2011/06/21/opinion/21Ackerman.html; Fisher, *Presidential War Power*, ch. 10.

110. Gregory Korte, "Trump Lawyers: Syria Missile Strikes Were Legal Because They Weren't 'War,'" *USA Today*, June 1, 2018, https://www.usatoday.com/story/news/politics/2018/06/01/trump-administration-explains-legal-basis-syrian-missile-strikes/664439002/.

111. Catie Edmondson, "Failing to Override a Veto, Senate Falls Short of Curbing Trump's Iran War Powers," *New York Times*, May 7, 2020, https://www.nytimes.com/2020/05/07/us/politics/senate-war-powers-trump.html.

Chapter Eleven

1. Stephen Skowronek and Karen Orren, "The Adaptability Paradox: Constitutional Resilience and Principles of Good Government in Twenty-First-Century America," *Perspectives on Politics* 18, no. 2 (June 2020): 354–69.

2. J. William Fulbright, "The Legislator as Educator," *Foreign Affairs*, March 1, 1979, 719–32, at 727.

3. Steven G. Calabresi and Christopher S. Yoo, *The Unitary Executive: Presidential Power from Washington to Bush* (New Haven, CT: Yale University Press, 2008).

4. *Morrison v. Olson* 487 U.S. 654, 705 (1988) (Scalia, J., dissenting). Emphasis in original.

5. Stephen Skowronek, "The Conservative Insurgency and Presidential Power: A Developmental Perspective on the Unitary Executive," *Harvard Law Review* 122, no. 8 (June 2009): 2070–103.

6. Daphna Renan, "The President's Two Bodies," *Columbia Law Review* 120, no. 5 (June 2020): 1119–214, at 1209–10.

7. Steven M. Teles, *The Rise of the Conservative Legal Movement* (Princeton, NJ: Princeton University Press, 2008); Amanda Hollis-Brusky, *Ideas with Consequences: The Federalist Society and the Conservative Counterrevolution* (New York: Oxford University Press, 2015).

8. Memorandum from John Ehrlichman to Cap Weinberger, June 26, 1972, quoted in Andrew Rudalevige, *The New Imperial Presidency: Renewing Presidential Power after Watergate* (Ann Arbor: University of Michigan Press, 2005), 61.

9. Edwin Meese III, "Address of the Honorable Edwin Meese III, Attorney General of the United States, before the Federal Bar Association," September 13, 1985, US Department of Justice, 5, 9, 3, https://www.justice.gov/sites/default/files/ag/legacy/2011/08/23/09-13-1985.pdf.

10. Dick Cheney, "Congressional Overreaching in Foreign Policy," undelivered draft of speech prepared for March 14–15, 1989 American Enterprise Institute Conference, 37, posted by Charlie Savage, *New York Times,* at http://s3.documentcloud.org/documents/339579/congressional-overreaching-cheney.pdf.

11. Stephen Skowronek, John A. Dearborn, and Desmond King, *Phantoms of a Beleaguered Republic: The Deep State and the Unitary Executive* (New York: Oxford University Press, 2021), 34–35.

12. Peter M. Shane, *Madison's Nightmare: How Executive Power Threatens American Democracy* (Chicago: University of Chicago Press, 2009), ch. 6; Andrew Rudalevige, "Beyond Structure and Process: The Early Institutionalization of Regulatory Review," *Journal of Policy History* 30, no. 4 (2018): 577–608.

13. Elena Kagan, "Presidential Administration," *Harvard Law Review* 114, no. 8 (June 2001): 2245–385, at 2385.

14. Lawrence Lessig and Cass R. Sunstein, "The President and the Administration," *Columbia Law Review* 94, no. 1 (January 1994): 1–123.

15. Kagan, "Presidential Administration," 2335.

16. Steven G. Calabresi, "Some Normative Arguments for the Unitary Executive," *Arkansas Law Review* 48, no. 1 (1995): 23–104, at 35.

17. Kagan, "Presidential Administration," 2335.

18. Calabresi, "Some Normative Arguments for the Unitary Executive," 35.

19. Skowronek, Dearborn, and King, *Phantoms,* 31–38. See also Julia R. Azari, *Delivering the People's Message: The Changing Politics of the Presidential Mandate* (Ithaca, NY: Cornell University Press, 2014), chs. 4–5.

20. Jeremy D. Bailey, *The Idea of Presidential Representation: An Intellectual and Political History* (Lawrence: University Press of Kansas, 2019), ch. 5.

21. Jide Nzelibe, "The Fable of the Nationalist President and the Parochial Congress," *UCLA Law Review* 53, no. 5 (June 2006): 1217–74, at 1217.

22. Jide Nzelibe, "Does the Unitary Presidency *Really* Need a Nationalist Justification?," *University of Pennsylvania Journal of Constitutional Law* 12, no. 2 (February 2010): 623–36, at

624. See also William P. Marshall, "Why the Assertion of a 'Nationalist' Presidency Does Not Support Claims for Expansive Presidential Power," *University of Pennsylvania Journal of Constitutional Law* 12, no. 2 (February 2010): 549–68.

23. *Seila Law LLC v. Consumer Financial Protection Bureau* 591 U.S. ___ (2020) (slip op., 22, 11) (Roberts, C. J., opinion of the Court). On the court's growing involvement in separation-of-powers disputes, see Nikolas Bowie and Daphna Renan, "The Separation-of-Powers Counter-revolution," *Yale Law Journal*, forthcoming.

24. Karen Orren and Stephen Skowronek, *The Policy State: An American Predicament* (Cambridge, MA: Harvard University Press, 2017), 123.

25. Orren and Skowronek, 137.

26. Andrew Reeves and Jon C. Rogowski, "The Public Cost of Unilateral Action," *American Journal of Political Science* 62, no. 2 (April 2018): 424–40; Sharece Thrower, "To Revoke or Not Revoke? The Political Determinants of Executive Order Longevity," *American Journal of Political Science* 61, no. 3 (July 2017): 642–56.

27. William G. Howell and Terry M. Moe, *Relic: How Our Constitution Undermines Effective Government and Why We Need a More Powerful Presidency* (New York: Basic Books, 2016), xix, 150.

28. William Howell and Terry M. Moe, "Why the President Needs More Power," *Boston Review*, July 2, 2018, http://bostonreview.net/politics/william-howell-terry-m-moe-why-president-needs-more-power. See also William G. Howell and Terry M. Moe, *Presidents, Populism, and the Crisis of Democracy* (Chicago: University of Chicago Press, 2020).

29. Blake Emerson and Jon D. Michaels, "Abandoning Presidential Administration: A Civic Governance Agenda to Promote Democratic Equality and Guard against Creeping Authoritarianism," *UCLA Law Review Discourse* 68 (2021): 418–47. On a proposed constitutional amendment, see Brian J. Cook, *The Fourth Branch: Reconstructing the Administrative State for the Commercial Republic* (Lawrence: University Press of Kansas, 2021).

30. Peter Baker, "A President of the People or a President of His People?," *New York Times*, April 16, 2019, https://www.nytimes.com/2019/04/16/us/politics/trump-presidency-base.html.

31. "Time and again the lesson is the same," Stephen Skowronek reminds us: "*the power to recreate order hinges on the authority to repudiate it.*" Stephen Skowronek, *The Politics Presidents Make: Leadership from John Adams to Bill Clinton* (Cambridge, MA: Belknap Press of Harvard University Press, 1997), 27. Emphasis in original.

32. For example, in an August 2020 poll, 62 percent of Americans agreed that "significant changes" that would address "the fundamental design and structure of the federal government" are needed. "Partisans Move Further Apart on Whether Government Needs Structural Change," Pew Research Center, September 2, 2020, https://www.pewresearch.org/politics/2020/09/02/in-views-of-u-s-democracy-widening-partisan-divides-over-freedom-to-peacefully-protest/pp_2020-09-02_democracy_0-09/.

33. John Maynard Keynes, *The General Theory of Employment, Interest, and Money* (London: Macmillan, 1936), 383.

Index

The letter *t* following a page number denotes a table; the letter *f* following a page number denotes a figure.